The Art and Technique of Digital Color Correction

The Art and Technique of Digital Color Correction

Steve Hullfish

Focal Press
Taylor & Francis Group

NEW YORK AND LONDON

First published 2012
This edition published 2013
by Focal Press
70 Blanchard Road, Suite 402, Burlington, MA 01803

Simultaneously published in the UK
By Focal Press
2 Park Square, Milton Park, Abingdon, Oxon OX14 4RN

Focal Press is an imprint of the Taylor & Francis Group, an informa business

Library of Congress Cataloging-in-Publication Data
Application submitted.

British Library Cataloguing-in-Publication Data
A catalogue record for this book is available from the British Library.

ISBN 13: 978-0-240-81715-6 (pbk)

Contents

CHAPTER 12
Tutorials   473

Acknowledgments

This book took a huge amount of effort and contribution by people other than the author. First, I must acknowledge the persistence, gentle guidance, and eagle eye of my original editor, Dorothy Cox, as well as the rest of the staff at Focal Press, especially Carlin Reagan, Melinda Rankin, Dennis McGonagle, and Paul Temme, who worked to make this a great looking and accurate read. And thanks also to my knowledgeable, meticulous, and enthusiastic tech editor, Jeff Greenberg, for keeping me honest and for keeping you, the reader, in mind at all times.

I must thank Bob Sliga, who started me down this road of color correction knowledge and who helped me with many elements of the book. I also owe a deep debt of gratitude to the rest of the colorists who contributed greatly by allowing me to interview them and watch them in sessions: Pankaj Bajpal, Greg Creaser, Terry Curren, Janet Falcon, Bob Festa, Larry Field, Pete Jannotta, Neal Kassner, Craig Leffel, Robert Lovejoy, Mike Most, Mike Matusek, Chris Pepperman, and Stefan Sonnenfeld. It is from their wisdom, experience, and skill that the reader of this book truly learns something valuable. And thanks to all of the employers of these colorists for allowing me free access to these busy and talented employees. Also, for providing an insightful interview on the viewpoint of the director of photography, thanks to David Mullen, ASC (American Society of Cinematographers).

Thanks to the many manufacturers and their representatives who provided invaluable assistance with their products: Roland Wood, of Silicon Color, for enabling many of the sessions with colorists around the country. Also from Tektronix, Steve Holmes, Leigh Havelick, and others for their support and knowledge in the field of monitoring. Thanks to Martin Euredjian for his use of his HD monitoring system, eCinema Display. And to the DR Group in Los Angeles for their support while doing the sessions in Los Angeles. Also Grady Sellers of Eastern Group for his help. Thanks to John Ladle and AJA for their gear and support, as well. To Avid for their Avid Artist's series Color Panel and to Black Magic Design for the DaVinci Resolve software and hardware. Also to Tangent Devices for the loan of a CP100 system and later for the Tangent WAVE. And to noted guru Gary Adcock, for helping with HD enlightenment and for the use of his Panasonic HVX-200. Also thanks to the folks at DSC Labs for their fantastic camera charts and to Eastman Kodak Company and the assistance of Carolyn A. Delvecchio for providing several film examples provided in the book.

There are many great examples of beautiful footage provided within these pages and on the DVD that were donated from several talented individuals and companies. Thanks to Artbeats and Julie Hill for providing several of their fantastic HD images for use by the readers and the colorists. All of the colorists were impressed by the quality of the color correction of the shots from their stock library. To three good friends, and fantastic cameramen, who are confident enough in their considerable shooting skills to let me use their footage for use in the tutorials: Rich Lerner, Randy Riesen, and Charles Vanderpool. Trying to find anything that needed "correcting" from the stuff they shoot is a difficult task.

Also, thanks to Barry Gilbert of Seduced and Exploited Films and his DP, Robin Miller, for the use of footage from his trailer for *Kiss Me in the Dark*. And through the kind assistance of Kyle Jackson and the folks at Tunnel Post for arranging permission to use the *Chasing Ghosts* footage. Also, thanks to the director and DP of *Chasing Ghosts* for the footage from their film.

To my family: my grandmother, Florence, for putting me up and keeping me company during my Philly/NJ/NYC sessions. And to my parents, Bill and Sue, who have always encouraged my writing, film making, and other creative pursuits, and taught me that you can do anything if you take it one step—or one page—or one turn of a bicycle wheel at a time. And of course, to my children, Haley and Quinn, who gave up their dad for the good part of a year and to my understanding wife, Jody, who has always been the quarterback of the family and had to take on far more than her share of the parenting as I wrote this book. I love you.

Using this Book and the DVD Materials

The Tutorial Clips on the DVD

The materials on the DVD are designed to let you follow along with the colorists. Some of the footage is standard definition. None of it is "log" footage (with the extra latitude in correction that is offered). Some of it is HD. All of it has been transcoded to ProRes LT. For most people, this will be relatively easy to use straight out of the box. For others, it may require downloading the proper QuickTime Codecs for use on a PC or on a Mac that doesn't have ProRes codecs loaded on it. ProRes—at least for now—won't work on a PC as an *output* format, but you can download and install the decoder that lets you see and use and transcode the files that are on the book's DVD using your PC.

For Mac or PC users who find they are unable to open the files on the DVD, please go to:

support.apple.com

Search for "ProRes QuickTime Decoder for Mac" or "ProRes Quick-Time Decoder for PC." Download and install as normal with most apps. This will allow you to see and use the files in your software. You shouldn't have to go through this step if you can simply see the footage on your computer when you click on it or try to load it.

I realize that standard definition is pretty passé by 2011, but when I started this project, this was the footage I used, and the wealth of information gleaned from these colorists was just too great to throw away. The point is not the quality of the footage but to see the ideas and methods of attack that the colorists used.

Obviously, HD 10- or 12-bit log footage gives you a lot more room to dig into the footage—the highlights, the shadows, the saturation—but having the limitations of working from an SD, 8-bit, compressed image should sharpen your skills. Please feel free to explore the ideas presented within the pages with footage that's your own. In the end, the footage on the DVD is just a starter. You really want to be trying these techniques and concepts on your own footage and everybody works on different types of footage. Working with the type of footage you usually see is the best idea. This book is aimed at a broad audience using different software and hardware. This book is not meant to show specific button presses for specific software, though you will get plenty of that.

Because of the broad appeal and scope of the book, I cannot discuss the dozens of color correction applications in depth. When I wrote the book initially, the assumption was that many readers would have Apple Color. Now, Apple Color has been EOL'd (end-of-lifed) by Apple, but it's still going to be a popular choice for a few years. For this edition of the book, I'm assuming that the majority of the readers will be using the light or paid version of DaVinci Resolve, though there will still be references to using Avid Symphony, Final Cut Pro (7 and X), After Effects, and Apple Color.

I'd like to explain quickly how to get the footage ready to use in two different applications on a Mac—Apple Color and DaVinci Resolve.

Using Tutorial Footage in Apple Color

1. Insert the DVD into your Mac, locate it on the Desktop, and open the disk.
2. On the disk are several folders. Drag or copy the footage labeled "DVD Tutorial Footage" onto your RAID or internal drive. A RAID is the best option for throughput of the video footage. You can also drag the other folders on the disk onto your RAID or internal, but they are not going to be used for color correction. Remember where you put the folder of tutorial footage and what you named it.
3. Launch Apple Color.
4. If you have a control surface, select it.
5. In the Projects Dialog box, click the New Project button.
6. In the New Project Dialog box, type a name such as "TUTORI-ALS" and click the Save button.
7. Color should launch into the Setup room with the Shots tab selected.
8. Hit the small icon of the red up arrow over a folder until you see the names of your drives on your computer or have some bearing on where in the file structure of your drives you are (Figure 0.1).
9. Double-click the drive—each drive is represented by the icon of a folder—to find the spot where you put the tutorial images.
10. Scroll through the drive using the small scroll bar next to the Modified Date to find your "DVD Tutorial Footage" folder, or whatever you renamed it to.
11. Double click on the "DVD Tutorial Footage" folder and you will see thumbnails of the footage in the folder (Figure 0.2).
12. If you wanted to, you could import each individual shot. Instead, click on the icon in the top left corner of the red up arrow over folder (Figure 0.3) and select the folder of tutorial footage,

Fig. 0.1

Fig. 0.2

Fig. 0.3

Fig. 0.4

probably called "DVD Tutorial Footage." Then click on the small button at the bottom right of the tab that says "Import Dir." (Figure 0.4). This will populate your Shots tab and your timeline with all of the shots on the DVD.

13. Because there is a mix of HD and SD sources, go to the Project Settings tab in the Setup room and set your Resolution Preset to 1920×1080 HD. This will call up a dialog box that asks if you would like to automatically scale all of your clips to the new resolution. Click on the "yes" button (Figure 0.5). Or you can go to the Geometry room and individually scale and change the aspect ratio on every shot.

14. With your timeline filled with all of the shots on the DVD, you can now quickly navigate through the timeline when you get to any chapter or example that you want to attempt yourself.

15. Click Command-S to Save your project or go to the File menu and choose Save.

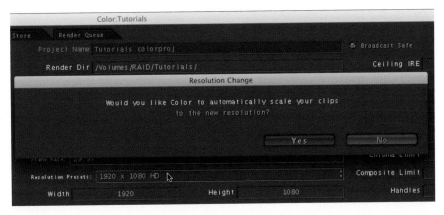

Fig. 0.5

Using Tutorial Footage in DaVinci Resolve

1. Insert the DVD into your Mac, locate it on the Desktop, and open the disk.
2. On the disk are several folders. Drag or copy the footage labeled "DVD Tutorial Footage" onto your RAID or internal drive. A RAID is the best option for throughput of the video footage. You can also drag the other folders on the disk onto your RAID or internal, but they are not going to be used for color correction. Remember where you put the folder of tutorial footage and what you named it.
3. Launch DaVinci Resolve.
4. If you haven't created a user for yourself, in the User Login Screen, click on Admin and click the "+" button at the bottom left side. Sign in as the Administrator and a New User Dialog will come up. Create a username and password (you don't need to enter anything for the password if you want to make it easy to log in). You should not do work as the Admin user. Either sign in as the Guest user or create your own account (Figure 0.6).
5. Double-click your new user to continue.
6. Resolve should open to the Config Screen.
7. Switch to the Browse screen using the buttons at the bottom of the screen (Figure 0.7). Note that the navigation to get to the Conform and Color screens as well as the others are located here.
8. If you've used Resolve before and configured it properly, your RAID drive and possibly some other storage options will be available at the top left in the Media Storage Area. Look in the drive where you saved the Tutorial folder (hopefully in your RAID) by clicking the small "+" button next to the name of the drive (Figure 0.8).

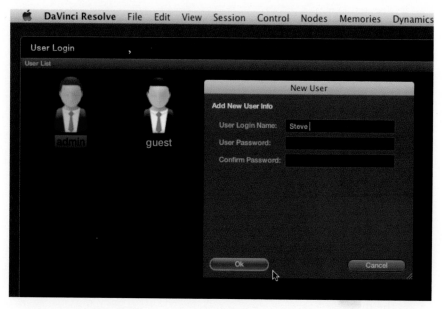

Fig. 0.6

Fig. 0.7

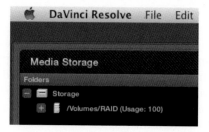

Fig. 0.8

9. If you've never configured the preferences in Resolve to allow it to see your drives, you need to do that first. Click on the top menu, next to the Apple menu choice that says "DaVinci Resolve," and select the Preferences option (Command-,). This launches the DaVinci Resolve Preferences dialog box. Using the "+" button on the left (Figure 0.9), you can add volumes that you want Resolve to look in for media and to use for rendering and other things. This is similar to the Scratch disk in Final Cut Pro. With your drive or drives added here, relaunch Resolve and follow steps 8 and 10.

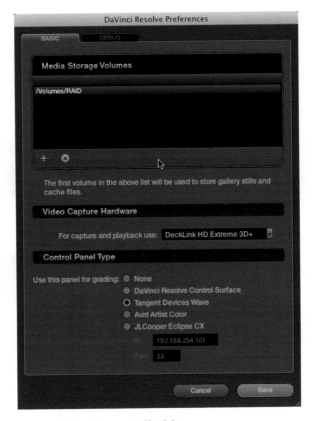

Fig. 0.9

10. Once you've found the drive where you put the tutorial footage, you can simply drag through the list to find the folder, or you can start typing the name and the list will automatically scroll down to it and highlight it.

11. Highlight the folder with the footage. Left-click (or control-click) to call up the contextual menu) and select "Add Folder Into Media Pool."

12. Resolve can not see folders inside of folders, and because of the way the Artbeats footage is licensed, it needs to be in its own folder, labeled "Artbeats." You will also have to navigate to the Artbeats folder inside of the Tutorials Footage folder (or whatever you renamed it) and left-click the Artbeats footage folder to select "Add Folder into Media Pool."

13. With all of the footage added to the Resolve's Media Pool, switch to the Conform Screen using the buttons at the bottom of the screen.

Fig. 0.10

14. In the Timeline Management section of the screen, click the "+" button to the left side of the screen just about perfectly in the middle vertically (Figure 0.10).

15. This opens a New Session Options dialog box. Click OK. The first session is always called the "Master Session," so you can't change that at the moment. This will populate the Conform EDL section of the screen and populate the Master Timeline with all of the shots.

16. You can scroll through the shots in the Master Timeline and play them in the Timeline Viewer. To start correcting them, you need to switch to the Color Screen at the bottom of the screen. Scroll through the timeline to switch between shots and follow along with the tutorials in the book.

17. Save the project using File > Save or Command-S. Name your saved project.

Other DVD Resources

The folder "CC_Session_text" contains text files (Word documents) of the complete transcribed color correction sessions and interviews with each of the colorists. The book uses only about a tenth of the complete information from the colorists. These text documents are *not* illustrated. But there are definitely examples of color grades and sections of interviews that are very interesting in these documents that are not used anywhere in the book. Happy reading. Please understand that these are my transcripts of what was said, so any spelling or grammatical errors or typos are clearly mine. Blame me, not them for any errors. I did not faithfully proofread the raw transcriptions (some of which were done by my students or outside transcription firms unfamiliar with the terms and lingo of postproduction). I corrected only the parts that were included in the book.

What This Book Is Not

I already wrote a book that is more technical in nature that discusses things like waveform and vectorscopes and gives detailed discussions on how to set up a proper viewing environment and calibrate your monitor (*Color Correction for Video*, 2nd edition, Focal Press).

Viewing Environment and Monitor Setup

To sum up the advice on viewing environment, you should grade in a room—or at least with your monitors against a wall—that is flat gray. Achieving perfect flat reflective response from paint is not easy, but try for a paint that is a nice 18 percent neutral gray. Do not have any brightly colored elements within your viewing radius, like a movie poster. Light the space with indirect D65 "daylight" lights. As a cheap solution, I use OTT lights (www.ottlite.com) in overhead cans. If you can splash a D65 source light on the wall behind your monitor, that's great.

As for setting up your monitors, that usually takes some specialized equipment and talent. There's a story that at Industrial Light & Magic or Pixar there was a lady who went around calibrating all of the monitors, and as soon as she finished the last monitor, she would go back around (months later) and start all over again. With today's LED, OLED, and plasma monitors, they "drift" much slower than the CRTs of old that needed basically weekly maintenance. So if you can get a professional to come in and set you up once, you should be fine for several years.

If you don't have the money for an engineer, then you'll need some combination of a color calibration device, like the X-Rite i1 Display Pro colorimeter (less than $200) or even their high-end Hubble (about $5,000). This will help you get the proper color on your computer displays, because the software in the computer can be connected to the colorimeter for feedback, but for your video monitors or projector, you will also need a way to feed the data from the colorimeter back to the monitor to be adjusted. It's possible to have that occur inside of your video card that feeds the monitor. With some monitors, they have methods of creating and displaying the changes in a LUT within the monitor and some monitors (consumer monitors generally) will need an external box that accepts the information from the loop created by the colorimeter and translates it into corrections on the monitor. Give a call to X-Rite and explain the specific pieces of gear you're trying to calibrate. There are too many permutations of equipment for me to lead a productive discussion on these pages.

I would love to give you detailed descriptions of how to use LUTs (look-up tables) and the tricks for navigating between compressed, 8-bit Canon DSLR footage and uncompressed, RAW, or log images from high-end cameras. However, a discussion of how to prepare a session for a digital intermediate would easily fill a book on its own. This is not that book.

Dealing with LUTs and the complexities of developing color management workflows for feature films or even primetime TV shows is the work of highly specialized consultants, color scientists and engineers. I have a book written by two Kodak color scientists that is bigger than this book and all it discusses is color management. (See the end of the last chapter for a bibliography.) Also, the tools and workflows for color management are changing almost daily. Each manufacturer comes up with new products and changes the names of their existing products. How many iterations and new releases of RED camera hardware like the REDrocket and REDcine cards and transcoding hardware and software have there been lately? New cameras with new sensors and new ways of recording the image in better and better ways come out almost monthly. I have no desire to keep up with Moore's Law when it comes to technology.

I do not deny that these are important issues. The proper color environment makes a difference in the way you see the image on your screen and the way your eyes fatigue and adjust as you work throughout the day.

LUTs are a very interesting subject; they help a colorist grade on a specific monitor while seeing a representation of the way the image will look on a different projector, film, or color space. Or a LUT can instantly take a RAW or log image and apply a grade to it automatically. Entire corporations are devoted to handling these technical issues. But the line has to be drawn somewhere, or this would become a 10,000-page color encyclopedia.

The point of this book is to show the *art* and *technique* of colorists. I want to show you how these colorists think and what their eyes see when they look at an image. Although many of these colorists know and understand the complex issues of color management and the engineering work that goes into their suites, most of them do not even think about these issues as they grade from day to day. They focus on the work. The craft. The art.

Thoughts on "Tech" and "Color Science"

Another of the very complex issues surrounding color correction at a high level (the level of digital intermediates for feature films) is *color space*. There are many difference color spaces. These color spaces are regularly "invented" as they're basically just mathematical descriptions of how you store, transform, and display a set of colors. This is mathematics at a high level. To me, not so interesting. Is it important? Yes, especially at the feature film level. But, it is also relatively controversial. Almost every high-end color correction and post house has a different recipe and a different preference for color spaces.

I have participated in discussions and arguments of these various color spaces and the discussions quickly get complicated and no clear winner ever emerges. Many post houses have developed their own specific methods and insist that their method is the only one that really works. However, every other post house feels the same way. Trying to either mediate those arguments or choose the best one or two to illustrate in the book seems fraught with peril.

For me to get in to the relative merits of P3, Rec709, sRGB, YCbCr, ACES, XYZ, and the myriad methods for transforming them would also be a book unto itself. Take a look at any scholarly paper that you can Google on color space and your eyes will gloss over before you get three paragraphs in.

I worked with one of the major players on integrating the ACES/IIF color workflows into feature films for the Academy of Motion Picture Arts and Sciences as they tried to implement this standard, and there were probably a hundred of the top color scientists working for years to figure out what all of the ramifications and permutations were of specific color space schemes and transforms.

That kind of knowledge is not condensable into a 5,000-word chapter. Here is the reason why understanding these spaces is critical, however: each of these spaces defines where gamma is set (i.e., 2.2, 2.4, 2.6); what the white reference is (i.e., D50, D60, D65); the purpose of the color space (i.e., capture, storage, transform, display); and the range or gamut of colors that can be faithfully reproduced. If your computer is sending out an image from one color space and your monitor is monitoring in another color space and your final output is in still a different color space, then the image you are trying to grade will really look nothing like the image that will be output at the end. If this freaks you out, simply do a test. Output a chip chart from your system and see what it looks like on your final output—whether that's the Web, video, film, or digital cinema.

How all of these color spaces work with each other and which ones are best—or at least acceptable—is a matter of contentious debate among some. The standards of the color spaces are set, but with new color space definitions and new "best practices" changing on a monthly basis, it's not something that can easily be discussed and certainly not something that can be definitively stated in the context of a book that would be out of date before it was ever published.

Waveform Tutorial Videos

Using waveforms and vectorscopes in color grading is a personal passion of mine. I discuss that subject in some depth in the early chapters. As usual, there are some tools that are better than others. I advocate for the use of external scopes, like Tektronix. Some people can't afford those at the beginning of their career. The internal scopes are a reasonable facsimile of external scopes. The main things they are missing are customizability (easy zooms, repositions, and one-touch presets), and resolution (both input resolution and display resolution). Other than that, the accuracy is not too far off generally. So feel free to use the internal scopes, especially during training.

For more on scopes and how they're used, Tektronix was gracious enough to allow me to include a series of tutorials that I created for them on the DVD. Please note that these were designed for use specifically by and for Tektronix scopes, but the general principles apply to all scopes. As full disclosure, I was paid by Tektronix to produce this series of videos. I felt that including them would add value to the book. I hope you agree.

The videos are in mp4 format, and should be easily viewed on most computers, iPads, and iPods. None of the content on the DVD for the book is suitable or playable for standalone DVD players.

CHAPTER 1

Primary Color Correction: Tonal Range Primer

Color correction is generally broken down into two distinct processes: primary and secondary color correction. These two processes will probably always be referred to as two *distinct* processes, but the technology itself is starting to change the perception of how and why these two processes are used and when the colorist moves from one process to another.

Primary color correction is the process of setting the overall tone, contrast, and color balance of the image. Secondary color correction is an additional step that refines the image in specific geographical regions of the image or in specific color vectors of the image. Don't let that word "vector" scare you. There are a number of definitions of the word "vector" that are used when discussing color space. It basically means the specific location or coordinates of a color. A vector can also mean the direction that something is heading, from one point in space towards another. So, essentially, in the color correction world, "vector" is just the technical word that defines a specific "color." Think of a vectorscope, which is a tool that allows you to kind of see the "color wheel" (Figure 1.1). The vectorscope shows you where parts of the picture are on the color wheel. So the vectorscope shows you the vector—or location on the color wheel—for the elements of your video image.

The first step in any color correction is to assess the tonal range of the picture. What are the problems with the tonal range and how can you address them? From a purely technical standpoint, it seems like an easy question to answer. As a matter of fact, many color correction plug-ins or color correction systems built into nonlinear editors have "automatic" buttons that will attempt to spread out the tonal range for you based on purely technical information. These automatic systems assume that the brightest parts of the picture should be as bright as possible while remaining "legal." The darkest part of the picture is also set automatically to be as low as possible while remaining "legal."

legal: For video-based images, "legal" means that the brightness and color saturation of an image does not exceed minimum or maximum levels that have been determined for a specific delivery channel for a video. This usually implies broadcast, but can also pertain to duplication. Each duplicator or broadcaster sets their own specific requirements for video levels, but in general these levels adhere to national and international standards and describe that the darkest portions of the luminance of the picture can not fall below 0IRE for NTSC digital video (and most other international video of any type) or 7.5IRE for composite NTSC in the United States. The brightest pixels are not to pass 100IRE when monitoring luminance only or, when combined with chroma, cannot pass 110IRE. (There are other ways to measure the signal other than IRE, such as in millivolts.) Also, as our delivery systems become more and more digitally based, "gamut" is also included in "legal" levels. Not all waveform monitors or vectorscopes can monitor gamut levels. These gamut levels are the legal amounts—or values—of certain colors. It is possible for the luminance of an image to be well under legal levels, but because of a combination of saturation and luminance, the legal gamut levels can be exceeded. We'll get into this more later in the book. In addition to "legal" levels, there is a second, similar term called "valid" levels.

vector: A position or coordinate in space or a direction between two coordinates. On a vectorscope, the vector is the specific position of a color in the two-dimensional circle defined by the vectorscope. The "targeted" vectors on the vectorscope are the three primary colors—red, green, and blue—and the secondary colors fall between them—magenta, cyan, and yellow.

valid levels: Levels that remain legal when transferred, translated, or transcoded between formats.

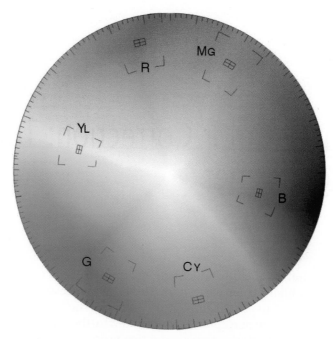

Fig. 1.1 The graticule of a vectorscope superimposed onto a color wheel. Notice that the "targets" on the vectorscope—the small boxes next to the black letters—correspond to the colors of the color wheel.

There are two big problems with this behavior. Simply setting the brightest pixel to 100 and the darkest pixel to 0 with all of the intermediate pixels spread evenly between them does not necessarily provide the best spread of the tonal range across *the most visually important parts of the image*. The other problem is that the image may not *need* to have either its brightest pixel at 100 or its darkest pixel at 0.

The first problem is solved with some experience. Great colorists know tricks that can enhance the perception of an image's tonal range. They know that they can sacrifice the detail in a certain tonal range where it may not be noticed so that they can use that tonal range to enhance a more visually important part of the picture. These are tricks that you will learn in this chapter and throughout the rest of the book, Automatic software doesn't know what is visually important, so it treats all areas of the image equally.

Even if the image should be spread from 0 to 100, that still leaves out one critical component: gamma. Spreading out the tonal range really serves to increase contrast, but the real impression of how bright or dark the image is relies largely on your gamma or midtone controls. Gamma really refers to a curve. The reason that midtones are sometimes referred to as "gamma" is because by lifting or lowering the midtones, you are

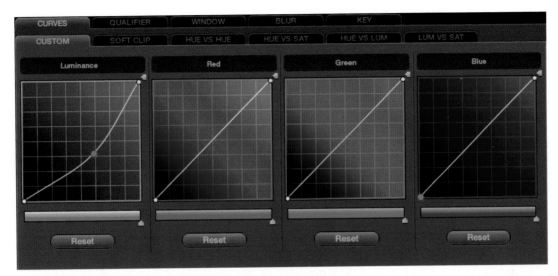

Fig. 1.2 Note that the luminance curve is curved because a point at the midtone was pulled down. The red, green, and blue curves are all straight lines from a black point at the bottom left to a white point at the top right.

creating a curve between the white point and the black point instead of a simple straight line (Figure 1.2).

Great colorists know tricks that can enhance the perception of an image's tonal range.

The second problem is that the image may not require an expanded tonal range (Figure 1.5). Most shots should have a pretty wide tonal latitude (range) with rich blacks and sparkling whites, but there are those images that should not take advantage of the full tonal range. Some examples: an igloo in a snow storm; a dark, moonlit close-up of a Navy SEAL creeping through the underbrush; a foggy, early morning rowboat ride; a long lens shot of a smoggy city at dusk. Each of these may only have a partial tonal range, lacking either a deep black or bright highlights. However, these examples are usually the exceptions to the rules. But they do require the colorist to consider the clues in the image itself to determine whether anything in the image deserves to be completely black or bright white.

The colorist must consider the clues in the image itself to determine whether anything in the image deserves to be completely black or bright white.

gamma: Technically gamma is a curve, but in some software programs, gamma is the label for the midtone adjustment slider. For all intents and purposes, gamma and midtone are synonymous in color correction.

Definition

tonal range (singular):
The tonal range is the difference between the brightest and darkest areas of the image, sometimes also called the dynamic range, luminance range, or contrast range, though these terms can have slightly different technical definitions. The tonal range of the image—and how those tones are spread throughout the tonal range—defines its contrast. For some applications of this phrase, tonal range indicates the actual number of *levels* of tones that a recording medium can record (256 per channel in the case of RGB 8-bit, or 1025 per channel in the case of RGB 10-bit). For our purposes, we will refer to tonal range (singular) as the range of tones between brightest and darkest. Ansel Adams and other proponents of the Zone System break the tonal range of an image into 11 distinct tonal ranges.

tonal ranges (plural):
The three commonly used tonal ranges that are used to break down the description (and control) of an image are shadows, midtones, and highlights. Sometimes shadows are referred to as blacks, pedestal, set-up, lift, or even lowlights. Midtones are often referred to as gamma, but also as grays or mids. Highlights are sometimes also referred to as whites, gain, luma, or even video. These are

Automatic Corrections Are Bad

Let's run an experiment to show that you are already a better colorist than the automatic color correction tools available in most software packages. Even if you aren't tempted to use these automatic features, this little experiment is an important lesson in using your *eyes* instead of the numbers or doing things technically perfectly.

Open the "Artbeats Popcorn" image (from Artbeats' beautiful Food1 collection; Figure 1.3) in any application that allows you to automatically color correct. Most of these tools automatically spread the tonal values and "white balance." But because these tools don't know what the image actually looks like, they do everything by the numbers. Sometimes using them can get you in the ballpark very quickly, and sometimes it makes an image look worse.

For my example, I brought the popcorn QuickTime into Avid Xpress Pro and color corrected it using the automatic color correction tools. To be fair to Avid and other applications with these tools, these automatic corrections can sometimes do a pretty good job. If you're in a rush, give each image a shot with them, but be prepared to take matters into your own hands. Doing things manually is actually a good thing. If all someone needed to do was push a button, then there'd be nothing special about the skills you're trying to develop.

Anyway, after running the popcorn image through the auto color correction, it doesn't look nearly as appetizing as the beautifully color corrected original image.

Most of these tools figure that you want something that's pretty "white" or neutral-looking and with a tonal range that's completely spread out. In the case of the popcorn image, the image *needs* to have a nice, warm golden tone. Also, the original image doesn't really go much beyond 80IRE in brightness, yet the autocorrection spreads the tonal values over the entire range, which causes the steam rising from the popcorn to take on a harsher feel and the brighter parts of the popcorn come close to clipping out, destroying detail by overexposing (Figure 1.4). (See definition of clipping on page 22.)

Fig. 1.3 Original image courtesy of Artbeats' Food1 collection.

Fig. 1.4 Color corrected using automatic correction tools.

This point is a good thing to keep in mind as you're color correcting things by hand. Not all images *need* to be at 100IRE and not all color casts are a bad thing. Some images need to be very contrasty and others need to have less contrast. You need to look for the clues in each image to help you find where the image wants to go. The long shadows of dawn or dusk should indicate warmer tones and lower contrast. The sharp shadows of the noonday sun should indicate higher contrast and maybe a hint of blue—or possibly yellow for heat.

The contrast for "golden hour" and "high noon" *can* be the reverse of what I just said. It depends on where the sun is. If the sun and camera are both pointing in the same direction at golden hour, things will be very evenly lit, like by a giant softlight. But if the camera is pointing toward the sun or perpendicular to it, instead of low contrast, it would have higher contrast because the difference between what was lit by the sun and the shadows would be great. The same goes for high noon. It can have great contrast, throwing deep shadows under the eyes, for example, or it can have lower contrast because the entire sky is acting as a big bounce light.

not necessarily technically correct terms, but they are terms that were used by the colorists as they were verbally conveying the use of these individual tonal ranges. The terminology in the book will *not* remain the same, because in real life, these terms are often interchanged—sometimes even by the same speakers.

Gamut: The complete range of colors that can be captured, displayed, or broadcast by a device or a system of devices. Most cameras or color correction devices have a much wider gamut (range of colors) than those that can be used further on in the production stream. For example, the gamut of colors later in the production stream that could require a limited gamut can be those: recorded to tape, burned to a DVD, encoded for the Web, broadcast from a TV transmitter, or viewed on a TV set. So there are multiple gamuts that have to be considered (see the previous definition for "legal" and "valid").

Keeping these exceptions in mind, let's consider the approach to most of the images that—as you will see—will benefit from spreading the tonal range as much as we can.

Monitoring

My first book on color correction, cowritten with Jaime Fowler—*Color Correction for Digital Video*—goes into detail about monitoring. I don't want to address those same issues as thoroughly in this book, but I will touch on them briefly.

Fig. 1.5 A classic example of when *not* to spread the tonal range: a polar bear in a snowstorm. No part of this image should be completely black. Image courtesy of Dan Zatz at WildlifeHD.com.

Video Monitor

Proper monitoring is crucial: you must have a well set up video monitor. There are instructions for doing this in my first book and on numerous websites and online instructions. Although LCD monitoring has been largely shunned by serious colorists, the production of CRT displays for video was halted several years ago, leaving many with no choice but to switch to LCDs or some other technology. The main issue with these LCD monitors is how colors and tones shift with the viewer's angle to the screen and how deep a black is able to be displayed. This problem is called *off-angle viewing*.

At a recent NAB (National Association of Broadcasters) convention, Sony revealed some beautiful OLED video monitors that largely resolved the off-angle viewing issue and improved performance in the blacks, which is a weakness of LCD video monitors. These monitors remain very expensive, but they're getting serious attention from the colorists and facilities that deliver high-end broadcast and film images.

Many LCD video monitors can be set-up with look-up tables (LUTs) or by using calibration hardware and software. The cost and accuracy of these calibration units varies widely from several thousand dollars to under a hundred dollars. For my computer, I use a midlevel unit by X-Rite called the i1Display Pro (about $240). It uses a hardware device and software to create a custom monitor profile that even takes ambient lighting into account. This device would not fulfill the expectations of a serious, full-time colorist, but it creates a profile that seems very accurate to me.

Many high-end video monitors also have hardware-based calibration options that can help properly calibrate them. As I mentioned earlier, for video monitors that aren't capable of being set up with a profile or LUT, my first color correction book offers an in-depth description of how to set up a monitor to color bars. There are also several resources for doing this available on the Web and from the monitor manufacturers. Ensemble Designs has an SDI to HDMI converter box that allows calibration of a consumer monitor. Instructions for calibration are included with the device.

At the higher end, the manufacturer Cine-tal has created a small box, called the Davio. A software application runs the Davio hardware and allows any monitor, even a consumer monitor, to be calibrated and matched to another monitor or to a specification. All of the calibration is done automatically and only takes a few minutes.

This type of device (or some kind of LUT box) is really necessary to get the most accurate color reproduction from your monitor. Simply adjusting the brightness, contrast, hue, and saturation on your monitor will not deliver dependable results. Instructions on using these devices for monitor calibration vary and are provided by the manufacturers. Entire seminar series are devoted to the topic of color management, so it's outside the scope of this book to provide it.

For serious color correction, consulting firms can be hired to set up your suite, making sure that the image is accurate at each stage of the postproduction process, creating a workflow that guarantees the integrity of the image throughout the process.

Viewing Environment

The viewing environment is also of critical importance. The lighting in a color-critical environment is daylight balanced, not tungsten. There is some debate over the exact temperature of "daylight," but it's about 6000–6500K. The daylight-balanced light is often used only as *reflected* light as opposed to *direct* light. For example, it is bounced off of a back wall behind the monitor. It is also fairly dim. The eCinema displays we used for most of the color correction sessions come with a separate, external, daylight-balanced backlight that actually matches the light used inside the monitor itself. It is designed to be placed behind the monitor, bouncing light onto the wall behind it. The light bouncing off the wall behind the monitor should be one-tenth the intensity the monitor when displaying 100 percent white.

Any additional lighting in the room can't increase this brightness level. The light sources should be 6500K bulbs or be filtered to reach that temperature. This color value is often referred to as D65. The "D" refers to daylight; "65" refers to 6,500 Kelvin. Actually D65's exact Kelvin rating is 6503.6. The actual color of daylight varies. D65 represents the color temperature at high noon in the northern sky.

No bulbs or light sources should be visible to the colorist's eyes while grading. Some color correction suites have a bulb near the colorist's desk that sends a beam of pure 6500K light to a small white card or tile near the colorist to act as a reference for pure white. This light can be turned on or off independently from the other lights in the room.

Walls should be a completely neutral gray: no tint at all. Paint mixers have a very hard time with this. Bring an 18 percent grey photo card to your local paint store and see if they can match it. Many color suites aren't painted at all but are instead covered in gray cloth, which cuts down on reflected light and glare.

High-level colorists are very sensitive to their viewing environment.

Here's a simple test to prove how important the viewing environment is to good color correction. Look at the following squares and determine whether the blocks to the right are darker than the blocks to the left (Figure 1.6). If you're familiar with optical illusions, you can probably guess the right answer despite what your eyes are really telling you.

The color chips inside the black surround (to the right) appear to be brighter than the ones on the white surround (to the left). The black surround also makes the contrast ratio of the chips appear slightly lower. This is due to a thing called *lateral-brightness adaptation*, which means that a particular retinal receptor in the eye is affected by the brightness of the receptors coming in to its neighboring receptors, which helps us detect edges better. (For more on the color theory involved, check out *Digital Color Management: Encoding Solutions* by Edward Giorgianni and Thomas Madden [Wiley]. Publication Date: January 27, 2009 | ISBN-10: 047051244X | ISBN-13: 978-0470512449)

High-level colorists are very sensitive to their viewing environment. This sensitivity extends to very small stimuli, such as glowing on/off switches on equipment and the color of the trace of the waveform or

Fig. 1.6 The environment around your monitor affects how you see what's in it.

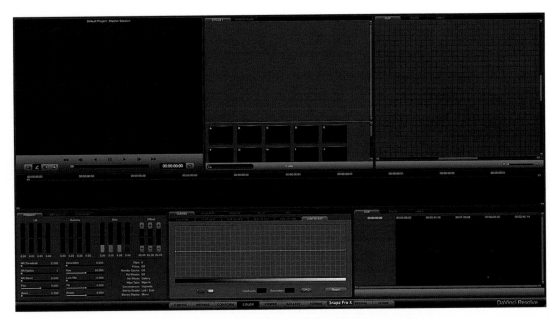

Fig. 1.7 The GUI for DaVinci Resolve is dark and essentially colorless.

vectorscope. Most colorists try to grade using waveform or vectorscopes that have a neutral trace and graticule color instead of the traditional green.

This obsession with surrounding environment used to include the option to turn off the bright white Mac menu bar at the top of the monitor when using Color (then FinalTouch). Color and some other color correction software applications, such as Avid Symphony, go so far as to allow the user to customize the application's graphical user interface (GUI) colors to be darker and less saturated. A look at the GUI for DaVinci Resolve makes this clear (Figure 1.7).

Definition

GUI: Graphical user interface. Basically, the screen that you see when working in an application that allows you to interact with the program and execute commands (Figure 1.7).

Surround Environment

Interview with Randy Starnes

To relate how important the surround is, when I first started, we worked in a room that was designed to resemble the living room, and the thought was, "You're going to watch television in an environment similar to this, so let's color grade in this environment. The monitor was set in a bookcase. It was a warmly lit room with a desk lamp, overhead tungsten lights. A beautiful room, very comfortable—it was like a den, a gentlemen's smoking room. And I think in those days, we even smoked in the rooms. The longer you would color correct something, the more red you would put into the pictures because your eyes became desensitized. At the start of the day, skin tones would look normal, but after six or eight hours, you were correcting skin tones oversaturated, like basketballs, because your perception has changed. The reason you have the neutral background is that you keep the same perception all along. You refer to something that is neutral. Otherwise, if you bathe the area in blue, you're going to compensate for that. You're going to lose your sensitivity to blue, or red, or warm. And then you become desensitized to that. If you sit in a yellow room, your pictures are going to end up yellow. Or you're going to be constantly fighting what you perceive. So the easiest way to avoid that is to surround the monitor with something that is neutral and daylight. You can also take your monitor to black and white to refresh your perspective. Sometimes I'll use the switcher to put a gray border or a white border around my image to judge what pure white should look like or pure gray. Sometimes that helps the colorist and sometimes that helps the client, whose perception is just as important to the process. If you have an environment that is not neutral, the hardest thing to get right are going to be the white scenes.

Randy Starnes has been the colorist on *Desperate Housewives*, *Extreme Makeover: Home Edition*, *Dr. Quinn: Medicine Woman*, *Touched by an Angel*, and others.

Waveform and Vectorscope Displays

Most of the waveform and vectorscope displays that are built in to the software of desktop applications are barely sufficient for color correction purposes. These scopes have two things going for them: they're free and they're convenient. Other than that, there's not much to recommend them. There are a number of reasons that they do not stand up to a professional's needs.

Depending on the specific application, many of the built-in scopes are not showing you full resolution. Some are designed to only show every other line or every *fourth* line of your video image! They also don't have the full complement of features that are available on an outboard scope, such as ability to zoom or position the trace to better evaluate the image. There can also be a problem with lag time between a correction and that correction being sensed by the scope, because the amount of computational horsepower that is required to display the scope is pretty intensive. The main problem with these built-in scopes for broadcast work is that they have no real relation to the signal that comes out of the computer, because they're not downstream of the video output. In the initial release of Color, the scopes inside Color didn't match the scopes for the exact same footage inside Final Cut Pro, though this was more of a Quicktime issue. Another serious issue for efficient color correction is the ease with which you can jump from

Definition

waveform monitor: A waveform monitor displays the amplitude level—brightness and darkness—along the vertical axis with the dark parts of the image near the bottom and the brighter parts of the signal near the top. Technically, the horizontal axis of the waveform displays "time," but practically speaking, the horizontal axis of the waveform corresponds to the horizontal placement of picture elements across the image with no regard to the vertical placement of elements in the image.

display to display or presets of displays. Largely, though, the issue with internal scopes is that they just don't have the resolution needed for color correction.

For a lot of reasons, I recommend having an external waveform and vectorscope. When choosing a scope, find features and tools that you think will be most useful to you. Some brands, like Tektronix, have patented displays such as the Lightning Display, Spearhead Display, Luma Qualified Vectorscopes, and the Arrowhead display that provide you with valuable information that you can't get from other manufacturers. So shop around for the tools in a scope that make the most sense to you as you color correct.

Also, make sure that the scope is monitoring the type of signal that you are recording to tape. It doesn't make much sense to be monitoring the composite or component video signal if you're laying HD-SDI or something else to tape.

> *I could see that their eyes were really watching the outboard scopes for critical decision making.*

I used several Tektronix model waveform monitors during the writing of this book, including the WFM7000 and the WVR7100 (Figures 1.8 and 1.9) and the WFM5200 that I own.

Though the colorists who participated in this book could use the internal scopes, I could see that their eyes were really watching the outboard scopes for critical decision making. Many of the colorists used specialized views or amplifications of views that simply were impossible to deliver with the internal scopes. Having a scope that was capable of displaying multiple views at the same time was also important.

Fig. 1.8 Tektronix WFM7000 rasterizer. Images courtesy Tektronix, Inc.

Fig. 1.9 Tektronix WVR7100.

Fig. 1.10 Senior colorist Pankaj Bajpai at Encore Hollywood grading images from the book using a Lustre. He has an OmniTek scope prominently displayed, set to show an RGB Parade and vectorscope. Pankaj has been the colorist for *Justified*, *Lie to Me*, *Sex and the City*, *Hung*, *Rome*, and *How to Make It in America*. Before his career as a colorist, he was a director of photography. Later in the book, Pankaj will walk you through some corrections, step by step starting on page 258 and 276.

All of the colorists, except Pankaj Bagpai and Bob Festa, who worked in their own personal suites with their own equipment, used a Tektronix scope for these sessions that enabled them to view four different panes of information on the monitor. They all configured the four-pane view to display an RGB Parade waveform display and a vectorscope. Some colorists set up an RGB Parade waveform showing the entire height of the waveform and then a second RGB Parade that was zoomed in and focused on the 0IRE line to better see how to balance their blacks. Most also set a fourth monitor pane to see the standard full waveform luminance display. This setup is similar to what I saw in the suites that the colorists worked in every day. Almost all of them had four dedicated outboard scopes—or a single display with four scopes—set to different views or displays (Figures 1.11–1.12), which allows them to see information in multiple presentations at a single glance without having to switch between views by pressing buttons on a single scope.

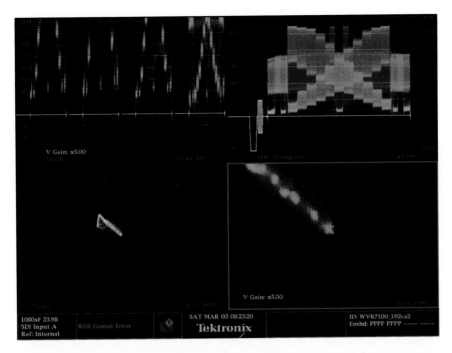

Fig. 1.11 Upper left quadrant: a YRGB Parade waveform monitor that has been zoomed in to focus on the shadows only. Upper right quadrant: the full-scale composite standard waveform. Lower left quadrant: a standard zoom on a vectorscope. Lower right quadrant: a 5x zoom to the center of the vectorscope.

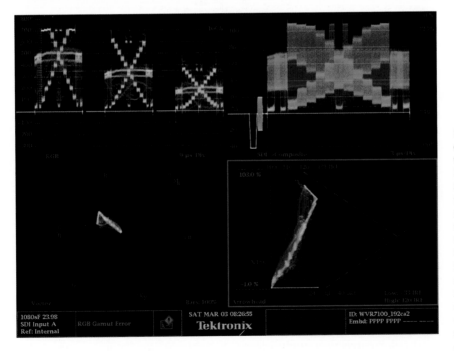

Fig. 1.12 Another set of views using the same video image input (a DSC Labs grayscale chart with a warm white balance) fed to the scope. Upper left quadrant: an RGB Parade waveform monitor showing the full scale (not zoomed). Upper right quadrant: the full scale-composite standard waveform (single field only). Lower left quadrant: a standard zoom on a vectorscope. Lower right quadrant: an Arrowhead gamut display.

Definition

RGB Parade mode (waveform): The RGB Parade is simply a display option of a standard waveform monitor. Colorists rely heavily on the RGB Parade viewing option on a waveform because it displays the individual levels of the red, green, and blue channels of the image. Each of these channels is displayed in its own "cell" horizontally with red, green, and blue in a "parade" from left to right across the screen. Each of these cells is essentially identical to the regular display of information on a waveform monitor, except that the values only pertain to the amount of that one color in the image. A variation on this display is the YRGB Parade display (Figure 1.13) that you will see throughout this book, which has four cells instead of three; the first being luminance (Y) followed by red, green, and blue.

vectorscope: Displays chrominance and hue. The saturation—or gain—of the chroma—or color—is measured by how far it extends from the center of the scope. Neutral images (black, white, and all levels of gray) register as a dot in the middle of the vectorscope. Hue is indicated by the position of the trace around the perimeter of the circle. Vectorscopes have graticules that show each of six different colors (red, green, blue, magenta, cyan, and yellow) in a different,

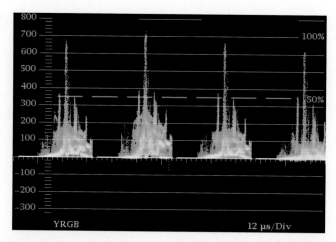

Fig. 1.13 Tektronix WVR7100 YRGB display, showing a separate cell for overall luminance *plus* each of the three color channels: red, green, and blue. Also note that this display is presenting the information on a scale of millivolts instead of percentage or IRE. This setting is a matter of personal preference. Most people find the IRE or percentage scale easier to understand and communicate. The Tektronix display is capable of displaying the graticule for either scale.

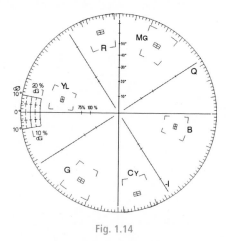

Fig. 1.14

Alternative Displays and Tools for Analysis

There are additional methods for analyzing the image. Most of these are specialized and are available only to specific applications. We'll address these methods throughout the rest of the book where they're applicable.

Some of the analytical tools for video images that are alternatives to the basic waveform and vectorscope include eyedroppering (available in most color correction applications), histograms (available in some color correction applications), and Luma Range view (available in a few color correction applications). Also, some applications such as Final Cut Pro can superimpose zebra patterns or warning symbols on video that has levels that are near or in excess of legal limits. Avid products have a similar warning system for illegal and out-of-gamut video levels. Tektronix scopes can also do this, with a setting called "Bright-up" displays.

Eyedropper tools (Figure 1.18) are a great way to look at a very specific part of the picture. You simply select the tool and click or drag to an area of your picture that you want to analyze, and then you use the same basic skills for balancing color on an RGB Parade waveform monitor. The goal is to get the levels—numerical, in this case—to match across all three color channels for any part of the image where you want a neutral balance. Be careful, because if you're analyzing only a single pixel, you may be looking at noise instead of the actual color. Move the eyedropper around a little to get a sense of the surrounding pixels. Also, eyedroppering can show you clipping. If the eyedropper numbers don't vary by much in a given area, that means there is probably clipping.

Histograms have some fans. I'm not one of them. The best thing a histogram can show you is whether there is clipping at either end in one of the color channels. If you have histogram analysis tools in your preferred color grading application, keep an eye on the histograms while you're doing a correction using one of the other methods, like with an RGB Parade. You'll start to see how you can balance the colors and to dial in a nice spread on your tonal range using the histograms. Histograms are actually quite good at setting the limits on your tonal ranges, but for balancing, I've found them to sometimes be quite deceptive. The basic concept for balancing with histograms is the same as with an RGB Parade. You are looking to match the starting and ending positions of the limits of each color channel. To compare the histogram to the RGB Parade, look at the image of the man with

fixed vector (position) around the vectorscope (Figure 1.14). Apple Color includes a cool 3D vectorscope that allows you to rotate the vectorscope in 3D space to see luminance displayed as well; 2D vectorscopes cannot display luminance information.

graticule: The overlay on the scope that indicates levels and positioning information. The graticule does not change unless the user changes it. It is usually customizable to display various scales and to provide information on how the trace signal is being displayed. It is analogous to the legends and lines on a chart or graph. The latitude and longitude lines on a map are the map's graticule.

trace: Part of the waveform or vectorscope display that reacts to the incoming video information. The trace is a representation of your video image on the waveform or vectorscope. Nontechnically, it's the squiggly stuff.

cell: This term is used to describe one of the three (or four) separate images on the RGB Parade waveform corresponding to the individual red, green, blue and—in the case of a YRGB display—luminance signals.

Fig. 1.15 The image represented in the RGB Parade and histogram.

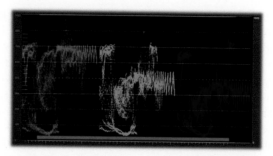

Fig. 1.16 Note that the black levels are balanced across the bottom of all three cells of the RGB Parade (red line). This is DaVinci Resolve's internal RGB Parade waveform monitor. Also that the levels across the bottom of the three cells is elevated quite a bit above 0, indicating a fairly "lifted" black level.

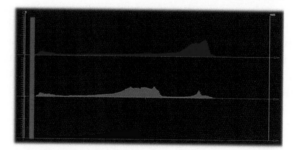

Fig. 1.17 Note that the histograms also show that each color channel starts at a similar horizontal position, indicating that they are balanced (red line). The left side of the screen indicates black and the right indicates white. The position of the first bump on the histogram isn't as far left as it could be, indicating the same elevated black levels as the RGB Parade. The difference in the balance of the bumps on the right side of the histogram indicates the warm skin tones and orange paint on the container in the highlight areas.

Fig. 1.18 The numbers from Avid's eyedropper, sampling the black in the shirt. These numbers are in 8-bit color space. The numbers in the red, green, and blue channels (33, 29, 30) are fairly close to each other, indicating that the blacks are balanced but are quite elevated compared to the true black indicated by the 16, 16, 16 numbers to the right of them. All of these tools are giving us the same information in different ways.

the sunglasses (Figure 1.15) and the corresponding image of the RGB Parade (Figure 1.16) and histogram from DaVinci Resolve's internal scope displays (Figure 1.17).

First Things First: Black Level

Nearly every colorist attacks an image by first determining where the blacks should be. "Blacks" refers to the deepest, darkest shadows and black portions of the image. As mentioned earlier, blacks are also sometimes referred to as setup, lift, shadows, pedestal, or lowlights. There is usually some portion of an image that you can pick out that should be corrected to the lowest legal level. If you don't correct at least *some* portion of the image to a black level that is low enough that it is almost devoid of detail, the shadows of the image will appear milky and the image will lack snap or pop. The trick is to lower the blacks to the proper point without losing detail that you want to keep.

Some colorists, when working with a monitor that they trust and with which they have a lot of experience, will judge this black level by eye. But although a good colorist knows how to judge these things from a trusted, proven monitor, black levels are generally set by looking at a waveform monitor, preferably one set to display in RGB Parade mode.

Mike Most on black balance and scopes: "The first place I go is black balance. I think it's pretty much the first place pretty much everybody goes. I like to use scopes to do that. Scopes don't lie. I can do it largely by eye, but it depends on what time of day it is, what I've been looking at for the last 20 minutes, and my mood. So for times when you're looking for a pure balance, a scope is kind of your best friend. I know a lot of people who tend to stay away from scopes entirely and I personally think it's kind of a mistake. I think you get a certain sloppiness that you don't need to have by doing that. I don't think you need to be a slave to scopes because a lot of it is just feel. But there are a lot of absolutes, and black balance is an absolute. Either the blacks are balanced or they're not and scopes don't lie. I trust the parade display. The vectorscope is a good guide, but for black balance, the parade display has to be the bible."

Looking at the waveform monitor in RGB Parade mode allows you to view the brightness of each of the three color channels: red, green, and blue. Separating the display into these channels allows you to see whether one channel has more detail in the darkest areas of the picture and whether any one color channel has the black levels elevated above the others. This is an important thing to be able to see, so that when you are using your color correction tools to lower the black levels, you do not crush the detail out of one channel that may be lower than the other two.

Definition

crush: To lower the black levels to the point where detail is lost in the deep shadow areas. "Crushing" clips the signal on the low end. Sometimes "crushing the blacks" is a desired result: creating a contrasty look. It is also sometimes a warning that the black levels are too low. For example: "As I lowered the blacks, the picture was looking nice and rich, but I pulled back a little on my correction because I saw that I was crushing the blacks and couldn't see any detail in the shadows."

Definition

Low Pass: A mode or setting on the waveform monitor that filters out all of the chroma information in the image as it displays the waveform, allowing you to analyze only the luminance values. The opposite of this setting is Flat, which does not filter out the chroma information. On some scopes, especially those internal to many desktop applications, the Flat mode is called Y/C, which stands for luma/chroma. This Y/C mode is often displayed with the luma and chroma information in different colors. On a standard waveform monitor in Flat mode, the luminance and chrominance values are indistinguishable by color on the display.

Reading the Waveform Monitor

Let's take a look at an image and determine the proper black level looking at both a standard waveform image in Low Pass—or luminance-only— mode and a waveform image in RGB Parade mode. First, we'll identify the picture elements in the video image and find the corresponding areas on the waveform monitor. This step will help us judge the effect of our corrections as our eyes move from the waveform monitor to the video image.

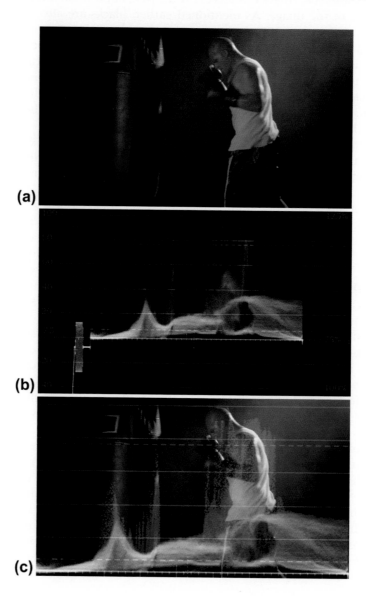

(a)

(b)

(c)

Fig. 1.19 (a) High-definition still from Artbeats' Sports 1 HD collection— SP120. (b) Waveform image grabbed from a Tektronix WVR7100. (c) Artbeats' image from Sports 1 HD collection overlaid with waveform display.

The images will give you a good idea of the correlation of the waveform monitor and the video image. The image of the boxer is a high-definition (HD) still grabbed from Artbeats' Sports1 HD collection, clip SP120H1 (Figure 1.19a). The image of the waveform was grabbed from a Tektronix WVR7100, the waveform image is simply an enlarged portion of that same scope (Figure 1.19b), and the third image is an overlay of the boxer and the waveform done in Photoshop (Figure 1.19c).

Take a look at the waveform from left to right and find the matching portions of the picture itself. The large rectangular shape on the waveform is not part of the image itself. This is the black burst. You can ignore that as you grade. The first small rises on the left correspond to the very shadowed boxing gloves hanging in the background. Then there is a small ramp leading up to a steeper spike. The small ramp is probably a little atmospheric smoke that is only barely perceptible in the HD image behind and about half way up the punching bag. The angled spike indicates the left highlight on the punching bag. The ramping of the waveform is because the highlight gradually gets brighter as the light reflects in growing intensity on the curve of the bag then falls away on the right side of the curve. The speckled area above the steep spike appears to be the portion of the yellow rectangle at the top of the bag. I can basically confirm this suspicion by looking at the YRGB parade.

Definition

grade: The act of color correcting an image. It can be used as both a noun and a verb. For example: "I like the grade you did on this image." "I'll pull some of the blue out as I grade this." "Grade" will be a common term used in this book because it's easier to type than "color correct." Also, this is a preferred term used by many colorists because it does not have the implication that something needed to be simply "corrected." I think it also tends to imply that it is more art than science. "Color correction" seems like a very engineering-based term. The term "grade" seems to have more favor in Europe, but it is widely used throughout the world, including the United States.

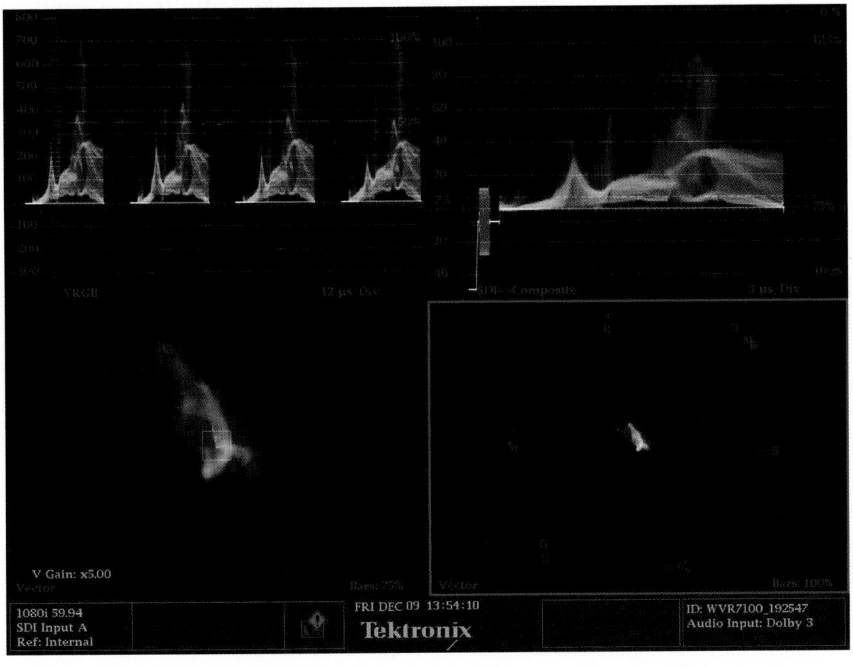

Fig. 1.20 Full display from a Tektronix WVR7100 showing (clockwise from upper left) a YRGB Parade, a composite (flat) display of the waveform, a vectorscope set to 5x gain (zoomed in), and a vectorscope set to normal gain.

If you look at the same horizontal area on the YRGB display (Figure 1.20 upper left corner)—the first of the three spikes—you will notice that the spike is taller in the red and green cells and shorter in the blue cell. I'll explain this in more detail in an upcoming sidebar, but the equal combination of red and green in RGB colorspace makes yellow. Now the yellowish nature of the spike is certainly partly due to the fact that the highlight on the bag is slightly yellowish, but the difference between the amount of red and green compared to blue at that point doesn't correspond to just a small yellowish tint to the highlight. It indicates something that is quite yellow, like the rectangles at the top of the punching bag.

Continuing on across the waveform from left to right, there are a four grayish spikes leading up to a thick spire that sits about one-third of the way across the image. These smallish spikes are the highlights in the wrinkles at the top of the punching bag: one along the seam in the middle of the bag and three short, but bright highlights just to the left of the other yellow rectangle. The tall spear in the waveform is the bright highlight at the top of the right side of the bag. Notice that in the tall spear, the discrepancy between the height of the red, green, and blue cells is minimized, because the yellow of the rectangle is obscured both by the bright highlight and in shadow. Your brain tells you that this has to be the same color yellow as the rectangle on the other side of the bag, but if you just look at the right-side rectangle, it's very difficult to make out any real yellow tint.

After the spike from the right-side bag highlight, there is a slightly elevated band in the waveform that goes between about 2 or 3IRE up to about 20IRE. (On the YRGB Parade, it goes from about 15 millivolts to about 150 millivolts if you use the measurement scale to the left, which goes from −300 to 800.) This band corresponds to the light caught by the atmospheric smoke between the boxer and the bag.

The complex shape to the right of that is the boxer. The highest portions of this shape indicate the reflected highlights from the top of his rear boxing glove, head, neck, shoulders, and left tricep. There are also bright portions indicating his white shirt, reflections on his pants, and the brighter flesh of his chest and forearm. The heavy band at the very bottom of the waveform is the shadow of his pants. On the right side of this shape, it falls off precipitously, with only a small ramp around 40–50IRE (Figure 1.19c). I think that ramp is the highlight from the top of his back leg.

The rest of the waveform display to the right is the bright haze of smoke. The top of the band is the bright smoke at the top of the picture gradually tapering down to the dark shadow at the bottom of the picture, behind the boxer. Notice that at about 20IRE on the waveform monitor about two-thirds of the way across there is a circular gap in this smoke band? That's where the boxer is blocking the haze.

Definition

IRE: One of the units of measurement that can describe a composite analog video signal's amplitude (brightness), where 0IRE generally represents black and white extends to +100IRE. 1IRE is equal to 1/140 of a volt or 7.14 millivolts in NTSC, though in all other systems, it corresponds to 7 millivolts. IRE stands for the Institute of Radio Engineers, which defined the unit.

Notice that the placement of picture elements in the vertical axis has no bearing on the waveform. In other words, there is no indication on the waveform whether a bright spot is at the top of the picture or at the bottom of the picture.

Looking at the black levels of this picture, you can see that they are already set about as low as they can go without crushing the detail out of the darker portions of the picture. This is no surprise, really, as this is stock footage from Artbeats that was shot on film and already benefited from a colorist's touch as it was transferred from film to tape.

Setting the Black Level

Let's look at an image that needs to have the black level adjusted. The most obvious candidate would be a picture that looks a little washed out. We're going to analyze the image in a number of ways and then look at several tools in various applications to correct the problem.

Please import the file "Brian interview overexposed" (Figure 1.21) from the DVD. It is a CCIR601 file size (NTSC, standard-definition video) and color space with interlaced fields, lower field first. You can use the color correction software that is most comfortable to you. I apologize to those of you in PAL or SECAM land. You will have to transcode the tutorial footage from these NTSC QuickTime files to something usable by your equipment.

The very first way that most colorists analyze an image is to view it on a broadcast monitor, which used to mean a CRT (cathode ray tube) display, but increasingly, even serious colorists are turning to LCD (liquid crystal display) monitors and projectors as CRTs have been phased out. Future monitor technologies, like SED (surface conduction electron emitter display), hold great promise, but are not available as of the

Fig. 1.21 An interview shot with available light on BetaSP back in 1996. I was the shooter and my brother Brian is the subject. This footage is available on the DVD as the file labeled "Brian interview overexposed."

Definition

clipping: An electronic limit on the maximum brightness of an image (usually imposed in the camera) to avoid overly bright or hot signals, or simply due to the fact that the imaging or recording medium can't perceive or record any greater brightness. Images recorded with portions where that level were exceeded will have lost picture information—detail—where the image exceeded the level. Clipping can usually be perceived on a waveform as a flattening out of the top of the trace into a sharp white horizontal line. Clipping is also possible on the low end of the signal, but that is generally referred to as "crushing." It is also possible for clipping to occur in individual color channels. An artifact of clipping is the flattening out of tonal or color detail.

writing of this book. OLED (organic light emitting diode) technology seems to be the current gold standard for reproducing the rich blacks that CRTs were able to achieve.

For now, you may use the image on the pages of the book itself, but you may also find this image on the DVD as a QuickTime file. The duration of each of the tutorial clips is quite short, in order to get as much data onto the disk as possible.

Import the file into whatever application you choose to use to do the tutorials. This might be Apple's Color, DaVinci's Resolve, IRIDAS's Speed-Grade (now owned by Adobe), Discreet's Lustre, Synthetic Aperture's Color Finesse, any of the Avid products, Apple's Final Cut Pro or Shake, or Adobe's Premiere or After Effects. There are obviously more desktop color correctors, compositors, and nonlinear editing systems with color correction capabilities as well. If you want to, you could even attempt these corrections with Adobe Photoshop.

Looking at this footage, you can see that the image has very little contrast and is quite washed out, with very little bottom (see the sidebar "The Language of Music and Color" on this page). There are no darker tones to anchor the midrange and highlights. The subject is poorly separated from the background elements. Looking at the waveform monitor indicates that there is probably some clipping of the highlights in the sky area, but there should be plenty of detail available in the rest of the image. The blacks are certainly not crushed because very little of the waveform trace is below 20IRE.

The Language of Music and Color

As someone who has hung out and performed with musicians most of his life, and who has had the chance to hear the unique language of colorists as well, I have noticed that the language of these two groups of artists is remarkably similar.

The example of the word "bottom" is used in both worlds. In music, it refers to having bass tones or low frequencies. To a colorist, it means blacks and deep shadows. Musicians and colorists also refer to images and music as being "warm" or "cool."

"Tone," "color," "midrange," "high end," "low end," and "shading" are often discussed by musicians. These words are obviously important to colorists as well. Adding "sparkle" or "depth" are things desired by both groups. "Spreading the tonal range" and "creating definition" are common goals. Having something that sounds or looks "thin" is bad for either group, while having an image or a sound that is "fat" is usually desirable. (And I don't mean "phat.") Other common words include "tension," "contrast," "texture," and "brightness."

To both groups, these are words that cross the artistic divide between the aural arts and the visual arts. What connects them is emotion.

Both color and music have a profound effect on our emotions. That is why they are both so important to storytellers and others who use media to influence and affect an audience.

Also, because collaboration and creative communication are important to both groups, it is important to learn to speak and understand a common language with your colleagues. The language used for creative communications is constantly evolving and is also varied by geography and by specific types of film and video professionals, so the exploration of these terms will need to be a personal one.

When you encounter a new word that is tossed at you by another creative professional, you can either ask what it means, if your ego will allow it, or "mirror" the phrase back with the meaning you *think* that the speaker intended. So if someone says "The bottom seems a little thin." You can say, "So you want me to pull down the shadows to beef it up a little?" If you get an affirmative response, then you know you've translated it correctly.

trace: The part of the waveform monitor that indicates the actual image being fed into the waveform. The other elements of the waveform monitor (IRE numbers and lines) are relatively fixed and are referred to as the graticule. ("Graticule" is also the word used for the longitude and latitude lines on a map.) On some waveform monitors, the graticule and the trace have separate brightness adjustments.

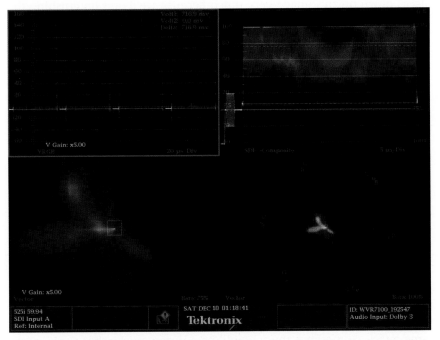

Fig. 1.22 Tektronix display showing (clockwise from upper left corner) a YRGB parade zoomed in 5x to the bottom of the waveform, a standard composite waveform with no zoom, a vectorscope with a 5x zoom, and a standard vectorscope display.

The standard composite waveform monitor (top right quadrant) shows that there is a small area in the middle of the image that appears to be almost on the 0IRE line where black should be, but most of the rest of the image doesn't reach all the way down to black (0IRE); see Figure 1.22.

An experienced colorist would actually tackle this color cast in the blacks at the same time, but we're going to break this task down into its components.

Looking at the YRGB Parade waveform (top left quadrant) shows that really nothing is hitting black except a small portion in the middle of the blue cell. This indicates that there really isn't a nice rich black anywhere in the picture and that the black balance has a heavy blue cast to it. We'll deal with the blue cast in the next chapter. For now our goal is to spread the tonal range, focusing on bringing the black level down to the proper level first.

An experienced colorist would actually tackle this color cast in the blacks at the same time, but we're going to break this task down into its components. Generally speaking, though, we wouldn't want to pull the overall blacks down on this image very much because we'll end up crushing the blacks in the blue channel while trying to bring down the overall level. That will mean we'll lose some detail there *and* cause some color problems.

So far we've used three methods to look at the black level in this image: we viewed the actual image on a broadcast monitor, we viewed a composite waveform display, and we viewed a YRGB waveform display. You'll learn more ways to analyze the image later in the book. Some of these methods have the widespread support of professional colorists; others are still gaining acceptance as the tools evolve.

Now that we have analyzed the image, it is time to actually *do* something to it. To affect the black levels, we are going to look at a few tools common to many of these applications. I will not show all of the tools from all of the applications, but I'll show you a broad array of tools that are available across the spectrum of applications. Your application may not have all of these tools. But you should be able to find one or two of them that look familiar, even if the specific tool is from a different application. That's all you'll need.

Often, when I'm teaching color correction, I tell the story of my martial arts training. I never got very far in the art that I studied—Hapkido—but I learned a lot of great lessons. One of the things that we did in Hapkido training was to learn many, many different ways to defend against the same attack. Sometimes there would be a dozen approaches to the same problem. We practiced all of these approaches over and over again, but the more we practiced, the more each of us felt comfortable with just two or three of the methods. That is the way the training was supposed to work. Depending on your physical build, strength, speed, weight, flexibility, and agility, certain methods would almost always work better. All of the methods were taught so that each of us could find what worked best for us. Sometimes the speed, strength, and skill of an opponent would dictate which defense was the best. The same goes for color correction. You'll see lots of tools and techniques. Some you won't be able to use because you don't have those tools at your disposal. Other tools or techniques just won't feel comfortable compared to others. And sometimes you'll use the same technique 99 percent of the time, but every once in a while, you'll need to try something different on a specific image because of the unique problems it presents. This Hapkido example is an important one to remember as you are exposed to the various ways to both analyze the image and to correct it.

All of the methods were taught so that each of us could find what worked best for us.

Now, back to setting the blacks on this particular image. We're going to watch the waveform monitor—and the broadcast monitor—and find a tool in your application that controls the setup, shadow, or black level. I'll tackle this correction in Apple's Color.

With the clip "Brian overexposed" called up into your application (Figure 1.23a), keep your eye on the RGB or YRGB waveform display (Figure 1.23b). Bring down the master setup level until the trace of the blue channel of the waveform display starts to flatten out at the bottom, then bring

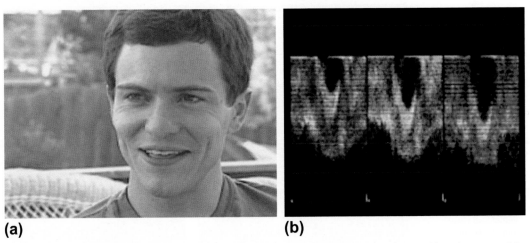

(a)   **(b)**

Fig. 1.23 (a) Here's the original source image again. Please remember that the translation between the RGB video color space and the CMYK print color space is not perfect. (b) Here's the internal RGB Parade waveform display that corresponds to the uncorrected image.

it back just a hair. If you don't have an RGB or YRGB display, then bring down the setup (or black or shadow) level until the overall waveform level starts to flatten out at the bottom, then bring it up just a touch.

In Color, there are two ways in the Primary Room that you can make this adjustment. One would be to drag inside of the black to white gradated bar in the Shadows group (Figure 1.24a). I pulled the shadows down to around –0.301 from 0 (Figure 1.24b).

Or, on the right side of the screen, you could pull the Master Lift down to about the same level. (This is done by dragging in the number window, holding down the center button or mouse scroll wheel.)

One of my favorite color correction analogies is that making adjustments—especially to blacks and highlights—is like focusing a camera. Point a camera at a subject and look in the viewfinder. The image may, by chance, appear to be in focus. But you don't *really* know if it's in focus or not unless you adjust the focus ring a little bit in each direction, then settle in on the proper focus. Doing color correction is similar. You need to see how far you can push an image *and* when you haven't pushed it far enough.

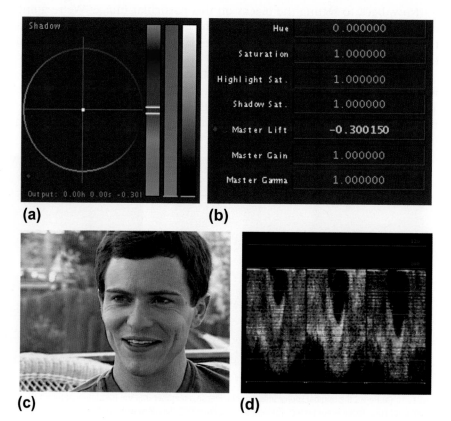

(a)   **(b)**

Fig. 1.24 (a) Shadow color wheel adjustment. (b) Master lift adjustment. (c) What the image should look like after the correction to shadows or lift. (d) The internal RGB Parade waveform display that corresponds to the first correction to shadows or lift.

(c)   **(d)**

The black levels can actually come down a little lower in the red and green channels, but we'll get to those kinds of adjustments in another tutorial. I chose to stop when the blue channel reached the bottom because I didn't want to clip or crush the blue shadows. Also, I was watching the detail area in the dark portions of the eyes, and that's as far as I could go before I started to lose details in the eyes.

Setting Highlights

With the black levels set, turn your attention to the highlights or gain controls. You can see from the waveform that the sky, especially on the right side, is clipped (Figure 1.25). This clipping is evident from the sharp white line at the top of the right side of the waveform display. It's never a good thing to see this kind of clipping, but it is very common in this kind of scenario of an interview shot outside with the sky in the shot. Trying to "unclip" this is not worth our time at the moment, so all we really want to do is set our gain control to get that clipped part of the sky to be the maximum legal level. We also want to use our "focusing" analogy to see if we can pull the highlights down to possibly eliminate the clipping. The clipping may be something that is fixable. You don't know until you try to get rid of it. If the shape of the top of the waveform stays flat, then the clipping occurred before it was brought in to the color corrector, probably during shooting.

When the maximum gain is reached, it may have affected your black levels, so adjust them a little bit to get them as close to 0IRE as possible

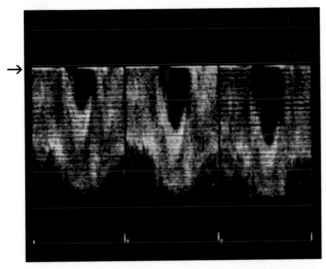

Fig. 1.25 The thin, hard white line at the top of the waveform display—indicated by the black arrow on the left side of the figure—shows where clipping of the highlights has occurred.

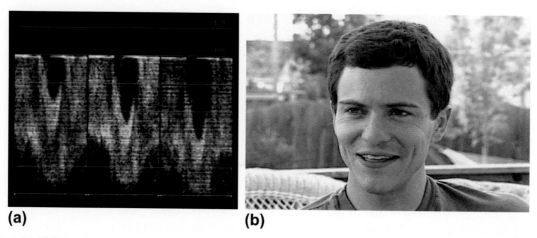

(a)   **(b)**

Fig. 1.26 (a) The resulting RGB Parade with a good spread between highlights and shadows. (b) The resulting image with the highlights and shadows spread out.

(assuming that your video signal is not set for 7.5IRE) without "crushing" any detail. Remember, we don't want to see the highlights or the shadows flatten out on the waveform monitor for now. The goal is to spread the tonal range from 0 to 100IRE.

Also, the shapes in the trace representing the brighter portions of your picture that are not already clipped will start to compress. Unless you are going for a specific "look," this clipping, flattening, or compressing is a bad thing. It means you are losing detail in those bright portions of the picture. This result is similar to the issues we discussed while setting black levels.

When you start to see this "flattening" in the waveform monitor, try to find the corresponding part of the image in the broadcast monitor and lift, then lower the gain while you watch the actual image (Figure 1.26). Do you notice the point at which the highlights begin to lose detail? Remember that camera focusing analogy here, too.

Making color correction adjustments is like focusing a camera.

If you don't have a limiter on your software, then the highlights can be adjusted far above "legal" without the waveform showing clipping (this may depend on your software or your settings in your software, to some extent). However, at some point in the broadcast or duplication or distribution chain, these super-bright highlights will get clipped. It's much better for the colorist to determine how and where the clipping occurs than to rely on some "dumb" device downstream to do this, because you'll have no control of the way the signal looks at that point. Plus, if you are doing these corrections with a client supervising the session, they may

Fig. 1.27 The table lamp behind the sleeping woman is referred to as a "practical."

Definition

practical lights: Sometimes called "practicals"; lights that are part of the scene, such as a table lamp in a scene next to an actor (Figure 1.27). Usually the brightness of practicals is closely controlled by the director of photography by changing the wattage of the bulb or putting it on a dimmer.

blow out: A nontechnical term for clipping or letting a bright highlight get so hot that it loses all or most of its detail. "The only way I can bring the level up enough to see the actor's face is to blow out the window."

love the look of what you're doing in the suite, but may be less than pleased when they see what the limiter does to their beautiful corrections.

For an image with highlights that are very high above the rest of the levels in the shot, you may want to set the main "brightness" using the midtones or gamma so that you have a pleasing level, then use the gain controls to bring just the highlights back down to a legal level. This example also can be an instance in which you break the rules in regards to clipping. If you have a scene that is perhaps mostly dark except for a couple of very bright practical lights that are seen in the shot or a scene with a very bright window behind a darker subject, you can make the decision to clip or "blow out" that window or practical in order to gain enough tonal range in the area that matters: your subject.

Make one last check to confirm that your setup change didn't affect your highlights, and then we'll find the correct gamma adjustment to make this look as rich and well lit as possible.

Setting Gamma or Midtones

After setting blacks and highlights, the final tonal correction is to set your midtones. This is how a lot of the mood of the shot is created. With the other two levels basically done by looking for their "extreme" legal limits, the overall tone of the piece is set using the gamma or midtone.

When *I* do color correction, I do not have to deal with too many outside opinions. My decision about the look is pretty much the final say. I realize that this is not the case for many colorists.

My personal preference when setting midtones in an image is to create a rich feel with a slightly lowered gamma. If your image seems a little dark, even with the highlights raised to the peak legal level, then raising your gamma can give you a brighter—though usually flatter—feel, sometimes somewhat akin to the look of a sitcom. The reason for this is that often the detail of the image is in the gamma and highlight areas, so the closer those two ranges are to each other, the less contrast there is in this critical portion of the image. Some images with more detail in darker portions of the image would actually look *less* flat by raising the gamma, but in my experience, this is the exception, not the rule.

When setting the gamma, there's really not much to go by except for personal taste. If you're trying to see into the shadows or trying to hide things a little in the shadows, then raising or lowering gamma—respectively—can accomplish much of what you want to do.

The final tonal correction is to set your midtones. This is how a lot of the mood of the shot is created.

Often I consider the gamma controls to be my "post lighting controls." If I feel like the on-set lighting was a little too contrasty or too flat, I can often use gamma to get it to look closer to what I want. Lowering the gamma usually increases the contrast in the shadow details of the flesh tones. Raising the gamma tends to flatten out those shadow details. A lot of that depends on the exact levels of the shadows on the flesh tones. On most "normal" footage, though, the shadows on flesh are in still in the midtone range, so lowering them tends to increase the contrast between the rest of the lit flesh tones, which are also in the midtones but are affected by the highlights as well.

To complete the correction on the Brian interview footage, let's set the gamma so that the flesh tones look rich and healthy but make sure that the footage isn't too dark. This is a pretty standard interview clip, so we want something that looks natural and not overly dramatic.

I brought the Master Gamma down about 0.05 in Color from 1.000 to 0.95. I used the "focusing" technique, looking at the eyes of the subject on the video monitor instead of at my waveform monitor. Actually, this was an instance in which the gamma looked good right where it was. When I brought it up higher than 1.0, the picture started to look washed out. When I brought it down around 0.90, it started to look too dark and I lost the detail and "sparkle" in his eyes. I ended up at around 0.955 (Figure 1.28). I want to point out that I wasn't being guided by the specific number of the gamma control. I was being guided by looking at the richness of the skin tone, the amount of texture and detail in the hair and eyes, and the overall brightness of the image. I am relating the numbers merely as a matter of reference after the fact.

Remember that if you are working with color correction software using only a mouse or single trackball to control tonal ranges one at a time, making adjustments to gamma will affect the levels for shadow and highlight that you've already set, so once you are done with your gamma adjustment,

(a)   **(b)**

Fig. 1.28 (a) The video image before correction. (b) The video image after correction. This is not a "final" correction; it is only the tonal correction in the primary room. The colors, saturation, and secondary color correction have not been affected yet.

you will need to revisit the corrections you did to highlights and shadows. Then readjust gamma. Then recheck highlight and shadow levels after that.

Something else that occurs with tonal range corrections—especially gamma corrections—is that the saturation of the image changes. If you are doing a tonal range correction and you start to dislike what you're seeing, try to determine whether it's the actual tonal range or if it's the increase in saturation. If it's saturation-based, try to ignore the saturation of the image and just look at the tonal range apart from that. You can always go back in and readjust the saturation independently when you are done with the tonal range correction.

Defining Contrast

Another important concept to understand in developing the tonality of an image is that contrast is not just a "global" parameter in an image. *Contrast* is generally defined as the range of an image from brightest to darkest. The wider the range, the more the contrast. But it is possible to increase the contrast in a specific area of an image by playing either the highlights against the gammas or the shadows against the gammas. This method can develop an increased amount of contrast in your shadows, your midtones, or your highlights. You can use it to draw attention to parts of the image that you want the viewer to focus on.

It is possible to increase the contrast in a specific area of an image by playing either the highlights against the gammas or the shadows against the gammas.

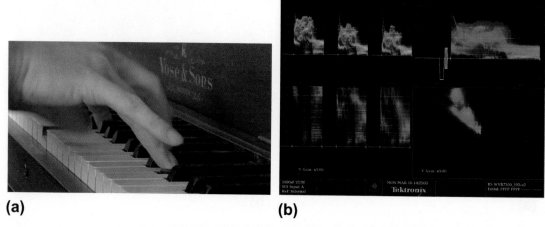

(a)   **(b)**

Fig. 1.29 (a) Warm piano image. b) Waveform images for warm piano images.

How does this method work? Think of the waveform image of a picture with low contrast. The entire trace on the waveform is squished into a small area. To increase the contrast across the entire image, you spread out the trace by making the shadows lower and the highlights higher. Now you can use this same concept to increase the contrast in a specific portion of the image. The goal in that area is to spread out the distance between the bottom of that portion and the top. So, if you want to increase contrast in your dark shadows, you lower the shadows and raise the midtones.

Now you have a choice of adding contrast to the area between midtones and shadow or midtones and highlights.

Notice that the difference in contrast between the tops of the black keys and the sides of the blacks keys is not that different (Figure 1.29a). If you wanted to increase that contrast so that the sides of the keys were more black and the tops seemed to have more light, then you would lower the shadow level (or Master Lift as it is called in Color) while raising the Master Gamma. In addition to seeing a difference in the image, notice that the spread of the trace in the lower portion of the waveform also becomes greater, indicating increased contrast.

I took this approach to an extreme in this case to make the difference clearly visible. In this instance, I introduced a lot of unwanted noise and a gamut error, but the contrast between the highlights of the black keys and the deeper shadows of the black keys is definitely sharper (compare the front highlight of the black keys in the middle, under the hands), while the hands have become more washed out.

Now change the contrasty portion of the picture to the highlights instead of the shadows.

Notice that one image emphasizes the keys and the other emphasizes the hands. The name of the piano is also clearer because the contrast has been increased between mid and high. Also, notice that the lower portions of the waveform monitor are stretched out when the contrast is in the shadows, as opposed to the stretched upper portion when the contrast is in the highlights.

Understanding how to gain contrast in the correct portion of the picture is essential as you develop your skills as a colorist. It isn't enough to simply increase the overall contrast. You need to be able to control contrast within the image because that helps in creating distinct "looks" in your images and also helps direct the viewer's eye where you want to focus it. Practicing this particular contrast "focusing" trick will also help you when a client asks you to "pop" something off of a background. To do that, you will need to understand the tonal range of the background and the tonal range of what is supposed to pop off of it and then figure out how to stretch that range. This trick is further supported by eliminating contrast in other areas of the picture so that the viewer's eye is drawn to the areas of the image that have more information. If you crush the shadows, then there is nothing to look at in that area and the viewer looks elsewhere.

I boosted the contrast even more in an attempt to get the piano name to pop even more off the background. One thing to be very aware of in doing these extreme contrast moves is that increasing contrast also increases the chroma levels. The hands got very heavily colored and unnatural as I pushed the contrast, so I had to also lower the saturation levels across the board. You can control the saturation of shadows, midtones, and highlights separately, so use this ability to create natural-looking color levels and reduce noise in unwanted areas. Some of the most objectionable noise is color noise, so reducing the saturation levels where you see noise can really clean up an image.

This concept of playing gammas against the highlights and shadows to increase contrast in specific regions of the picture is very important to your ability to quickly and easily manipulate the "look" of an image. It will help you execute a look that a client has in mind, and it will help you match the look of two or more shots in a sequence. Because of the importance of this concept, you should really practice this on your own.

The three images you will need to develop this skill are a ramp like the one on the DVD called "BWRamp" or "ramp from 0-254.psd." Most non-linear editing systems (NLEs) have a similar test image built in to them, or you can even make your own. The ramp should start at 0 percent luminance on one side (usually the left) and then go all the way to 100 percent luminance on the other side (usually the right). The other image that you will need is the image of the chip chart from the DVD called "grayscale_neutral." And finally, use some of the real video from the DVD or—better yet—from your own projects to see how these gamma versus highlights or shadows corrections affect a natural image.

Think of it as a rubber band. At first the image is "loose" and low contrast. Then you stretch the tonal range so that it goes from 0 to 100 or whatever is natural. Now the rubber band is tightened and contrast is increased. But you can also grab the *middle* of the rubber band and pull it up or down as well, stretching values (adding contrast) in one direction and compressing them (lowered contrast) in another.

This practice will be greatly enhanced by using a manual control device with the ability to adjust the highlights, gammas, and shadows all at the same time, like the Tangent Devices CP-200 or CP-100 that the colorists in this book used. The reason for this is that adjusting the gammas will obviously have an effect on the highlights and shadows, so if you can move only one at a time, it will require numerous adjustments back and forth as the various tonal range corrections interact.

Practice with the ramp image and try to get the dark part of the ramp compressed in a tight dark band on one end while the bright area is spread out more. Then reverse that. If you can copy and paste your color corrections in your application, try applying these corrections to real-life images or to the grayscale chart.

Do the same thing with the grayscale chart. Try to get the chips at the bottom to all be very close together while spreading the distance between each chip in the highs and mid-highs. Then do the opposite.

Try to practice on real-life images from the DVD or your own collection. What if you want to add lots of contrast to the skin tones? What if you wanted to see lots of detail in the shadows? How could you get more detail out of the clouds in the sky? Playing gamma against the other two tonal ranges will deliver these effects. Taking the highlights or shadows *past* the point of clipping and *then* playing with gammas will take these corrections even further by stretching the contrast over an even greater area.

CHAPTER 2

Primary Color Correction: Tonal Correction Tools

This chapter describes the tonal correction tools available in several of the applications and plug-ins for doing color correction. It also describes their respective strengths and weaknesses.

Main Tools for Tonal Corrections

Across the range of products, there are lots of tools. Some of them help to alter tonal range; some are more commonly used to control the "color" of the image, generically meaning that they'd be used to control hue and saturation, though they'd also have some effect on the tonal range as well.

For tonal corrections, almost every application that has color correction abilities has some slider or numerical controls to adjust brightness, contrast, black level (sometimes also called lift, shadows, pedestal, blacks, or setup, as mentioned in Chapter 1), and gamma. Some applications may also include numerous sliders and numerical entry windows for various tweaks to the gamma, including knee, shoulder, softness, and the width or specific range of each of these gamma adjustments.

In addition to the typical sliders controls—which are sometimes controllable by knobs or dials on an external manual interface like those made by Tangent Devices (Figure 2.1), JLCooper, and Avid—some applications also give you tonal control via the manipulation of histograms, which some applications call Levels. Most of these Level controls allow you to adjust the output level, which is a fairly intuitive thing to do, but some also include the ability to adjust the actual *input* Levels using a histogram, which will work the reverse of the way you would think.

Another very common way in computer applications to adjust tonal ranges is via curves. Curves is a popular tonal correction tool because it offers incredibly precise control and is very intuitive. So you'd figure that it is *the* tool to use for tonal corrections, but there is a caveat: you can *really* screw up your images with this tool. Most applications that have curves allow you to place as many as 16 distinct points on the curve to control it. All of these points can do some very funky things to your image, including creating severe posterization or banding. Patrick Palmer, formerly of IRIDAS and now with Adobe, points to these issues as the reason Speedgrade does not have Curves. Curves is a favorite tool of Photoshop users, After Effects users, and those who move back and forth between Photoshop and video applications. Full-time colorists are much less enamored of this tool, though with exposure to it through Apple's Color and DaVinci Resolve, that may change.

posterization: Posterization happens when an image breaks down from having *continuous* tones to having specific regions of tones where each region has a *distinct transition* to the next (Figure 2.2b). This effect is similar to banding.

Fig. 2.1 Tangent Devices Elements control panel.

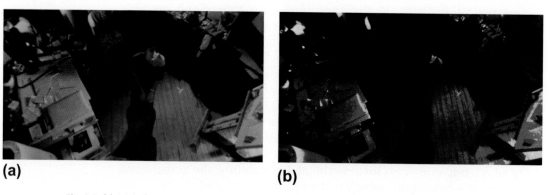

(a)   **(b)**

Fig. 2.2 (a) Original image (16 mm film transfer to HD courtesy Vanderpool Films). (b) Posterized image.

(a)   (b)

Fig. 2.3   (a) Original image, DV resolution (Courtesy Randy Riesen). (b) Sky exhibiting banding.

Sliders and Numerical Controls for Tonal Range

Let's start the exploration of these tonal correction tools with simple sliders and numerical input. There are two test patterns that can help you understand the specifics of what these tools can do as you start to explore.

Load the chip chart image from the DVD tutorial media folder ("gray-scale_neutral") and load a ramp pattern. See if your application has one of these ramps. It will have been created for the specific way that your application treats video black. If not, you can use one of the ramps on the DVD ("ramp from 0-254.psd").

banding: Similar to posterization, banding occurs when a continuous tone image breaks down into bands of distinct, individual tones. This effect usually occurs in gradients such as the sky. For example, the image begins as a continuous gradation from light blue to dark blue, then through overcorrection (or a radical change in color space or compression) turns into individually discernable bands of color (Figure 2.3b). Banding is more likely to happen with lower-bit-depth images (8-bit instead of 10-bit images).

Definition

chip chart: A camera setup chart that has several different gray "chips" that range from white to black. The chart that is used throughout this book is DSC Labs CamAlign GrayScale Test Pattern chart (Figure 2.4). It has 11 gray patches or "chips" that have specific reflectance values.

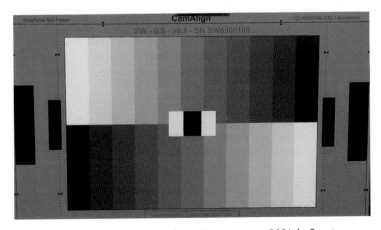

Fig. 2.4   DSC CamAlign GreyScale Test Pattern, courtesy DSC Labs, Toronto.

Don't Use Brightness or Contrast Controls

Of all of the controls available in most applications, the Brightness and Contrast controls are the ones that should be avoided. Why? Because they limit the control you have, compared to other sliders.

Watch what happens on a waveform when you use the brightness slider to adjust the image of the ramp or the chip chart. The entire trace of the waveform moves up and down uniformly. Compare this effect to adjusting the gain. When using gain, there is some movement in the other tonal ranges of the picture, but the largest percentage of adjustment occurs only in the highlights of the picture.

Now grade the chip chart or ramp image using the Contrast control. The Contrast control will compress or expand the entire trace of the waveform equally from each end of the tonal range by raising the blacks by an equal amount as it lowers the whites, or vice versa. Good color correction is all about having control, and Brightness and Contrast rob you of control.

Good color correction is all about having control, and Brightness and Contrast rob you of control.

So what do you do if you want to make the picture brighter or add contrast? Well, "brightness" comes from several things. Bringing the gain up to its highest legal level is a key one. Sometimes, because of some very bright highlights, the picture will still seem too dark once you have raised the gain on those highlights to 100IRE because the middle tones of the picture—containing much of the real information—were not raised much. In that case, the real sense of how bright the picture looks is done in the midtones (more on that in a moment). Sometimes, getting a picture bright enough may even involve increasing the gain so much that some of the brightest parts of the image will clip. That is a judgment call that you need to make in deciding what parts of the image "deserve" to have the most detail. If the highlights are not important, then you can clip them to the point where detail is lost in order to rescue detail from the high midtones and midtones, because clipping out the highest highlights will also raise the levels of the middle highlights and midtones.

Greater contrast usually comes from setting nice rich shadows using the setup control and then getting as much of a range as possible between the darkest portions of the picture and the brightest portions of the picture. The contrast control rarely works for this purpose because if your blacks are muddy but your highlights are almost at their maximum level, for example, then you can only slightly increase contrast before the highlights can't go any higher without clipping. If you want *lots* of contrast, you can ignore all of the warnings about clipping either end of the signal and really stretch out the tonal range. You will have better results doing an extreme contrast move with a system that does its color correction computations in a higher color space. DaVinci Resolve works in 32-bit floating point, as do Apple Color and Color Finesse. Avid works at 10-bit. All of them have to convert these color corrections back to the original bit depth of the source footage or the highest output bit depth, which is often 8-bit, 10-bit, or 12-bit.

Knowing all of that, if you find the need to raise the entire tonal range of the picture *equally*, or to compress or expand the contrast (entire tonal range) of your picture *equally*, then feel free to use Brightness and Contrast controls. An example of this could be in a nonlinear editor: if you want to reduce the overall contrast of an image quickly so that a title or text "pops" over the background more, then lowering contrast would be an ideal tool.

Although you might do your color correction with only one of the following products, I hope you'll check out the description of how the corrections are done in each of the products. I can't give descriptions of *all* of the products out there, so I'll show you specific GUI tools from a certain representative sample of products. The way your particular product works may not be included in the list, but the basic operating principles will probably be similar to one of the other products mentioned here. Some applications or plug-ins have very "proprietary" tools that I'll sometimes mention and show. Other times, the basic tools operate nearly identically across all color correction products. In that case, it's hardly worth describing the same process over and over, so I'll select an application that is representative of them all. Interfaces change from release to release and products come and go, so I'll try to just give an overview here.

As I've mentioned, there are a *lot* of NLEs, standalone color correctors, plug-ins, and compositors out there with color correction tools. Covering them all—and knowing them all thoroughly—is impossible, but I will show you some of the main ways that you can affect your tonal corrections in each of several applications.

Just before I finished writing this edition of the book, Adobe purchased IRIDAS and its color correction application, SpeedGrade. Because of the timing of the acquisition, I won't be discussing Adobe's color correction application in this book, but the principles of operating it will be the same as using the tools in many of the other applications included in the following chapters.

Let's start with the tools in DaVinci Resolve. You should really read about all of the different applications, because certain tips and material may be covered only when I discuss that specific application, even though that information may pertain to more than one application. I also believe that colorists might become more like editors, who need to know multiple

Definition

bit depth: The number of bits (the smallest data amount, basically on or off binary information) used to describe a color. There's a little confusion about bit depth numbers. Sometimes what is referred to as 8-bit is the same as 24-bit because they are saying that 8 bits per color channel multiply to 24 bits (8 × 3); 8 bits of color depth gives you 256 shades of gray. Then you multiply those 256 shades of gray times the three color channels (256 × 256 × 256) to show how many colors you can describe in that color space (16.7 million colors). And 10-bit video has 1024 shades of gray instead of 256. Obviously, 10-bit video is going to be preferable for color correction. The bit depth computations here generate numbers that are on the theoretical limits. You are really limited in the actual number of levels of tones and colors by your recording and display devices and the color spaces that they represent.

applications in order to stay viable and employed, Obviously, that doesn't apply to everyone, but many colorists will be able to make a good living by diversifying the products with which they make their living, so knowing the capabilities and limitations of each will be a valuable career enhancer.

DaVinci Resolve

In DaVinci Resolve, primary color correction is done in the Color screen (Figure 2.5); screens are accessed from the buttons in the middle along the bottom of the UI.

Inside the Color screen interface, at the bottom left corner, is an area of three tabs labeled Primary, 3-Way Color, and RGB Mixer. For tonal range controls, let's first look at the Luma Lift, Luma Gamma, and Luma Gain sliders. They're the vertical sliders to the left of the RGB sliders for Lift, Gamma, and Gain. These controls are best accessed from a hardware color correction control surface, like the Avid Artist series (Figure 2.6) or, of course, DaVinci's own controllers (Figure 2.7), but you can definitely just grab each slider in the middle (the default position) and drag it up or down.

A very interesting feature is the LUM MIX control, which allows you to mix the tonal range corrections made with the Luma sliders back in

Fig. 2.5 DaVinci Resolve's Primary controls are in the Color screen, accessed through the buttons at the bottom center of the screen.

Fig. 2.6 The Avid MC Color control surface works with several color correction applications, including DaVinci Resolve.

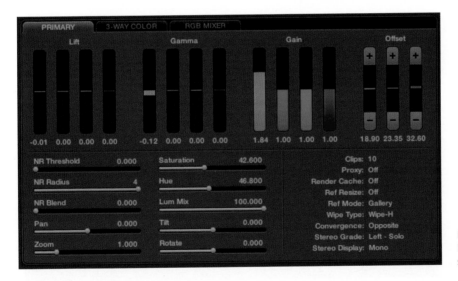

Fig. 2.7 DaVinci Resolve's Primary Tab in the Color screen.

with the original tonal ranges of the image. This mix allows for some very interesting effects. I haven't found in other color correction systems, though it could exist or might have been added since I wrote this.

The 3-Way Color tab (Figure 2.8) is also part of the Primary controls. This tab will look familiar to almost anyone who's spent any time in Final Cut Pro, Avid, Color, or any number of other color correction interfaces. Although the wheels can't help you with your tonal corrections, you can use the dials below the wheels to adjust lift, gamma, and highlights. The 3-Way Color tab also has a LUM MIX control to blend corrections.

Fig. 2.8 Resolve 3-Way Color tab, added in version 8.01. The tonal controls are the dials directly below each color wheel.

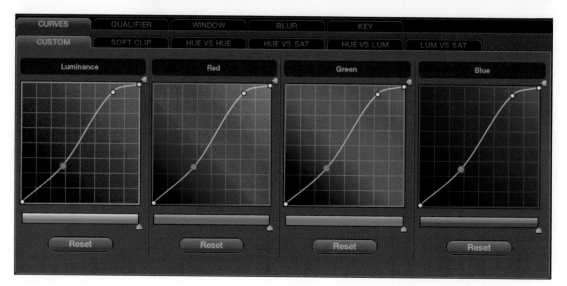

Fig. 2.9 Resolve's Custom Curve controls allow you a more graphical, intuitive representation of your tonal range control.

Finally, in the next control panel to the right from the Primary panel, in the Curves/Custom tabs, are similar color curve controls to those featured in Photoshop, Avid, and Color (Figure 2.9). The three colored curves give you control over the balance of your image, but the gray curve to the left is the Luminance curve, which can be used to adjust tonal values. In addition to the traditional points that can be manipulated on the curves, there is also a small triangle to the right top of each curve that can be used to compress the tonal scale and even invert it to a negative image by dragging vertically on the triangle. The other unique control device is the small bar directly below the curve with a triangle to the right side. These controls are the LUM MIX controls, allowing you to blend the correction back with some of the original image.

For more details on how to use curves, see the sidebar on page 54 "How Curves Work" as well as two other curve-related tutorials and tips.

Color Primary In Room

There are three tools to use for the most intuitive tonal corrections. The first is the colored sliders at the top of the screen to the right of each of the three color wheels. The first, rainbow-colored vertical bar in each group adjusts hue. The middle bars adjust the chroma or saturation level of the image. And the black/white bars to the right of each group adjust the level of the black point, midtone (gamma) distribution or white point in the shadow, and midtone or highlight tonal ranges, respectively (Figure 2.10).

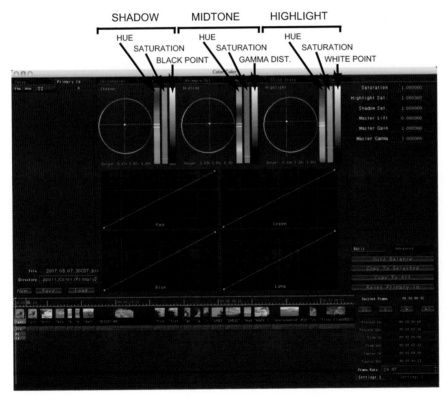

Fig. 2.10 **Color's Primary In Room** Apple discontinued Apple Color when it launched Final Cut Pro X in 2011, but many colorists are still using it, and the concepts discussed in this section apply to other color correction applications. This book was originally made possible when Color's predecessor, FinalTouch, allowed me to bring a professional color correction system around the country to visit many of the colorists featured in this book.

Definition

hue offset wheels: A circular user interface patterned like a color wheel or vectorscope that allows for the control of both hue and saturation. Hue values are indicated around the perimeter of the circle and saturation is indicated by the respective distance from the center of the circle. With some color correctors with manual user interfaces, these hue offset wheels can be controlled by multiple trackballs. Each wheel controls a different tonal range.

gamma: Gamma has several definitions, but the primary one that is used by colorists is to describe the midtones or midrange tones of a picture. Gamma can also refer to the curve or steepness of the transition from black to white. These are similar definitions in a way, because by altering the gamma—or midrange—of a picture, the curve or transition from shadow to highlight is also affected. Directors of Photography usually refer to gamma to mean the response curve from black to white instead of meaning the midtones, specifically.

Each group—consisting of a circular color wheel (sometimes referred to as *hue offset wheels*) and three vertical bars—controls one of the three tonal ranges. The far left group is for shadows. The middle group is for midtones or gamma. And the right group is for highlights.

If you have an Avid Artist Color controller, a JLCooper MCS Spectrum controller or Eclipse-CX, or a Tangent Devices Element, Wave (Figure 2.11), CP100, or CP200-BK controller, the dials and trackballs on the controller are linked to the various controls on the GUI. For most controllers, each trackball controls the corresponding Hue Offset wheel on the GUI. The rings around each trackball control the black point, gamma distribution, and white point (from left to right). And the dials at the top of the device control saturation. On all of these devices, the dials, buttons, and knobs are customizable and serve several functions, depending on the way it is customized by the user or by "the factory."

If you are using Color with just a mouse or a trackball, you can bring the shadows or blacks up or down by dragging the small, horizontal cyan line that is at the bottom of the black/white bar on the left. There is a similar small, horizontal cyan line across the middle of the middle black/white bar. Drag this up or down to control the midtones of your image. To control highlights, drag the cyan line at the top of the righthand black/white bar up or down.

The second way to control tonal corrections is to use the entry windows for master lift, master gamma, and master gain controls along the right side of the screen, near the top. You can type in numbers, but that is hardly intuitive. The best way to control these sliders with a mouse is to use the scroll wheel. Hover the mouse over the numeric lift, gamma, or gain number, click down on the scroll wheel, and drag the mouse left and right to adjust in gross increments, or scroll the wheel itself up and down for fine increments.

The default tab in this location is the Basic tab, but you can also make corrections with the Advanced tab. We'll get into that a little more in

Fig. 2.11 The Tangent Devices Wave control surface is compatible with Apple Color and several other color correction applications.

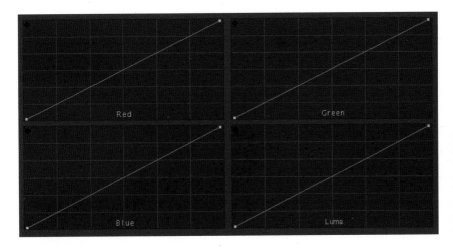

Fig. 2.12 Because we're discussing only tonal corrections in this chapter, tonal corrections would be made using the Luma Curve, which is the bottom right control of the four curves.

Chapter 4, as the Advanced tab is more for making color corrections than tonal corrections.

Much of the use of these specific tools was covered in the previous chapter when we corrected the overexposed interview footage of Brian.

The third way to control tonal corrections is to use the Curves controls (Figure 2.12), which are located in the middle of the Primary In room.

Although the previous two methods of controlling tone in the Primary In room of Color allow control over three tonal ranges, the Luma Curve allows you to alter the black and white points by moving the bottom and top corner of the curve. But it also allows multiple custom selected points in between those points that can be adjusted in any direction.

For more on the use of curves, see the Curves control section later in this chapter.

The Avid Symphony and Color Finesse HSL Control Tab

There are actually a number of subtabs in this area. You can affect the master HSL levels, which include controls for the master highlights, midtones and shadows, or you can gain more discrete control by adjusting the same controls inside the specific tonal ranges. This means you can control the highlights, midtones, and shadows of the highlights; the highlights, midtones, and shadows of the midtones; and the highlights, midtones, and shadows of the shadows. How are there highlights of shadows? There aren't, really. But instead of simply giving you three tonal ranges, the extra tabs let you restrict your corrections to *nine* discrete tonal ranges: the high highs, mid highs, low highs, high mids, mid mids, low mids, high shadows, mid shadows, and low shadows. IRIDAS Speedgrade (now owned by Adobe) has these same types of tonal range controls.

D e f i n i t i o n

HSL: Hue, saturation, and luminance. Sometimes referred to as HSB, or hue, saturation, and brightness.

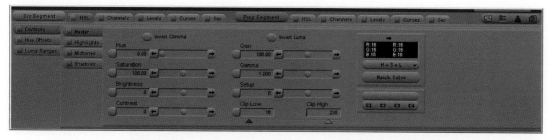

Fig. 2.13 **HSL controls in Avid Symphony.** For basic adjustments to tonal ranges using sliders or numerical values, Symphony and Color Finesse have several options, depending on how much control you want to exercise. The quick and dirty place to start is the HSL Controls tab of the color correction mode.

If you have Symphony or Color Finesse, you can get a better sense for how all these crazy "shadows of the highlights" and "highlights of the shadows" controls work by putting up the grayscale "chip chart" in the color correction mode and watching your waveform monitor as you adjust each of the controls.

There are a couple of controls on this tab that you should not use, even though they may seem to be the most obvious ones to start with. The Hue and Saturation controls are not really for doing tonal corrections, so I'll discuss those later. And as I already mentioned at the start of this section, Brightness and Contrast really limit your control over specific tonal ranges, as they affect all areas of the picture equally.

Histograms or Levels

I'm not much of a fan of the Levels controls that are available in many NLEs. But if you are comfortable with viewing the levels in histograms, this could be a powerful way for you to have intuitive control over the same basic gain, midrange, and shadow control that was available in the HSL Controls tab (Figure 2.14).

If you are unfamiliar with the concept of histograms, then you may want to read the sidebar that details how to read them.

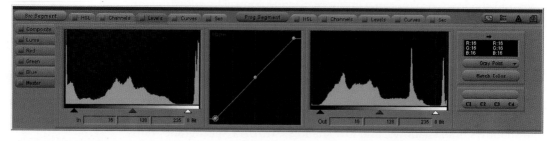

Fig. 2.14 The Symphony Levels control allows you to adjust levels while viewing histograms.

Histograms

A histogram is a very simple graph. Horizontally across the *x* axis (redundant, I know, but I'm trying to be clear) indicates the image's tonal range with black to the left and white to the right. The vertical axis, or *y* axis, shows the number of pixels at each tonal value. Most histograms of a well-exposed image will look somewhat like a bell curve, with some pixels at absolute black and some at absolute white, and then most of the pixels will be in the midrange of the picture. There are some beautiful images that may not look like a bell curve, but if you have a histogram that looks like a bell curve, it should be a pretty well-exposed image.

When analyzing an image on a histogram, though, the bell curve shape is less important than identifying the danger signs of a histogram: sharp peaks or "cliffs" at either end of the histogram. These indicate that clipping is occurring. So you can use this "cliff" effect to help you judge when your correction starts to clip.

Look at the following example, which uses the "Steve dark at the park" clip from the DVD.

In the Master tab, at default, the numbers under each histogram are the same (16, 128, and 235); see Figure 2.15. This indicates that black (16 in NTSC levels for a 7.5IRE setup) on the source is mapped to black on the output side.

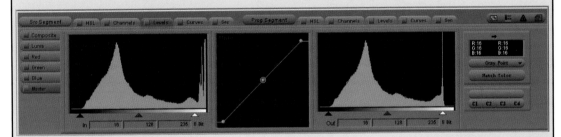

Fig. 2.15

Now, on the input side, slowly move the black triangle to the right, releasing when the source black side reads 25 (Figure 2.16).

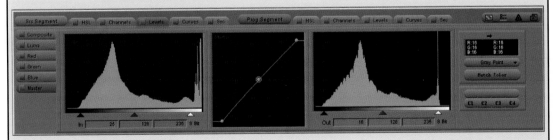

Fig. 2.16

Now the slope on the output side has a nice clean incline, from the black triangle to the peak, but if you slowly move the input slider up from 25 through 30 and 40, you will see that the output side starts to have a significant spike of pixels above the black triangle.

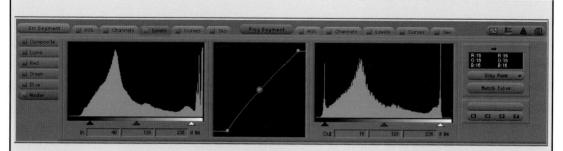

Fig. 2.17

That's because all of the pixels to the left of the black triangle on the input side have "piled up" at pure black on the output side (Figure 2.17). The more technical description of what's happening is that the levels are being remapped; all of the pixels in the source footage between 0 and 40 have now been remapped to 0. And all of the pixels between 40 and 255 have been remapped between 0 and 255. So all of the levels of tonality that are in the slope to the left of the input black triangle have been compressed, or clipped down to black on the output side. This means you have lost all the detail in the darkest pixels, because where there used to be subtle differences between these very dark pixels, now all of them are at 0. Usually this "crushing" of detail is a bad thing, but it can also be useful to create a punchy, crushed black look. As long as you don't mind losing the detail in the deepest black areas, you're fine. But if you want to preserve that detail, then stop before the big spike gets too big.

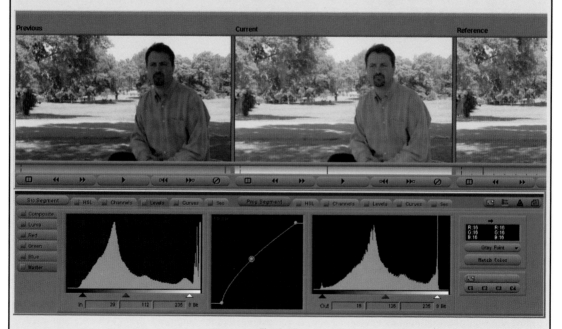

Fig. 2.18

Here is the final position of the Levels (Figure 2.18), including a midtone correction to lift the face out of the shadows. I wouldn't call this a final correction, but that's as far as we'll take it in Levels. Notice that there is a small spike to the left of the output histogram. I chose to let some of the blacks lose detail, but not a lot. I assume that most of those pixels are in the black leg at the bottom of the frame and possibly in my (yes, that's me—or it *was*, back in about 2005) black hair.

Another way to gain an understanding of histograms is to look at the grayscale chart (Figure 2.19) as a histogram (Figure 2.20). There is a video version of this file called "grayscale_neutral" on the DVD.

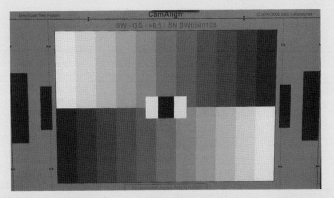

Fig. 2.19

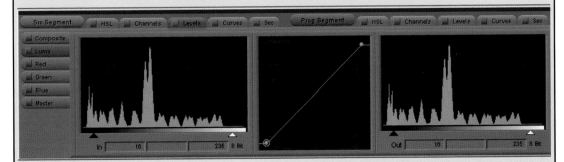

Fig. 2.20

If you look at the Luma tab, you can see the five small double spikes to the right of the big middle spike and the five small double spikes to the left of the middle spike. These five left spikes are the five darker chips. The five spikes to the right are the five brighter chips. The big middle spike is the middle gray chip *plus* the surrounding gray background. That's why the middle spike is so much bigger. In this case, the spike does not indicate clipping but simply a large area that is supposed to have the same color to it. Remember that the vertical axis of the graph doesn't indicate brightness, but the number of pixels at a given brightness level. So, because there is a greater area of middle gray on the chart, the histogram shows many more pixels at this middle tonal range. Having spikes that do not indicate clipping is very rare in most "natural" video images. Usually, there is some kind of gradation or imperfection to the color.

There is also a larger bump to the far left side, indicating the larger patches of black on the sides and in the middle of the chart and possibly even some of the black text on the chart.

Forms and Functions of Histograms

In some programs, the histogram is not limited to displaying the master histogram. For example, in many applications, you can also display histograms of the Composite level (saturation and luminance together), Luma, and individual levels for each of the red, green, and blue channels.

... the danger signs of a histogram: sharp peaks or "cliffs" at either end ...

These individual histograms can be useful for spotting problems with the individual channels. As I mentioned in the sidebar, sharp spikes at either end of the histogram indicate clipping (lots of pixels jammed into the same tight tonal range). You can look at the individual color channels' histograms and see whether a specific color channel is more clipped than another, or if there is an entire tonal range that is weak in a certain color channel. I've actually seen footage from cameras with severe technical problems where there was absolutely *no* information in a particular color channel.

The trick with Symphony's Levels controls is that there are both input and output Level controls. These are tied together. The input controls seem counterintuitive; as you move the shadow triangle to the left, the level of blacks goes up, and moving it to the right makes black levels go down. The reason for this is that when you move the black level to the right on the input side, you are telling Symphony to map all of the levels to the left of the triangle to a lower level.

However, if you move the same black triangle on the *output* side to the right, you are telling Symphony that all of the levels of black that are at or to the left of the input black triangle should now be mapped to a higher level.

A way to understand this is to look at the curve in between the two histograms as you move the input, then the output black triangle. On the input side, moving the black triangle to the left or right moves the black point on the curve go left or right. But moving the black curve on the output side moves the black point on the curve up and down.

To best study how this works and get it "under your fingers" is to call up a black-to-white ramp or chip chart and simply slide the faders around, watching the waveform carefully as well as looking at the result on the video monitor.

D e f i n i t i o n

under your fingers:
This is a term that musicians use to describe practicing something enough times that the movements become second nature. Basically, it means developing muscle memory, in which your body knows what to do without your brain consciously thinking about it.

Curves Tab

Curves in Apple's Color, Avid, Resolve, and Synthetic Aperture's Color Finesse are similar to the Curves controls of several other products, like Adobe's After Effects and Photoshop. They allow pinpoint control over

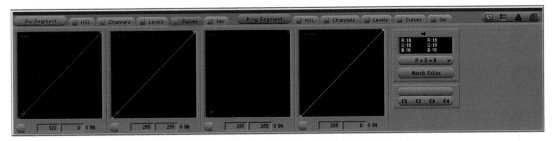

Fig. 2.21 The Symphony Curves controls allow very precise control over specific tonal ranges.

specific tonal ranges. This power of control is a wonderful thing, but like any kind of power, it can be abused.

DaVinci Resolve, Color, Avid, and Color Finesse give you a curve for each color channel and a fourth curve for the Master (or Luma). Looking at the default position of curves makes you wonder why they are called curves—they're straight!

That's because at their default position, the curves are simple graphs that indicate that the input level or source level, which is indicated along the horizontal axis of the graph and is mapped perfectly to the output level, which is indicated along the vertical axis of the graph.

Imagine if you were to draw numbers from 1 to 100 along the horizontal axis and then do the same along the vertical axis. As you trace vertically up from the 50 level on the source side, the diagonal line intersects perfectly with the horizontal 50 level on the output side. Similarly, 0 horizontally matches up with 0 vertically and 100 horizontally matches up with 100 vertically, giving you a perfect diagonal graph.

But if you "curve" that graph—by adding or selecting a point along the diagonal line and moving it—you remap the input or source levels to new output levels. For example, to lower the gamma of an image, create and drag a point in the middle of the curve and pull it down a little. Note the numerical values at the bottom of the curve. If you pull the center of

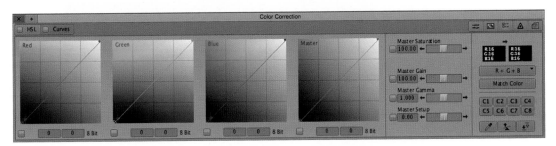

Fig. 2.22 The Curves tab in Avid Media Composer 6. Avid color codes the curves so that it's easier to see what will happen when you move a curve. For example, pulling the green curve down or to the right will make the image more magenta.

the graph—128—down to 120, that will mean that the pixels that were originally at a brightness value of 128 are now mapped lower, to 120. That also means that all of the other values that were between 128 and 0 are slightly compressed into a smaller tonal range between 120 and 0 and all of the values between 128 and 255 have been lowered but into an *expanded* range between 120 and 255. So each time you place and move a point on the curve, you are not only remapping the tonal values of that point but also compressing and expanding the tonal ranges on either side of the point on the curve.

A valuable thing to understand about using curves is that the steeper the angle in a curve, the greater the contrast of the image in that range. Although few professional colorists use curves, they utilize the concept of expanding tonal range where it is needed and collapsing it where the eye does not need the information as much.

This concept is the basis for a great little tip about how to quickly make images look better quickly using curves.

S Curve Tip

In the master curve, place a point—by clicking on the diagonal line of the curve—about a quarter to a third the way up from the bottom of the curve and another about a quarter or a third the way down from the top. Now drag the top point slightly upwards and the bottom point slightly downwards. This creates a shallow "S" curve. The curve makes the blacks rich and the whites brighter (possibly clipping detail in each of these areas, depending on how much the points are moved) and then spreading the tonal values out over a wider range across the middle of the picture.

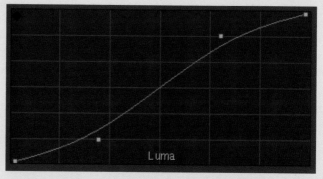

Luma

Fig. 2.23 This is what the S curve looks like in Color's Luma curve in the Primary In room.

A valuable thing to understand about using curves is that the steeper the angle in a curve, the greater the contrast of the image in that range.

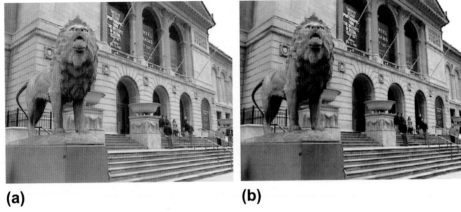

(a)　　　　　　　　　　　　　**(b)**

Fig. 2.24 a) The video image as it was shot. A fairly washed out, low-con image. b) The video image with the simple S curve applied. The blacks are richer, the highlights pop more, and the contrast in the midtones is improved.

Of the colorists who participated in sessions for this book, the biggest proponent of using curves as the primary place for doing color correction is Los Angeles–based Avid Symphony Nitris editor, Terry Curren of Alpha Dogs in Burbank. Although his primary job is as an editor, Terry's corrections stood up very well against those done by the full-time colorists, and he made his corrections very quickly and efficiently using curves. Before Apple bought FinalTouch from Silicon Color, Terry's biggest complaint about the product was that it lacked curves, which are integral to his approach to color correction. Under Apple's first release of Color, curves were added.

We will get into using individual color channel curves to fix color cast issues in Chapter 4, page 131, but the master curve can also be easily and intuitively used to do either quick or very complex tonal adjustments to a picture.

Curves Tutorial

In the previous chapter, we corrected the "brian_interview_overexposed." Let's try this same correction again using the curves in Color Finesse HD+.

Launch Color Finesse. Start a new project or open a previous one and import the shot "brian_interview_overexposed." In the upper left corner, call up the LUMA WFM, or Luminance Waveform. I recommend doing all of these corrections looking at an external waveform/vectorscope, such as the Tektronix WM7000 used throughout the rest of the book, but I will explain these corrections using the built-in scopes in Color Finesse.

Below the built-in scopes, in the lower left corner, are tabs that allow you to select tools with which to do your corrections (Figure 2.25). Select Curves. The Curves tool presents you with four graphs. As I mentioned

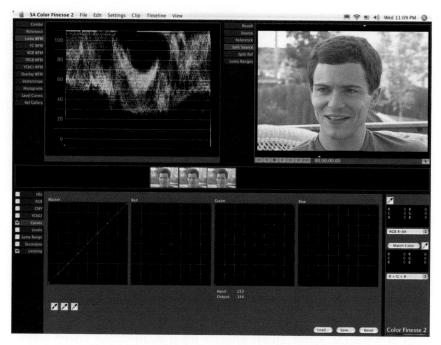

Fig. 2.25 Curves interface for Synthetic Aperture's Color Finesse.

earlier, there are Curves tools in many different applications. If you prefer to follow along in Color's Primary In room or in the Avid Curves tool or one of the other applications, the process will be very similar.

The leftmost graph, which has a white diagonal line and is called Master, gives you control over the overall signal—the composite of red, green, and blue. The next three graphs to the right give you control over the individual color channels: red, green, and blue, respectively. Each graph has a diagonal colored line indicating the color channel it controls.

How Curves Work

The graphs are interactive. Clicking on a point in the graph and dragging it in a direction alters the relationship between the incoming and outgoing levels. The incoming (source) level is represented along the *y* axis (up and down) while the outgoing (corrected) signal is represented along the *x* axis (side to side). So if we want to raise the black level, we click on the point at the bottom left corner and raise it. To lower it, we click on the same point and drag it straight to the right. This remaps the 0 value of the incoming signal, basically saying "all of the values to the left of where I drag this point should be mapped to 0." If you drag the top right corner down, you remap what was 100 on the source down to where you leave the point. If you drag the top right corner point to the left along the top, you are saying "every source value to the right of this point should be mapped to 100." In turn, every value along the line to the next point is also remapped.

The best way to see this visually is to load the "ramp_from_0-254" file. I created this image in Photoshop; it has a gentle S shape to it if you look at it with the waveform monitor. Make some adjustments to it in the Curves tool. Watch the Luminance Waveform monitor (LUMA WFM in Color Finesse) while moving the bottom left point of the graph to the right, straight along the bottom of the graph. Notice that the waveform flattens along the bottom right, corresponding to how far you move the point along the Master Graph. Also notice that in the video monitor, the amount of the ramp that is completely black has increased. Now move it straight up along the left edge. The black level in the waveform rises and the video monitor becomes washed out because there's no longer anything mapped to pure black. In both cases, notice that the most extreme change, visually, is in the blacks or shadows. The gammas move fairly significantly and the highlights don't change much.

Now do the same for the point at the top right corner of the graph, representing the highlights. Move it down along the right edge, watching as the waveform monitor drops along the right edge from 100 and the video monitor becomes less contrasty because there are no longer any bright whites. Then move the top righthand point to the left along the top edge. Notice that the image in the waveform monitor flattens along the top as all of the values are clipped to 100. Also notice how it changes in your video monitor. The pure white band to the right of the ramped gradation becomes broader and broader as you move the point to the left.

For now, we will concern ourselves only with the first graph, which controls the master level.

We'll start by determining where our black level (shadows) should be. Looking at the LUMA WFM display, you can see that there is almost no part of the image registering below 30IRE. You can also see that there is significant clipping of the highlights by looking at the tight, flat line along the top of the waveform at 100IRE. That means that we probably will not be able pull any detail out of the sky.

Let's start with fixing the black levels first. This item is usually the first thing that should be fixed, but it's doubly important to start with in this instance because that's where the majority of the problem with this image resides.

So, to lower the black level using curves, you click on the point at the lower left corner and drag it to the right, along the bottom of the graph. If you wanted to raise the black level instead, you'd drag the same point straight up, along the left hand edge of the graph.

Under the graph, you can see a numerical value for your adjustment. When you get to about 40 input, 0 output, some of the darker portions of the waveform display start to crush along the bottom. This is where you *start* to lose detail in some of the blacks. From here, the amount that you crush that

TIP

Some applications allow you to lock the axis in which you drag the cursor to either horizontal-only or vertical-only by holding down the Shift key.

detail is a personal preference. The image still looks washed out to me and the majority of the darker portion of the image is still around 10 or 12IRE.

Lower the blacks even more. Somewhere between 58 and 73 on the input of the graph, I think the black is pulled down low enough and the clipping isn't too extreme. As you try to focus your adjustment for black somewhere in that range, change from watching the waveform monitor to watching the video monitor. Try to rack "focus" back and forth while looking at some critical areas. In this image, for me, the critical areas are the hair just above his forehead, his eyes, and his skin tone. I don't want the texture of the hair to be lost by pulling the blacks too low. I also don't want to pull the blacks down so low that I lose the sparkle in his eyes. There are a lot of reflections in his eyes that give the image life, and if the blacks come down too far, you will lose them. Other colorists that I watched work on this image were less concerned with the eyes and brought the blacks down a lot farther than I did. The other tonal region you need to look at in addition to those two areas is the skin tones in the midtones. You want a nice, rich skin tone that doesn't look too washed out. There are other things you can do to enhance the skin, so instead of trying to get it perfect right now, use the detail areas of the hair and eyes to determine how low to bring your black levels. I settled on a value of 60 for input and 0 for output. That means that in the source footage, everything (on Color Finesse's scale from 1–255) that was below 60 is now remapped down to 0. Then the entire range of the source from 60–255 is now spread from 0–255 (Figure 2.26).

Fig. 2.26 Note the difference in the image in the split screen between the source image on the left and the effect that the black correction has on the right.

Now let's turn our attention to the highlights, which are controlled by the top-right point on the graph. Here's where that camera focus analogy comes into play. We can see that the highlights are already clipped, so we don't really need to try to drag the white point to the left along the top. That would just cause the clipping to worsen. But we can try to focus the adjustment down a little to see if we can undo some of the clipping. Pulling the white point down a little (Figure 2.27) basically just lowers the overall level and doesn't unclip the whites. But the original level was at 110IRE, so I brought my white level down to 231 to bring the image into legal range. (This is just legal for luminance. Chroma information could still be illegal.)

To set the midtones of the image—similar to what you did with the gamma adjustment in Color—click on a point about halfway up the diagonal line. Pick a spot at about 160 input, 120 output (looking at the small numbers below the master curve). The values of this point actually tell you a little about the mathematics of how the signal is being remapped as you make your corrections. If you hadn't moved the highlights or shadows, all of the points along the diagonal line should match perfectly. The input number and the output number should be identical. But you remapped the shadow values to have a big difference in value (60 input, 0 output); the highlights had a small drop (255 to 231) and the middle of

Fig. 2.27 Note the split screen showing the source and the correction.

the graph kind of split the difference with a 40-point difference. So you can see that by lowering the shadows, we've also already lowered the midtone values somewhat.

You don't need to pay too much attention to the waveform monitor as you adjust the gammas. There's not much that they can tell you. Sometimes, if you adjust the gamma enough, you will create clipping or illegal levels in the shadows if you lower the gamma a lot or in the highlights if you raise the gamma significantly, but as we're pretty close to the correct level for gamma, all you need to watch is the same detail areas we were monitoring before when we were concerned with setting the shadow (black) level. Watch the eyes and hair for loss of detail and the skin tones for richness as you lift or lower the point in the middle of the line. You can also move the middle point left or right. The move in the blacks richened up a lot of the midtones, and the move in the highlights brought down the overall levels as well. Because of this, even though I usually end up pulling down gammas to richen up the image, with this one I ended up bringing them up a little bit so that the skin tones didn't look too dark (Figure 2.28).

With curves, you can also make adjustments to very specific tonal ranges. For example, you may be able to soften some of the clipping in the sky areas by adjusting a point near the top of the graph. You won't

Fig. 2.28

be able to bring back any detail into the blown-out sky, but you may be able to create some texture in the areas where the clipped sky rolls off or transitions to another element, like the edges of the trees.

> *The thing you want to avoid when you use two points on a curve that are fairly close to each other, is "posterizing."*

Try placing a point on the Master Graph less than a quarter of the way from the top. Then pull that point down a little while you watch the areas that transition from the clipped sky. The thing you want to avoid when you use two points on a curve that are fairly close to each other, is "posterizing." (See definition for posterization at the top of this chapter.) If you adjust the point too radically, it will posterize. As much as you may want to eliminate the clipping in the sky, having posterization is much worse. If you find a good balance before the posterizing occurs, you may be able to create some texture in the areas surrounding the clipped sky. I was able to bring it down by only a very little bit. You can also watch the top of the waveform while doing this and you will see the compressed, clipped area at the top of the waveform start to stretch out (Figure 2.29). Don't get "target lock" while doing this. You'll be

Fig. 2.29 **Final Curves adjustment in Color Finesse.**

thinking: "Wow! I'm unclipping all of the detail in the sky." But you need to see on the picture monitor whether you are really just introducing noise and banding or posterizing. Be like a doctor: "First, do no harm!"

One of the problems that begins to emerge in this image as the tonal range improves is that a lot of noise and artifacting of the video becomes evident. If you have no means of correcting this noise, then you may have to either limit how far you take your correction or determine that the noise is a small price to pay for the improved contrast. Many color correction systems have noise reduction built in to them, and you can use that feature to fix the noisiness that you introduced. The thing with noise reduction is that it must be used with a very gentle hand. Always check the image before and after noise reduction to make sure you haven't applied too much.

Isolating Tonal Ranges with Curves

Another cool thing about working with curves is that you can isolate specific tonal ranges using points that you don't move so that other corrections on either side don't affect them.

Let's try an example. To best understand exactly what this isolation is doing, open the "grayscale_neutral" file from the DVD and load it into an application with curves, like Color, Avid, Photoshop, or After Effects.

With this example, what we want to see is how we can isolate a specific tonal range so that it is not affected by the corrections that you make in another area. First, let's see what happens when we don't isolate the tonal range.

With the "grayscale_neutral" clip loaded, look at the image on the waveform monitor and on the video monitor. The levels are almost correct. The highlights are a little below 100IRE, but the black levels are correct and the gammas are just about right (Figure 2.30).

Now, let's adjust the shadow area with a point about 25 percent up from the bottom of the master curve. Because the range is 1–255, that that would equal an input value about 63. Hover the cursor over the diagonal line in the master curve while watching the input value just below the master curve graph. When it gets to around 63, click on the line and drag that point down to around 40 while watching how the trace of the waveform monitor reacts. You'll notice that while the majority of the correction is in the bottom of the waveform monitor (the shadows), the midtones and even the highlights are affected to some extent (Figure 2.31).

In some real-world corrections, you may want to adjust the deep shadows without changing your midtones or highlights. The key to doing this with curves is to add points on the curve that you do not move at all. These points will protect the rest of the curve from moving.

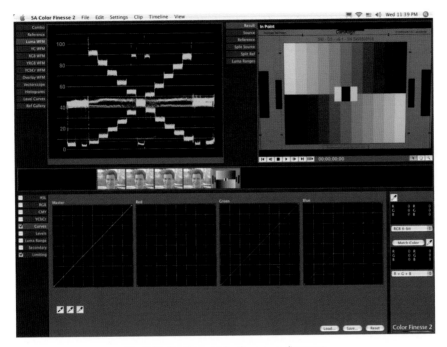

Fig. 2.30 Starting point for the curves adjustment.

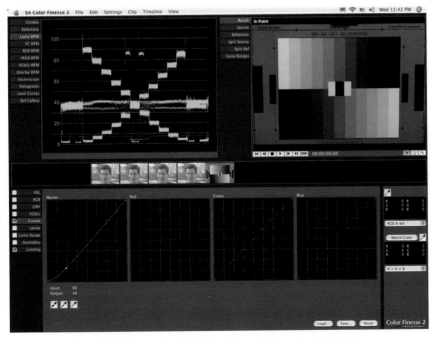

Fig. 2.31 First Curves adjustment in the deep shadows to make the black deeper.

Reset the master curve. In Color Finesse, this is done with the reset button at the lower right. In Avid, Alt-click on the activated tab to reset. In many other applications, click on the altered point and hit the delete key on your keyboard. In Color, click on the small diamond in the upper lefthand corner of the curve to reset the entire curve or just drag the point off the graph to remove it. In Color Finesse, right-click a point on the curve and choose Delete Point from the pulldown menu.

This time, let's place a point on the graph that is just below the halfway point. I set my point at 120. This point will isolate the mid-tones and highlights from the corrections we make lower on the curve (Figure 2.32).

Now, click on the same point (63) that you adjusted before and drag the point up and down as you watch the waveform monitor and video monitor. You'll notice that the changes to the midtones and highlights are much less obvious than before. They still move a little bit depending on what application you use because the point is controlling the curve like a Bezier curve, so the point is not really a hard and fast cutoff of the correction. Some applications add much less of a Bezier effect to the curve. Avid should really require only a single point to isolate the correction. If you want to, you can add a second point just above the first isolation point.

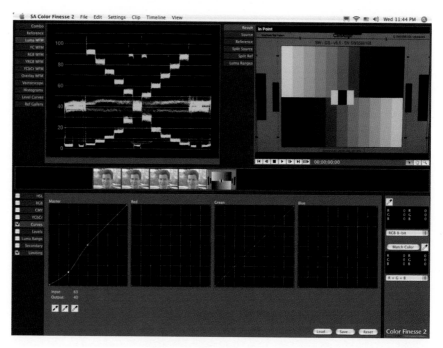

Fig. 2.32

Try 130 or 140. This will limit the amount that the Bezier curve affects the curve about the higher mark. Now, move the lower (shadow) point again while watching the waveform monitor. Also watch the video monitor; you can see that the shadows are being deepened, while the highlights and most of the midtones don't move at all.

If you bring the shadows down far enough, you will see that you start to crush the middle chip that is at 0IRE. The crushing or clipping is indicated by the waveform trace starting to flatten out. If you want to protect the deepest blacks from clipping, you could also place a point on the curve that is very low. This will protect the detail in the deep blacks while allowing you to pull the rest of your shadows deeper. I placed my point at 16. Then, as I brought my shadow point (input 67) down to an output of 51, the darkest black did not clip (Figure 2.33).

To practice this some more, continue this same correction without resetting it and try to get the brightest chip on the right side (the chart was lit a little brighter on the right side) to 100IRE and the next three chips to land at 80, 70, and 60.

The key to this exercise is figuring out what point on the master curve corresponds to the luminance value of the chip as it is viewed in the waveform monitor. This is a very valuable skill to have. You should be able to

WARNING

A reminder about moving points that are too close together: There are only so many levels of gray between points, and if you stretch them too far or condense them too closely, your image will fall apart. By "fall apart," I mean that it will either exhibit a lot of noise or posterization or banding. These faults in the picture will be much more noticeable than any errors that you're trying to correct, so try to avoid taking the image beyond where it can go.

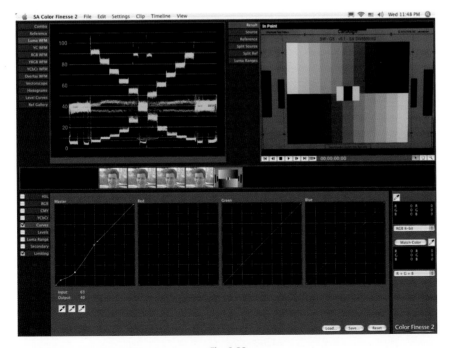

Fig. 2.33

look at a waveform display and figure out approximately what parts of the image on the video monitor correspond to the waveform display.

Luma Range Display

The skill of knowing what parts of the image on a waveform will be affected by a specific tonal correction isn't important only in using curves. You also have to be able to do this if you're just using shadows, midtones, and highlights. Color Finesse and Avid Symphony have a nice function that allows you to develop this skill. It's called Luma Ranges. In Color Finesse, this is one of the main viewing modes at the bottom of the list of tabs in the upper right pane. When you view your source using Luma Ranges, it shows you each of the three tonal ranges as a shade of black and white. So parts of the image that you would control with the shadows control are black. Parts that are considered midtones are displayed in gray, and parts that are considered highlights are white (Figure 2.34).

Import some of the test images from the DVD, or bring in some movies and images of your own and try to guess what the resulting Luma Range display will look like. This is a fairly simple exercise with a well-lit image, but if it's over or underexposed, your eye will get fooled into spreading the tonal range. For example, on an underexposed image, you will be surprised how little of the image is considered a highlight.

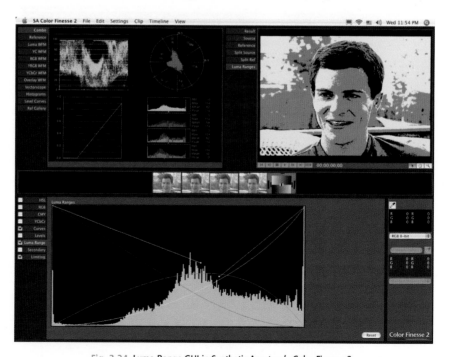

Fig. 2.34 Luma Range GUI in Synthetic Aperture's Color Finesse 2.

In the image of Brian in Figure 2.34, I used the Luma Range editing tools so that there would be a good distribution of black, gray, and white in the image. The actual source image shows up as mostly gray and white when no Luma Range editing is done.

Luma Range Editing

With Color Finesse and Avid Symphony, there are ways to alter the *definitions* of the three Luma Ranges: shadows, midtones and highlights. In other words, *you* can determine what the application considers to be shadow and where it transitions to being a midtone and then where midtones become highlights. For most normal images, you don't need this kind of control. The definitions make sense and give you the kind of control you want. But for certain shots, you may want to alter the definitions of these tonal ranges so that you can gain greater control over specific parts of the picture. I don't have specific technical information from the manufacturers, but I would assume that most applications consider the range from 0IRE to about 25IRE to be shadows, from 25IRE to 75IRE to be gammas and from 75IRE to 100IRE to be highlights. Obviously, these numbers (even if they're right) wouldn't be hard cutoff points. It would work something like this: if you move the shadow control, the darkest 10 percent would be affected 100 percent by the control, the next 10 percent of the darkest part of the image would be affected 90 percent by the control and so on, until the brightest parts of the picture aren't affected by the shadow control at all.

Avid Symphony and Color Finesse both have tools to define Luma Ranges. They are essentially the same, though Symphony gives a little bit of added control. At the current time, there is no ability to edit Luma Ranges in the lower-end Avid products.

Figure 2.35 shows the Luma Range control for Color Finesse. It shows a histogram of the image with three curving lines overlaid and two

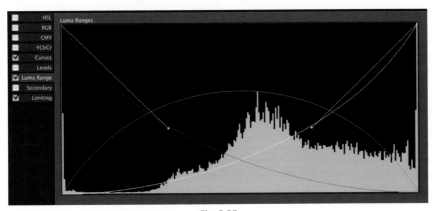

Fig. 2.35

straight lines that are the controls for the Bezier curves of the shadow and highlight curves.

The curving arcs represent the definition of the shadows, midtones, and highlights. The tonal ranges are represented by overlapping curves instead of as strictly defined and delineated areas because if the definitions of the tonal ranges were defined with a sharp cutoff, corrections to individual tonal ranges would cause sharp, visible transition lines in the picture at the point where one tonal range was defined from another.

In Color Finesse, the curves of Luma Range are interactive. The only way to alter the definition of the midtones is by altering the curve for highlights and/or shadows. In Symphony, each curve can be radically altered by setting numerous points on any of the curves. This is a lot of power, but it can really cause bizarre artifacts in the shot because the curves can be set to overlap with each other or cut off with abrupt transitions or even leave entire portions of the picture that are not defined by *any* tonal range at all!

The value of this control is that it is possible to define very specific portions of the picture. One example of where this ability would be useful would be in a shot with a hot window. If the rest of the shot was

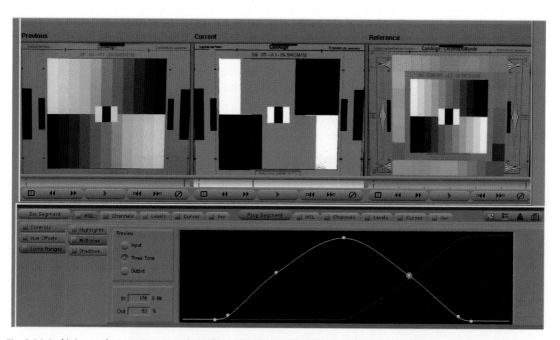

Fig. 2.36 In this image, the Luma Ranges are basically unedited. Notice what parts of the grayscale image the Symphony considers shadows, midtones, and highlights in its default mode.

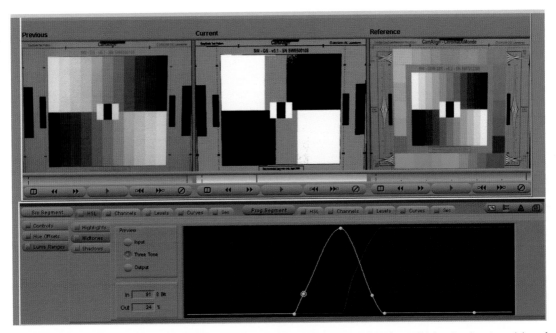

Fig. 2.37 Here is the same grayscale image with no color correction, but the Luma Ranges have been edited so that there is much less of the image that is considered by the software to be midtones. This would be useful if you wanted to make an adjustment that affected only a very small range of tones in the absolute middle of the picture.

very well lit and you tried to use your highlight control to bring down the intensity of the window, it might also bring down other highlights in the rest of the room. If you want to limit your correction to the window alone, you could use Luma Ranges (Figures 2.36 and 2.37) to define the highlights of the picture to only include the window values. Then you could use your midtone and shadow controls to control the rest of the image.

Alternative to Luma Range

Experienced colorists get a lot of this same ability to isolate a very specific tonal range by creating a matte that qualifies a specific tonal range (Figure 2.38). Because this type of correction is really defined as a secondary correction, we'll discuss it further in the next chapter.

Definition

qualify: This term means that an area of the picture is specifically isolated for a correction by any number of methods. You could qualify something for correction using its hue, chroma strength, or tonal value. You could also qualify an area of the image using a window or garbage matte. For example: "I qualified the brightest highlights by making a matte of everything over 90IRE and added a bit of yellow to them."

Fig. 2.38 A key that was created in the Color Secondary Room to qualify the highlights of the "brian_interview_over-exposed" shot. The areas defined in white would be the only areas qualified for the correction.

Thinking about the Budget

One consideration before you start to play with the Luma Range editing capabilities is that—like most things—color correction is usually done on a deadline and with a budget.

To stay on budget or deadline with your corrections, you should stick with the main or primary color correction capabilities of your application. A sure way to kill that budget is to define the specific Luma Range of every shot, or to add color effects or secondary color correction to every shot. Secondary color corrections and Luma Range definition are fantastic tools that help you accomplish specific tasks, but you need to consider how long you have to grade the entire project and how much time you can devote to each shot. Hopefully, you can make each shot of a longer form project look pretty good in under a minute. I typically had about two days to grade a 600-shot, 48-minute documentary. That works out to about a minute and a half per shot or 20 minutes of color correction work for each finished minute of programming. American dramatic primetime shows are usually in the range of 1000 shots in a one-hour show and are usually graded in 12 to 16 hours, averaging a bit better than a shot a minute. Reality shows are closer to 1200 shots in an hour-long show and only usually budget for a single day, including laying it off to tape, which works out to about 170 shots an hour or close to 3 shots a minute. Color correction for digital intermediates can vary greatly, but can average about 20 minutes (about two reels) per day.

Neal Kassner, a colorist for CBS's *48 Hours* estimates that he has about 16 hours to color correct that show's 1200 to 1500 shots per episode. That's 75 to 90 shots an hour. Other colorists I've spoken to have mentioned averages for a nationally telecast documentary as 6 to 8 minutes to correct one minute of finished program time. On spots, the average is 3 to 8 hours for a single 30-second spot or a series of spots based on the same material. Some facilities expect certain output from their colorists, such as 100 shots an hour.

Craig Leffel, of Chicago's Optimus, says that it depends if the corrections are from tape or server or if the OCN has to actually be racked on the telecine. For film negative, the average is 4 to 6 shots an hour if there are only a few shots per reel.

Legendary colorist Bob Festa, formerly of R!OT in Santa Monica, says that for spots he corrects off the telecine, the average is 10 shots an hour. "Unfortunately, in today's world, I'm still racking up film on a day-by-day basis. Today I was working with dailies rolls and we had 30 shots in 3 hours basically. So that's pretty much to my formula of 10 shots per hour." (Most colorists working from telecine have an assistant that threads up the telecine for them.) In a new interview for this edition of the book, Festa says that the majority of his work is spots, and he grades a typical 30-second spot in 3 to 5 hours. His company, New Hat, also does DI work, which typically takes 40 to 80 hours to grade a midlevel 2-hour feature film. Festa's company doesn't do TV series regularly, but his colleagues at his former home, R!OT, generally grade a 30-minute HBO series in about 8 hours.

Pankaj Bajpai, who is also featured throughout this book, grades top-tier episodic television at Encore in Hollywood. According to Bajpai, "It depends on the project; it depends on the budget for the project because you can do an episodic in ten or 14 hours. We average about 16 to 18 hours on an hour long episodic but you can go up to 25 or 30 hours on a budget. I have done that obviously on a show like *Rome* where you're not gonna get it done in 20 hours because every detail is just finessed to the *n*th degree so it go 25 to 30 hours. If it's a period drama like *Carnivale* from HBO, it was a period drama set in the Dust Bowl era and everything was heavily processed on color, and we did it in 24 to 26 hours per episode, but it was an enormous amount of work to create a time and place. In Santa Clarita, they would shoot hills of green for the Dust Bowl. The reality of it is you have to be able to manage your time, and the way you do that in my view is that you don't spend a lot of time talking about it, you show options and find out if this is what they are talking about and then move, you have to constantly keep moving on and I find that if you get stuck, one thing and people start to obsess on one frame then you're hosed. So you've gotta keep moving and move in way that people don't feel rushed. That's the other aspect of coloring. I don't think were talking as much about color here but about the other aspect of coloring which is important to know."

Some of these numbers have changed somewhat over the years, as colorists are transitioning from a workflow that was originally almost entirely "straight off the tele-cine" to a current workflow where telecine transfers get transferred "flat" to either a digital disk recorder, some kind of a server as a file or to a tape format like D5, then the colorist basically does a tape-to-tape color correction or color corrects from a file. Back in the day, a rule of thumb for telecine transfers was 1 hour to grade 11 minutes (one 1000-foot 35 mm reel).

Definition

OCN: Original Camera Negative.

racked: Physically placing the spool or reel of film on the telecine and threading it.

telecine: This is the machine—or sometimes used as a description of the process—that transfers film to video in real time. The telecine feeds the image to the color correction hardware. I've heard at least three different pronunciations and everyone will tell you that the way *they* pronounce it is correct. TELL-uh-sin-ee. Tell-uh-SEEN. TELL-uh-sin-uh. Most of the interviewees, including Bob Festa, who's probably been at it longer than anyone else, pronounced it "TELL-uh-sin-ee," with the heavy accent on "tell" and a lesser accent on "sin." The other way to transfer film to video (or data, actually) is with a film scanner, which, as of the writing of this book, is not real time, but is getting close.

In even more recent history, the technology and workflow of color correction has transitioned yet again. Instead of the telecine transfers or film scans, colorists are primarily seeing file-based footage from cameras such as the RED, ARRI ALEXA, and other HD and digital cinema cameras. Festa claims he hasn't touched a roll of OCN since 2007 or 2008.

Regardless of the technology or the originating format, the trick to grading an entire project on budget is to leave enough extra time to work on the shots that really need the additional attention.

Until you get more experienced at estimating how long you need to really tweak an entire project, try to get a first pass at all the shots done in half of your budgeted time. Then use the second half of the time to polish the overall corrections and devote extra time to "trouble" shots or those that have high emotional significance or importance to the story,

Also, don't forget to leave time for revisions, especially if you don't have absolutely every single decision maker in the session.

CHAPTER 3

Primary Color Correction: Color Control Primer

Many of the concepts discussed in the tonal chapters continue to be applicable as we advance the discussion of how to control the hue and saturation of the image. These changes in hue and saturation are rarely done globally. In other words, across the entire image equally, we'll use elements of the tonal corrections to isolate and "qualify" our corrections as we continue.

Balancing the Image

One of the most basic chores a colorist must accomplish is to "balance" the image. This means that any *unwanted* color cast is eliminated from the image.

Along with spreading the tonal range of the picture, which was covered in the first chapter, "balancing" the image is the other main aspect of primary color correction. Balancing involves removing unwanted color casts from the picture. Notice the word "unwanted" in that sentence. Very often, color casts are a *good* thing that provide context, mood, and interest to the image, such as the warmth of a scene lit by a sunset.

Color casts are rarely of the same strength, or even the same hue, in each of the tonal ranges of the picture. Just as we started our tonal corrections by working on the blacks or shadows first, we will begin to balance the image starting with the blacks. Before starting the correction, you need to analyze the image to know what you need to do.

Analyzing Color Casts

The three standard tools for analyzing color casts are the RGB Parade waveform monitor (or the YRGB Parade waveform monitor), the vectorscope, and of course the video monitor itself.

primary color correction: Generally, any correction to the entire image. The other phase of color correction—secondary color correction—is applied only to specific color vectors or geographic areas within the frame. So primary corrections are global in nature and secondary corrections are more specific. Not all images require secondary color correction. And, as the tools have changed in the industry, the concept of separating secondary color correction from primary color correction has become passé. Today's software tools are blending these two concepts into a single process.

Regional Color Differences

Neal Kassner
colorist of CBS's 48 Hours

One of the things I find helpful to do is to look at life as objectively as you can. What color blue is the sky? Because that can be a very regional thing, I've found. If you're working in the Miami market, I think they want more punchy colors than, for instance, in New York. We (CBS) did something where some material that was shot in Manhattan was color corrected by an LA colorist, and although the colors were technically correct, it didn't have what I felt was a New York feel. So I had the opportunity to go back and regrade it and make it a little more of what I think New York looks like. In a recent episode of *Studio 60 on the Sunset Strip*—it's set in Los Angeles, but they had a scene in a corporate board room that took place in New York, which they set up with the standard stock shot of the East River from under the Brooklyn Bridge. But the color difference really struck me. Not that I was so aware of the LA look, but the New York look was cleaner. It was more contrasty, and it was bluer. And that right away (that said to me)— "Oh, this is Manhattan." Even the fact that the Brooklyn Bridge was right there in the middle of the shot—that was secondary to the fact that this was just a much cleaner, sharper, crisper-looking image than the LA stuff.

But getting back to what I was originally going to say: What color blue is the sky? Grass isn't really green in television. There's a *lot* of yellow in grass. So if you try to make it look green, it's going to look phony. It's going to look like Astroturf™. You need to look around. You have a white barn in the middle of a field. At noon, it's going to be white. Late afternoon, it's still going to be a white barn, but it's not going to look white to your eye. Your brain is going to filter what your eye sees.

To best understand what these displays are showing you, let's check out some standard test images with color casts.

Using Your Eyes

For some images, it will be very easy for even an untrained eye to spot the color cast, but on subtle color casts, it definitely takes some training. You should really spend some time looking at almost any kind of image— but especially film and video images—and try to understand what makes them look the way they do.

Is the image very contrasty? Does it have a color cast? Does just one of the tonal ranges really show the color cast? Where are the blacks, or shadows? Are they crushed? Is there a colored or graded filter on the sky? Watch TV commercials. Other than print advertisements, TV spots have had the most time spent in refining the look. Also, if you're checking out images on a video monitor or TV set, make sure it is properly calibrated. Another good visual training tool is to watch an image on your professional video monitor, then transfer it to a DVD and watch it on several of the regular TV sets in your home. Look to see how the image changes on each set. It can be a little bit of a depressing exercise to see the way your carefully honed images look "at home." Try to keep your home TV sets set up properly so that you're always watching the broadcast images as close to the way the colorist intended them.

Also, study print advertisements. Though these advertisements often have images that are hard or impossible to replicate on video, you can learn valuable techniques by studying the way print advertisements are retouched. (Retouchers are the print equivalent of colorists.) Also, because the print advertisement doesn't move, it's much easier to analyze for a lengthy time period.

One of the ways to train your eyes to better understand and analyze the image is to confirm what you are seeing with some other method of analyzing the image, like a waveform, vectorscope, eyedropper, or histogram.

Let's take that list in order.

Color and the Waveform

I've already discussed the basics of the waveform monitor in the first chapter, but that was just to understand the tonal range of the image as it was displayed. It is also possible to find many critical clues about the color of your image using the waveform monitor.

The standard waveform display is not going to tell you a lot about color, but switching to RGB Parade mode or YRGB Parade mode is a favorite colorist tool for analyzing color. My guess is that if most colorists were stranded on a desert island with only one scope, they'd choose the RGB Parade. The main reason is that the red, green, and blue cells of the RGB Parade waveform correspond easily to the red, green, and blue controls available on most color control panels. The RGB Parade also gives intuitive visual clues as to which tonal range is exhibiting a specific color cast.

Let's run through a quick tutorial to see how the RGB Parade waveform displays color information.

The standard waveform display is not going to tell you a lot about color, but switching to RGB Parade mode or YRGB Parade mode is a favorite colorist tool for analyzing color.

Call up the "grayscale_neutral" and "grayscale_cool" movies from the DVD's tutorial media folder. Hopefully, you've got a nice external waveform monitor to use, but the internal one will certainly work for this tutorial. Read your app's manual to see the image using an RGB or YRGB waveform monitor. If you use a YRGB view, remember that the first cell represents "luminance" and the next three cells are red, green, and blue. I will be doing this tutorial using an RGB view, and I'll do this correction using Color.

With the "grayscale_cool" movie in the timeline and Color's Primary In Room active, you can see that the chip chart does not look the same in each of the color channels. Switch to the "grayscale_neutral" movie. Notice how all three waveforms are identical. This means that in each tonal range, the amounts of red, green, and blue are the same.

The chip chart is made up of shades of gray, from black to white. Pure white is the presence of red, green, and blue light in *equal* amounts at "full power." Measured on an RGB waveform set to IRE or percentages, this means that red, green, and blue are each at 100IRE or 100 percent. If you were measuring in RGB color space in 8-bit, red, green, and blue would each be at 255. In video color space at 8-bit, they would be at 235. In 10-bit RGB color space, white has red, green, and blue at 1023. In video space, they would be at 940.

Black is the absence of any color, so in RGB color space at 8-bit or 10-bit, that would be 0 for all colors. If the black has "setup" added to it for NTSC, then black is 16 in 8-bit and 64 in 10-bit.

So, that last paragraph had a lot of numbers thrown at you. The gist of them all is that pure white, pure black, and pure gray means that the red, green, and blue channels all match, no matter what level they're at. Knowing this makes it easy to watch the RGB Parade waveform and balance the color by making the top and bottom of the waveform monitor match across all three color channels. You can't really do this with gammas in real-world images, usually, because the midtones tend to have a specific cast to them for a reason, like skin tones. You don't want to balance a skin tone so that all three color channels are the same, or the skin tone would be gray.

Pure white, pure black, and pure gray means that the red, green, and blue channels all match...

Having learned that black, white, and gray should match across the channels, let's try to use RGB levels to balance the shot. There are other tools that could also do this, but we'll save them for later. In Color, go to the Primary In room and use the Advanced Tab which is on the right side of the control screen about half way down.

This calls up a list of numerical selection boxes allowing you to change the lift, gamma and gain for each of the separate color channels. Let's look at the correctly balanced chip chart image first (Figure 3.1a) to see what our goal is.

Look at the RGB Parade waveform monitor and notice the shape that the test chart makes in each color channel. They are all basically the same shape and relative height. The dark black chip in the middle should be all the way at the bottom of the waveform. The white chips should be at the top. Each chip should be at the same level across all channels. The slightly higher red channel compared to the green and blue channels indicates that although the camera was white-balanced, there is a *very* slightly red cast to this "neutral" chart.

Now, call up the "grayscale_cool" shot (Figure 3.2a) and notice the height difference between each of the color channels in the RGB Parade waveform.

To the right of the color wheels in Color's Primary In room is the Basic Tab. Under the Basic tab, select the Advanced tab (Figure 3.2b). Use the red, green, and blue lift controls to even out the difference in height between the red, green, and blue cells of the waveform monitor. In Color, center-clicking on the numerical box and dragging left and right will change the level in large increments. If you have a scroll wheel on your mouse, you can use it to move in finer increments.

At the top of the Advanced tab are three sliders for Red Lift, Green Lift, and Blue Lift. Pull each Lift color channel down so that you "balance" the shadows to near black (0) without being crushed or clipped. With each slider, take your correction *too far down* to see where the clipping occurs, then pull it back up so that the shape of the trace at the bottom of the waveform "unflattens." This "focusing" helps you see how far you can go with each correction. It's always easier to see where the correction should end up once you've taken it too far in each direction.

Definition

lift: Another term for setup or pedestal or shadows or blacks. I use these terms relatively interchange-ably. The lingo of specific professionals that you deal with will depend on their background, age, and how "hip" they think they are. I try to use whatever terminology my clients and colleagues prefer, to make communication easier even if the terms aren't quite technically correct.

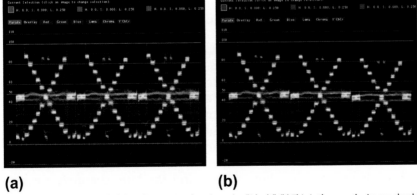

(a) **(b)**

Fig. 3.1 (a) This image is slightly color corrected to show the "ideal." (b) This is the way the image should look off the DVD. Though to the naked eye, it looks neutral, it is ever so slightly warm.

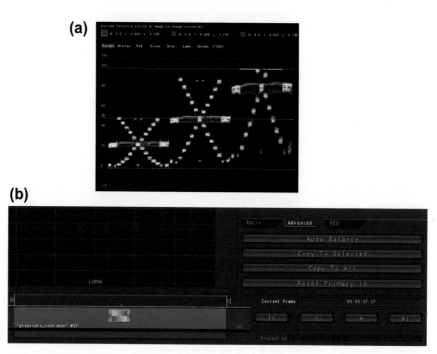

Fig. 3.2 (a) The red channel is low, the green channel is actually almost correct, and the blue channel is elevated with the highlights very clipped. (b) To the right of the Primary Color room are two or three tabs. The first tab is Basic. The second is Advanced and the third (possible) tab is RED.

Remember that the Lift controls are for controlling the *bottom* of the waveform—the shadows. Looking at the image on the RGB Parade, the shadows of the red are very close to being correct. They could come down a very little bit. The green channel is about three times as high in the blacks in the red channel and the blue channel is about three times as high as green. When you are done with your corrections, the red channel should have the least change and the blue channel should have the most (Figure 3.3).

The results for my blacks correction look something like Figure 3.3.

Note that the blackest chip, in the middle of the blue channel, is still fairly elevated, but if I lower the lift any further in the blues, the chips on the sides start to crush. With the blacks balanced, now you can set the highlight balance. Using the same technique as setting the blacks, use the red, green, and blue gain sliders to properly set the whites all to the same level. The top red levels are 50 percent of where they should be. The green channel is actually quite close to the correct level, but still needs to come up about 15IRE, and the blue channels are very clipped.

TIP

If you have a waveform monitor that lets you zoom in or expand the scale of the waveform monitor, zoom in on the bottom of the waveform when balancing blacks and zoom in on the top when balancing highlights.

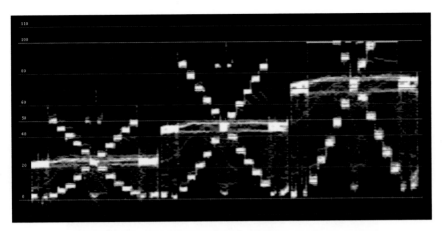

Fig. 3.3

Because of the blue clipping, you will never be able to get the blue highlights all the way up while still getting proper black and gamma levels. Because the blue highlight information is already compromised, we'll concentrate on getting proper levels in the blacks and gammas. When you get the gain for red and green to the proper balance, recheck your black levels; the red channel will be slightly higher than where you left it originally because of the severe amount of gain needed to get it to the proper level. Green didn't need much alteration in the highlights, so the shadows shouldn't have moved. (Remember, all tonal ranges have some interaction with each other.) Use the blue gain controls to try to get the midtone area—the sixth chip from the top or bottom—to 50 percent. The midtone on this image is also where the waveform shows a double line all the way across the middle of the waveform display (Figure 3.4).

With gamma, the main swatch of gray that is the background for the chips should be even across all three channels on the RGB parade waveform. As I just pointed out, that gray is indicated on the waveform by the two parallel lines that go all the way across the cell. The most difficult channel to correct will be the blue channel, which was the farthest from correct. Also, due to the clipping, just try to get the gammas and lift correct for the blue. You'll end up with a pretty good balance except for in the highlights, where the blue channel is clipped so badly.

The "cheat" for fixing the yellow cast in the highlights is to go back to the Basic tab and pull the Highlight Sat. control down to 0 or close to it. In real-world images, this cheat will often work. If you pull the Saturation control down to 0, you'll see your waveform for the blue channel miraculously seem to "unclip." But sometimes, this will not work in a real-world image, because there will be no saturation at all.

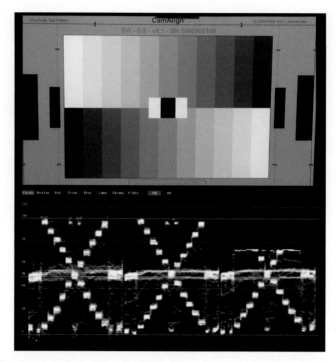

Fig. 3.4 This RGB Parade display shows that the shadows and midtones of all three color channels match fairly well, but the clipped highlights of the blue channel are low, resulting in yellowish highlights.

That's all well and good for a test image, but you would think that with the wide range of colors and hues in a real-world video or film image, this same concept wouldn't really work. But it does.

I'll correct this cool image of Chicago's famous Art Institute lion (Figures 3.5 and 3.6) using DaVinci Resolve. But you can execute this correction with your personal favorite color correction application.

In Resolve's Browse window—switch to it at the very bottom of the screen—look for the folder you copied to your RAID or internal hard drive from the tutorial DVD (Figure 3.7). Double-click it to call up all of the footage into the Media Pool. Anything you want to color correct has to be in the Media Pool.

There are lots of different colored elements in the picture with no obvious white, black, or gray reference point . . . but believe me, they're there.

Fig. 3.5 Here's the image we're going to correct. On the DVD, this is "Art_institute_blue.mov."

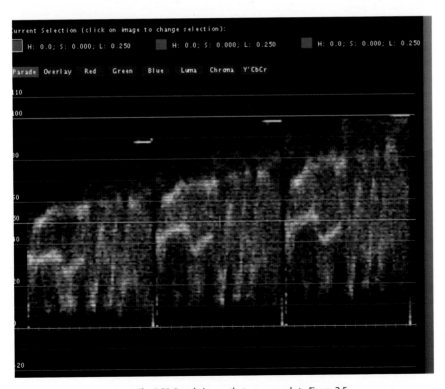

Fig. 3.6 The RGB Parade image that corresponds to Figure 3.5.

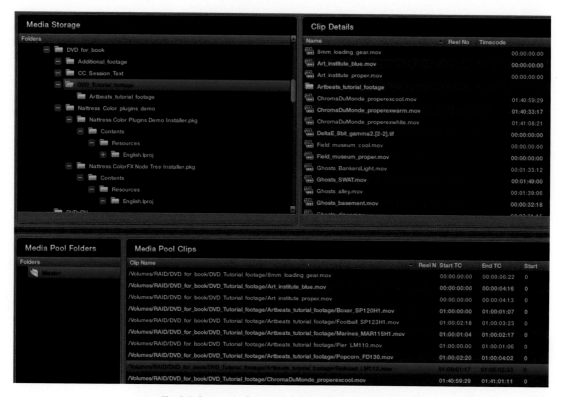

Fig. 3.7 Start out in the Browse Window of DaVinci Resolve.

Now switch to the Conform window—again, using the buttons at the very bottom of the screen—and you should see that the top left corner is the Media Pool with all of the same clips that were in the Browse window's Media Pool.

In the Timeline Management section—to the left, below Media Pool in the Conform Window—select NEW+ to create a news Master Session (Figure 3.8). All of the clips in the Media Pool will be added to it and be displayed in the timeline at the bottom right.

Now, switch to the Color window using the buttons at the very bottom of the screen. Through the center of the screen, you can see the timeline. Click on the clip of the "Art_institute_blue.mov" in the timeline to see it in the viewer.

This image is definitely incorrectly white balanced. Check out the "Art_institute_proper.mov" shot (Figure 3.9)—which should also be in the timeline if you put all of the footage from the DVD into the Media Pool—to see the same scene with the proper white balance.

This image has the proper white balance. The façade of the building seems warm, but note that the lettering of the banners is white.

Fig. 3.8 Select the NEW + button in the Timeline Management Tab.

Fig. 3.9

Notice that the building behind the lion (Chicago's famous Art Institute—a great place to study the use of color and tonality in images, by the way) is not really gray, but a warm, yellowish sandstone. There are lots of different-colored elements in the picture with no obvious white, black, or gray reference point . . . but believe me, they're there.

With the "blue cast" lion shot called up in Resolve, let's use the same type of sliders that we used in the Advanced tab of Color along with the RGB Parade waveform to get a sense for how to balance a real-world image using a different color correction application.

In Resolve, let's work with the Primary tab (Figure 3.10), which has the same essential controls as Color's Advanced tab in the Primary Room. Notice that there are red, green, and blue controls for lift, gamma, and gain.

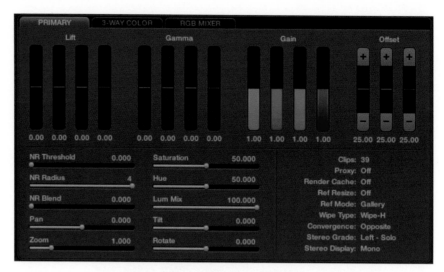

Fig. 3.10 DaVinci Resolve's Primary tab

Looking at the RGB Parade waveform monitor, the color channels almost seem to stair-step, with the red low, the green in the middle, and the blue levels quite elevated (Figure 3.6). We are going to treat this just like the chip chart and see how close that gets us to the correct color.

The first thing that probably needs work is the "lift" of the blue channel. Bring the level down so that the bottom of the blue cell touches the 0IRE line. You can "focus" it up and down a little to make sure you haven't clipped or crushed it. When you start to work with the green lift, you'll notice that Resolve's behavior is a bit different than Color's. The other two color channels move when you get the green channel's lift low enough. Don't worry so much about the specific level of the green channel's lift; just try to get the levels the same for red, green, and blue (Figure 3.13). Once they're all balanced, you can use the tonal lift control—the gray slider to the left of the RGB sliders—to bring the overall levels of the lift down (Figure 3.11).

On the image of the Art Institute, the lowest black point in the center (Figure 3.12) probably represents one of the blackish areas inside one of the arched doorways at the top of the stairs or the black area in the arches above them (Figure 3.9).

Now we'll make the same kinds of changes to the highlights of each channel.

This time, I'll start with the red channel gain and bring it up until the part of the image that sits around 60IRE is up closer to 80, which is where the green channel is. On many images, you'll want to match all of the channels so that the *basic* top of them is at 100IRE. In the case of this

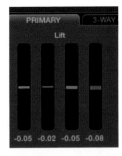

Fig. 3.11 Here's what the red, green, and blue lift corrections look like.

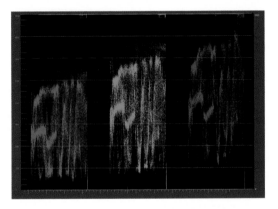

Fig. 3.12 Here's what the RGB Parade looks like on the uncorrected original.

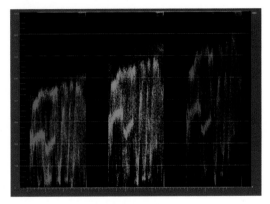

Fig. 3.13 Here's the RGB Parade after the lift corrections.

image, there is something clipped on the far right side at 100IRE in all three channels, but you do *not* want to simply match that in each image. That area is heavily clipped, but you do *not* know if the amount of each color channel is clipped *equally*, so you'll need to ignore the clipped area as you correct.

To get a good sense of where we want this image to end up, look for the "warm lion" shot in the timeline. If you didn't put it in the media pool before, go back and add it so that the two Art Institute lion shots are in the timeline. Though the typical shot would have levels that essentially match, this image is largely composed of the reddish yellow sandstone of the Art Institute. Reddish-yellow means that the lowest of your color channels should be blue (the opposite of yellow) and as it's more red than pure yellow, the red channel should be the highest. Checking out the RGB Parade waveform confirms that is exactly the case. Notice that in the RGB Parade of the uncorrected "warm" Art Institute lion shot, the blacks are very elevated, but pretty well balanced.

The RGB Parade waveforms for the two different Art Institute shots are basically unbalanced in opposite directions. The warm one is strongest in the reds and weakest in the blues (Figure 3.15). The cool one is weakest in the reds and strongest in the blues (Figure 3.14).

I like the warm look, but if we want to, we can correct both of them to a more balanced, neutral, grayer, "urban" feel. With the lift balanced and lowered in either shot, simply use the RGB gain controls to make the tops of the RGB Parade color channels match at around 80 or 90IRE or percent.

There are some bright highlights in the stairs at the bottom of the picture, but they probably shouldn't be pure white. You may prefer to balance the highlights at some level higher or lower than I did. To make that determination, you'll need to look at the image in the picture monitor to decide when it starts getting too bright.

To execute the more neutral balance—instead of trying to match the warmer image—set the red gain levels to match the green gain levels. Look at the various shapes in the waveform of the red and green channel and see how closely you can get them to match with the red gain control.

Now use the blue gain control to match the blue highlights back to where the red and green channels are. At this point, the clipped areas of the sky are around 100IRE for red, 95IRE for green, and 85IRE for blue. This is not a good color for the sky. We'll show you how to fix this problem in the secondary section of the book. For now, we're trying to complete those basic, primary color corrections.

You should realize that a primary color correction is often done to get *most* of the image looking good, even if it means that it takes another,

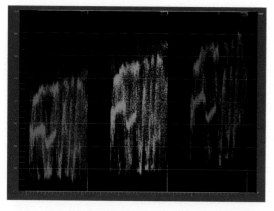

Fig. 3.14 The RGB Parade for the uncorrected warm Art Institute shot.

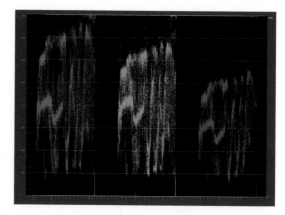

Fig. 3.15 The RGB Parade for the uncorrected cool Art Institute shot.

secondary color correction to fix something that you "broke" in the original.

Another interesting shape to notice is the zig-zag Z shape in the waveform monitor to the left side, in the middle (vertically) of the RGB Parade. This shape is the weathered, copper-colored lion. You don't want this Z shape to match across the three color channels in the RGB Parade, because the lion is blue-green in color, so that Z shape should definitely be higher in the green and blue channels than it is in the red channel.

Here's where I ended up (Figure 3.16). This is the cool Art Institute shot corrected. The sky is an odd yellowish color because of the clipping in the original image, but this can be fixed with a secondary color correction that isolates that portion of the image or by reducing the saturation in the highlights.

Figure 3.17 is the RGB Parade that corresponds to the corrected Art Institute shot. The red, green, and blue channels are not balanced in the midtones and highlights because I wanted to keep some of the warmth of the sandstone façade.

Something else to note is that when we made the gain adjustments to the reds and blues, the shadows or lift was also affected. The shadows of the reds got higher and the shadows of the blues went a little lower. So take a moment to get the shadows balanced again.

A color correction is often done to get most of the image looking good, even if it means that it takes another color correction to fix something that you "broke" in the original.

Fig. 3.16

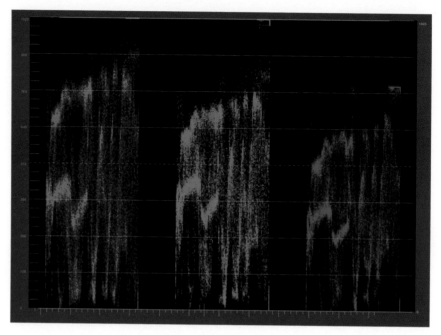

Fig. 3.17

Comparing the original image with the new balanced image shows a marked improvement in both color balance and contrast. Comparing it to the "correct" shot shows that the "real" image is perhaps a bit warmer. There are exercises in matching shots later in the book. We won't try that right now, but you could pull up the gammas in the red channel a bit to warm up the picture. Also, looking at the lettering in the banners in the arched areas at the top of the picture, you might also see that the lettering on the banners that is supposed to be white is fairly bluish, so you could use the blue gain to pull down the amount of blue in the white of the lettering.

This is a tutorial for a specific purpose—balancing using the RGB parade and individual channel levels—so we are not going to finish the correction right now. This image is not ready for prime time, but we made significant improvements. If you think that it is too dark, you could use the Basic Tab's Master Gain and Master Gamma to tweak the overall level. You could also bring down the level of the Highlight Sat. control as a quick fix to the yellow tint of the sky.

Making these corrections while monitoring the RGB Parade and making corrections with the red, green, and blue gain, gamma, and lift "sliders" is very intuitive. But this is only one of the ways that you can balance color. The other way is actually the more common way for an experienced colorist to use, but instead of using the RGB waveform, it's much more intuitive to use the vectorscope when using this other tool.

Your Eyes

It's very important to "reset" your eyes at least every hour. After a long time of staring at a computer and video screen, your eyes become tired and need to get a fresh perspective on the colors that they are seeing on the monitors. The best way to do this is to stop for even a minute or two and look out a window or actually go outside. Refocus your eyes on something far away for a few seconds and remember what real-life images look like in daylight. Some color correction suites provide a small pool of daylight balanced light on a surface of the color correction desk for this same purpose.

If you can't get up and rest and reset your eyes, another trick that colorists use is to add a white or black border to their corrections with a wipe, so that your eyes get a sense for "absolute" white and black. This is easier done in a typical DaVinci color correction suite that often includes a small video switcher. If you are color correcting in a nonlinear editor, you may want to create and save two effects that add a white border and a black border to your image.

Another popular technique among colorists is to pull all of the saturation out of your image in the color correction application, or to have a preset on your monitor that you can quickly switch from full-color to black-and-white. Especially when looking at images with color casts, this technique effectively gives your eyes some perspective on where black and white should be. It's easy for your eyes to become accustomed to a specific color misbalance, making it seem as though it's correct.

Color and the Vectorscope

Let's look at the blue balanced chip chart image again (the "grayscale_cool" clip on the DVD), but this time we'll analyze the signal and fix the image using a vectorscope. When you look at the image on the vectorscope, you see that some of the trace of the scope is fairly close to the center of the vectorscope, but most of it is decidedly closer to the blue and cyan targets, along the –I line (Figure 3.18).

On the vectorscope, the "grayscale_cool" clip has a distinct blue-cyan color bias. Notice the portion of the trace that extends along the –I line, between the blue (B) and cyan (Cy) targets on the vectorscope.

With the vectorscope, pure white, pure black, and pure gray all show up as a tiny point in the absolute center. There is no distinction on the vectorscope of the brightness of an image, so pure black and pure white both look identical to the vectorscope. The further the trace extends from the center, the higher the amount of chroma or intensity of color.

Each of the three primary additive colors—red, green, and blue—have a target on the vectorscope's graticule (Figure 3.19). Red is at about 11 o'clock. Blue is at about 4 o'clock. And green is at about 7 o'clock.

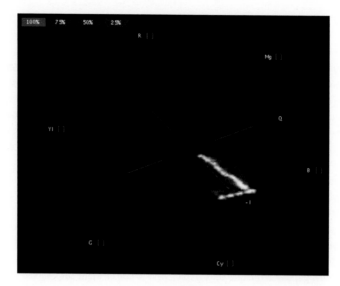

Fig. 3.18

Then the secondary colors to red, green, and blue are in between them. Magenta is between red and blue. Cyan is between blue and green. And yellow is between green and red.

Using the color wheels (sometimes called *hue offset wheels*) for each tonal range while looking at the vectorscope will allow you to "dial in" the color balance for each tonal range. As we have done in the past, let's start with the blacks or shadows.

The way to make corrections using these hue offset wheels is to move the cursor that sits in the center of the wheel in the opposite direction of the color cast. So, look at the vectorscope and you'll see that the trace of the vectorscope is in the blue "vector." In Color's Primary In room, click on the center of the shadow wheel, which is the one to the left of the interface. If you have a manual user interface, like a Tangent Devices WAVE panel, Avid MC Color (Figure 3.21), or JLCooper Eclipse, these adjustments would be done with the three trackballs controlling the three respective color wheels.

So, knowing that the image should be completely free of any color in the case of the chip chart, the entire trace needs to be exactly in the middle of the vectorscope. Because it's off toward the blue vector, we can balance the image by dragging the shadow cursor on the hue offset wheel toward yellow in the opposite direction of the color cast. Slowly "focus" or "aim" the trace as closely on the center point of the vectorscope as you can. Not all of the trace will move because you're trying to balance only the shadows at the moment.

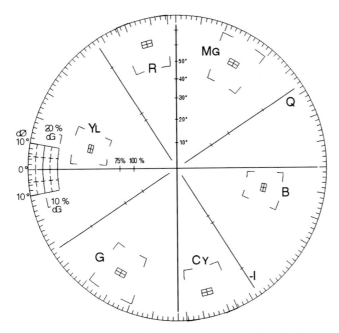

Fig. 3.19 The vectorscope is a great visual way to remember the relationships between colors.

If you are trying to remember which primary colors blend together to make a secondary color, all you have to do is look at a vectorscope. The secondary color is between the two primary colors that make it (Figure 3.19).

If you are trying to remember a color's opposite color, you can look directly across the vectorscope. Any color that is 180 degrees from another color on the vectorscope is its opposite. This tip is handy if you are trying to eliminate a blue cast and you want to add a color to "cancel it out": the answer is directly opposite blue on the vectorscope—yellow (Figure 3.20).

Sometimes if you want to make an image more red, it may not be good to actually add red, because doing so will also increase the luminance. If you want to make an image more red and reduce the luminance, you can also decrease the other two primary colors in equal amounts. Using the vectorscope to remember these color relationships is helpful. If you want to increase yellow, you can either decrease blue, which is opposite yellow, or you can increase the two primary colors on either side of yellow, which are red and green.

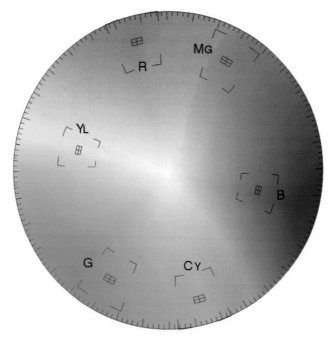

Fig. 3.20 Use the vectorscope to remember that the opposite of blue is yellow. The opposite of green is magenta. The opposite of cyan is red.

Fig. 3.21 Avid MC Color user interface. Devices like this one dramatically improve color grading efficiency by allowing multiple controls to be manipulated simultaneously.

Once that is done, balance the highlights in the same way. The highlights are also blue, so the move needs to be towards yellow again. It is *possible* that the color cast is not the same *color* in each of the three tonal ranges. It is *highly likely* that the cast is a different *strength* in each of the ranges. Slowly focus the trace in to the center of the image. The key to many of these corrections is subtlety.

The image is almost balanced, so now use the midtone wheel and focus the trace so that the remaining blue cast is balanced out. It's possible that the corrections from the highlights or midtones affected the shadows, so go to each tonal range again and tweak it slightly to better focus the trace in the vectorscope right in the middle of the crosshairs.

If you have one of the manual user interfaces, you will find that the easiest and fastest way to do these corrections is to manipulate multiple trackballs at the same time. It takes a bit of coordination to pull this trick off, but one of the reasons that experienced colorists can do color correction so much faster than a novice is their ability to manipulate multiple controls at once.

Now let's try a real-world image to see how that compares. With real world images, balancing with the vectorscope is a little trickier because instead of a nice, sharp monochromatic image, all of the natural colors in the image turns the trace of the vectorscope into a big fuzzy ball. But with experience and practice, you can see the white and black points in the trace and "dial them in" to a well-balanced image.

Call up the images "Field Museum proper" (Figure 3.24) and "Field museum blue." (Figure 3.26) Compare the images on the vectorscope (Figure 3.25 and Figure 3.27).

The "proper" image has some of the trace in the middle and the rest skews off toward yellow and green, which makes sense because the Field museum is made from the same yellowish stone that the Art Institute has and the green is coming from the pine trees in the

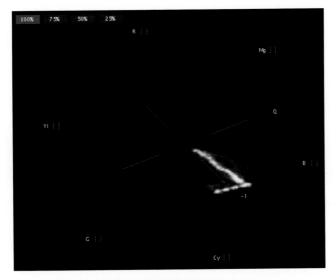

Fig. 3.22 Standard zoom of the "grayscale_cool" image.

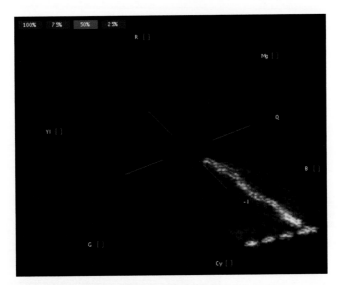

Fig. 3.23 Same image zoomed 2x in Color's internal vectorscope is called "50 percent zoom."

foreground. Compare that to the "blue" image and you can see that the vectorscope is favoring the blue and cyan vectors with almost no yellow or green.

The key to many of these corrections is subtlety.

Fig. 3.24 Chicago's Field Museum of Natural History with the proper white balance.

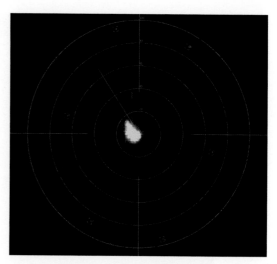

Fig. 3.25 Final Cut Pro's internal vectorscope display of the properly white balanced Field Museum shot.

Fig. 3.26 The same shot with an improper blue white balance

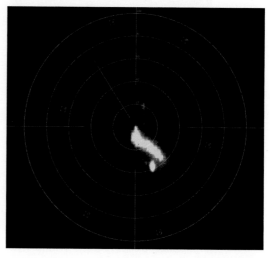

Fig. 3.27 Final Cut Pro vectorscope image of the improper, blue white balanced image. Notice that the trace aims more toward the cyan/blue vector.

Without looking at the RGB waveform or even the image on the video monitor, let's see what happens if we simply try to dial this image into the middle of the vectorscope using Avid's hue offset wheels. Start with the shadow wheel, then do the highlight wheel before finishing with the midtone wheel. If you don't have Avid Media Composer software, then try this same correction using the color wheels or trackballs of the system that you prefer. The concepts will be the same.

The highlights required the most correction. The small "blob" of trace under the main centered portion of the trace is the sky, which should have some blue in it (Figure 3.28). Trying to center that part will result in the museum façade becoming quite magenta. Watch the façade of the museum on your video monitor to protect against getting a magenta cast. This image is starting to lean towards magenta here.

What you'll end up with is an image that's a little on the cool side (bluish) and also fairly washed out. Let's correct the contrast by using the shadow, midtone, and highlight sliders to the right of the hue offset wheels. Pull the blacks down and the highlights up and move the midtones to where they look natural to you. If your correction has become tinged with magenta, this is a very unnatural color, and you should steer clear of it.

Now warm up the image a little by dragging the cursor on the midtone hue offset wheel up towards red, but watch the pine trees to make sure that they don't go red. The trick here is that you want to warm up the midtones of the museum façade, but the brighter pine needles are

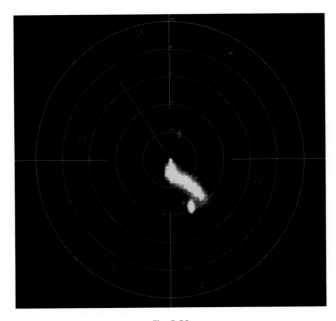

Fig. 3.28

also in this tonal range, so they will start going too red. There is a lot of the façade that is affected by highlights controls, but moving the highlights too red makes the sky look an odd yellow color. Normally, we'd try to qualify the sky or the façade or the pine trees with a secondary color correction, but for now, just try to find a nice balance using your primary color correction tools.

With the tonal fixes and the color balancing, this is now a much more pleasant image (Figure 3.29).

Fig. 3.29

Visual Clues to Color and Contrast

Although we usually want to balance the colors so that our blacks and highlights are neutral and the tonal range is nicely spread out, there are certain clues that we need to look for when determining color balance and tone. One of the main clues is the position of the sun in outdoor shots. By looking at the shadows in the image, you can tell whether the sun is high (deep, close shadows) or whether it is low (long shadows).

Those long shadows usually indicate a nice, warm "golden hour" feel. The shadows are rich and the colors are reddish-yellow.

Even indoors, you can use shadows and the presence of practical lights in the scene to guide your corrections. Although you don't want an entire scene shot with fluorescent light to look bright green, it's natural to include some of this green cast if your characters are working in an environment typically lit by fluorescents, like a police station.

Similarly, with a nice table lamp next to a subject, your audience will be expecting a nice warm light to be coming from it. As long as these colors make sense in the emotional context of the story, use the lighting clues to give you a direction on color and contrast.

Histograms

I am not a major fan of histograms. There is no perfect histogram. About the only thing that histograms are good for is checking clipping, and your eyes or the waveform monitor can pretty much give you the same information.

As mentioned in the tonal chapter, if you used the teachings of Ansel Adams about the Zone system, a perfect histogram would be a beautiful bell curve with small amounts of deep, rich black at one end, a lot of nice midtones in the middle and a small amount of pure white highlight at the other end.

But beautiful images can make a horrendous-looking histogram. Looking at the following histogram, it would seem that the image is terribly underexposed with almost no white or bright portions of the picture (Figure 3.30).

But in reality, the image is a beautifully exposed shot of a woman in a window at night (Figure 3.31).

The waveform image of the same picture (Figure 3.32) indicates that although much of the image is dark, the part that is bright is bright enough.

The histogram gives you no clear sense of where the bright or dark pixels are or how bad the clipping in an image is. You can get a general

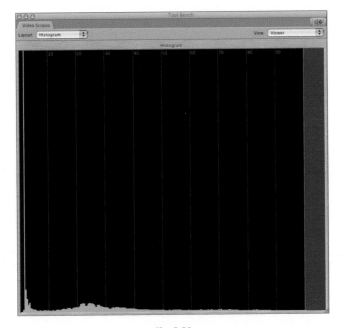

Fig. 3.30

Fig. 3.31 The image has lots of black and perfectly exposed whites and few midtones. Image courtesy Artbeats' LifeStyles Mixed Cuts collection (LM119).

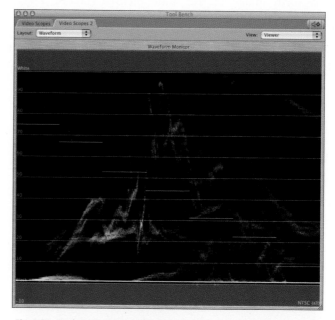

Fig. 3.32 Final Cut Pro's internal waveform monitor displaying the same clip.

sense of clipping from histograms by looking out for large, sharp "cliffs" in the data at either end of the histogram. Spikes aren't a bad thing in a histogram as long as they have a steady rise in the shape. Clipping is seen as a sharp vertical climb or drop at either end of the histogram. The histogram of the image in question does show a sharp spike in the deepest blacks, and the shadows in the waveform also indicate that there is probably clipping in the blacks as well, but the image is very well exposed. You can see that in the waveform, but the histogram gives no sense that the image is well exposed.

The other problem with histograms is that there's not a lot of variety in the way that they can be displayed in most software. You can't zoom in on portions of the waveform to get a better view like you can with waveform monitors and vectorscopes. They are also rarely calibrated with any sort of indication about specific levels or numbers of pixels. Even if they had that kind of information, it still wouldn't help much. Why would you care if there were 6000 pixels that were a certain shade of middle gray?

In defense of the histogram, many people who do retouching like to use the histogram to set blacks and highlights because it allows them to see when there's room to either pull the blacks down or the highlights up. As soon as they start to see clipping occur (a sharp spike at either end), then they can either stop to retain detail or continue pushing the contrast, knowing that they're clipping their image. For me, and most experienced colorists, you get the same amount of information from a waveform monitor, with the added bonus that you know the specific area (horizontally) that the clipping occurs. This gives you some guidance when you're trying to assimilate what the scope is telling you with what the video monitor is telling you.

You can also get a sense of color balance by looking at the histogram to see whether the shadow end or highlight end of one of the color channels is higher or lower than one of the other channels.

For a quick tutorial, try to use the histogram in Color to balance the shot of the Field Museum. I tried doing it with the Final Cut Pro hue offset wheels with a little success, and I got even closer using the blacks, mids, and whites sliders. In any room in Color, you can switch one of the scopes to histogram view by right-clicking on the scope that you want to change to a Histogram and choosing "Histogram" from the contextual pulldown menu that appears where your mouse was positioned (Figure 3.33).

You can view the histograms with all three channels at once using "RGB" (Figure 3.34) or you can see larger images of each of the color channels individually using the R, G, or B buttons at the top left corner of the histogram. You can also view the luminance of the image using the "Luma" button.

Use the three "lift" sliders for each color in the Advanced Tab to bring the shadow end of the histogram down so that each of the spikes on the left side of the histogram were even with each other. Notice that the large "mounds" to the left—black—are one above the other. See Figure 3.35.

Then adjust the three gain controls so that the tall "skyscraper" at the right side of each color channel lines up one above the other (Figure 3.36).

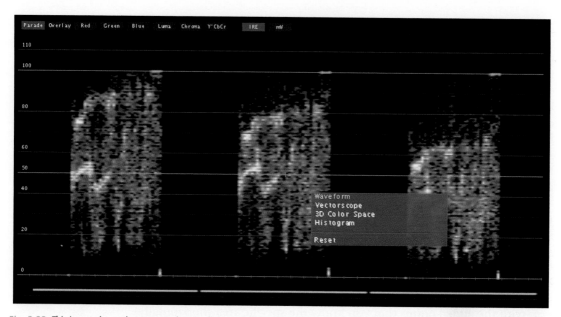

Fig. 3.33 This image shows the contextual menu that opens if you right-click on a scope in the Apple Color UI, allowing you to switch to a histogram.

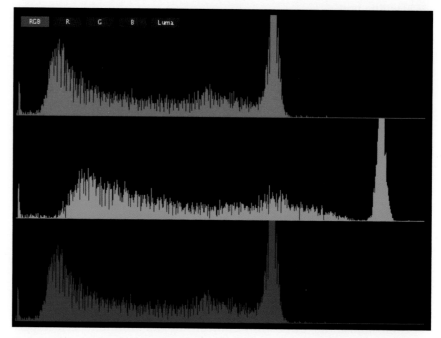

Fig. 3.34 The uncorrected histogram. Notice that each color channel starts and stops in a different horizontal position. To balance this shot, each channel should start and stop at the same horizontal position.

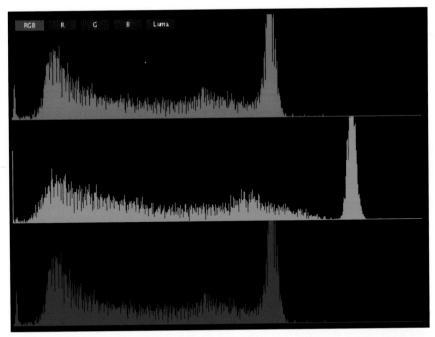

Fig. 3.35 This histogram shows the correction to the shadow side (lift) of all three color channels. Note that on the left side of each color channel, the histogram starts in the same place. On the right side (gain), the histograms still don't match.

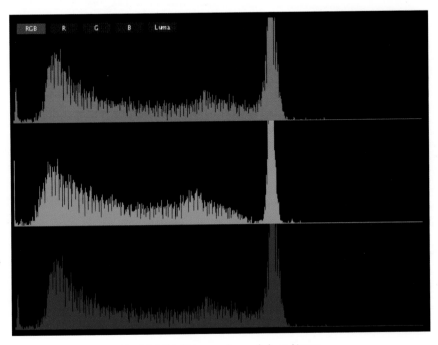

Fig. 3.36 This histogram shows a balanced image.

Looking at the histogram itself, there's really no way of telling what to do with your midtones. The shapes in the histograms in the middle of the graph seem to be lining up pretty well. At this point, the image seems a little magenta in the midtones. You can use the gamma controls for the individual channels to tweak the image using your eyes on the video monitor to complete the correction. Remember, if you see magenta in the midtones, you need to either lower the red and blue of the midtones or raise the green of the midtones because red and blue make magenta and green is the opposite of magenta. Which you use depends on whether you want to raise the overall feel of the midtones or lower them. If you add green to counteract magenta, you will also be increasing the level of the midtones. If you lower red and blue equally, you will be reducing magenta *and* reducing the overall level at the midtones.

In reality, you simply don't use a single tool to guide you through an entire correction. You have to rely on how the image looks in the video monitor and compare that with the information you're getting from the RGB Parade waveform and the vectorscope. You can check out images that have severe problems with histograms to get an idea of what might be wrong with a specific channel, but most colorists would be able to glean this same information from the RGB Parade.

Eyedropper

One of the relatively new and very precise methods of analyzing color in most of these software-based color correction applications is to use the eyedropper.

Apple's Color and Final Cut Pro, Avid, and Color Finesse, among others, allow you to see the numerical values for sampled pixels. This is valuable information. The eyedropper allows you to sample very precise sections of the image. The big caveat to the eyedropper is that it depends on the specific pixel you sample. Some apps—like Avid—allow you to average the eyedropper sample across a 3×3 grid of pixels around the exact tip of the eyedropper. Other apps allow you to choose a 5×5 grid. This averaging is usually a good thing, because noise and other odd variations can mean that the exact pixel you chose isn't really representative of the other pixels that appear identical around it. The danger with the larger sampled grids is that they can include pixels of very different colors that are adjacent to the one you chose. For example, if you sample near the edge of a dark line, the sample grid of 5×5 pixels might be reading half of the pixels on the bright edge and half the pixels on the dark edge, giving you a reading that really doesn't correspond to either area.

Aside from those caveats, eyedroppering can give you some very good information about your picture. For this tutorial, we'll use Color Finesse.

Using Eyedroppering in Color

To use the eyedropper information in Color, choose 3D Color Space (Figure 3.37) as one of your scope quadrants on the right screen and choose RGB mode from the buttons on the upper left of the scope. The other choices are HSL, Y'CbCr, and IPT. These choices affect how the eyedropper information is displayed. RGB is the most useful when you're manipulating the red, green, and blue controls. Color allows you to select three different points on the image to track via the eyedroppers. These points are accessed along the bottom of the 3D color space scope. Click on a square to select it and then drag around on the image. It would make sense to use these three points to track a white point, black point, and neutral midtone. As the image plays or as you make adjustments to the image, the numbers to the right of each square update. Many applications provide you with 8- or 10-bit numbers for each color channel, but in Color, they are provided as decimals with 0 being black and 1.0 being white.

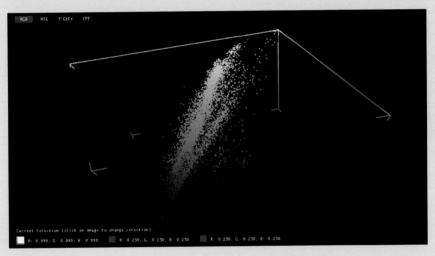

Fig. 3.37

In Apple Color, the eyedropper functionality is in the 3D Vectorscope. Click on the small white, black, and gray boxes at the bottom, then click or drag on the image in the viewer. The small box will change to the color of the sampled pixel.

The eyedropper swatches in the 3D Color Space scope match the points on the image.

Using Eyedropper in DaVinci Resolve

DaVinci Resolve really only has eyedroppering in a limited form as part of the Color Tab in the Qualifier tab. To use this feature, select the Qualifier tab, then the RGB tab. There is a Color Picker icon in the bottom right corner of the tab. This Color Picker is supposed to be used to select colors for secondary color correction, but using it to analyze a specific pixel or group of pixels is definitely possible. See Figure 3.38.

Fig. 3.38

When the eyedropper icon is black, it is active. Move the cursor up to the Viewer in the upper left corner and the cursor will be a black-and-white crosshair. Click or drag over any portion of the picture to analyze it. The red, green, and blue bars in the RGB tab show a proportional graph of how much red, green, and blue is in that pixel or area of pixels. However, the bars don't show whether the pixels are dark or light. They just show the relative "weight" of each color channel to each other. To the right of the colored bars are numerical sliders. These sliders provide some numerical data about the selected pixels, but the numerical data is really supposed to be used to qualify (choose) pixel ranges for secondary color correction.

Let's sample some pixels in a few images. Call up the "ChromaDu-Monde_chart" and the "ChromaDuMonde_Warm_chart" in Color Finesse or some other application that allows you to see the samples from an eyedropper.

One thing to make sure of is that the eyedropper is sampling at a color bit depth that you are familiar with.

One thing to make sure of is that the eyedropper is sampling at a color bit depth that you are familiar with. Basically this means 8-bit for most people. If you are used to seeing eyedroppered images with whites around 255, then set Color Finesse for RGB 8-bit (Figure 3.39). In Color Finesse, you set this with a twirl-down menu just below the eyedropper on the right side of the UI (Figure 3.40). In Color, the numbers do not use an 8- or 10-bit scale but a decimal scale with black at 0.000 and white at 1.000.

Don't worry about viewing a lower bit depth scale due to quality issues. The numbers are all being crunched by the application at a higher

Fig. 3.39 Set the bit choice depending on the numerical scale you're used to reading. 8-bit is a scale from 0–255. Video levels in that scale should be from 16–235.

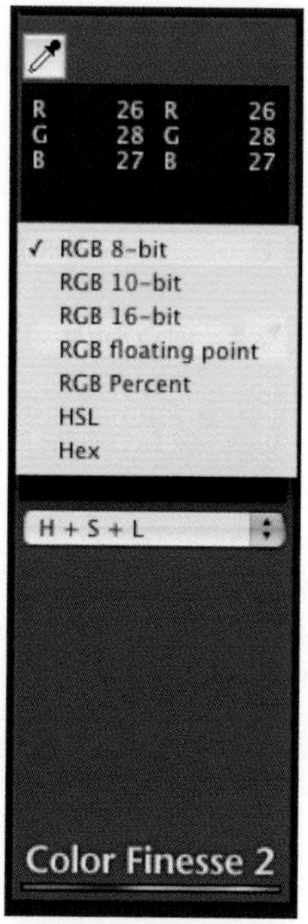

Fig. 3.40 Your other choices are 10-bit, 16-bit, floating-point, RGB percentage, HSL, and Hex. RGB percentage would certainly be an easy way to read the numbers from the sampled pixels.

TIP

One way to get a general idea of the color in an area is to drag the eyedropper throughout the area slowly and watch the samples as they change. Try to get an average of the area in your head. This is a good way to avoid being fooled by a strange sample.

TIP

To tell if an area has been clipped or crushed, drag the eyedropper around the area. If the number values are "locked in" and don't move at all, then there is no detail in that area.

bit depth. The numbers that are being displayed are purely for reference and do not limit the quality of the correction.

Sample the pure white chip on the ChromaDuMonde chart. In Color Finesse, you click on the eyedropper once, then move over the area you want to sample, and then drag around and release when you've found the area you want. Or you can click once on the eyedropper and then click again on the spot you want to sample without dragging.

As discussed in other areas of the book, you can tell if you are looking at balanced black, gray, or white if the red, green, and blue channels are the same. In the case of the eyedropper information, this is a numerical readout. So if the sample reads around 235 in each of the channels in 8-bit space, then the white is exposed correctly and it is balanced. If your specific sample does not match across all three channels, you may want to drag the eyedropper around the area. You'll probably see a little movement in the numbers. Try to average them out in your head. Do the numbers flip-flop sometimes? Is one channel consistently higher or lower than the others? You don't want to adjust your levels based on a single pixel.

Check some other areas of the same chart. Drag the eyedropper around the gray background. Check the color of the blackest chip. Check out some of the colored chips. The ChromaDuMonde series has a couple of colored chips that represent skin tones. Seeing what the sampled numbers are on these skin tone chips is valuable information to store away for later.

> *Seeing what the sampled numbers are on these skin tone chips is valuable information to store away for later.*

To use this information for color balancing, call up the "ChromaDu-Monde_Warm_chart." Now sample the "black," "white," and "gray" areas of the chart. You'll see that the numbers no longer are a close numerical match from one color channel to the next. Now the sampled colors are skewed with larger numbers in the red and green channel and lower values for blue.

In most color correction apps, you don't get real-time feedback of your sample as you change it with the color correction app, but Color Finesse *does* update the numbers of your sample as you grade, which is a very cool thing. The numbers to the left are the original sample values and the numbers to the right are the result of your correction. You can also compare the right and left color swatches under the eyedropper values to see "where you took" the correction. If you like eyedroppering as a way to analyze the image, Color Finesse is probably the app for you.

Sample the black chip in the center of the chart. I got 26 for red, 28 for green, and 15 for blue. I scrubbed around in the area, and though the numbers did change, the blue number was rarely above 16, and even though the red and green numbers occasionally matched, the green number was usually slightly higher than red. This indicates that the blacks are slightly elevated (they should be at 16) and they have a yellowish tint (green and red in nearly even amounts). The blue channel is actually probably just about perfect.

Now, in Color Finesse's RGB tab, you can call up the red pedestal slider, pulling down the slider until you get the sampled number for red down to around 16. Then bring the green pedestal down to 16 as well. I ended up lowering the green and red pedestal to –0.04 and raising the blue pedestal to 0.01.

Sample a white chip on the "warm" chart. For me, the sample showed 254 for red, 245 for green, and 186 for blue. This means that the chart is fairly yellow (both red and green are elevated, making yellow) and that red is a little higher than green, so it's a reddish-yellow. You can confirm this finding by simply looking at the chip. So to get a legal level, we need to bring down the red quite a bit, bring down the green a touch, and raise the blue levels quite a bit. Let's use our eyes as we do this, or you could check out the RGB Parade and then resample the chip. Keep at this until all three color channels read at about 235.

Even after these two corrections, the midtones still look very red. We'll sample the middle gray tone and adjust the gammas to eliminate the cast. I scrubbed around and settled on a gray sample of 136 for red, 118 for green, and 102 for blue. As there's no absolute value given on the chart for gray, I'm going to match red and blue gamma to green gamma.

It would also be possible to attempt this correction using the hue offset wheels. This method requires some real knowledge of how the colors combine to make each other. Moving the wheels to match the numbers of the sample is a little like trying to solve the Rubik's cube puzzle. Sometimes as you get close to "solving" one color, one of the other colors drifts away, and it doesn't seem like you can move the hue offset wheels in a direction that solves all three colors. For example, when trying to get highlights of red and green down and blue up, I pulled down toward blue until the number for blue got close to 235, and then I had to maintain the distance from the center while I swung the hue offset wheels clockwise and counterclockwise to get the red and green numbers to match. This is actually a good exercise to learn the hue offset wheels. You can also adjust the hue numerically with the arrow keys.

Using very subtle movements in the wheels, try to match numerical values of each channel. Of course, you want to make sure that your sample is of a black, white, or gray image and that when you are controlling the midtones, the sample is of a midtone area. You shouldn't sample a black chip and try to balance it using the midtone wheel, of course.

Another good exercise is to load up a chip chart like the "ChromaDuMonde_warm" clip from the exercise in this section and use the hue offset wheels to balance while looking at an RGB parade. This exercise is considerably simpler with a manual interface like the WAVE or Element by Tangent Devices (Figure 3.41), Avid MC Color, or JLCooper Eclipse that allows you to control all three hue offset wheels at once.

Fig. 3.41 Tangent Devices' Element color control panel.

Balancing Color with a Flat Pass Waveform Monitor

Another way to tell that an image has a color cast is with the standard composite waveform monitor set to flat pass (sometimes called YC in some software applications).

Of all of the colorists that were interviewed for this book, the only person that utilized this technique regularly was Neal Kassner, the colorist at CBS's *48 Hours*, but it's also a technique that I've employed occasionally. Both of us were taught this technique in the days before the widespread acceptance and use of RGB waveform monitors when we were learning to "shade" or "paint" multicamera shoots.

Shading or painting generally involved pointing all of the cameras in a multicamera shoot at a single chip chart such as the grayscale chart or the ChromaDuMonde chart by DSC Labs, which is used throughout this book. Then a technician in the truck or control room uses overall pedestal, gamma, and gain controls as well as controls for the individual red, green, and blue color channels to make all the cameras look the same. This step was often done without an RGB Parade waveform monitor and usually in conjunction with a vectorscope.

With the waveform set to Flat Pass—where you are able to see chroma information in the scope—the shader would match the level of each chip chart on the waveform monitor and then would balance the color channels by attempting to get the flattest line possible in the shadows, midtones, and highlights.

Let's attempt to dial in a color correction using nothing but a waveform monitor in Flat Pass mode. Call up the "grayscaleneutral" clip and the "grayscalecool" clip into Color Finesse or whatever software you're using.

shade: To set up a camera to properly match other cameras in a multicamera environment. It is also applied increasingly often to single-camera shoots where a digital imaging technician (DIT) assists the director of photography in achieving the look he or she desires from a video camera—usually an HD video camera. Shading involves manually white balancing the camera and setting the blacks, mids, and white levels. It's kind of like pre—color correcting the camera. Many of the same skills apply to both color correction and camera shading.

paint: See "shade" above.

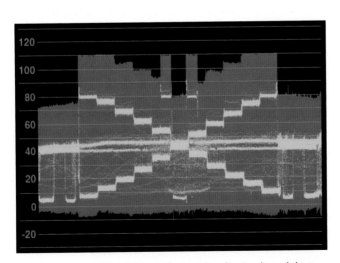

Fig. 3.42 Color Finesse's YC waveform monitor showing the cool chart.

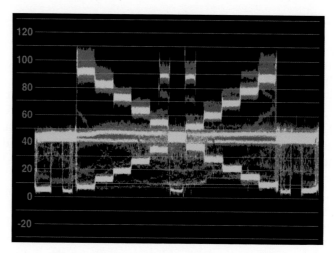

Fig. 3.43 The same YC display showing the neutral chart.

If you use Color, you'll need an external waveform monitor, because Flat Pass is not an option for viewing any of the built-in waveform monitors in Color, though "overlay" is close to what you need. In Color Finesse, the waveform to use is called YC Waveform. An external waveform monitor is definitely preferable for this exercise. If you don't have access to a YC waveform or Flat Pass composite waveform display, you can use an "overlay" type waveform as is available in Color and Color Finesse. The overlay waveform basically takes the three channels of the RGB Parade waveform and lays them over each other. The goal with the overlay waveform is similar to the composite Flat Filter waveform: make a thin line. With the overlay, you can see the difference in the three channels, and the goal—at least with a pure white, gray, or black portion of the image—is to have them all lay perfectly on top of each other.

Looking at the "Neutral_Gray" clip followed by the "Cool_Grayscale clip" while viewing the YC or Flat Pass composite waveform monitor shows you that the neutral clip has much less excursion in the trace (Figure 3.43)—in other words, the trace is skinny on the neutral clip and fat in the cool clip (Figure 3.42).

It took some serious movement in the midtones and the highlights of the hue offset wheels to flatten out the display in the waveform monitor. Note that Color Finesse has four hue offset wheels and that the first one is an overall—or master—wheel. In order to get enough range out of the midtones, I had to do some of the correction in the master and then counteract that correction in the blacks.

Trying to flatten out the color with the composite waveform is something that you would generally only attempt with a pure white or black portion of the image in a real-life image. To do this effectively, you need

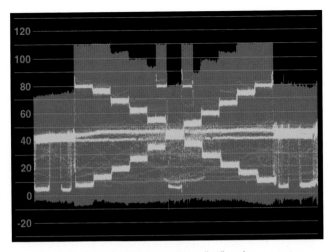

Fig. 3.44 Before correction—"YC" mode.

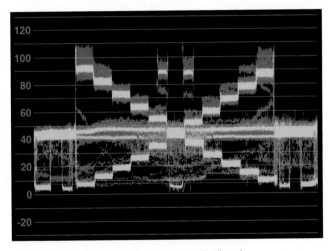

Fig. 3.45 After correction—"YC" mode.

to figure out the part of the image in the waveform that is white or black. This is a similar exercise to what we did with the boxer image in the first chapter. Once you have identified a section of the waveform that should be black, you can use various tools in the shadows tonal range to flatten out the signal in that area. Then do the same with whites. Once you have balanced the blacks and whites on most images, the midtones will fall into place naturally or at least be close enough that you can complete the correction using only your eyes and the video monitor.

Kassner provided another helpful tip to refine this "flattening" technique of eliminating color casts. His tip is just one more reason to use an external scope. Although many of the colorists liked to zoom in on their waveforms vertically—in other words, expanding the waveform to closely examine only the top or bottom—Kassner also likes to zoom in *horizontally* to better find and examine the color in a specific horizontal location on the waveform monitor. If your waveform monitor allows you to zoom in horizontally, so that you are not seeing the entire field, give this tip a try and see how much easier it is to isolate what is happening in the magnified area.

Color Contrast

When doing primary color correction—or secondaries, for that matter—another thought to keep in mind is that the contrast of colors in an image is just as important as the contrast of tones. If an entire image is warm or cool, the impact of that color temperature can be further strengthened by having some contrasting color to give your eye something to compare.

This concept is applicable to balancing colors in an image. If you are trying to introduce or enhance a color cast, it often creates interest and a heightened sense of the color cast if one of the tonal ranges—usually shadows or highlights—is either perfectly balanced or has a slight color cast in the opposite direction. This contrast of colors can often help your eye see the color cast better by "anchoring" it with a pure balance. The reason this works is that if all of the tonal ranges have the same color cast, your brain starts to color balance the scene automatically, but if your eye has a pure black or white to hold on to, then the color cast elsewhere in the picture can't be filtered away.

In addition to general color casts in an image, color contrast can be enhanced to add interest. The best way to do this kind of isolated color work is in secondaries, however, so we will discuss that in Chapter 5.

CHAPTER 4

Primary Color Correction: Color Manipulation Tools

In the previous chapter, we discussed two of the most important color manipulation tools: the hue offset wheels and the individual red, green, and blue gain, gamma, and shadow controls. In this chapter, we'll continue to explore those tools and will also look at other tools that are available in Color and other applications.

Color Wheels

The color wheels are analogous to the triple trackballs that most DaVinci and other serious colorists use as their main color manipulation tools. Whatever your software calls them, they are the GUI analogy of the triple trackballs on all color correction panels.

We did a correction tutorial already with trackballs or color wheels using a chip chart in the last chapter, so let's dive right in to a real-world correction using trackballs or color wheels. I'll be working in DaVinci Resolve, but you can use any application that has this same functionality.

The color wheels functionality in DaVinci Resolve is in the 3-Way Color tab. It's also known as the 3-Way Color Corrector in Final Cut Pro. Apple Color just calls them color wheels in the Primary Room, and in Avid and Color Finesse, they are the hue offset wheels in the HSL Tab.

With the "Ghost_diner" clip (Figures 4.1 and 4.2) loaded up in your color correction app, make sure that no previous color correction work is still applied to it. If you have a global "reset" button, use that before continuing so that all parameters are at the factory defaults.

I'm going to do this correction with the Tangent Devices WAVE control panel attached (Figures 4.3 and 4.4), but the corrections will work just the same by using your mouse with the GUI on the screen.

Fig. 4.1 Starting point for the "Ghost_diner" clip. Fairly dark and cool.

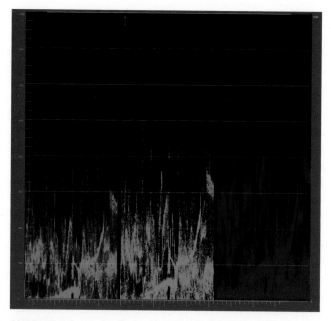

Fig. 4.2 Matching RGB Parade waveform for "Ghost_diner" clip. Note that the blue channel is the highest of the three color channels.

Fig. 4.3 The Tangent Devices WAVE controller is compatible with many color correction applications, including DaVinci Resolve.

Fig. 4.4 The three large dials above the trackballs control the levels of the three tonal ranges. On many other controllers, like Avid MC Color, these dials surround each trackball.

In the Resolve software, the 3-way color wheels themselves (Figure 4.5) don't have any way to correct for the tone of the picture. On the WAVE panel, I'll use the large dials that are directly above the trackballs to control the levels of the shadows, midtones, and highlights (Figure 4.3). In Resolve's Color screen, in the 3-Way Color Corrector tab, you can use the thumb wheels under the color wheels to control these same functions.

I started by bring up the master lift control, using the large dial above the left trackball. The black levels are sitting nice and low, but I wanted to see if the blacks were being crushed, so I lifted them a bit to check. Doing that, I can see that the red and green channels are a little crushed and the blue

Fig. 4.5 In Resolve's UI, in the 3-Way Color Corrector in the Color screen, the three thumbwheels under the color wheels control the lift, gamma, and gain.

channel is just slightly elevated, indicating that there is some blue in the shadows. To fix that, I will roll the lift trackball up just a bit toward the 10 o'clock position. This evens out the bottoms of the red, green, and blue channels. Then I'll pull the black levels back down by rotating the lift dial counter-clockwise until they reached 0% on the RGB Parade waveform. (That's "anti-clock-wise" for our friends speaking the Queen's English.)

Using the highlight trackball, I rolled the highlights up toward 10 o'clock just like I did for lift. On the far left side of each color channel is a thin highlight that is easiest to see in the green channel and hardest to see in the red channel. I manipulated the highlight trackball until all three of the color channels had the highlight at 100 percent on the RGB Parade waveform. This is one of those instances when the better resolution of an external waveform monitor really helps.

With those two changes made, the image looks much better balanced. The last fix is to the gamma or midtones. Let's worry about balance first. To balance this, I look at the angled diamond shape about halfway up each color channel on the far right of the RGB Parade. This shape probably represents the wall above the mirrored hutch to the right side of the frame, near the top of the picture. I would guess that that wall should either be neutral or maybe even slightly warm if it was painted in a eggshell or cream color. If that's the case, then the diamond shapes should either match across all three channels or maybe be slightly higher in the red and or yellow channel. To start with, let's manipulate the midtone or gamma trackball to make the three diamond shapes in the RGB Parade waveform monitor match (Figure 4.7). Then maybe we can look at the image and push it slightly warmer to see if it works. Finally, I'll

Fig. 4.6 The "Ghost_Diner" final correction. The print image may look a little saturated. This image is definitely more balanced, though the original intent of the director of photography may have been to maintain the cooler look.

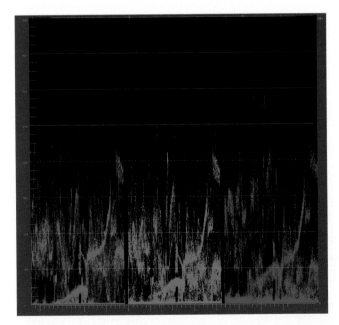

Fig. 4.7 The RGB Parade, showing the balanced image. Note the three diamond-shaped sections of trace about midway up on the right side of each color channel. In this image, those diamond shapes have matching vertical position. In the original (Figure 4.2), the red channel was the weakest and the blue channel was the strongest. Refer back to Figure 4.2 on page 112 to compare.

dial in the level of the midtones watching our hero—facing us in the booth—so that we have detail in his clothing, but keeping skin tones natural. Also, keep an eye on the other elements of the image so that things like the guy at the counter or the bread in the foreground don't get too much visual attention by lifting the gamma too much. My main concern in determining that level is watching the hero's skin tones and shadow detail (Figure 4.6).

Angle of Attack

Terry Curren from Alpha Dogs in Burbank, California, has a rule of thumb for balancing images on the RGB Parade waveform: "Even though the whites and the blacks end up even, the mids have this little angle to them with slightly higher reds, mid greens, and lower blues." Terry demonstrated this by holding a pen up to his RGB Parade scope, showing about a 15-degree angle from the midtone blue cell to the midtone red cell, with the green midtone perfectly in between. The angle of the pen was similar to the red line showing the same angle in the gammas on this RGB Waveform display (Figure 4.8). Obviously, there are times when the midtones have one of the other channels that is more dominant than in this example, but as we went through correction after correction, this angle on the midtones with reds above greens above blues seemed to be the most common by far.

This angle makes sense when you think about how much skin tone there is in the midrange of most of our images. Skin tones are reddish-yellow. Yellow is higher red and green than blue. And a warmer, redder yellow tone would be slightly more red than that.

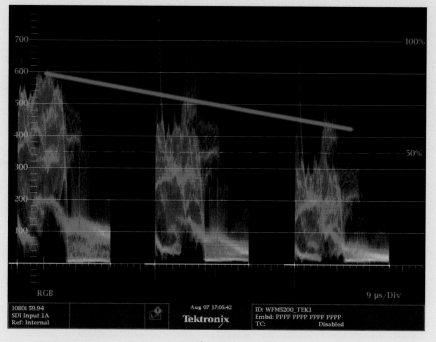

Fig. 4.8

Color Wheels and Trackballs with RGB Parade

One of the tricky things with the color wheels—or trackballs—is to figure out which way you need to move when watching the RGB Parade waveform. Using hue offsets while monitoring a vectorscope is very easy. It's almost like you're directly manipulating the image on the vectorscope with the wheels. It's the same kind of direct manipulation and response you get with RGB controls or curves while watching the RGB waveform.

Using the trackballs or hue offsets is one of the most universal, hands-on ways to do color correction, and the RGB Parade waveform is arguably the most important piece of test equipment for color correction—not counting the video monitor itself. So you really should have a good understanding of how these two pieces of equipment work together.

Load the "grayscale_neutral" clip into your preferred color correction software that has hue offset wheels (or some form of "color wheel" correction). The goal here is to make the movement of the trackballs or color wheels correspond in your brain to the resulting desired movement for each cell in the RGB Parade waveform. This is not something that's going to happen quickly for many people. If you are a musician, think of it like practicing a musical instrument. You need to get the feel of this "under your fingers." It's a question of muscle memory that will develop over some time. The directions should make sense, because they adhere to the color theory that we've already discussed elsewhere. It may appear to be backward, but if you understand what the color wheels are actually doing, it will make more sense.

Consider pulling the shadow trackball straight toward green (moving toward the 8 o'clock position on the wheel). What do you think should happen to the RGB Parade waveform? If you consider that pulling the wheel toward green is adding green and that you are doing this in the shadow wheel, then you should guess correctly that the green cell will rise at the bottom and the red and blue cells will come down, because the opposite of green is magenta, which is composed equally of red and blue.

From that position, swing the point on the color wheel from 8 o'clock toward 9 o'clock. Green stays the same basically and red (which is in that basic direction) moves up and blue (which is in the opposite direction) moves down. Swinging from 8 o'clock toward 6 o'clock raises the blue channel while keeping green fairly even and lowering red.

Using the trackballs or hue offsets is one of the most universal, hands-on ways to do color correction.

After you've tried those moves, reset the shadow wheel to the default. Practice trying to move specific combinations of cells with specific moves of the wheels or trackballs:

- Moving toward green raises green while lowering red and blue (Figure 4.13).
- Moving toward yellow raises red and green while lowering blue (Figure 4.11).
- Moving toward red raises red while lowering blue and green (Figure 4.21).
- Moving toward magenta raises red and blue while lowering green (Figure 4.19).
- Moving toward blue raises blue while lowering red and yellow (Figure 4.17).
- Moving toward cyan raises blue and green while lowering red (Figure 4.15).

Another important trick to learn is this: if you want to maintain the position of one cell while moving the other two, imagine a line drawn from the color that you want to remain stationary across to the color opposite it. For our example, we'll try to keep the green channel stationary while having the red and blue channels move up and down on either side of it. So draw the imaginary line from green to magenta. To move red and blue while maintaining the green cell's position, move the trackball or wheel perpendicular to the imaginary line. For us, this perpendicular line is from about 10 o'clock (raising red and lowering blue) to 4 o'clock (raising blue and lowering red). This corresponds almost perfectly to the "I" line on the vectorscope.

Thinking about what you are doing from a color theory perspective, this makes sense. You are not moving toward or away from yellow at all. You are maintaining the cursor's distance from green while moving it toward yellow-red or blue-cyan.

Trying to maintain the position of the red channel while moving green and blue in different directions means a move that corresponds to the Q line of the vectorscope. This is approximately from 2 o'clock (lowering green) to 8 o'clock (lowering blue). Let's make a shorthand for these clock positions by dropping the quote marks and the "o'clock." For the next couple of paragraphs, numerical entries will refer to clock positions around the color wheel or vectorscope. (Technically it would be best to use degrees, but clock positions are easier, I think.)

Trying to maintain the position of the blue channel while moving green and red in different directions means a move from 1 (lowering green) to 7 (lowering red).

If you are not following along with the tutorial in an application right now, you may need some visual support. Here are some examples.

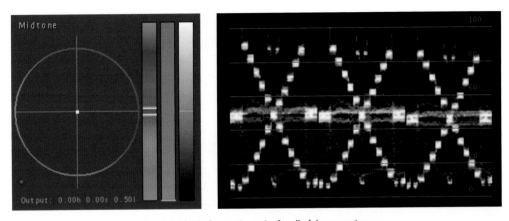

Fig. 4.9 This is the starting point for all of the corrections.

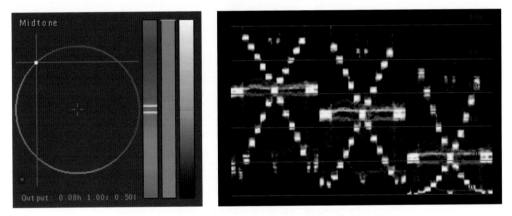

Fig. 4.10 This correction raised red, lowered blue, and green stayed the same.

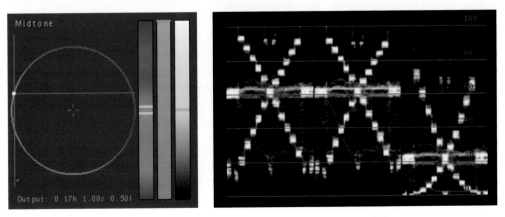

Fig. 4.11 This correction raised green and red equally and lowered blue.

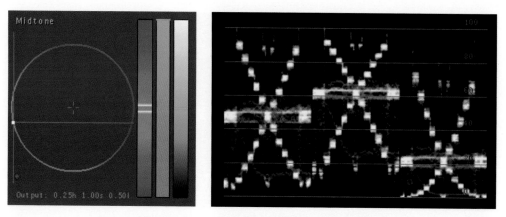

Fig. 4.12 This correction raised green, lowered blue, and red stayed the same.

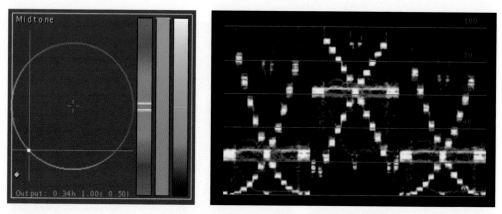

Fig. 4.13 This correction raised green, and lowered red and blue equally.

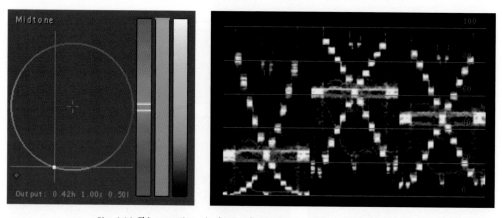

Fig. 4.14 This correction raised green, lowered red, and blue stayed the same.

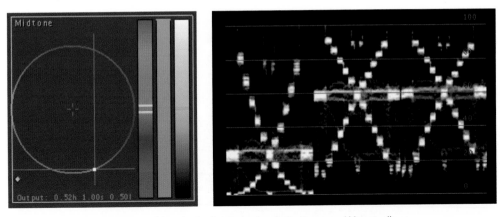

Fig. 4.15 This correction lowered red, and raised green and blue equally.

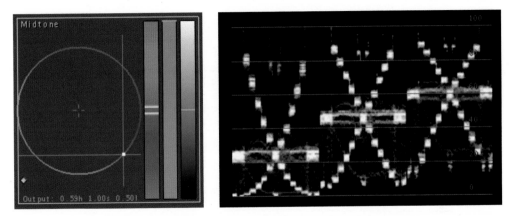

Fig. 4.16 This correction lowered red, raised blue, and green stayed the same.

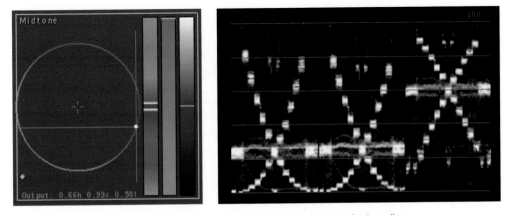

Fig. 4.17 This correction raised blue and lowered green and red equally.

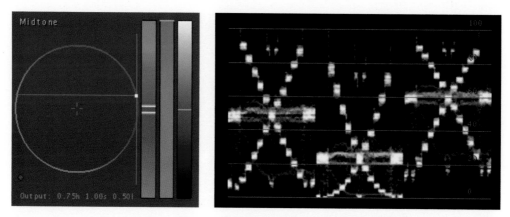

Fig. 4.18 This correction lowered green, raised blue, and red stayed the same.

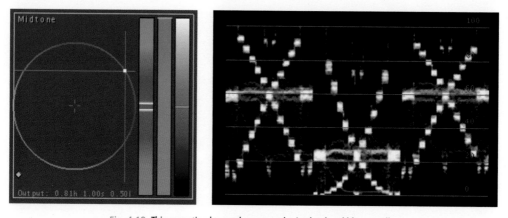

Fig. 4.19 This correction lowered green, and raised red and blue equally.

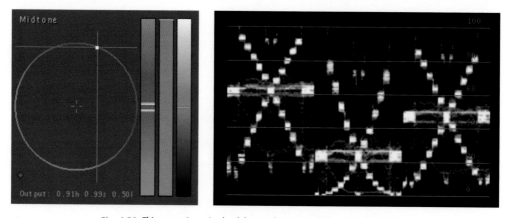

Fig. 4.20 This correction raised red, lowered green, and blue stayed the same.

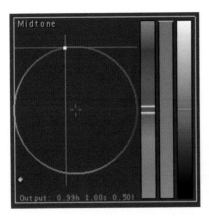 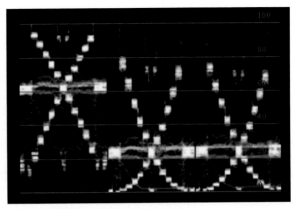

Fig. 4.21 This correction raised red and lowered green and blue equally.

I will drag the midtone hue offset wheel to extreme values around the circumference of the color wheel and show the corresponding RGB Parade waveform. Remember that the starting point for all of the midtones is about 50IRE and not quite perfectly balanced, but close. Note the direction of the hue offset change (exact degrees are indicated by a number under the hue offset wheel) compared to the movement of the midtones in the RGB Parade.

Saturation Controls

Before we discuss some of the other tools for making color corrections that are available in some of the color correction applications and plug-ins, we have to discuss saturation controls. Any good color correction application should have the ability to control saturation in the highlights, in the shadows, and across the entire image as well.

It's kind of fitting that I've left the discussion of saturation so late in the section about color, because as I watched the expert colorists, most of them didn't do changes to saturation until fairly late in the process. As with so many things in color correction, this is not a hard and fast rule, but it does make a lot of sense because of the way that many of the other primary color corrections can alter saturation. Changes in black level, brightness, contrast, and color balancing can all affect saturation. So until these things are all set, the real saturation of the image remains fluid.

Changes in black level, brightness, contrast, and color balancing can all affect saturation.

Once the tonal range and color balance are set, there are several reasons for adjusting the saturation controls. Obviously, we need to have "legal" colors, and if raising the gain has also raised the saturation of certain colors, then we need to use saturation to bring those levels in to the correct range. Also, corrections such as raising the blacks or stretching gamma can increase saturation and cause color noise in various portions of the picture. Using the high or low saturation controls can help diminish the appearance of noise in these areas.

One of the other important reasons for adjusting saturation is in matching shots. If you are trying to match shots that were white balanced differently, adjusting saturation in certain tonal ranges after balancing the colors will often help tweak the match in a way that simply balancing the colors cannot do.

The other important reason for adjusting saturation is in creating a look. So many of the great looks that the colorists developed for the later chapters of this book relied on the creative use of saturation. Usually this meant lowering the saturation, but sometimes it meant taking saturation to the extreme upper limits.

Saturation adjustments are also important when you're trying to take an image in a very different color direction than it was intended to have. The reason for this is that if you are trying to introduce a totally new color scheme to an image, the old colors must be nulled out so that they don't "pollute" the colors you're trying to add. For example, if you are trying to create an icy-blue skin tone on a person with a normal skin tone, the reds and yellows of that skin tone will blend in with the correction you're trying to make. If you first lower the saturation in the areas of that skin tone, or across the entire image, you will find that your icy-blue look will be much easier to achieve and much more satisfactory in the end.

Obviously, one of the important reasons to adjust saturation is simply "to make it look good." Saturation levels are very subjective—like gamma levels. When you're doing primary color correction, you sometimes "break" something that needs to be fixed elsewhere. That is often the case with saturation. If you had to add warmth to the midtones of an image in order to get a nice healthy skin tone, it's possible that other areas of your midtones will need to have saturation reduced. Or possibly the addition of warmth in the midtones meant that some cool element in the midtones became desaturated, so you may be able to bring the saturation up in that case, though the only real way to fight this would probably be a secondary color correction, which we will discuss in the next chapter.

Histograms

Most histograms used in color correction applications are just tools for analysis (Figures 4.22 and 4.23), but there are some that allow you to actually manipulate the image with the histogram interface. Color Finesse actually gives you both. As part of their analytical tools, along with RGB Parade waveforms and vectorscopes, Color Finesse offers up a histogram for

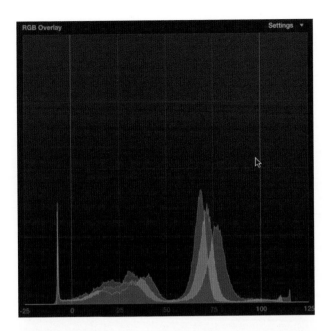

Fig. 4.22 Final Cut Pro X histogram display.

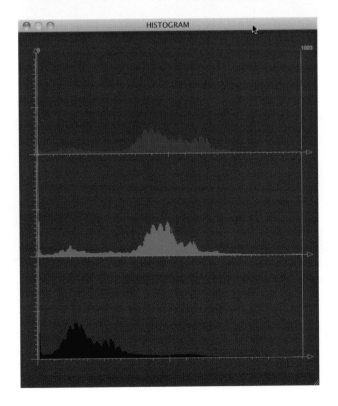

Fig. 4.23 DaVinci Resolve histogram display.

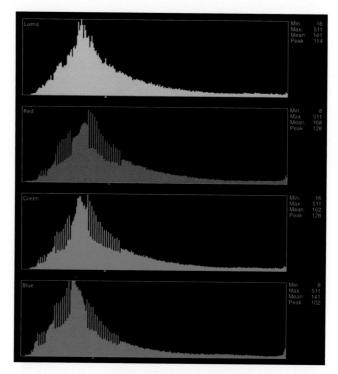

Fig. 4.24 Color Finesse histogram display for analysis.

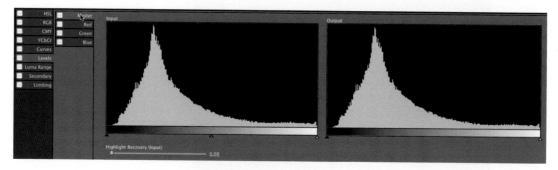

Fig. 4.25 Color Finesse histogram display—called "Levels"—for direct manipulation.

analysis (Figure 4.24), but in its correction tools, it provides "Levels," which allow you to manipulate the image in a histogram display (Figure 4.25).

Avid Symphony's tool to manipulate color using a histogram display is also called Levels.

Trying to do color balancing with histograms would definitely not be my choice, but it's certainly possible if your application has the tools. I should also point out that using histograms as a tool to do color correction (as opposed to just analyze a color correction) is a favorite of print retouchers, who are the "colorists" of the print world.

The basic concept for using histograms to fix color casts is similar to using curves. You are remapping the incoming levels to different outgoing levels. With curves, the relationship is on a grid where the horizontal and vertical axes define the relationship between incoming and outgoing signals. In a histogram, you basically have two horizontal axes and you attempt to match the position that the histogram levels sit with their ideal location.

In the tonal range correction that we did with the histogram, the goal was to spread out the tonal range across the histogram as much as possible. With color cast corrections you attempt to do the same thing in three different color channel histograms—this work gets very difficult with severely un-white balanced images.

Call up the "ChromaDuMonde_cool" clip into an application that allows histograms to be manipulated and look at each color channel. The green channel appears pretty good, but the red and blue channels don't have much that's recognizable to match to the green channel (Figure 4.26).

The way I approached this correction was to try to match the blacks, whites, and grays using an eyedropper tool, constantly adjusting the levels and resampling. The things to adjust are the small triangles under the histogram. The default positions for the outgoing black and white histogram triangles correspond to the correct legal levels of black and white. That's why I did most of my corrections on the input (left) side.

The basic concept is to match the points on the histogram on the left side so that the histogram on the right looks like you want it to look. Figures 4.27 through 4.29 show the results of my correction.

The whites, dark grays, and blacks are correct, but there is a blue cast to the upper grays. This is probably because the blue channel is clipped in the high end (due to the cool white balance), so all of the colors between

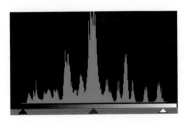

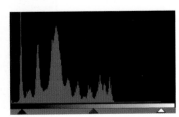

Fig. 4.26

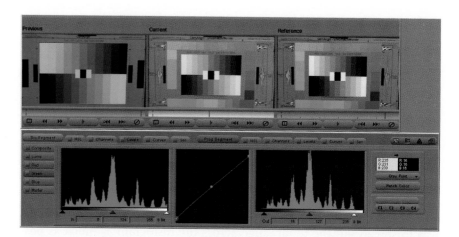

Fig. 4.27

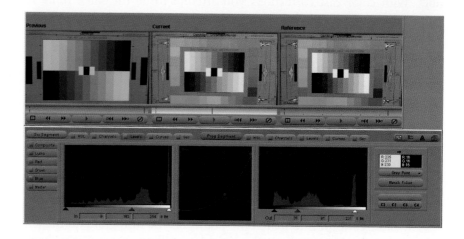

Fig. 4.28

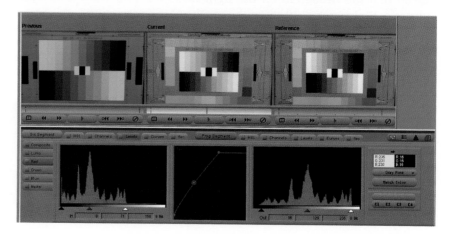

Fig. 4.29

the clipped blues and the midtones are more blue than they should be. The only way to fix this problem would be to try to lose the blue cast in the upper midtones by making the whites too warm, then using a secondary color correction to either pull all of the saturation out of the clipped area, or try to balance just the highest whites.

One of the ways we can check to see what the clipping in the blue channel looks like is to look at another color correction tool in Avid Symphony called Channels, which is similar to After Effects' ability to display the individual color channels using the controls at the bottom of the Composition window (Figure 4.30).

After Effects can show you what the individual color channels look like using the Show Channel and Color Management Settings under the Main Comp window.

Looking at the individual color channels as black and white images gives you a good idea of what kind of damage has been done to specific channels. It is also a good way to see which channel has the worst noise problems. Often, noise needs to be corrected only in specific channels.

Figures 4.31, 4.32, and 4.33 are the red, green, and blue channels, respectively, of the "chromadumonde_cool" image. You can see that the green channel is very nicely exposed across all tonal ranges. The red channel is also fairly evenly exposed—though darker and less contrasty. And the blue channel is overexposed throughout, with the highlights completely clipped. On a properly exposed chart, all of these color channels should look identical because the amount of red, green, and blue in each of the black, gray, or white chips should be identical. Obviously, the color chips around the edge of the chart will have different exposures due to the different amounts of each channel in each chip.

Fig. 4.30 After Effects Show Channel Control.

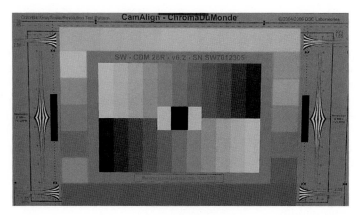

Fig. 4.31 Red channel.

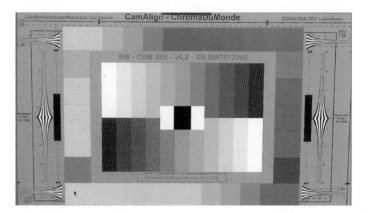

Fig. 4.32 Green channel.

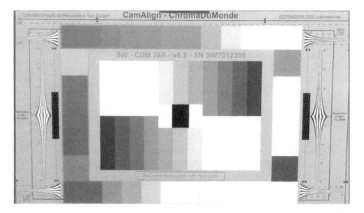

Fig. 4.33 Blue channel.

Curves

Curves seem to be the Rodney Dangerfield of color correction. They just don't get any respect. I'm not entirely sure why this is. I've spoken to many colorists. Though curves have been around for quite some time on DaVinci and other color correction systems, experienced colorists have largely shunned them. Possibly this has happened because they are most comfortable with the hands-on speed of manipulating images with their color correction panels alone (Figures 4.34 and 4.35), which don't have an easy way to control the curves interface.

The most common Curves tool is probably the one available in Adobe Photoshop. This tool is also available in Resolve, Color, After Effects, Color Finesse, and all Avid products (Figures 4.36–4.41).

Fig. 4.34 DaVinci 2K panels. Image courtesy of DaVinci Systems.

Fig. 4.35 DaVinci Resolve. Image courtesy of DaVinci Systems.

Fig. 4.36 Adobe Photoshop Curves.

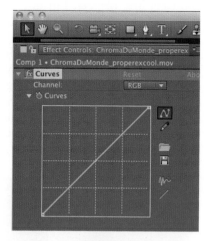

Fig. 4.37 Adobe After Effects Curves.

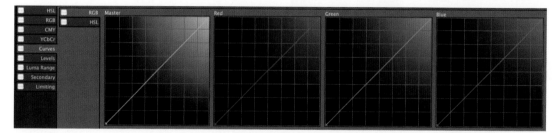

Fig. 4.38 Color Finesse Curves.

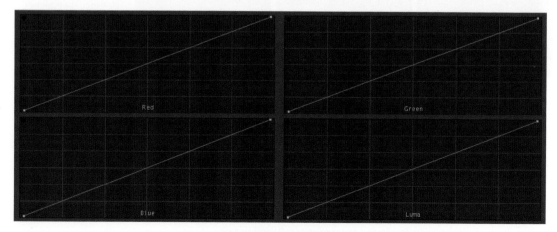

Fig. 4.39 Apple Color Curves.

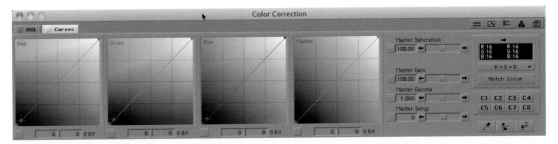

Fig. 4.40 Avid Media Composer Curves.

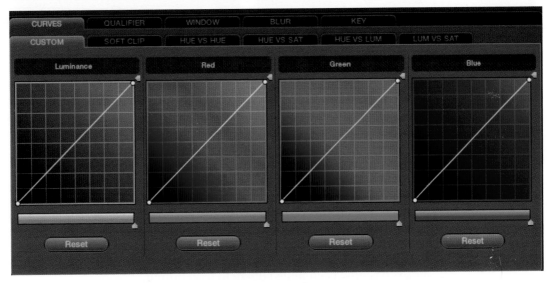

Fig. 4.41 DaVinci Resolve Curves.

We've discussed curves in the Tonal Tools chapter, but that was in the context of making adjustments to the tonal range of the picture. Curves can also be used to adjust color in a very quick and intuitive way.

To show you the power of curves, let's run through a quick tutorial. Call up the "flowerbench" file in an application like Resolve, Color, After Effects, Color Finesse, or Avid Media Composer that has curves. As shown in Chapter 2 page 53, curves can make tonal corrections easily in the master curve. I'll be doing this tutorial in Avid Media Composer because I like the nice color coding of the curves in that application.

When dealing with curves, the RGB or YRGB Parade waveform is the most intuitive way to monitor your image while you are making corrections.

Take a look at the RGB Parade waveform with the "flowerbench" image up (Figure 4.42).

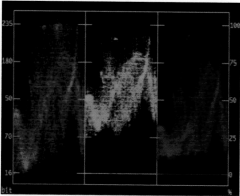

Fig. 4.42 Flowerbench image and Avid Media Composer internal RGB Parade.

All of the black levels are elevated, but the red is the closest to being down at 0IRE where it probably should be, followed closely by blue, and the greens are highest of all. The red highlights appear to be clipped, and they are as high as they can go. The greens highlights are low and so are the blue highlights. Let's take care of those things first, then see what else the image needs when we get those things taken care of.

Drag the bottom of the red curve to the right to pull down the shadows in the red channel (Figure 4.43). Watch the red cell of the RGB Parade waveform until the lowest part of the shape gets to the bottom. Your image will not look any better, but the tonal range of the red channel is much improved. My correction pulled the 0 black level in red over to 24. That means that everything that was between 24 and 0 on the original image has now been pulled down to 0 on output.

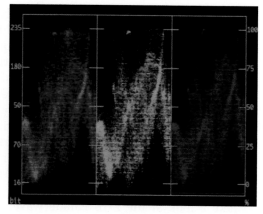

Fig. 4.43

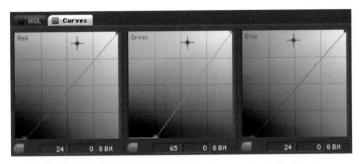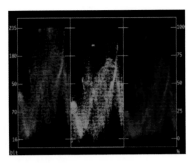

Fig. 4.44

Now, drag the same points to the right on the green and blue Curves. I took the black point of the green curve to 65 and the blue curve to 24. The image starts to look better and the three cells of the RGB Parade waveform are much more even (Figure 4.44).

Grab the upper right corner of the red curve and pull it down just a little to see if you can get rid of some of the clipping in the highlights. You don't want to bring it down too low. There are lots of bright whites in this image, and you need some part of all three RGB channels at the very top. I ended up bringing the top of the red curve down to 252. Greens are pretty low. To bring a highlight level up in curves, you need to drag it to the left along the top, because you can't drag it any higher. Drag it to the left while watching the highest spot in the middle of the green RGB Parade cell. Line the high spot on the green channel with the high spot on the red channel. This point corresponds to the bright white leg of the bench at the middle bottom of the image. My correction put the top of the green curve to 230. Do the same thing with the blue channel. My correction put the top of the blue curve to 240 (Figure 4.45).

The image is looking even better at this point, but still seems a little yellow. If you look at the RGB Parade waveform, this yellow tint is evident by the fact that the red and green channels appear stronger. (And red

Note

DaVinci's curves only go up and down at the extremes. Shadows can't be dragged right and highlights can't be dragged left.

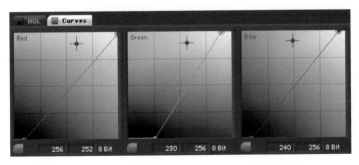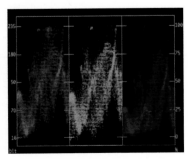

Fig. 4.45

and green make yellow. With the addition of a weak blue channel, this means that the color opposite from blue—yellow—is stronger.)

Looking at some of the shapes in the waveform monitor, we can try to see if the corresponding parts of the image are white or black and figure out what we need to do to get them to be balanced white or black. Notice that the far left side of the red and green channels on the RGB Parade are higher than the blue channel. On the red and green channel, that portion of the trace comes up to about 40IRE. On the blue channel, it's at about 25. To pull this part of the waveform up, click on the blue curve about 25 percent of the way up the diagonal line and drag it straight up (Figure 4.46). We'll watch the blue channel of the RGB Parade, but we'll also watch the video image. That part of the waveform is on the left side, so we need to be looking at the left side of the video image as well. We're also pulling up part of the image that is fairly dark, so we want to keep our eyes on the shadows on the left side of the video image.

I was able to get the blue channel to match the red and green channels, but when I did, I noticed that the shadows in the pine tree in the background to the left became very blue. So I undid that correction.

What I know about the real-world scene is that the extreme left side of the image is actually the siding of my house. That siding is painted a warm tan color (reddish yellow). The bluish tinge to the shadows gave us the clue that we didn't want that part of the waveform to match.

Let's try something else. Looking at the RGB Parade waveform, we can see that even though we have the brightest part of the blue channel up as high as it can go, the rest of the blue highlights aren't as strong as the highlights in the red and green channels. Knowing that the bench has a lot of white in it and the garage door in the background is also probably white tells us that we need to bring up the highlights of the blue channel.

Grab a point on the blue curve about 75 percent of the way up the diagonal line and drag it upward. We're trying to get the area on all three channels to look about the same at 75IRE. Before doing this correction, there's a kind of a "peak" in both the red and green channels at about 75IRE. Bring

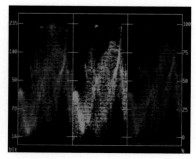

Fig. 4.46

that same area of the trace in the blue channel up to match them. My adjustment was to bring the point at 185 on the blue curve up to 207. When I did that, I also brought the highest highlights on the blue channel up too far, so I made an adjustment at the top point of the blue curve back down to 246.

You could look at the RGB Parade and decide that the highlights in the red channel are too strong, but I think that the extra "weight" at the top of the red channel trace on the waveform is probably due to the red and pink flowers that are in a corresponding position to the strongest parts of the red channel of the waveform monitor. If you want to, you could play with the red channel to get it back into line with the blue and green channels, but you'll see that the white highlights in the picture quickly turn cyan, which is the opposite of red.

The image looks significantly better at this point. But there's a lot of green in the tin flower can on the bench and I don't think the green foliage pops very well. Let's see if we can pull out some of the green in the midtone areas.

Start with a point in the green curve that's about halfway up and pull it down a little. Using the information in the tip box on this page (in the margin to the right), you know that you're moving the midtones of green down, so you need to be looking at the midtones of your video image to prevent the image from going too magenta, which is the opposite of green. As soon as you see the midtones turn magenta, you have to back off the correction. For me, the magenta cast started almost immediately when I pulled the gammas down, so I returned it to its original place. (Undo—Command-Z or Control-Z—should work on most applications, or you can select the point and delete it.)

I still feel that there's a bit of a green cast to the middle shadows, so this time, let's place a point that's much lower on the green curve and pull it down subtly. I brought the point from around 106 down to 57, which may not seem like a very subtle move, but remember that the black level of green was already pulled down quite a bit, which pulls down all of the other points on the curve as well.

Looking at our original image (Figure 4.47) compared to our correction shows a significant improvement (Figure 4.48). These are changes that would not be quite as easy to make using the traditional hue offset wheels because the changes to the midtones of the blue and green channels wouldn't work as well as the specific changes we made to the high midtones of the blue channel and the low midtones of the green channel (Figure 4.49).

The important thing to remember when choosing a point is to determine a specific portion of the picture you're trying to change—like the tin watering can in the previous example—and to try to guess where that tonal range lies on the curve. Don't be afraid to make mistakes. Pick a point and move it a bit. If it's not affecting the tonal range you want, then delete it and pick another point. Use the information you gathered from

> **TIP**
>
> Whenever you are making a correction, be aware of what tonal range you are adjusting and which color you're adjusting. When you're looking at your video monitor, you want to be especially tuned to the subtle changes in *that* specific tonal range and with *that* specific color. Sometimes if your eyes are looking at the entire image, you'll miss subtle changes that you would notice if you were looking in the right place. You also don't want to be blind to what the correction does to the larger image. Sometimes this means tweaking the image back and forth looking at just the shadows the first time you tweak it and then at the overall image the next time you tweak it.

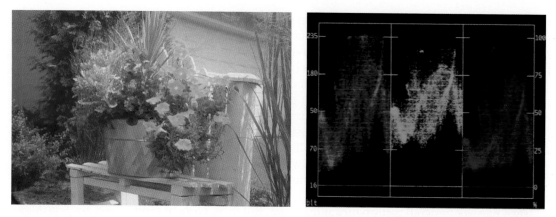

Fig. 4.47 Flower bench, original.

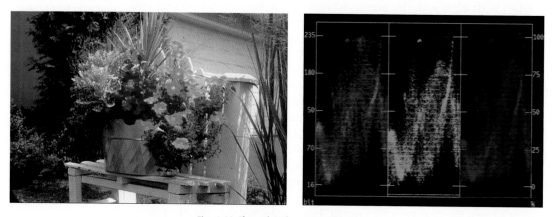

Fig. 4.48 Flower bench, corrected final.

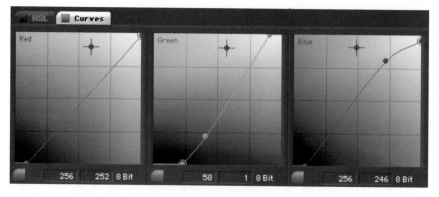

Fig. 4.49 Final corrected curves.

the first point to determine where the second point should go. Did the first point affect a tonal range that was slightly above or below the range you really wanted? That will guide you in picking the correct spot.

Use extra points on the curve to protect portions of the curve that you don't want to affect.

You also want to remember the tip from Chapter 2 about curves: use extra points on the curve to protect portions of the curve that you *don't* want to affect. For example, if a correction to the midtones of the red curve is working great for the midtones, but it is adding too much red to the highlights, then place a point on the red curve between the top of the Curve and the area that you are moving in order to protect the red highlights from being affected by the red midtone point. When you do this, be careful not to place the points too close to each other or it will cause banding or posterization. You can use the previous tip about eyedroppering the image to determine where the "protection point" should go.

RGB Lift, Gamma, and Gain Sliders

A tool that works similarly to curves are the red, green, and blue numerical or slider controls for lift, gamma, and gain. Virtually all color correction software includes sliders like these. In DaVinci Resolve, they are in the Color Screen in the Primary tab. They are available in the Advance tab of Color's Primary Room. They are available in Color Finesse and many Avid and Final Cut Pro color correction plug-ins, such as 3Prong's Color-FiX AVX plug-in or Magic Bullet's Colorista plug-in for Final Cut Pro.

Note that I'm not talking about simply adjusting lift, gamma, and gain, but adjusting the *individual color channels* of red, green, and blue in each of those tonal ranges.

Figures 4.50 through 4.56 show a range of options from various products and plug-ins that allow you to color balance your images using RGB sliders or numerical values in each tonal range. Although we're going to do this correction in Color, any of these applications—or others with a similar RGB-level UI—will work similarly.

For this tutorial, we'll use the "ChromaDuMonde_properexwarm" clip from the DVD.

Looking at the ChromaDuMonde chart is a little more complicated on the vectorscope and RGB Parade, but it is still very similar to the grayscale chart. To familiarize yourself with how the chart should look on the scopes, import the "ChromaDuMonde_properexwhite" clip from the DVD. Notice the way that the color from the color chips surrounds the center of the

T I P

Some applications, such as Avid Media Composer, allow you to eyedropper a point on the image and see exactly where on the curve that point lies. This feature is a great instructional tool to develop your ability to know where these points would fall without letting the software do it for you. A good photographer knows how to use a light meter, but most also pride themselves on being able to set exposure by eye if they have to. Developing a good sense of the luminance levels of various parts of an image will make you much faster as a colorist, because your corrections will be more intuitive.

vectorscope evenly and how they aim toward the six color vector targets. Also, the various skin tone chips should form a line that follows the I line of the vectorscope. The I line runs the diagonally across the vectorscope from about the 5 o'clock position to about 10 o'clock. Many people refer to this

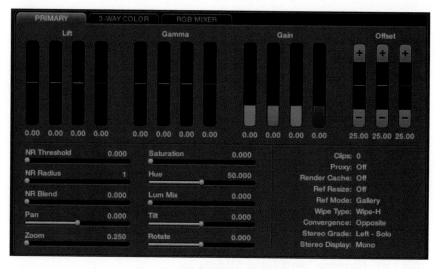

Fig. 4.50 RGB sliders in DaVinci Resolve.

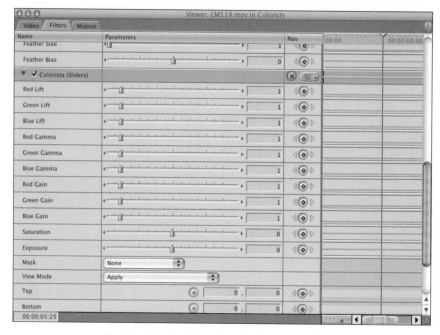

Fig. 4.51 RGB sliders for the Final Cut Pro Colorista plug-in.

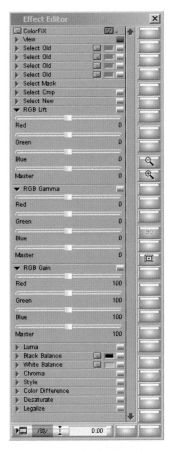

Fig. 4.52 RGB sliders for 3Prong's ColorFiX plug-in for Avid.

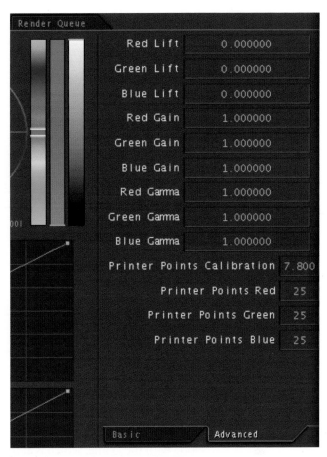

Fig. 4.53 Color's RGB sliders are in the Advanced tab of the Primary In room.

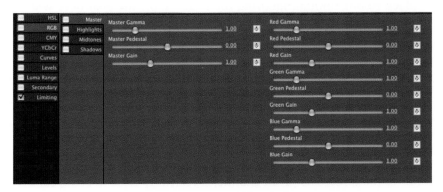

Fig. 4.54 Color Finesse's RGB sliders.

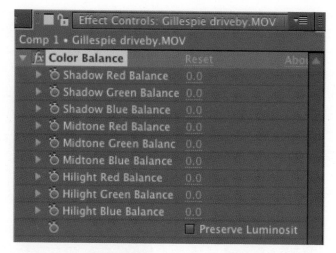

Fig. 4.55 After Effect's built-in RGB color balance UI.

Fig. 4.56 IRIDAS's SpeedGrade DI primary color correction controls. IRIDAS has been purchased by Adobe but had not been integrated into its product line when this book was written.

as the "skin tone" line on the vectorscope. Technically though, this line, along with the Q line, which is at a 90-degree angle to the I line, are actually the in-phase and quadrature phase lines for the color difference signals in NTSC. What does that mean? Nothing to a colorist, so we might as well call the top half of the I line the skin tone line—for us, that's what it's good for.

Back to our tutorial. Ignoring the color chips, the goal here will be similar to the tutorial we did with curves. We want to use the red, green, and blue channel sliders or numerical entry boxes in each of the tonal ranges to color balance the gray chips. We'll use the red, green, and blue "lift" data boxes to control the bottom of the trace as it appears in the RGB Parade display.

Compare the waveform of the properly exposed chart (Figure 4.57a) with the improperly exposed chart (Figure 4.57b). Notice in the top left RGB Parade display (Figure 4.57b) the difference in levels between the channels, with the red channel (the first cell) having higher levels in all three tonal ranges and the blue channel (the third cell) having the lowest levels of the three. The green channel is relatively close to being correct. If you look at the RGB Parade display at the lower left, you are looking

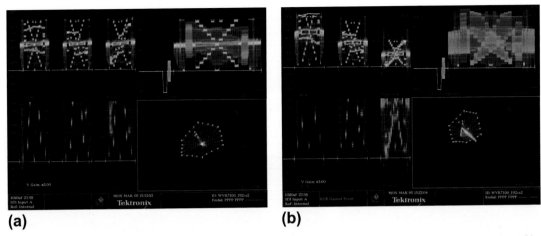

(a)   **(b)**

Fig. 4.57 Tektronix WVR7100 displays of both the balanced ChromaDuMonde chart (a) and the chart with a warm white balance (b).

at a 5x vertical gain. You can see that the black levels of all the red and green channels are elevated somewhat. Looking at the composite waveform display in the upper right corner, you can tell that there is some kind of color cast, because of the excursion in the trace for each chip chart. Compare it to the tight, well-defined steps of the X in the upper right scope of Figure 4.57a. The vectorscope shows the red color cast because the color chips are all pushed up toward the red vector instead of being evenly distributed around the center of the scope.

For this tutorial, our main focus will be the standard RGB Parade waveform display because it will match up very nicely with the specific red, green, and blue sliders or numerical entry controls.

The controls in the Advanced Tab of Color's Primary In room are actually laid out in the order you should use them: with lift first, gain next, and gamma last. Watching the RGB Parade waveform, bring the red, green, and blue lift down until the center black chip rests on the 0IRE line. Remember the focusing analogy and bring the level only low enough to get a good clean black without clipping the signal or creating an illegal black level. The center black chip in the blue channel reads much higher than the darkest chip to the left. In the red and green channels, the lowest chip is the center chip. We may have to determine which chip we try to put at 0 for the blue channel. For now, we'll put the center chip for the blue channel at 0. Remember, once the relative positions of various parts of the lower part of the trace start to change, you need to stop, because that is showing clipping. See Figure 4.58.

Next are the gain controls. Bring them up so that the brightest part of the white chip is at 100IRE. Note that the chart is not quite evenly lit, so the left side of the chart is slightly brighter than the right side of the chart.

Red Lift	-0.037700
Green Lift	-0.037700
Blue Lift	-0.033350

Fig. 4.58 My numbers for the lift correction from Color.

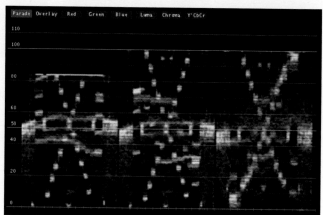

Red Lift	-0.021750
Green Lift	-0.058000
Blue Lift	-0.010150
Red Gain	0.811500
Green Gain	1.179799
Blue Gain	1.829400
Red Gamma	1.000000
Green Gamma	1.000000
Blue Gamma	1.000000

Fig. 4.59 My numbers for the gain correction and the resulting waveform from my gain corrections.

Seeing this slight difference in luminance between the right and left sides of the chart is very difficult to do visually, but is quite obvious with your scopes. Also, you may notice that as you start to bring up the green channel gain, you can't really get to the top (100IRE) before the green channel starts to compress and a strange interaction starts happening with the red channel gain, which almost seems to start unclipping. Once this happens, stop raising your green gain and bring your red gain down quite a bit (I brought mine down to about 80IRE) until you can get the green channel to 100IRE without compressing. Then bring your blue channel up to match green. See Figure 4.59.

As you make changes to the gain—and especially to the gamma—you may notice that your lift (black) has changed. This is because the gain corrections were so drastic that they affected the lift. This effect is common. If you were grading these sequences with a manual user interface that allowed you to tweak the red gain and red lift at the same time, you could do this much faster. By using a single mouse, you'll need to go back and forth between the gain and lift controls until you've got both of them in equilibrium. See Figure 4.60.

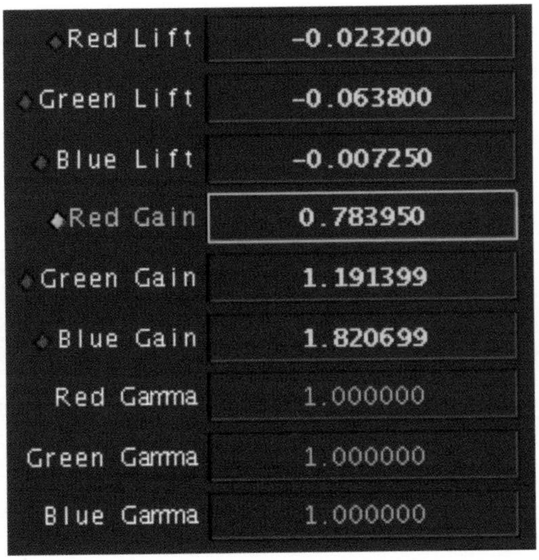

◆Red Lift	−0.023200
◆Green Lift	−0.063800
◆Blue Lift	−0.007250
◆Red Gain	0.783950
◆Green Gain	1.191399
◆Blue Gain	1.820699
Red Gamma	1.000000
Green Gamma	1.000000
Blue Gamma	1.000000

Fig. 4.60 The numbers for gain and lift. Check the minor difference between these and the numbers in the previous illustration. Now it's time to make sure that the midtones are also balanced. With the highlights and shadows balanced already, the midtones should be pretty close.

Notice, though, that the similar shapes that sit just under the 60IRE line in the RGB parade are not quite at the same level in all three channels, even though the white chips and black chips are even. I'm going to match the red and blue midtone shapes to the green midtone. The midtone corrections will have a fairly strong effect on both the highlights and shadows, so I'll have to do some back and forth corrections between the three tonal ranges until I have the shadows, midtones, and highlights all even across the three color channels. Figure 4.61 shows my final result with the numbers and RGB waveform.

With the amount of clipping in the red channel, this correction is problematic, but you can see from the vectorscope and the 3D Color Space that most of what is supposed to be neutral is actually fairly neutral. There is a slight red cast in some of the chips still, due to the clipping of the red channel. In a real-world image, you could determine whether this slight warming was appropriate and what you were willing to sacrifice in other colors or tonal ranges to try to get these into "spec."

Let's apply this to grading a real-world image with these same tools. Call up "piano_cool" from the DVD into your chosen color correction application or plug-in. I'll do this one in Color Finesse.

Figure 4.62b is the starting RGB Parade waveform display for the piano cool image. It shows that the black levels are slightly elevated across all

Red Lift	−0.005800
Green Lift	−0.050750
Blue Lift	−0.015950
Red Gain	0.782500
Green Gain	1.179800
Blue Gain	1.807650
Red Gamma	0.923150
Green Gamma	0.939100
Blue Gamma	0.988400

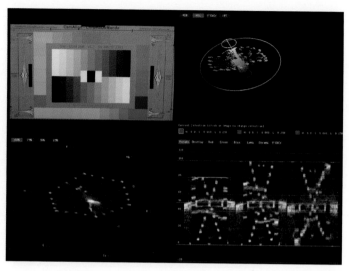

Fig. 4.61

(a)

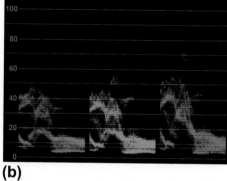

Fig. 4.62

three channels. Looking at the right side of the shadows, the blue channel starts at about the same level as the other channels at its lowest point, but the portion of the trace from about 0IRE to about 20IRE shows that the deep shadows above black are elevated above the other two tracks. Also, looking at the highlights, the red channel is the lowest, and the blue channel is the highest. Midtones are a bit hard to judge at the moment. Let's set our black, lift, or pedestal level first across all three channels. We have the nice black piano keys on the right to use as a very clean black, so that should be relatively easy.

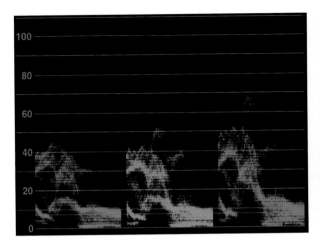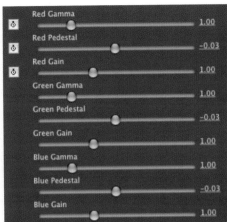

Fig. 4.63

Figure 4.63 shows what the numbers and RGB Parade look like at the end of the pedestal correction. Now we'll move to the highlight or gain correction. Once again, we have nice white keys to use as we set our highlights.

The blue channel is closest to being correct and the red channel needs the most help. Let's set all of these so that the highlights on the white keys in the middle of the frame are at 100IRE. That might be too bright, but we'll start with that goal to spread out the tonal range as much as possible, then we can look at the video monitor and determine whether 100IRE is too bright for this image.

Here's where I left the gain controls (Figure 4.64). There is some green above 100IRE, but the main shapes across the 100IRE line match across all three channels. Notice that the blacks in the red channel are slightly elevated now, because the gain change was so radical. We'll need to fix that, then decide what we want to do with the gammas.

Now that I'm satisfied that the gains and pedestals match across the three color channels, we need to decide what to do with the gammas. First, let's look at the RGB parade display (Figure 4.65) and figure out what we're looking at. We have only a couple of elements to figure out. There are the hands, the brown piano wood, and the black and white keys. What is what in the waveform?

Well, the area between 0IRE and 20IRE to the right of each cell is the black keys and probably some of the dark wood to the right of the image. The area in the middle of each cell between 90IRE and 100IRE is the highlight on the white keys in the middle of the screen. The area to the left and extending past the middle of each channel between about 80IRE and 30IRE is the hands. In the red channel, this shape goes up to about 90IRE, probably due to the highlight on the "pinky" side of the hand.

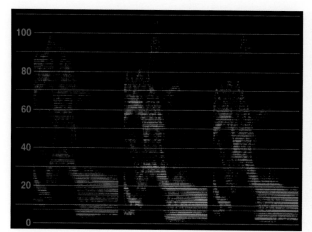

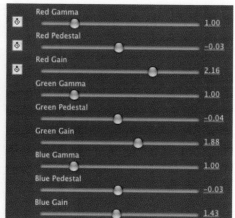

Fig. 4.64

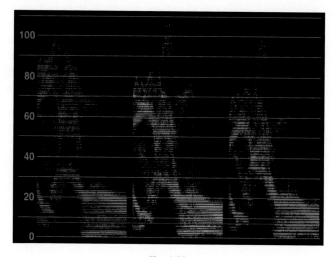

Fig. 4.65

You may think that we need to even out the discrepancy in the levels in that 80IRE to 30IRE zone—which is definitely defined as "gamma"—but consider the color of flesh. It's pretty red and fairly yellow, without much blue. Considering that, the RGB Parade may be sitting just about right.

But we wouldn't be doing our job—and I would be contradicting my own advice—if we didn't try to focus our correction and see what we can do with the skin tones and any other colors in the gammas. But trying to focus color in gammas is not something you can generally do with scopes. This is where you have to turn your eyes to the actual image and find where the image is most pleasing or correct visually.

I started by making an adjustment to the blue gammas, and the skin tone, and the tops of the piano keys quickly started getting too yellow as I dropped the blue gammas. Raising the blue gammas added too much coolness to the flesh tones in the hands.

Changing the green gammas downward pulled some green noise out of the wood and skin tones, though going just slightly too far started making the image go very magenta very quickly. Lowering the green gamma also added a nice richness to the dark wood of the piano. Raising the greens instantly started looking sickly.

Bringing the red tones down certainly doesn't help the skin tones. Raising them creates a nice warm glow to the dark piano wood, but moving it too much adds an unnatural oversaturated look to the hands first and then to the wood.

Here's where we started and where we ended up (Figure 4.66).

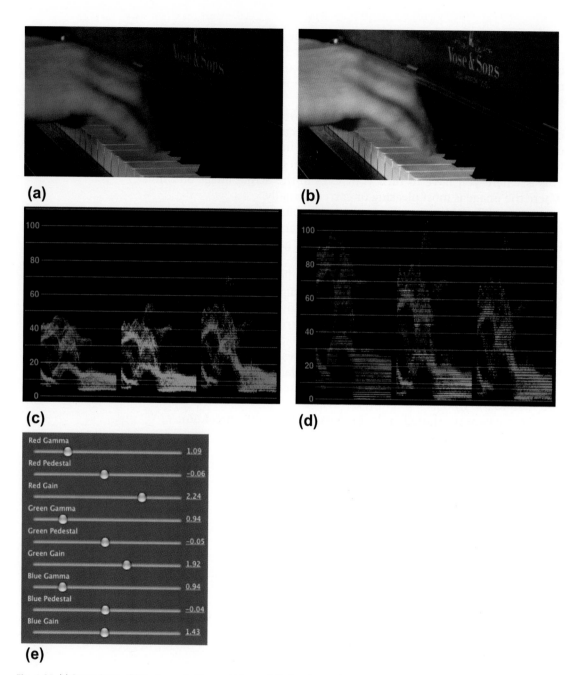

Fig. 4.66 (a) Source image. (b) Final corrected image. (c) Source RGB Parade waveform before correction. (d) RGB Parade after correction. (e) Color Finesse RGB sliders in their corrected positions.

Channels or Channel Mixers

Avid Symphony and After Effects allow you to see the individual channels as black and white images, and Symphony allows you to blend the channels together in combinations that include not only red, green, and blue, but also Luma, Cr, Cb, and an offset percentage.

DaVinci Resolve also provides a similar toolset (Figure 4.67), though it is called the RBG Mixer and is available in the Color Screen in the RGB Mixer tab.

The black and white views are handy visual tools, but don't give you too much more information than the RGB waveform. Here are the individual channels for red, green, and blue (Figure 4.68).

Green looks pretty much like you would expect for a black and white representation of the ChromaDuMonde chip chart (Figure 4.68b), except

Fig. 4.67 DaVinci Resolve RGB Mixer tab in the Color Screen.

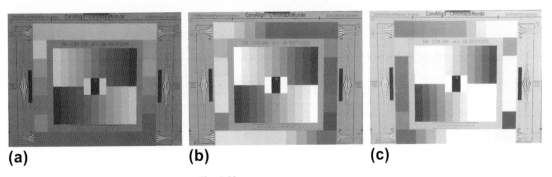

(a)   (b)   (c)

Fig. 4.68

that the dark grays are a little stretched out and the upper grays are a little compressed. The red channel looks like nothing is really clipped or badly crushed (Figure 4.68a), but all of it is pretty dark compared to the green channel. The blue channel really shows the clipping in the upper whites (Figure 4.68c), just as I suspected it would, but notice that the chips from the blacks up to the midtones match pretty well between the green channel and the blue channel. But nearly all of the upper gray chips are almost the same luminance value in the blue channel. This explains why our previous correction looks like it does.

Compare what the three channels are showing you visually against the Tektronix RGB Parade waveform image.

In the RGB Parade waveform, in the upper left of Figure 4.69, you can see how compressed the chips above the midtone are in the blue channel. This effect is giving you more information, actually—it's just not so visually simple to digest. The waveform is showing you that even though the green channel image looked pretty good, it actually has quite a bit of clipping going on in the upper grays.

Fixing these issues with Channels is a different matter than *seeing* them, though. With Channels, the way to fix the problems is to combine channels with each other. This is basically way too unintuitive for most

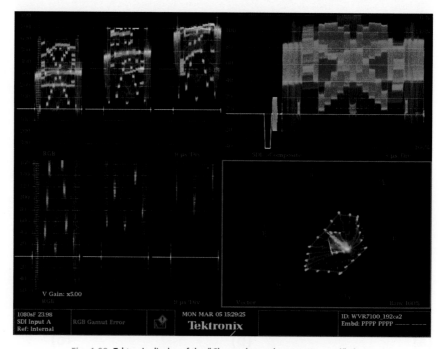

Fig. 4.69 Tektronix display of the "Chromadumonde_properex_cool" chart.

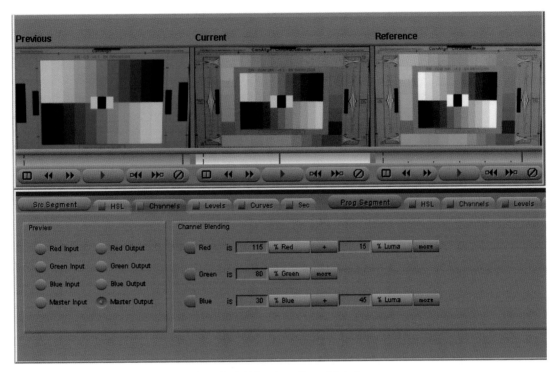

Fig. 4.70 Avid Symphony Channels interface.

color corrections, but it can save you—if you have access to a Channels-like interface (Figure 4.70)—for some really nasty corrections. There are two main situations where I find myself turning to Channels. The first is when a color channel is completely missing or is almost completely missing. Sometimes this happens on multi-camera shoots, where a single color channel gets shorted out going to the iso deck. The camera seems fine going into the switcher, but not the iso deck. I can try to fake the missing color channel using Channels.

I also use Channels with very noisy video. Nine times out of ten, the noise primarily resides in a single channel. By reducing the strength of the noisy channel and mixing it with the cleaner channels, I can take out the noise.

You should know that Channels is only going to get you so far in saving things. In almost every color correction that I start in Channels, I have to use other tools to fix what I broke in the image.

I'm not going to get into a detailed explanation of this tool because very few applications have it. What I did above was to look at what was wrong with a given channel and try to correct it by reducing the percentage of the problem channel and mixing it with a percentage of a channel that had attributes that would address the missing elements of the bad channel. Sometimes this causes some whacked-out color shifts. The goal here is to try to make the picture look more normal than what you started with. Channels is really only a last-ditch attempt to fix bad technical problems for me. If you have access to Channels or an RGB Mixer, as in Resolve, and want more information on how to use it properly, I would suggest checking out one of the many Photoshop color correction books, such as *Photoshop Color Correction* by Michael Kieran. There is an entire chapter on blending channels in that book. Photoshop offers a much greater capability to blend many different channels using options beyond those available in Avid Symphony, Color Finesse, and Resolve.

After Effects also has a similar color correction tool called Channel Mixer that can be found at Effects > Adjust > Channel Mixer. The Channel Mixer defaults to having the red channel be 100 percent red, the green channel be 100 percent green, and the blue channel be 100 percent blue. You can also combine each color channel with one of the other two color channels by percentage or you can choose the Constant ("Const") option with specifies the amount of the input channel to be added to the output. Color can't do this type of correction, but there is a channel mixer plugin for Final Cut Pro that does this.

Printer Lights

There is another option on several color correction systems, including DaVinci Resolve, Apple Color, and IRIDAS's SpeedGrade. You can choose to alter the color the way the film industry has done it for decades: with Printer Lights. This is *not* going to give you a lot of control.

Basically, this approach turns your highly specialized, finely tuned digital color correction workhorse into an analog processor that harkens back to the dawn of color film: changing the color correction of scenes with a paper tape reader (Figure 4.71) controlling the relative light levels of the red, green, and blue printer lights that create the film print from the negative. This additive color timing of a film print uses printer points or printer lights from 1 up to 50 for each channel. Typically the printer is set up to the "default" exposure of 25 red, 25 green, and 25 blue, which is right where Color's default levels are set. To raise any given channel, you lower its numerical value. If you want to raise the overall brightness of a scene, you lower all three color channels evenly. There is no ability to change relative levels for each tonal range. Of course, in SpeedGrade and Color you can combine the use of printer lights with any other tools in the system.

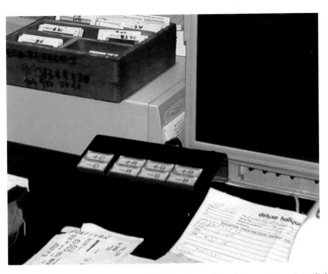

Fig. 4.71 The actual control device for color correcting major motion pictures using printer lights. I took this at Deluxe Labs in Hollywood while timing a trailer print.

Filters

In addition to the various tools that give you primary color correction control, there are numerous effects plug-ins for color correction, editing, and compositing software that allow you to place filters on your image to make global corrections such as duotone, bleach bypass, sepia tone, film look, and gradated filter looks ("grads"). There are really too many of these to mention, and the filter choices are constantly expanding and evolving, but the ability to use them creatively to affect color in your images certainly exists and I felt I should at least mention the possibility of its use.

Fig. 4.72 Original image.

duotone: A process that reduces the color palette of an image to two tones. Sepia tone is a duotone image with yellow or gold and black (Figure 4.73).

sepia tone: A duotone image using yellow or gold and black. The purpose of sepia tone is usually to give something an aged or antique look. Sepia itself is a brownish pigment or color. The specific HTML color list RGB coordinates for sepia are 112, 66, 20 (Figure 4.74).

bleach bypass: AKA skip bleach. A film developing process that bypasses the bleach bath creating an image that is more contrasty and less saturated because the silver is retained along with the color dyes of the film, creating an image similar to laying black and white on top of color (Figure 4.75)

gradated filters: Filters that are usually placed in the matte box of a film or video camera, a piece of glass that is gradated either from dark to light or from one color to another or from a color to transparent. It is generally referred to as a "grad" and its purpose is often to take some of the brightness out of a harsh sky or to add color interest to a scene. (sometimes called graduated or graded filters) (Figure 4.76b).

Fig. 4.73 Duotone filter.

Fig. 4.74 Sepia filter.

Fig. 4.75 Bleach bypassfilter.

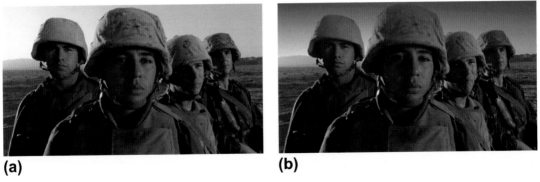

(a)   **(b)**

Fig. 4.76

Additional Tools

Many color correction applications have specific, patented tools that make it stand out from the other applications that are available. DaVinci Resolve has the ability to combine nodes and to composite different looks using the same compositing tools that are available, for example, in Adobe Photoshop: add, subtract, difference, multiply, screen, overlay, darken, and lighten effects. This really increases the ability to create very complex grades.

Apple Color also has the very cool and powerful Color FX Room, with its nodal effects tree that allowed multiple effects to be combined in intricate ways.

Because these tools are not widely available across multiple applications, I am not going to cover them. There are application-specific training books and DVDs by myself and others that teach these tools, but this book was created to be product- and platform-agnostic, so the aim with this book is to cover features, workflows, tools, and tips that can be accessed by most colorists, regardless of the software or hardware that they have access to.

CHAPTER 5

Secondary Color Correction Primer

Although primary color correction affects the entire raster, secondary color correction is limited to specific geographic regions—for example, vignettes or windows—or specific color vectors. Secondary color correction can also affect specific tonal regions, but these secondary regions are more specific than the shadows, midtones, and highlights that are used to qualify corrections in primary color correction.

As the tools have become more nonlinear, the distinctions between what is primary and what is secondary are beginning to blur. For the purposes of defining workflow, this distinction will probably never totally evaporate, but the boundaries between these two terms are more vague than they have been in the past. As a matter of fact, the boundaries where secondary color correction ends are also beginning to fall as more color correction applications are offering the ability to add effects and filters to create exciting new looks. Another aspect of the blurring lines between primary and secondary color correction is that some definitions of secondary color correction describe it as being corrections made downstream of the telecine. Color grading in the years since 2000 have become increasingly detached from the telecine or scanner so that now, virtually everything is done apart from a tele-cine—if a telecine is involved at all. As of 2012, colorists rarely work from telecined material. Either film scans or digital camera origination is the primary source of material fed into modern color grading suites. Even the telecined material is rarely graded directly from the telecine, instead being transferred "flat" to an HD digital tape or directly to a server. The flat grade is then corrected by the colorist without access to the telecine.

Here are a few of the interfaces for secondary color correction (Figures 5.1–5.7).

Definition

raster: Computer terminology that has crossed over to video to represent an image created from horizontal lines of individual pixels. The raster refers to the entire video image.

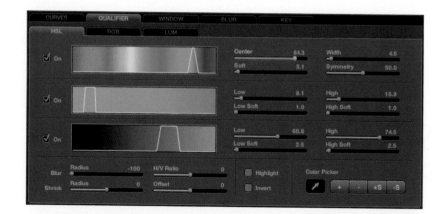

Fig. 5.1 DaVinci Resolve Secondary Qualifier tab. This tab is typically behind the Curves tab.

Fig. 5.2 DaVinci Resolve Secondary Window tab. This tab is typically behind the Curves tab.

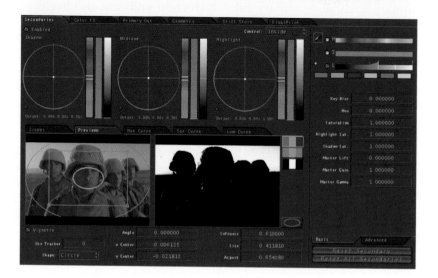

Fig. 5.3 Color's Secondaries Room, image courtesy Artbeats.

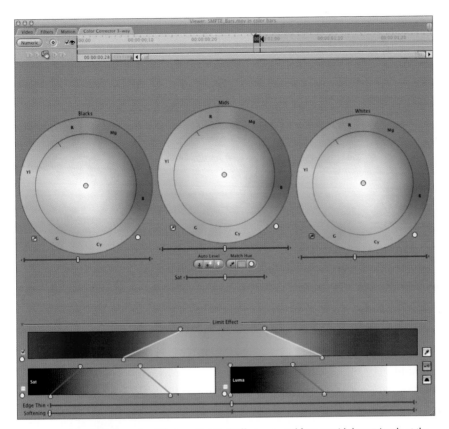

Fig. 5.4 Final Cut Pro's Secondary Effect—called Limit Effect, accessed from a twirl-down triangle at the bottom of the three-way color corrector.

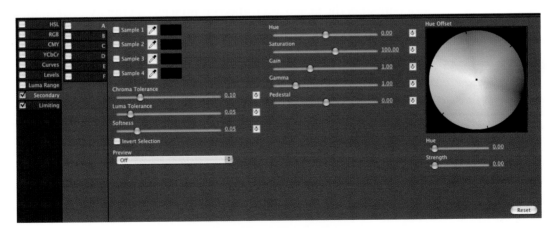

Fig. 5.5 Color Finesse's Secondary tab.

Fig. 5.6 Avid Symphony's Secondary color correction tab.

Fig. 5.7 IRIDAS's SpeedGrade DI Secondary correction mode. IRIDAS has been purchased by Adobe. Plans for integration into Adobe products or as a standalone Adobe color corrector were not known at time of publication.

I briefly touched on this issue at the end of the previous chapter, but it could easily be argued that this new effects capability belongs in a discussion of secondary correction instead of primaries. Where it belongs depends on whether you feel that "primary color correction" is a workflow term. If "primary" and "secondary" simply define logical steps in a workflow, then effects work is decidedly in the secondary category. On the other hand, if you regard primary color correction as global corrections to the image and secondary corrections as qualified or targeted corrections to a portion of the image, then effects is probably a primary correction, as many of these filters and effects are applied to the entire image. To many colorists, it is not a distinction that even needs to be made. Everything is simply a tool and categorization is not necessary.

The Purpose of Secondary Correction

In nearly every demo of a color correction application or NLE with color correction capabilities, there is a point in which they turn a car or a shirt or a product package a different color using secondaries.

When I first started color correcting, I rarely used secondaries because I didn't find myself correcting car commercials in which they filmed a car with the wrong color. I soon learned that serious colorists

Definition

secondaries: Shorthand for secondary color corrections. The plural is often used because most applications allow you to have multiple secondary color corrections—secondaries—on a single image.

rarely use secondary color correction for such obvious chores. Instead, secondaries are used subtly for much more natural corrections. Some of the main targets for secondary color corrections are skin tones, sky, water, and grass.

Primary color correction often must be done with an eye on the big picture and an understanding that the goal is to make *most* of the image look good but also that certain things, like skin tones, may need additional work with secondaries. As you may have noticed, the items I mentioned in the previous paragraph—skin, sky, water, and grass—are all things that people have a natural understanding about and preconceived notions regarding what colors these things should be. Often, getting a primary color correction to look good across most of the image will take these specific items out of the color range that most people are expecting. Sometimes, if you want to warm up an entire image, the skin tones will go much too orange. Or, by pulling the unwanted blue cast out of an outdoor scene, the grass will turn yellowish. Or, by bringing up the levels of the foreground elements of the picture, the sky will become overexposed. All of these things call for a secondary color correction that isolates or qualifies the problem area and fixes *just* that portion while leaving the rest of the primary correction alone.

Secondary color correction is often used to fix the things that the colorist "broke" in the primary correction. For example, in trying to match the colors and luminance values of two shots, a colorist may use primary color correction to get the majority of the shot to match, but will find that the only way to do that is to have the sky of one shot be a strange color. In this case, the colorist would match most of the shot using primaries, then use secondaries to fix the problem with the sky. This situation often happens with images that have a color cast in addition to clipping, because the clipping in the dominant color cast will cause any corrections to the unclipped portions of the image to deliver some very strange colors to the clipped areas.

Secondaries are also often used to make the subject of the shot "pop" or to focus the viewer's attention on something important. This task is often done with a vignette, which slightly darkens the edges of the image and points the viewer's eyes to the main focus of the shot. It can also be done by qualifying an important part of the image and increasing the saturation or contrast in that portion of the image to draw the viewer's attention to it.

Many colorists I spoke with love getting into specific parts of the picture to work in isolation on that area, but not everyone is in complete agreement about the technique.

Stefan Sonnenfeld

One of the hottest colorists in the world for the last decade has been Stefan Sonnenfeld, (Figure 5.8), whose grading kit of choice is the DaVinci Resolve. His filmography as a colorist (as of late 2011) is a staggering 115 titles, including some of Hollywood's biggest box office hits and films with definitive creative looks: *Pirates of the Caribbean* (all four), *Transformers*, *Star Trek*, *300*, *Fast and the Furious*, *National Treasure: Book of Secrets*, *Invincible*, and *Alice in Wonderland*.

He has worked with the top tier of A-list directors and producers, including Jerry Bruckheimer, Michael Mann, Hans Zimmer, Michael Bay, Steven Spielberg, Gor Verbinsky, Tony Scott, and Spike Jonze.

In addition to his film work, he has also graded TV series, including *CSI: NY*, *Cold Case*, *Without a Trace*, and the pilot of *Prison Break*.

Sonnenfeld is the president and principal of Company 3 in Santa Monica, with offices in New York, London, and Atlanta. Company 3 includes a wealth of top-level colorists, including Siggy Fersti and Stephen Nakamura (who was featured in my first color correction book). Sonnenfeld was named by *Entertainment Weekly* as one of the 50 Smartest People in Hollywood.

Fig. 5.8 Company 3 president and colorist, Stefan Sonnenfeld.

On his own use of secondaries, Sonnenfeld says, "I do not use a ton of secondaries. I am also not known to be the craziest colorist. I am telling you that you can go into my room and look at twenty different sessions and you will not find any of that and that is just what it is."

With the speed at which he works, trying to qualify secondaries would seem impossible. Sonnenfeld explains, "I never have enough time. I have 140 shots that they have given me two hours to do. I have back-to-back 150-shot sessions with four hours to do them, so that is 300 shots in four hours with very difficult work. I know I will get through it, but I do not spend a lot of time on the frames. There are people who will not work with me because I do not sit in a room and key things with 18 windows, just because I am not into that. Let's do it and move on to the next one, because you can overthink stuff."

Are You Qualified?

For me, the biggest issue of secondary color correction is *qualification*. I'm not talking about whether the colorist is skilled enough to do it. I'm talking about what portion of the image you are trying to qualify—in other words, "choose"—as the section in which you make alterations.

In case you missed the earlier glossary item for this word in Chapter 2, "to qualify" or "qualification" means that an area of the picture is specifically isolated for a correction by any number of methods. You could qualify something for correction using its hue, saturation, tonal value, or a combination of all three. You could also qualify an area of the image using a "window" or garbage matte. This is an important concept to grasp. So much of this chapter will be devoted to methods and techniques for qualifying parts of the image. Once a portion of the image is well qualified, altering it is largely based on the skill sets of the previous four chapters.

Once a portion of the image is well qualified, altering it is largely based on the skill sets of the previous four chapters.

Creating effective qualifications when doing secondary color corrections requires a good understanding of your tools and of your ability to analyze the image and understand what can be selected and how.

As this book is not really about developing specialized skill sets with specific tools, I'll leave that exploration up to you. As for developing an ability for understanding what can be isolated in a shot, that is a matter of some experience and—for even the best colorist—a good deal of experimentation. Of course, the more experienced you are at making these qualifications, the less experimentation you need. Getting that knowledge and practical experience is what the rest of this chapter is about.

Definition

vignette: One of the layperson's meanings for this word is for a photograph or other image with edges that shade off gradually. To a colorist, "vignette" is both a noun and a verb. The noun describes a shape placed in the picture to allow a different correction inside and out. Most often, this correction is used to create the effect of fading out (darkening usually) the edges of the image. As a verb, it is simply the action of making the vignette or the effect the vignette has on the image, as in "I vignetted it so that the center of the image pops a little better." Additionally, Color uses the word to describe *any* use of a shape to create or modify a secondary. For other software, these are considered windows or masks.

TIP

Increased contrast is one of the brain's visual cues that something is closer to us (and therefore inherently more important).

Qualifications in secondaries are done in three basic ways:

1. Isolating a specific color vector or luminance range or a combination of the two
2. Using a shape to define a portion of the image
3. Using a combination of the two

For all three of these methods, the basic concept is to create a matte or mask that limits the correction to a specific portion of the image.

There are also three basic steps to doing a secondary color correction:

1. Determine what you are trying to accomplish
2. Figure out how you can qualify the correct portion of the image without qualifying unwanted areas
3. Make a correction inside and/or outside of that qualified area

Let's take a look at the three methods of color correction and walk through each of the three steps with each method.

Color Vector Isolation

One of the main secondary color correction qualification methods is to isolate a specific color vector and alter it in some way. This is a very good way to do secondaries as opposed to "vignettes" or "spot" color correction, because you don't have to worry about camera movement or things crossing the foreground. The color corrections that you apply to a specific color vector isolation or qualification stay with those pixels as long as those pixels stay relatively the same color. They don't need to be tracked or rotoscoped. Passing shadows or other active lighting effects or semi-transparent foreground effects like smoke or fog will have an effect on color vector isolations, though, as they will change the color of the image behind it.

Each color correction application has a slightly different set of controls to accomplish isolating specific color vectors, but most of them work very similarly to Color. You can try to isolate the vector in the old-school way by guessing at the correct hue and saturation and luminance values and moving the HSL sliders until you have a clean matte, but nearly everyone will start his or her qualification of the selected color by sampling it with the eyedropper first.

Nearly all color correction applications have the ability to sample a portion of an image with an eyedropper. Symphony uses a "syringe" for sampling large areas. Each application has slight differences in how the eyedropper works. Some—like Color—allow you to add and subtract from your qualifications using the eyedropper and certain modifier keys.

Some apps allow you to click on a color only with the eyedropper; others allow you to drag over large areas to qualify multiple shades of a color. Some of these eyedroppers sample only the precise pixel that is at the tip of the eyedropper; others allow you to set a user preference of sampling and averaging a 3×3 grid of pixels around the tip of the eyedropper or even a 5×5 sample. Consult the users' manual for your application on how the eyedropper works. (And stay on top of your application's current way of doing things, as applications evolve and gain new abilities or ways of doing things all the time.) Learn the options for the eyedropper tool when creating qualifications. This book is not about specific button pushes in specific applications, so I will not go into them here.

Let's try doing an old-school color vector qualification, so that if you're in an application that doesn't have an eyedropper, you can get something accomplished. Also, learning to do it the hard way helps understand exactly what's going on and makes doing it the easy way even easier.

Load the "art_institute_lion_proper" clip into your color correction application. I'll be using Color for this secondary tutorial. In Color, you go to the Secondaries Room (which is like a tab) and enable one of the secondary tabs just above the timeline (there are eight). Apple Color processes each of theses secondary tabs in numerical order, so some colorists like to leave the first secondary tab free in case they want to go back in and stick a secondary in before their first secondary. If that sounds like smart advice to you, select the tab for Secondary 2.

Fig. 5.9

As pointed out earlier, the first step of making a secondary correction is to determine what you are trying to accomplish. For this tutorial, our goal is to make the lion on the Art Institute steps be "the star of the show"—we want the viewer to notice the lion as the focal point of the shot.

The second step is to figure out how to make a qualification that will enable you to accomplish that goal. Looking at the image, the lion is fairly green-blue, and there doesn't appear to be too much else in the image that is the same hue or saturation as the lion. Much of the rest of the image contains similar luminance levels, so the obvious place to start is to create a key using the hue information.

To view the matte that you create with your qualification, make sure that the Previews tab under the shadow hue offset wheel is active. In the Previews tab, the left window shows you the clip and allows you to see and manipulate any vignettes or garbage mattes you've created. The right window shows you the matte of any isolations you've made by color vector selections or luminance selections. To the right of that window, there are three small icons called the Matte Preview Mode buttons (Figure 5.11). The top one has red, green, and blue rectangles for viewing the image normally in RGB, which is essentially the same image that is in the Scopes window. The middle one has gray, green, and gray rectangles. This is called the Desaturated Preview. It is a view of your qualified areas in full color and your unqualified areas in black and white (monochrome). The bottom icon has black, white, and black rectangles. This is the Matte Only

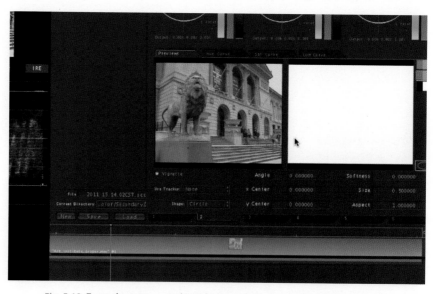

Fig. 5.10 To see the matte created in Color Secondaries Room, select the Previews tab.

Fig. 5.11 Matte Preview buttons show you what has been selected by the qualification.

button and displays the isolation as a black and white matte image, with qualified portions in white and unqualified in black.

Click on the icon to see the black and white matte on the second monitor. The display is white, indicating that the entire image is selected.

Start by selecting only the hue slider and drag the small white lefthand line above the hue bar towards the right (Figure 5.12) to narrow the hue selection, and pull in the small white line on the righthand side to the left and equal amount. Then drag the white line inside the hue bar so that it is over the bluish green area of the hue bar. Now use the white lines on top of the hue bar to adjust the width of the hue selection. Moving either white line will move them both. If you want to move just one side of the hue selection, hold down Shift while you drag. The smaller white lines above the hue bar control the fall off of the selection and will be crucial to creating a nice matte. If you can't see the fall off controls, then use the eyedropper and click on the lion. This will add two little gray triangles with gray handles above the HSL bars. You can adjust the fall off in the same way as the hue selection.

Disable the luminance and saturation controls, if you used the eyedropper. Just adjust hue until you get the best selection possible. Use that focusing analogy. Try to get the greatest amount of the lion selected with the least selection of other picture elements. Some of the things to look for in this particular image when selecting with hue are the sky and the banners in the arches of the museum. Even the grayish shadows on the inside of the lower arches have some green in them. They can become qualified depending on the angle and spread of the hue, but you should be able to do a good job of isolating just the lion. Here's my isolation (Figure 5.13).

This correction is not perfect. We want to see if we can isolate the lion more and get less of anything that is not the lion. Also, we need to soften this matte or the correction will look very nasty (Figure 5.14). In Color, choosing a Key Blur of about 1.0 or 2.0 is a good starting point. Key Blur is located just below the HSL selectors.

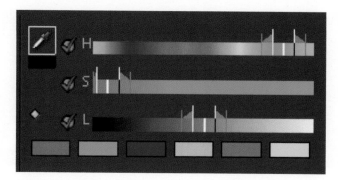

Fig. 5.12

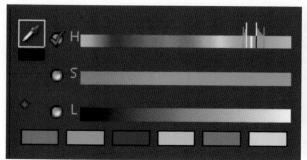

Fig. 5.13

Fig. 5.14

We could further qualify just the lion using a garbage matte created in the vignette section, but for now, see if adjusting the saturation or luminance controls will clean up this qualification any further. After a bit of experimenting, I found that the hue control by itself worked to get the best key (note the check mark in Figure 5.13).

Before we try to improve the qualification any more, let's see if we can accomplish what we want to do to the lion with the qualification we already have. This step is part of the time management of color correction. You could try to really dial in a perfect matte for the lion, but it is possible that the fairly rough qualification that we have now will suffice, so why waste any more time on it? Later on, you may discover that in order to really take the secondary correction where you want it to go, you need a better qualification so that your adjustment does not pollute other areas of the image.

Our goal with this correction was to make the lion pop from the background and be more prominent. I started by taking the midtone hue offset wheel all the way down to cyan on the outside edge of the wheel, but then I decided that I didn't want to have the lion's hue swing to a new direction—I just wanted to increase the saturation and contrast of the color that already existed. So I reset my hue offset wheel and just increased the saturation and lowered the gamma, lift and even the gain a bit. Here are the numbers (Figure 5.15).

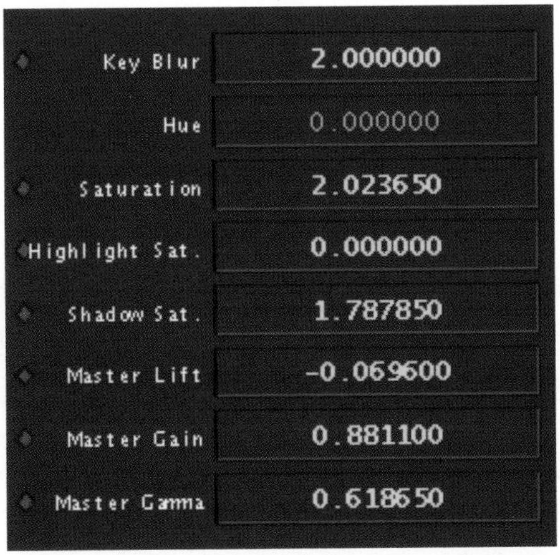

Key Blur	2.000000
Hue	0.000000
Saturation	2.023650
Highlight Sat.	0.000000
Shadow Sat.	1.787850
Master Lift	−0.069600
Master Gain	0.881100
Master Gamma	0.618650

Fig. 5.15

Here's the before and after (Figure 5.16). This isn't a final correction—just a secondary on the lion. I also included a diagonal split image to see the difference.

Before moving on to the spot color corrections—or vignettes as they're known in Color, or Power Windows, as they're known in DaVinci—let's take a look at color vector isolations in Avid Symphony. I realize that Symphony is not a widely popular application for color correction, but even if you don't have a Symphony, don't skip ahead, because Symphony has an interesting graphical interface that allows you to better understand and visualize what you are doing as you isolate these color vectors.

Figure 5.17 shows the Avid Symphony's Secondary UI. Notice the two vectorscope-like images in the bottom center. The one to the left shows the vector you've selected. The one to the right shows the way you have moved that selected vector. Actually, the entire bottom of the

Fig. 5.16

N o t e
At the bottom of the right side of this UI is a section called Selected Vectors. This section logically belongs on the left side, because it allows you to *define* a vector by clicking on one of the colored squares, but they didn't have room for it on the proper side and there was space to the right. These Selected Vectors was how I actually selected the green vector for this image. You can see that the green color square is highlighted in white.

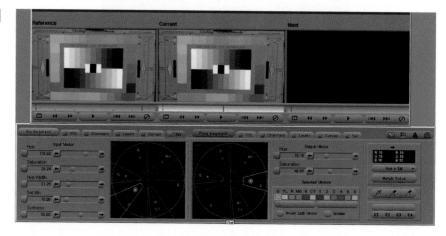

Fig. 5.17

UI is split in two to divide the functionalities of the two sides. To the left, all of the sliders under the words "Input Vector" are controls to *define* the vector that you want to qualify or isolate. To the right, under the words "Output Vector" all of the controls *affect* that selected vector. Not all applications break it down into this nice, obvious division of tasks, but they all work the same way. You need to figure out in your application which are the "defining" tools and which are the "affecting" or "controlling" tools. Once you understand that, everything will make sense.

To understand what defining and moving the vector does, look at the Reference image of the ChromaDuMonde chart at the upper-left (upper-left corner of Figure 5.17). This is the source image. Notice the green color chips at the lower-left of the ChromaDuMonde chart. These are the colors that fall within the area defined by the green vector that has been selected for correction (Figure 5.18).

Looking at the vectorscope, you can see the location of the green color chips on the vectorscope. The three selected color chips fall within the area on the vectorscope defined by the green vector area on the Symphony UI.

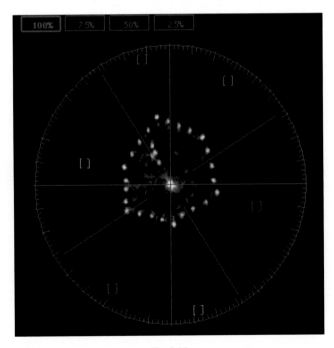

Fig. 5.18

Notice these same color chips in the center image in the UI (upper center of Figure 5.17). The green color chips are bluish-purple because the green vector was swung towards the blue-purple vector in the "output vector."

Notice the numbers on the input and output sides. On the input side, the numbers define a specific degree of hue and amount of saturation that has been selected. On the output side, you see the new angle to which the hue has been swung and the fact that the saturation has been increased (Figure 5.19). This saturation increase is also displayed visually by the vectorscope image, which has the green vector pulled out slightly further on the output side than the input side. Just like a vectorscope, the distance from the center of the vectorscope shows the amount or power of the saturation.

To get a better understanding of this, it is possible in the Symphony UI to isolate the vector you are trying to define and to display all of the unselected vectors as gray. To make it more clear what we are selecting, we'll switch to the "isolate" mode. (Many other applications have a similar mode.)

In this example, we spread the input vector—which could also be known as our isolation or defined or qualified vector—and rotated the hue a bit so that we isolated only the bottom row of green color chips. Notice the numbers for hue are slightly different than in our first

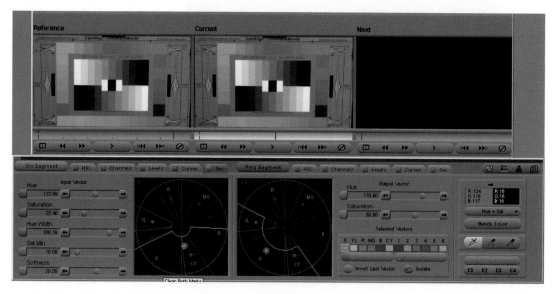

Fig. 5.19

example. I needed to rotate the hue slightly so that only the color chips in the bottom row were isolated. Also notice the hue width number is much larger, which allowed us to select all nine of the bottom color chips instead of just the three that were selected in the first example. You can see this visually on the left vectorscope-like image in the UI, which has expanded to cover a larger portion of the vectorscope. (The small dot with the circle around it in the middle of the chosen vector is the control point for moving the vector.) You can see in the Current window at the upper-center of the UI that all of the color chips at the bottom have been chosen.

If we were to rotate the hue one direction or another, we would deselect some of the chips along the bottom and start to select chips going up one side or the other of the ChromaDuMonde chart. In Figure 5.20, the vector was swung towards blue. Notice that we haven't changed or affected the colors in this example. We are simply defining a slightly different set of colors by rotating the hue.

Symphony also has a set of vectors called "custom vectors," which are basically the vector selections you create when you use the syringe or eyedroppers to pick colors off of the source clip. Instead of looking like arcs joined by straight lines, custom vectors are round or oval shaped. I created a custom vector by clicking on the upper left skin tone color chip on the ChromaDuMonde chart. (The color chips ringing the ChromaDuMonde

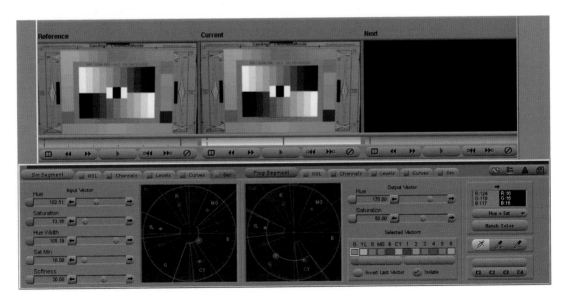

Fig. 5.20

chart are meant to mimic the colors around the vectorscope, except for the four chips just above or below the corners. These four chips are skin tone color chips, representing various racial skin tones—or just people with really good tans.)

I picked a skin tone because skin tones are common things to target for secondary color corrections. Notice the very tight selection area on the source vectorscope image (Figure 5.21). This step has selected only the upper left color chip, while leaving the other three skin tone chips unselected. This is one of the goals of isolating a vector for secondary color correction.

To select the other skin tone chips, you could see if swinging the hue or increasing the hue width would select them, but as I've mentioned before, almost all skin tones line up right along the I line of the vectorscope, regardless of race. So, to select the other skin tones, the other choice is to increase the saturation width. Notice how the custom vector in this image selects more levels of saturation extending from the middle of the vectorscope outwards (Figure 5.22). This effectively selects the other skin tone chips as well as one of the regular color chips that is also very similar to skin tone.

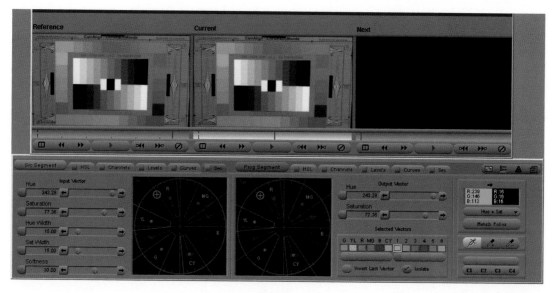

Fig. 5.21

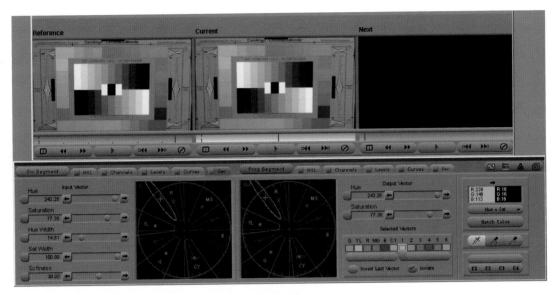

Fig. 5.22

Isolating a Vector in DaVinci Resolve

DaVinci Resolve has great secondary color correction capabilities. Let's explore the basics of qualifying something in Resolve based on its color.

Let's start with the "ultralight_barn" QuickTime file (Figure 5.23).

Fig. 5.23

Fig. 5.24

We want to make the canopy of the ultralight pop better from the surrounding field and trees. To do that, we'll make the grass greener and the canopy bluer. The first part of this process is to qualify—that is, select—the canopy. The easiest way to do this is with the eyedropper button at the bottom right of the Qualifier tab of Resolve's Color screen.

First, select the HSL tab of the Qualifier tab and make sure that the "On" checkboxes to the left of the hue, saturation, and luminance bars are selected (Figure 5.24). Click on the eyedropper icon then click on or drag over the canopy in the small viewer window in the upper left corner of the Color screen. By the way, the Viewer screen also has an eyedropper icon, and you can use that if you want a larger "canvas" on which to use the eyedropper. Obviously, the image on the Viewer screen is bigger than the smaller image on the Color screen.

When you've selected some pixels from the canopy, notice the changes to the hue, saturation, and luminance bars. They indicate—with a white "bell graph"—the values of the pixels that have been selected by the eyedropper.

To see what this qualification looks like on the image itself, click on the Highlight check box at the bottom of the HSL tab, near the eyedropper icon. This changes the viewer window so that the selected pixels are shown in their normal color state and the unselected pixels are grayed out (Figure 5.25).

This feature makes it easier to see how well we are qualifying the image as we continue to manipulate the controls. We want to select as much of the canopy and as little of the rest of the image as possible.

To continue to finesse this qualification, we will use the + and—and + S and –S buttons to the right of the eyedropper button. These are the color

Fig. 5.25

picker modes. The+button allows you to add new values to the range. The—button allows you to deselect values from the range. The+S and –S buttons do the same thing with softness.

Experiment with these buttons for a while to see how much of the canopy you can select and how little of the rest of the picture is included in the selection. Command-Z or Control-Z will work to undo simple mistakes or clicks.

The other things we want to experiment with are the sliders to the right of the hue, saturation, and luminance bars. These allow you to adjust the selected values numerically.

Try adjusting the Center slider to the right of the hue bar, "focusing it" back and forth to optimize the best selection of pixels. Then adjust the Width slider until you start to see parts of the barn buildings being selected. Then adjust the symmetry and softness sliders. Watching the white outline on the Hue bar gives a good idea about what these sliders are doing in their selections.

Next to the Saturation bar (the second colored bar under hue), adjust the Low and High sliders. On the low side, the adjustments start to pick up more of the barn buildings because we are telling Resolve to include more low saturation pixels. Because the barn buildings are mostly white, they have some blue in them but are mostly desaturated. By adjusting the Low slider, we are picking up pixels with values that are *less* desaturated. Adjusting the High slider, we can go all the way to the top of the range because there are no other highly saturated blue pixels in the image. We might as well leave this slider as high as it can go to ensure that we've selected as much of the saturated canopy as we can get. But on other images, you will need to focus this adjustment to get the best selection possible. High soft and Low soft sliders control the fall-off of the selection.

Finally, next to the Luminance bar—the black to white bar at the bottom—manipulate the Low, High, Low Soft, and High Soft sliders to maximize your selection. With this image, the hue and saturation of the canopy is so distinct that after some experimentation, you'll see that you can actually deselect the "on" button on the Luminance bar entirely. It really has no effect. Trying the same thing on the Saturation bar, however, will instantly show that quite a bit of the background pixels have been deselected based on saturation.

The sliders at the bottom of the HSL tab are for the Qualifier blur. The sliders are for the blur amount (radius) and the horizontal and vertical ratio of the blur. There is also a slider to shrink or grow the qualification and another offset control. You can see the effect that these sliders have on your qualification if you make and extreme change to the qualified area, like cranking up the luminance level.

With your qualification complete, deselect the Highlight checkbox to see your image in full color in the viewer. Now we can manipulate the just the color of the canopy without affecting the rest of the image.

To make the canopy stand out, use the Color Wheels in the three-way color corrector tab to swing the gamma towards blue (Figure 5.26). Also, lower the gamma a bit. You can also try corrections in the shadows and highlights. Because of the tonal range of the pixels in the canopy, shadow

Fig. 5.26 The CMYK reproduction of the correction is not great. Obviously, you need to just tweak the colors enough to make them pop without having them look unrealistic.

corrections won't do too much, but the highlight controls will alter the image almost as much as the gamma controls.

For colorists who are migrating over from Apple Color, it's a little easier to manage multiple secondaries in Apple Color than it is in Resolve, but that's because using multiple secondaries in Resolve is a lot more powerful and therefore more complex. The method for using multiple secondaries in Resolve is to use the Node Graph to allow mapping of secondaries in very specific ways, including serially or in parallel. In Color, it is possible to map secondaries only with each secondary being fed into the next in *series* (serially, or in a row). With Resolve, these serial or parallel positions can be remapped at will and can make a real difference in the way the corrections look.

Imagine a case in which your first secondary takes out all of the color of all of the pixels in the image. Then, from that point on, none of the secondaries would have any color information to work with. In Resolve, you can have multiple secondaries running in parallel with each other, or you can rearrange the order of serial connections by disconnecting and reconnecting the links between each node. This approach takes a bit more work, but delivers a lot more power and control.

To do this, you start with a basic correction in the node graph. This first node is always there by default. Now you can either use right clicks on the nodes or in the node graph *or* you can use the Nodes menu choice at the menu bar at the top of the screen to add specific types of nodes (Figure 5.27).

For a simple set of secondaries, the node graph I've built (Figure 5.28) allowed me to add specific vector-based qualifications and corrections to three different areas of the image and then combine them with a unique compositing mode.

Add Serial	⇧S
Add Before Current	^⇧S
Add Parallel	⇧P
Add Layer	⇧L
Append Node	⇧A
Node + CPW	⇧C
Node + LPW	⇧Q
Node + PPW	⇧G
Node + PCW	⇧B
Add Outside	⇧O
Add Matte	⇧M
Enable/Disable Current	^D
Disable All	
Enable All	
Delete Current	⇧D

Fig. 5.27 DaVinci Resolve's Nodes pulldown menu.

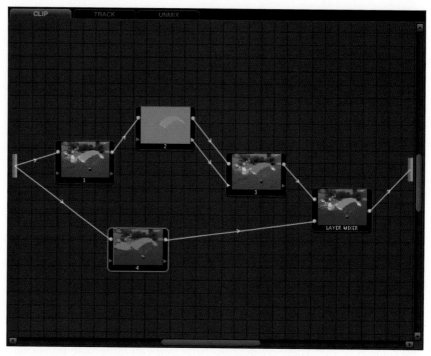

Fig. 5.28 DaVinci Resolve's Node graph with multiple secondaries combined both in series and in parallel.

Isolation Practice

To practice the ability to isolate a single color in an image, use the "ChromaDuMonde_ properexwhite" clip from the DVD and work with your secondary color vector selection tools to isolate individual color chips or to specifically choose sets of two or three or more chips from the others.

Using the ChromaDuMonde chart is good for getting the basics of hue selection under your fingers, but you'll need something more natural for making other selections based on various levels of saturation. The ChromaDuMonde color chips are all basically the same saturation, except for the skin tone chips.

Plus, one of the other skills that you need to practice is determining the right fall-off or softness levels that allow you to grab (for example) all of the skin tones on a face that is half in shadow or to grab all of the tones of a shirt that has numerous levels of chroma and luminance because of folds and shadows and highlights.

Choose some other clips from the DVD and see if you can isolate various portions of the image. Want a challenge? Try these:

- Isolate the skin tones in "piano_correct." The highlights of the skin are similar to the aged yellow of the tops of the white piano keys. As I've stated before, skin tones are one of the big things that colorists like to tweak as a secondary.

- In any of the ultralight clips, try to isolate the entire "wing" of the ultralight while keeping other colors out of the selection. This is a common correction for a number of reasons. If the video is for the ultralight manufacturer, they might require the color to be a very specific shade to properly represent the product they're delivering. For other purposes, the producer may just want to pop the ultralight out of the image, calling attention to it through color contrast.

- In the "Jackie_interview" clip, try to isolate her skin tones without selecting the same tones in the wall to the left or in the door behind her. (This can't be done without the addition of a garbage mask of some sort, but practicing with this real-world image is a great experience.) What would you do if a director of photography (DP) asked for a specific correction to the skin but didn't want to see that correction in the rest of the image?

- In the "Railroad_LM112 Artbeats" clip, isolate the suitcase. In an image like this, it would be common to ask for more emphasis to be placed on an important prop so that the audience would think of how it relates to

Fig. 5.29 Courtesy of Bruce Lindbloom (www.brucelindbloom.com).

the storyline or so that they remember its presence in the scene at some later point.

- In the "8mm_loading_gear" clip, attempt to isolate the yellow jacket or orange life jackets. With the jacket, I found it helpful to turn off saturation (in other words, to *not* limit by saturation) because the jacket's saturation levels go from white to yellow. Yellow is one of the colors that people often wish to tweak specifically. Often a shade of yellow with more red in it is desired, yet that red cast is *not* desired in the rest of the image.

- In the "Football_SP123H1" clip from Artbeats, try to isolate the football and hand from the grass. To attempt the impossible, try to isolate the ball from the hand. This isolation figures prominently in some of the upcoming corrections by our panel of colorists later in the book.

Fig. 5.30 Courtesy Getty Images.

Another good image to use for many experiments is this image created by noted color scientist Bruce Lindbloom. Because there is shading in the image and various levels of saturation in many different hues, this is a good overall image with which to experiment. This image is also on the DVD ("DeltaE_8bit_gamma2.2.tif").

Another test image that you can use if you need skin tones or are trying to isolate things with secondaries is this image from Getty Images. The image is on the DVD as well ("Getty_Test_Image.jpg"). It is intended for use in setting up printers and doing color management for Getty Images stock site.

Spot Color Correction (Vignettes or Power Windows)

Another form of secondary color correction is called *spot color correction*. In Color, they're known as vignettes; in DaVinci, they're called Power Windows or Windows (Figure 5.31). The basic concept is to draw a shape on the screen and color correct inside or outside of that shape (Figure 5.32). In the early days of Power Windows, you could use only geometric shapes—variations on circles and squares. Now, most of the file-based color correctors like Color and others allow you to draw custom shapes using Bezier curves or B-spline curves. Many of these vignettes, windows, or spot correction shapes can also be tracked to the movement of the shot, which is important in many shots. With some software, like Resolve, you can also combine these shapes, adding them or subtracting them from one another, to create complex windows.

Shot movement—whether it's camera movement or movement within the frame of a locked-down shot—will be a big factor in whether you choose to use a spot color correction. In the example we did earlier in the chapter of the lion at the Art Institute, the camera is locked down, the lion doesn't move,

Fig. 5.31 DaVinci Resolve Window tab.

Fig. 5.32 DaVinci Resolve UI showing Circular window with softness on a shot.

and no one crosses in front of the lion or even gets near it, so that shot is a great candidate for a spot correction or for use of a garbage matte to further isolate the color vector correction. (We'll discuss that in the next tutorial.)

There are a couple of reasons to use a spot color correction. One of the ways is to use it very globally to darken the corners of the image and focus attention on the subject in the middle. This method is usually done with a very soft oval shape placed right in the middle of the image. With this use, you don't really have to worry too much about shot movement because the "spot" is supposed to look more like an in-camera effect, anyway. Another technique for a spot correction is to pick a portion of the frame and affect it in much the same way as the color vector secondary would be used—to pick an area to enhance or fix a problem with the primary correction. The third way to use spot correction is almost as a "post-lighting tool." You can add this kind of selection to almost spotlight certain regions of the frame. If you are familiar with making prints in a darkroom, this can be similar to dodging and burning.

Let's do a tutorial for each of these reasons.

The Vignette

Vignette is Color's term for spot correction. One of the meanings of the English word "vignette" means a photograph whose edges fade off gradually. The following tutorial is about—not Color's meaning—but the creation of a "vignetted" image.

The vignette is often used to focus the audience's attention in the middle of the screen. It can also create the point of view (POV) feeling that you are watching the image through your own eyes (as opposed to being a third-person participant). Vignetting is also a common trick to salvage large flat areas of a shot, like a boring sky or a huge, blank wall that was lit flatly. The vignette adds interest and texture to images like that.

Call up the "Kiss" clip (Figure 5.33) from the DVD into Color or some other application that allows you to make spot color corrections.

Fig. 5.33

Faking Spot Corrections

If you don't have a color correction application that allows for spot color correction, you can usually fake it with the tools in most nonlinear editing systems. Copy a clip from your timeline and edit it on a track directly above the clip from which you copied it. Correct one of the clips for the optimum look of the "inside" of the correction and correct the other clip for the look that you want on the "outside" of the correction. Then use a soft-edged wipe to transition between the two of them. You may need to actually create a matte and place it on another track. Each NLE deals with mattes differently, so consult your user manual about the channel on which to place the matte and the channels for the "darkened" and "proper" versions of your color corrections.

On an Avid, for example, the recipe would be to put the correct clip on the bottom track (V1), the darkened clip on the second clip above it (V2), and a matte clip with black around the edges and a soft, white center on the top track (V2). Then add a matte key effect to the top track.

So: Figure 5.34a plus Figure 5.34b keyed with Figure 5.34c gives you Figure 5.34d.

(The matte for this effect is available on the DVD as "mattekeyvignette.psd.")

In Final Cut Pro, the effect would be accomplished slightly differently. Place the dark clip on the bottom (V1), the correctly graded clip on the *top* track (V3), and the matte clip in between (Figure 5.35). Then right-click or control-click on the top clip and select "Composite Mode" from the pulldown menu, then "Travelling Matte—Luma." In Final Cut Pro, you could also generate your gradient for the second track right inside of Final Cut Pro using the Generator button on the Viewer and choosing Render, then creating a radial shape and placing the start point somewhere near the middle or wherever you want it.

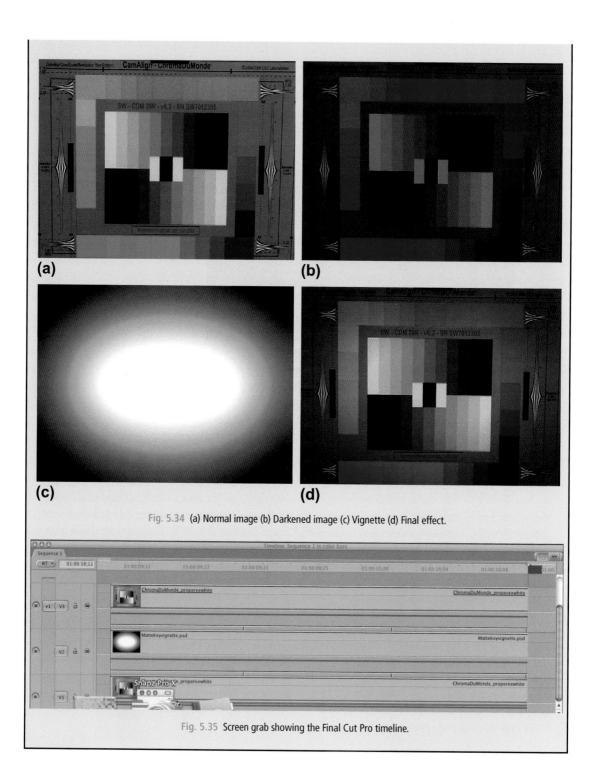

Fig. 5.34 (a) Normal image (b) Darkened image (c) Vignette (d) Final effect.

Fig. 5.35 Screen grab showing the Final Cut Pro timeline.

In Color, go to a secondary and enable it and enable the vignette. Then draw an oval that goes from edge to edge and almost from top to bottom (Figure 5.36).

You can soften this circle by either center-dragging (center-dragging on many mice is the scroll wheel) in the circle or by changing the softness in the vignette control area (Figure 5.37).

Once you have at least a starting point for the shape and softness, you can choose the Control pulldown at the upper right of the secondary tab near the HSL controls and specify whether you want to correct either the inside or outside of the vignette. You can choose to do both inside and outside corrections if you want to. I actually chose to lower the gain and midtones outside of the oval and bring up the chroma a bit inside the oval.

This is the image with a pretty strong vignette (Figure 5.38). We'll be seeing example of vignettes in the color corrections that our panel of colorists executes in the coming chapters as well. I made this vignette pretty bold to emphasize what I was trying to do, but most of the vignettes that you'll see later in the book are much more subtle. These vignettes are very hard to show in print unless they're fairly obvious, which is the *opposite* thing that most colorists are trying to accomplish with vignettes.

Instead of a very broad oval that covers a lot of the image, you could also aim the center of the vignette to the focal point of the image. In the following image, the correction remains the same as above, but the oval is centered

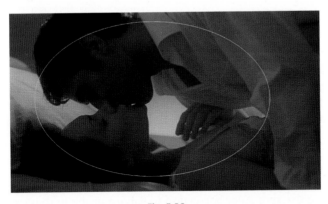

Fig. 5.36

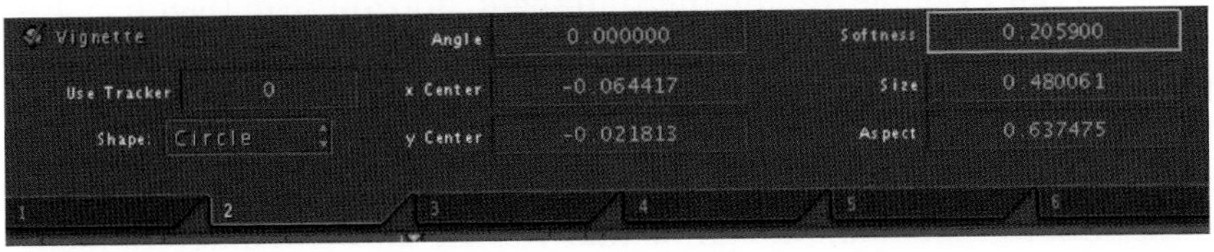

Fig. 5.37

Fig. 5.38

Fig. 5.39

on the kiss and the softness is expanded. The yellow lines are optional UI overlays that let you know the boundaries and shape of the vignette.

You can see that this can be a very effective way of enhancing a shot (Figure 5.39).

Geographical Color Fix

You can also use spot color correction to solve a problem that exists in just a specific area of the picture, or to enhance just a specific area of the picture. For our example, call up the "ultralight_horizon" clip (Figure 5.40).

This is not the best way to select the grass and/or sky, but it will work for the purpose of the tutorial. The best way to do this correction "in real life" is to use the same method that we used earlier in the chapter when explaining the Final Cut Pro Limit Effect using the same clip. Let's continue with this method, though, so that you see how two different methods can be used to the same end result.

Fig. 5.40

This image is very washed out, but it also looks like the top of the image needs to be treated in a much different way than the bottom of the picture, below the horizon. Normally, you would try to balance the picture and expand the contrast first in a primary color correction, but I'm going to take this right to a secondary color correction to make my point.

The first thing to do is to select the grass area with a window of some sort. I will do this correction in Color, so go into secondaries, enable a secondary, and enable Vignette. Then choose a square shape and drag it out and position it so that the top of the resulting rectangle is roughly placed on the horizon which is slightly off-angle. Color has an angle control that can be used to precisely align the top of the rectangle with the horizon. You can also add a slight softness to the rectangle.

For the purpose of this tutorial, we'll address a single frame of the shot, but the camera does actually tilt up over the course of the shot, so in a real-life situation, you would need to track the rectangle to follow the tilt (Color is capable of doing this) or add keyframes in a program that was not able to track so that the shot's horizon would stay lined up with your spot correction's "horizon."

With the grass defined as the inside of the correction (Figure 5.41), you can adjust the contrast and colors of the grass alone, just as you would in a normal primary color correction. Originally, I started by trying to use the hue offset wheels to pull the grass towards green, but when I added a pretty heavy correction in the master lift, the saturation of my green color looked really bad. I reset my hue offset wheels and worked on contrast first. I chose to lower the master lift and slightly lower gamma and barely raise gain. With the contrast and tone set, I pulled the midtones away from blue just a little to improve the color of the grass. I also did similar, very minor corrections to highlights and shadows in the same direction.

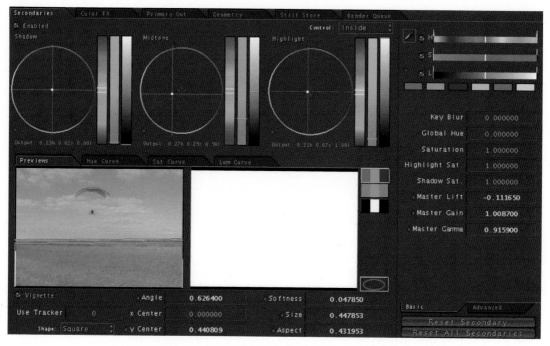

Fig. 5.41 The shape of the vignette is hard to see since it sits right on the horizon.

The darker overall shade of my grass correction helps focus attention up towards the ultralight.

Once the color of the of the grass is complete, switch the secondary control from "inside" to "outside." With the sky, I started working on the contrast first. I brought the master lift down a *lot*. This popped the ultralight against the sky because it's the only really dark element in the top half of the image. I brought the gain up so that the clouds would "read" better against the blue of the sky and brought the gammas down a bit to stretch the contrast between the sky and the clouds even further. Then I pulled the midtones towards blue pretty severely. The midtones only really affected the blue sky (remember that the grass is being "protected" from the midtone correction by the spot correction). Then I pulled the highlights—which was basically just the clouds—away from blue so that the clouds would be more cleanly balanced towards white (Figure 5.42).

The result is something that could not be executed in a primary color correction, which is pretty obvious when you see the wildly different corrections that went into the top and bottom of the image (Figure 5.43).

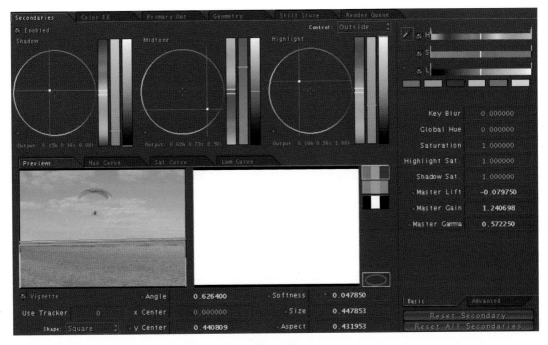

Fig. 5.42

Fig. 5.43   Before and After shots of the ultralight with secondary corrections.

User-Defined Shapes

Many file-based systems, like Lustre, Baselight, Resolve, Color, or Symphony allow you to hand-draw organic shapes to define these geographical areas on the screen. This feature is a very powerful tool that I both encourage you to use and discourage you from using.

On one hand, these custom shapes are very valuable for at least two reasons. The first is that using squares and circles is obviously fairly limiting when you are trying to isolate a specific portion of the screen. The other great reason for using custom shapes is that they are much less likely to be noticed as spot corrections. Obviously you don't want *any* spot color correction to be noticed. That is a sure sign that it hasn't been done properly. But even watching the best of TV spots with a trained eye, you can see vignetting that has been done by a skilled colorist, if you know what to look for. But with a custom shape, it is very hard to see even a fairly extreme spot correction, because the shape is not uniform. This is the same concept as camouflage in military and hunting use. A camouflaged person or truck is just as visible as any other person or truck, but the camouflage pattern works by breaking up the easily defined shapes that humans and animals are used to identifying as another human being or truck.

Pankaj Bajpai

Pankaj Bajpai is Senior Colorist at Encore in Hollywood. He was instrumental in establishing their file-based workflows and DI-style approach to grading TV episodes. He has also provided his expertise to AMPAS's ACES/IIF color workflow.

In 15 years as a colorist, Bajpai has graded multiple seasons and various episodes of hit TV series, including *Lie to Me*, *Carnivale*, *Sex and the City*, *Hung*, *The Beast*, *In Treatment*, *Justified*, *Rome*, and *The Wire*.

Before becoming a colorist, Bajpai worked as a DP on documentary films around the world.

Fig. 5.44 Encore's Pankaj Bajpai at the controls of his Lustre.

I sat in with Pankaj Bajpai at Encore in Los Angeles. Pankaj drives a Lustre, and one of his favorite tools in its arsenal is Lustre's ease of creating masks and windows. He explains, "I do a lot of masks and a lot of Power Window type work because so often it is very important to bring that three-dimensionality, because when your pictures feel three-dimensional, then you almost automatically start to feel like it's real."

Figure 5.45 gives you an idea of the complexity of the shapes that Bajpai is drawing to get these organic looks.

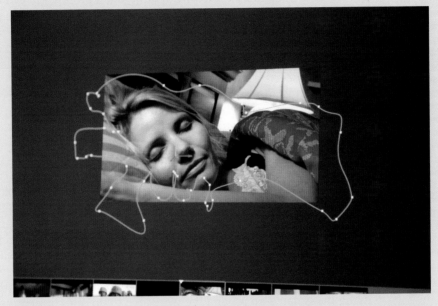

Fig. 5.45

Another adamant user of these custom shapes for secondary color correction is veteran Chicago colorist Pete Jannotta, who says, "I always prefer to draw (custom shapes) because even in Da Vinci I don't use a fixed circle ever anymore. What I like to do is draw the shape and then move it around so I can see how the light is working. I don't care what the shape is, but if it's an oval, then it's fixed and I can't control it."

But the flip side of this control is the cost in time. If you've got time on your side, then custom shapes are great.

Using Spot Color Correction to Relight

One of the subsets of reasons to use a spot color correction is in the ability to effectively relight the image in post. This is not to cast aspersions on the director of photography in any way. They are under the same time constraints for lighting the scene that we are for grading it in post, so sometimes what the DP *wants* to do just doesn't happen on the set.

Many directors of photography complain that the budget isn't there to pay them to sit in with the colorist for the transfer to act as a guide to ensure the integrity of the final image. Often they are already working on the next project when it's time to color correct their footage. Sometimes all that the DP has time for is a phone call to the colorist. There are several applications designed to provide a technical link between the DP and the colorist. Kodak has a software system that a production can license to allow the DP to do some basic "look creation" on the set and then deliver that image to the colorist as a guide. IRIDAS has a similar system.

Color Vector with Window or Vignette

Sometimes it is impossible to qualify something with a color vector isolation alone, and that is where the third method comes in, which is a combination of the color vector isolation assisted by a vignette (in Color) or a Window (in Resolve).

Let's go back to the first image we tried in this chapter, the Art Institute lions. Load the "art_institute_lion_proper" clip into your color correction application. Now try to select the lion again with a color vector isolation or if you saved your isolation from the first example, then load it up.

The best isolation that I could come up with looked like Figure 5.47.

Notice that the lion was pretty well selected, but I also selected some of the grayish-green pedestal that the lion is standing on as well as some grayish-green tones in the steps, under the arches and in the eaves of the building. In the first example, we corrected the lion without further qualifying the isolated areas, and we were able to do our corrections without damaging the rest of the image too much.

In this exercise, we want to get a much cleaner key, and the only way to do that is to add a garbage matte to that will key out the rest of the isolation

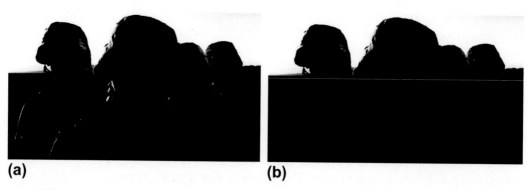

(a)   **(b)**

Fig. 5.46 (a) This is a matte created from luma of MAR115H1 from Artbeats. Notice the unwanted highlight areas lower on the Marines' clothing. (b) This is the same matte with a garbage matte applied so that only the portions of the luma matte above the yellow line will be used for the qualification.

that we don't want. In Color, this is done by enabling the vignette portion of the same secondary in which the color vector isolation was executed.

If the secondary is enabled and you're looking at the Preview mode with the matte view selected (showing the matte on the second monitor), you will instantly see what the garbage matte does (Figure 5.48).

Of course, that's not exactly what you want it to do, so we need to modify it a bit. If you are working in Color or some other application that allows you to draw vignettes or mattes with custom shapes, then you are in luck. If you are limited to using only geometric shapes, you'll still be fine completing the rest of this tutorial. Just use an oval and shape it, position it, rotate it, and soften it so that it isolates as much as possible without "eating in" to the matte you already created for the lion.

Figure 5.49 is the matte image with the circle garbage matte. The inside and outside softness of the circular garbage matte are defined by the yellow lines.

where it wasn't wanted or add a little extra punch to a face or to eyes that didn't quite get enough light on set.

Encore's Bajpai is quick to point out that he doesn't feel that his grades are actually relighting: "I am not intending to relight a DPs work. That is not the idea. The idea is to enhance it and in that enhancement, if you look at this image versus where it started, the lights already in there, the lamp is already lit that way so when you're looking at that and you're looking at this. All it is, it's fallen into . . . it's not exactly relit. It is more like what that lighting needs to be in the context of that scene or the emotional feel that happens to be in that scene."

spill: Light falling outside of the area it is wanted; light from an uncontrolled or undercontrolled light source. With greenscreen work, it refers to unwanted light bouncing from the background onto foreground elements.

Fig. 5.47

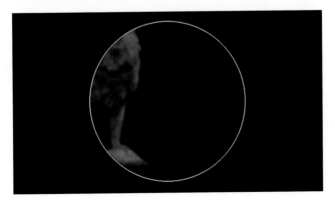

Fig. 5.48

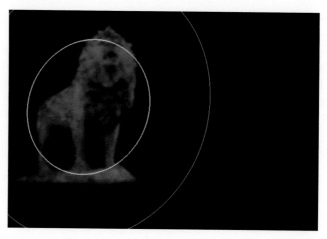

Fig. 5.49

In Color, when you are in the Vignette area and select "User shape" from the Shape pulldown menu just below the Vignette check box, you are instantly transported to the Geometry room where you have a little larger image to work with to set your points. Just start clicking on the image of the lion in the Geometry room UI to create your shape (Figure 5.50). When you get back to almost where you started, choose "Close Shape" from the button to the right of the lion image.

Once your shape is drawn, use the "Attach" button at the top right of the UI to have the shape "attached" to your secondary correction. This step is necessary because you can choose multiple saved or created shapes to attach to your correction.

Then you can go back to the Secondary room and soften the edges of the shape so that there is not a hard edge to the garbage matte. You can see the difference in the cleanliness of the matte by viewing the matte in the right-hand (non-UI) monitor while toggling the Vignette check box off and on.

The discernable difference in the final image is actually quite small. Remember that the original secondary correction without the garbage matte was to darken the lion and pump up the saturation. In small areas under the lion and in the eaves of the roof, this also darkened those areas and brought up the green cast. With the garbage matte in place, those areas are fixed. Was it worth the effort for the minimal gain? Only you and your client can say. I suggest that you try to make your qualifications as clean as possible, but sometimes your schedule and budget will not allow it. You can certainly see the difference when you toggle between the shots with and without the garbage matte, but if you edited the non–garbage matte version into a show, then put in a second shot and then cut back to the garbage matte version, there is no way anyone would see the difference.

Fig. 5.50

Secondaries Are Crucial

Knowing what to use secondaries for and how to decide what to isolate and how is really critical to good color correction. That is why the next chapter will finally bring in the full expertise of our expert panel of colorists. We'll have them walk you through a number of color corrections that use secondaries. The tools for each application are really either limited to tools that are available exclusively to a specific application (see the sidebar on Color's "Secondary Curves") or they are very limited to the color vector isolation and shape-drawing tools that have already been covered extensively in this chapter. I've sprinkled in some great advice from some top colorists in these early chapters, but in the chapters to come, we'll let these talented, dedicated experts show how to deliver creative results with technical expertise.

Secondary Curves

One of the interesting sets of secondary tools in DaVinci Resolve and Apple Color are the Hue, Saturation, and Luminance curves. These are unlike the curves that we discussed in the previous chapter. These curves allow you to select a specific hue with a click of a button and either rotate its hue, alter its saturation, or change its luminance value (Figure 5.51).

A few pictures will be worth way more than the thousand words that it would take me to explain this further.

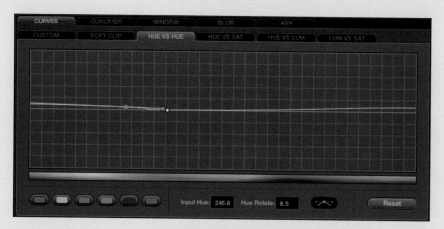

Fig. 5.51 DaVinci Resolve Hue curve UI.

Here's the unaltered image (Figure 5.52). All of these ultralight images are courtesy of Randy Riesen, who is one of my top three cameramen in Chicago. Digging through 20 hours of raw footage to find a couple of shots that needed some work was difficult. Virtually everything was picture perfect, despite the extreme conditions he was shooting under.

Fig. 5.52

Color allows very quick adjustments to specific hues. In the Hue curve, clicking on the point of the curve that corresponds to the hue of the ultralight's wing and adjusting it (Figure 5.53). changes the hue of the wing (and quite a bit else); see Figure 5.54.

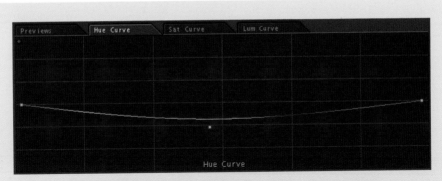

Fig. 5.53

Fig. 5.54

Adjusting the Saturation curve (Figure 5.55) at the same point makes the wing more saturated (Figure 5.56) instead of changing its hue.

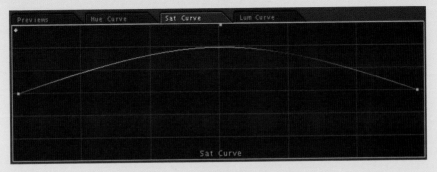

Fig. 5.55

Fig. 5.56

And adjusting the same point on the Luminance curve (Figure 5.57) makes the wing darker (Figure 5.58). This step required setting a second point to isolate the luminance correction on the wing from the other colors in the image that were similar.

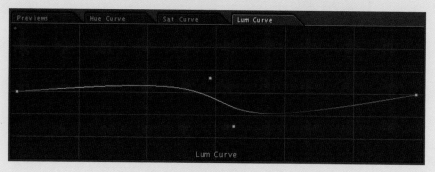

Fig. 5.57

Fig. 5.58

CHAPTER 6

Secondaries with the Pros

In the earlier chapters, we broke up color correction into various components or tasks, which makes sense when you are trying to learn something. In reality, these tasks are not performed in isolation, but in a more all-encompassing, holistic approach that includes revising work that was already done and fixing issues that actually developed throughout the color correction process.

Because of that, the following chapters, which are led mostly by our expert panel of colorists, will have a *primary* focus—such as secondary correction, or look creation—but will also include *other* elements—such as primary correction—or may jump into other elements of the correction, because that's how the colorists actually worked on the images and to break the tasks up like in the previous chapters would be to take their entire thought process out of context.

I organized this chapter into two basic secondary concepts that we outlined in the previous chapter:

1. Vignettes (or spot corrections or windows)
2. Vector and luma qualifications (based on HSL values)

Both of these methods actually create mattes, inside of which the secondary correction is done.

Almost every colorist in this book used vignettes in their work, but many of them seemed almost a little embarrassed that they used them.

Vignettes

One of the methods of secondary color correction is vignetting or spot color correction. In a DaVinci suite, it is called Power Windows. Whatever

> **Note**
>
> Something to keep in mind as you see where each colorist took an image is that they were asked to be fairly self-directed in what they thought the image should look like. This instruction is fairly unusual for a colorist, as a director of photography or director or producer is usually guiding the session and providing the colorist with context for the shot or a vision that had been developed prior to the shot.

Definition

vignette: (noun) An image in which the edges are darkened or faded. (verb) The act of darkening the edges of an image. This term is slightly confusing now for Color users, because Color uses the term to define creating a geometric or user-defined shape in which to do a secondary color correction.

TIP

Look in the corners of an image and you'll see that they are often darker than the middle. This should be visible on at least one shot in about 50 percent of all TV commercials.

the term, the tools allow for the correction of a specific geographic portion of the image that is usually defined or qualified by a geometric shape or possibly by a user-defined shape that is created by combining geometric shapes or by the use of Bezier or B-spline curves (Figure 6.1).

Apple's Color uses the term "vignette" to define any of these geographic corrections, but when most colorists are discussing vignetting, they don't mean *any* geographic correction, but the specific act of darkening the edges and focusing the viewer's attention on the middle of the screen (Figures 6.2 and 6.3). Sometimes the technique is done with a defocus vignette that blurs the outside edges instead of—or in addition to—darkening them.

Almost every colorist in this book used vignettes in their work, but many of them seemed almost a little embarrassed that they used them, although vignetting is a tried-and-true technique that you can see in practically any national TV spot on the air.

I asked veteran colorist Bob Festa of New Hat, a Santa Monica telecine boutique, about this aversion to vignettes.

"Well, I'm one of the original architects of one of the most abused techniques in color grading," Festa explained jokingly. "The beauty of it is that in any given shot—if it's done well—you can't point to it and say, 'That's got a vignette on it.' It's a very subliminal, subconscious 3D thing. And quite frankly, I used it as recently as 20 minutes ago. I'm not going to let it drop."

Fig. 6.1 The yellow and green lines in this window describe user-defined windows in DaVinci Resolve. Secondary color correction can be applied inside and outside of these shapes. Image courtesy of Seduced and Exploited Films from *Kiss Me in the Dark*.

Fig. 6.2 Source image without vignette, image courtesy of Artbeats.

Fig. 6.3 Vignetted image with very strong vignette effect, image courtesy of Artbeats.

For the colorists that used this technique in the sessions I watched, the vignetting clearly improved the final image, which I could confirm by disabling the secondaries with the vignettes in them.

It makes the image seem to have more depth to it. If there are big bland areas, like a gray sky, it gives more texture to it, and it focuses the attention where it's supposed to be. Festa agreed with this assessment:

Bob Festa

When DaVinci announced their inaugural Master Colorist Awards, Bob Festa (Figure 6.4) was the winner of the commercial category.

Bob Festa is one of the most recognized names in color correction and is highly respected among his peers. His credits include virtually all of the world's best-known brands and spots, including the original Levis 501 Blues campaign. He has worked with some of the industry's finest directors including Leslie Dektor, Bob Giraldi, Erich Joiner, Joe Pytka, and Jeff Zwart.

His input has helped define many of the modern tools that colorists use every day.

Festa has a masters degree in Public Communication from Pepperdine University and honed his grading skills at Deluxe Laboratories, Action Video, Editel Los Angeles, Complete Post, Hollywood Digital, and R!OT Santa Monica.

He currently works as owner/colorist at his telecine boutique, New Hat, in Santa Monica.

Fig. 6.4 Photo by Steve Hullfish

Fig. 6.5 Football image without vignette. Image courtesy of Artbeats.

Fig. 6.6 Football image with vignette. Image courtesy of Artbeats. This vignette is pretty strong and obvious for the purposes of being seen in print. This was created with an oval Window in Resolve, darkening mids and shadows outside of the oval.

"It's clearly more filmic. Maybe it's because early on in Pandora (Pandora's grading system was called Pogle), people had to use square windows and a lot of people had a problem getting a good vignette with a square based window. But in the round, oval-based world, I have no problem making it work within the confines of safe action in a tasteful way."

Another colorist who is unapologetic for using vignettes is Chris Pepperman–formerly of NFL Films, now senior colorist at NASCAR–despite chiding from some of his colorist coworkers.

I use vignetting on everything that I do in my commercial work.
– Chris Pepperman, NASCAR

Definition

Pandora: Pandora is one of the major, high-end color correction manufacturers. Though they have several product lines, the best known was Pogle. Now their software product is called Revolution. When Apple's Color was being developed, Pogle and DaVinci colorists were the main ones solicited for feedback.

"They think it's just darkening the edges. My idea of a vignette is: I don't want you to see it. I'm using it as an option like a DP would. I'm using it as a lighting tool. That's what I consider vignetting." Pepperman continues, "Being able to help isolate your eye towards the specific product, person, or whatever you want in the picture. So that's why I use it all the time. I use vignetting on everything that I do in my commercial work, whether it's a square or a circle, or whether it's a shape that consists of a combination of shapes. (DaVinci lets you combine geometric shapes in a variety of ways.) I always do it because when I look at a picture, I'm always trying to help what I'm looking at. If I was working on a picture of a beautiful mountain landscape, I would do the same thing. I would try to isolate, vignette the sky, and bring it down or the ground and bring it up. I'm just always using it because it's just such a powerful tool for the colorist. Why wouldn't you?"

Vignetting the Ultralight Flyover Scene

Craig Leffel, of Chicago's Optimus, demonstrates this classic technique as part of his correction of the "ultralight flyover" shot (Figure 6.7). (You can follow along with these corrections by loading the tutorial scenes from the DVD into your color correction application or plug-in.) When creating these vignettes, some of the colorists chose to create the shape and leave the edges sharp while affecting the secondary or setting the shape and size of the vignette. This sharp edge made it very easy to see exactly how much they were affecting the image. Other colorists preferred to set the softness on the vignette's edge *before* affecting any

Fig. 6.7 Source image courtesy of Randy Riesen.

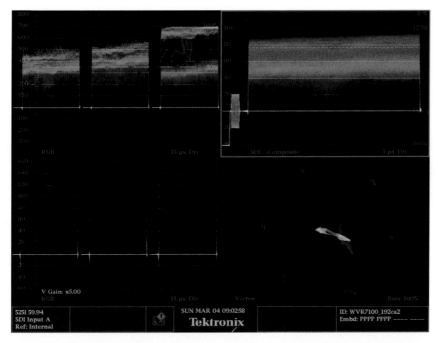

Fig. 6.8 Scopes showing source image, from Tektronix WVR 7100. Upper left is RGB Parade. Lower left is RGB Parade expanded to show black level. Upper right is composite waveform. Lower right is a vectorscope at standard zoom.

change so that they had a better sense for the way the correction would actually look when it was complete. Leffel puts himself in the first camp, saying, "I find it easier to change the shape before I change the softness of a vignette. But I'm kind of in both camps. It depends on what I'm trying to do. If I'm trying to do something that's really extreme, then I don't need to see it, but if I'm trying to do something subtle, or I'm trying to just fix something, the more subtle it is, the more I like to have less softness so I can see what I'm actually doing instead of assuming it's working with the softness turned up. This one I'm gonna start hard just to see."

First, Leffel does a primary correction. This correction mostly involved the master black, gamma, and highlight levels. Leffel also tweaked the highlight balance toward red and slightly moved blacks the same direction (Figure 6.9).

All colorists worked in FinalTouch HD, because Color was not yet released. This screenshot is from the Primary room of FinalTouch HD.

He continues the correction with a secondary qualification on the grass (Figure 6.10). He grades inside and outside that qualification.

Craig Leffel

Craig Leffel started as an assistant editor at venerable Chicago post house, Cutters, back in the days when they were still cutting on KEMs. He then moved on to colorist jobs at two Chicago powerhouses, Skyview and Editel, then became senior colorist and partner at Optimus.

He has worked primarily in spots, using DaVinci, Spirit, Baselight, Lustre, Color, Scratch, and others. Leffel is currently the director of production for the production arm of Optimus called One.

Leffel graduated from Indiana University at Bloomington.

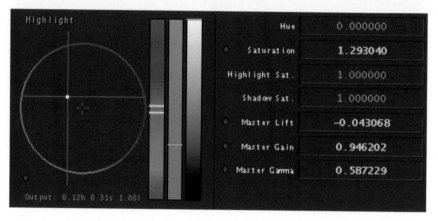

Fig. 6.9

Leffel continues his correction. "Now that I've got an isolation and a sort of base level correction I'm doing an outside vignette because in the original image, the sides are real flat. There's an even exposure across the whole thing. It's always nice to have a vignette there to blend out—not to do an *obvious* vignette, to darken the edges obviously—but to do a soft vignette (Figure 6.14).

"So, I brought down gamma and black and a little bit of gain, but not much. Mostly gamma. This image is mostly gamma anyway. There's not a whole lot of black and not a whole lot of white, so almost all of this image is easily manipulated with gamma."

You don't really sense the vignette there. You just sense richness.
– Craig Leffel, Optimus

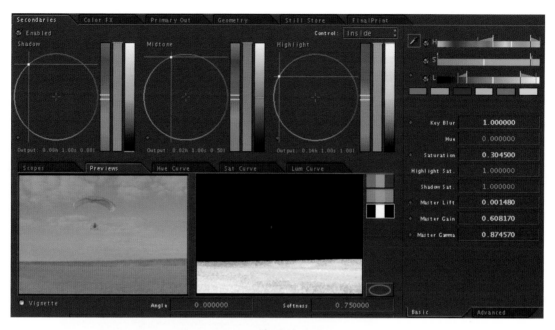

Fig. 6.10

Fig. 6.11 This is the correction inside of the qualification—the white areas.

Although Leffel keeps the edge sharp on his vignette while he drops the level at the beginning, he gets to a point where he needs to see the vignette softness closer to the way it will look in the end. "I'm going to make that vignette as soft as I can make it and what this is going to do is

Fig. 6.12

Fig. 6.13 This is the small correction made outside the qualification—black areas.

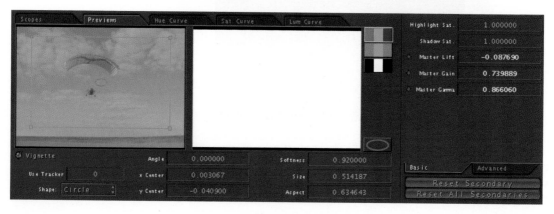

Fig. 6.14

Fig. 6.15 **Final correction.**

just add richness to the whole image. We brought it down from what the original was. Now we're going to add even more richness. The interesting thing is going to be to see what happens when the ultralight flies. If you do the vignette soft enough, then the vignette doesn't become an issue with the motion. You don't really sense the vignette there. You just sense richness. The brighter center is just sort of a natural feeling which is what I'm after."

Vignetting the "Kiss" Bedroom Scene

Of all of the colorists who used vignettes to focus attention on the subject, the most intricate example was probably done by Mike Matusek of Chicago's Nolo Digital Film. Matusek worked with several vignettes to shape the bedroom scene from "Kiss Me In the Dark" (Figure 6.16). We'll walk through the entire correction, including the vignettes he creates at the end of the grade.

"I don't use the vectorscope much," Matusek mentions, before he starts grading the image. "Before I start any shot, I quickly glance at the waveform. See where the whites and the blacks are? I noticed that the blacks are a little warmer, so I thought I'd balance them. Sometimes I'll whack out the blacks just to give it a look, but I'll always try to start by balancing it. Overall I thought it looked a little washed, so I'm bringing the midtones down a little bit as opposed to crushing the blacks.

"On the Nucoda system that I work on, I'll zoom in and sample an area. So now I'm going to work on gain. The midtones are a little warmer

Fig. 6.16 Bedroom scene from "Kiss Me In the Dark." Image courtesy of Seduced and Exploited Entertainment.

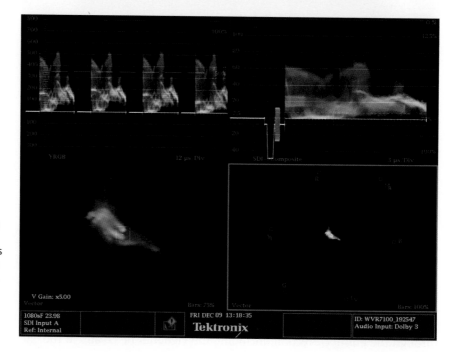

Fig. 6.17 Scopes showing source image from Tektronix WVR 7100. Upper left is YRGB Parade. Lower left is vectorscope zoomed in 5x. Upper right is composite waveform. Lower right is a vectorscope at standard zoom.

than I'd like. I like playing off these little blue accents, these highlights," he says, pointing to her négligée. "So what I'd like to do is overall go a little cooler." Matusek simultaneously pushes warmth into the shadows and then adds blue into the midtones. "And I got some green out of the highlights, just because I didn't like that. I noticed that there is some green in the blanket or maybe there's some green fill and then I pulled green from those highlights, but the whole image starts to look magenta, because I'm losing green," Matusek explains, backing off of his green highlight correction.

Fig. 6.18 Final primary correction.

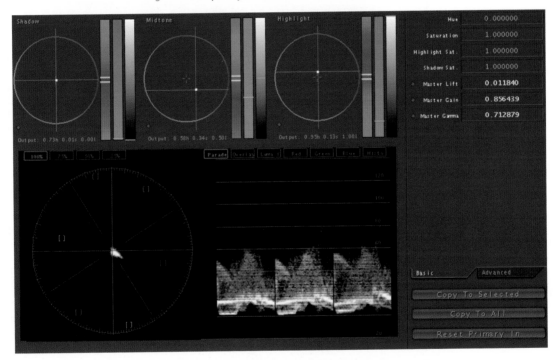

Fig. 6.19 FinalTouch UI showing primary data.

The trend, I felt, was that in independent film it was more about setting the mood and emotion.

– Mike Matusek, Nolo Digital Film

Matusek switches between the original source and his correction (Figure 6.18). "See? That's getting a lot moodier."

Kiss Me In the Dark

The short film "Kiss Me In the Dark" is a production of Seduced and Exploited Films. It was directed by Barry Gilbert, and the DP was Robin Miller.

Gilbert has been working as a director and producer for several years on independent features and spots. Currently, he works out of New York City.

Gilbert explains that this short film has its genesis in a feature script he was shopping. The aesthetic of the film was influenced by Gilbert's love of Ingmar Bergman films.

Many of Gilbert's earlier projects were heavily reliant on dialog, so for this film, he sought out the challenge of making a film completely without dialog.

If you want the context of the footage from the short as you are attempting to grade it, here is Gilbert's synopsis of the film:

It's a woman who lives in a big, old empty house and apparently spends all of her time thumbing through old photos and watching videotapes of her and her dead husband. What we see rather quickly on is that apparently the husband is back in the house and comes and embraces her. But the issue is clouded when she wakes up and wonders if she was merely dreaming, and it becomes apparent that this is not an isolated incident, that this is a pattern. This is the night that she decides, after quite a few drinks, that she is going to settle the issue once and for all. She's wired the house and there are all these surveillance cameras and she has ordered some fancy night vision goggles, which on one level is absurd, because if it was that easy, then everyone would have night vision goggles. It's really a question for the audience. Is she privy to a ghost that wants to be found, or is she so torn by her desire to reconnect with him that she's gone through these kind of sad attempts to rationalize? The point is that she's probably just as afraid of finding out that she's wrong than that there really is a ghost.

Before Matusek starts adding secondary vignettes, he shuttles through the footage past the first frame and sees that a man comes down into the frame from above. Matusek is glad he checked the shot: "The thing that's a big pain in the ass is when you spend ten minutes on a shot like this and hit play and then the guy comes in the frame and screws up what you did, so what I would typically do is go through the whole shot to see what I'm getting myself in to. So he does come in, but I notice that he doesn't really go in front of the pillow. What I notice is that my eye goes to this pillow (above her forehead) and even down here (the sheet under her neck and shoulders), so what I'd like to do is put a window here (on the pillow) and drop the exposure. Put a window here (foreground sheet) and drop the exposure. I really hate this highlight on the back wall, so I'd put a Bezier shape and bring that highlight down (Figure 6.20) and really soften it, and if I had to, I could keyframe it to stay where I wanted it to stay. First I'll put those other two windows, because I know they'll actually work."

Matusek explains that about half of the work he does is commercials and half is independent films. "The trend, I felt, was that in independent film it was more about setting the mood and emotion and with commercials, it's about getting a really cool look to grab people's attention. Hopefully, it's to help sell the product with the look having to do with the story of the spot, but mostly give it a hip, cool look and focus the attention on the product. And if you give it a really cool look, when you get to the product shot, make it look nice and pretty and bright. So basically commercials are a lot brighter, contrastier. Long form is a little bit moodier."

At this point, Matusek adds a soft, low, wide vignette to darken the sheet below her body, bringing the highlights down to about half and the midrange down a little, commenting, "Now your eye goes to her and I still don't like that pillow, so I'll do one more window there." He draws a custom shape for the pillow and brings the master gain down. "I think I went a little too flat." He checks back and forth—toggling the vignette off and on before revising it by increasing the contrast inside the window.

> *You've got to push it to the point where it looks pretty bad and then bring it back. Especially with clients.*
>
> *– Mike Matusek, Nolo Digital Films*

"There's nothing wrong with saying 'You wanna go darker with that? You wanna go darker?' But you've got to push it to the point where it looks pretty bad and then bring it back. Especially with clients. All colorists can see subtle changes in what they did. We're staring at the image for the whole time, while they're reading a magazine or they're on their laptop and they're looking up and down, so they miss those subtle changes. So it's good to show them—not extreme differences—but enough differences so they can see it."

Fig. 6.20 **With the vignette. Only the Master Gain was brought down to about 75 percent inside the vignette.**

Matusek then adds another vignette, bringing down the edges some more. "When you go back and forth you kind of get a feel for the balance, like 'That feels a little top heavy.'" To fix the "top-heaviness" of the image, Matusek repositions the vignette lower in the frame, then toggles back and forth to check the correction. "Here (without the vignette) it looks a little bit overlit. Here (with the vignette) it's a little more dynamic. There's more depth."

Matusek continues to evaluate the image to see how it can be improved. "Now that I'm happy with all this other stuff, this highlight (on the négli-gée on her breast) is bothering me. So now there're two things I could do. I can add a luma key on the highlights and defocus them. Or maybe just put another window and bring it down." Matusek adds another window, on the négligée (Figure 6.21), explaining, "By putting that window on her hand and her breast, your eye goes to her face."

Fig. 6.21 Vignette on négligée. Only Master Gain was brought down to about 70 percent inside the vignette.

Fig. 6.22 An overall vignette was added to focus attention and give texture. The outside of the vignette has the Master Gain lowered to about 50 percent.

Fig. 6.23 Original Source from Seduced & Exploited Entertainment's "Kiss Me In the Dark."

Fig. 6.24 Matusek's final correction.

When he is done with the vignettes, he summarizes what he did, and what he looks for before he moves on to the next shot (Figure 6.24). "I kind of shaped it. First you start off getting the density of the image. Then I get the color balance where I want it. Then the mood and where you want to put the gamma and the midtones. Then I kind of shape it. And now I'll go back to my primary and maybe I'll go even cooler with it, just for the heck of it and see what it looks like."

Mike Matusek

Mike Matusek is the principal colorist at Nolo Digital Film in Chicago. Nolo specializes in digital intermediates for features and creative color grading. He has extensive experience as a telecine and DI colorist grading commercials, feature films, and documentaries. He has experience with DaVinci's 2K color corrector but hehas done most of his recent grading on the Nucoda Film Master.

Commercial projects include clients such as Disney, Nintendo, McDonalds, AT&T, GoDaddy.com, Kelloggs, Miller Lite, Sears, and Bally's Total Fitness. Feature films include *Chicago Overcoat*, *Of Boys and Men*, *Baby on Board*, *The War Tapes*, and *Kubuku Rides* (the first film from Steppenwolf Films).

He's also corrected ESPN's edgy *30 for 30* doc, "The Trial of Allen Iverson."

Matusek is a graduate of Southern Illinois University.

Fun with Windows

Larry Field, the colorist on FOX's *24*, was reminded of a trick he'd done with a Power Window on his DaVinci color corrector. "On one of my shows I needed a sunrise, so we picked a spot behind a mountain and I grabbed a Power Window with a pretty broad soft edge to it and created a pinpoint and dropped another window and graded off that and basically produced a sunrise using Power Windows."

Vignette to Create Day-for-Night

NASCAR senior colorist Chris Pepperman (formerly of NFL Films) used vignettes to create a day-for-night look in the "Michigan Ave. Pumpkin Lights" scene (Figures 6.25–6.28). Normally, in a day-for-night shot, you would want to avoid shooting the sky, because even if you darken down the entire shot, the contrast between the sky and the rest of the image is usually a clear giveaway that the scene was not shot at night. To bring that contrast under control, Pepperman used several vignettes throughout the image.

"So the first thing I'm going to do is create a circle. I'm going to take it down below the pumpkins and I'm going to rotate it and now I'm going to stretch it. I'm situating this window where I can now work on the outside of it and I really want to knock down the sky even more. I'm gonna really crush the you-know-what out of it." As he does this, he notices something that bothers him. "Can you see the noise in there a little bit? So what I'm going to do is come up on the black levels to get rid of that noise and leave the black levels alone, because there are some blacks here in the building. I'm going to bury (the highlights) and add even more dark blue." But as he does this, he sees another problem develop (Figure 6.29). "I don't like what it's doing here. I should be able to track more of that blue in there. And I see some posterizing going on."

Fig. 6.25 Source image courtesy Randy Riesen.

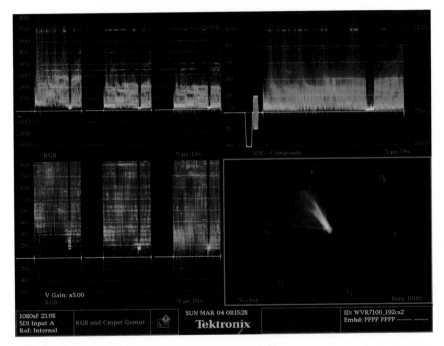

Fig. 6.26 Scopes showing source image from Tektronix WVR 7100.
Upper left is RGB Parade. Lower left is RGB Parade expanded to show black level. Upper right is composite waveform. Lower right is a vectorscope at standard zoom.

Fig. 6.27 Pepperman starts out with a primary correction.

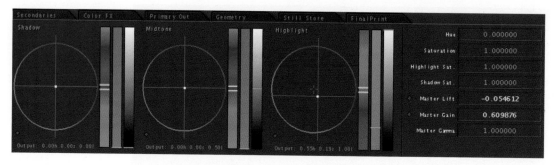

Fig. 6.28 Data from FinalTouch Primary room UI.

I want to almost see the curvature of the vignette because I want to put some texture in the sky.

– Chris Pepperman, NASCAR

Because of these issues, he backs off the more extreme correction that he was trying to do before continuing. "So the next thing I'm going to do is soften that out. But I want to almost see the curvature of the vignette because I want to put some texture in the sky. I want it to be almost organic. I don't want it to look flat like you're keying something in. I like having it darker to lighter. It gives it more of a true appearance." I comment that the vignette he's created looks like something a DP might have done with a filter. He'd been working outside of the vignette he created, but switches back to the inside to work on the lower part of the frame.

"Now inside the vignette, I might bring up the black levels a little bit. I'm going to push a little more blue to give it a perception more of night.

Fig. 6.29 First secondary correction finished. Corrections were made inside and outside the qualified area made by the oval vignette.

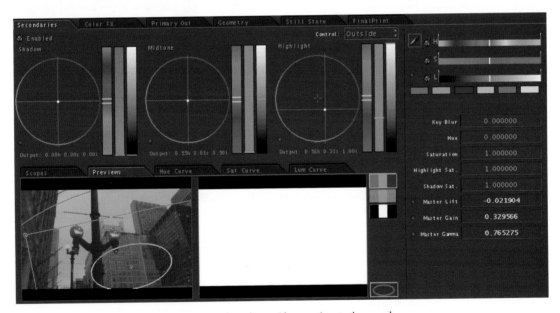

Fig. 6.30 Data from the outside corrections to the secondary.

I don't want to contaminate the blacks too much, 'cause I don't want to change the color of the building either. Now I'll start to bury the blacks again so you can really almost see the shadow on that. I really like that, but I still think we can push it more. So I'm going to go back outside the window and I'm going to bring the midrange down and the whites. I'm just going to make it a little more blue. And now I'm going to drop the window down.

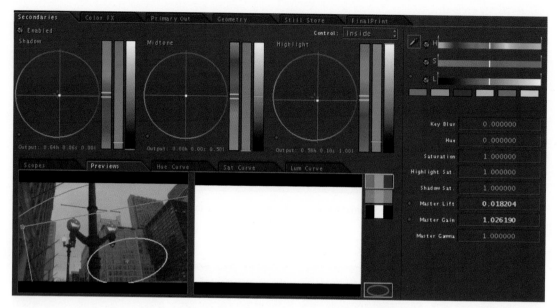

Fig. 6.31 Data from the inside corrections to the secondary.

"What I'm going to do is an isolation appearance. This is something I like to do." Pepperman creates a custom user shape for the next vignette, defining one of the buildings. "What I'm doing is brightening the building to give it the appearance that the lights are on." Pepperman creates this illusion by raising the highlights and crushing the blacks inside the vignette (Figures 6.32 and 6.33). "I'm going to make sure that the blacks are deep, so it doesn't look like it's got a spotlight on it. And the midrange might even help that. Now, that looks pretty good. I'm going to soften it. So I like that."

Fig. 6.32 This has the second vignette added to the top-right building.

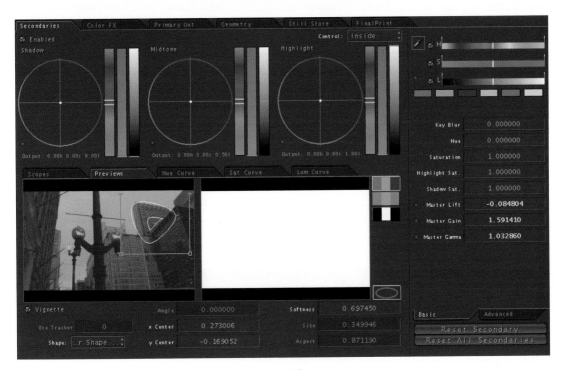

Fig. 6.33

You can see the triangular window and the changes to the master levels to create the impression that the lights are on bright inside the building.

Fig. 6.34 The third vignette added to the leftmost building.

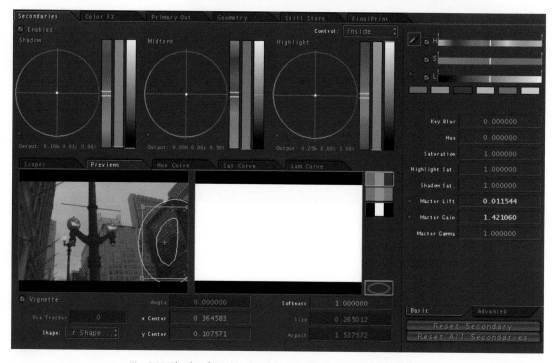

Fig. 6.35 The data from the secondary, including the shape of the window.

As his next step in the correction, Pepperman plans to bring up the blacks on the building to the left and raises the highlights (Figures 6.34 and 6.35). "I'm going to use the trackballs to clean up the blue and now I'll soften it."

"And then I just want to do one more thing." Pepperman creates a custom shape in the middle of the frame and darkens it (Figures 6.36 and 6.37). "Now it doesn't look like it's darker on the edges. You've got a darker feel in the middle, too."

Fig. 6.36 The effect of the fourth secondary vignette.

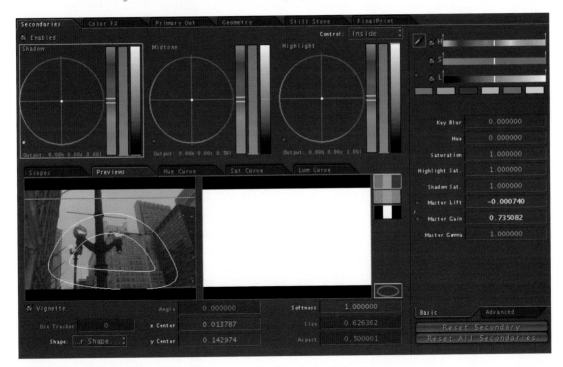

Fig. 6.37 The data from the fourth vignette.

"If I really wanted to, I could isolate the pumpkins and bring them up. I don't like the way they clip. I would brighten them back up to where they're clipping. Like they would in real life. Because when it's clipped like that but it's low, it just doesn't look right. So if I brighten the pumpkins up, this picture would say day-for-night much better. It would simulate it much better." As he blows out the pumpkin lights, the shot looks much more realistic as day-for-night (Figures 6.38–6.41).

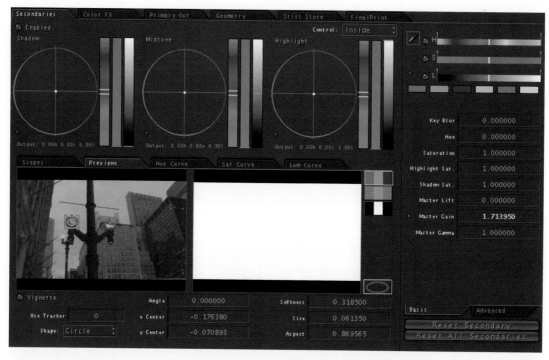

Fig. 6.38 The data for one of the pumpkin lights.

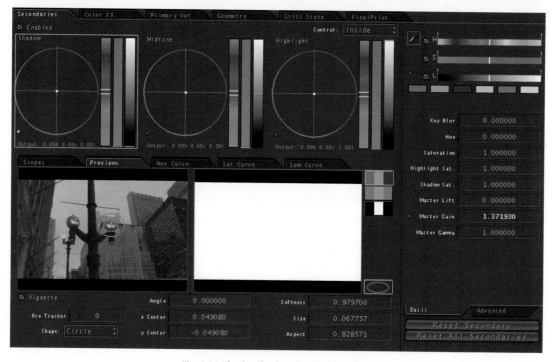

Fig. 6.39 The data for the other pumpkin light.

Fig. 6.40 Starting point for image.

Fig. 6.41 The final correction, including the last two pumpkin light vignettes.

Vector and Luma Qualified Secondaries

One of the reasons to use secondaries is because balancing an entire tonal range—highlights, midtones, or shadows—is not specific enough to fix more isolated color casts within that range. When that happens, secondaries allow the colorist greater precision to manipulate more specific ranges of color. One example of this is in the scene from *Chasing Ghosts* that I call "Banker's Light" (Figure 6.42).

Janet Falcon, formerly a Miami-based colorist who is now at Shooters Post in Philadelphia, liked the challenge of bringing this scene to life and used secondary color correction to execute her vision. She starts with a basic primary correction (Figures 6.44 and 6.45), then moves on the secondaries.

"The highlighted areas in the shirt don't have much green in them," she begins. "It's the midtone shadow areas that have more green. If I just take green out of the highlights, that'll go further away. I just want to take green out of the lower lit areas (of the shirt)."

Falcon pulls green out with a secondary qualification based on the greens of the shirt. She pulls some of the green out, but when she does, she sees that her qualification of the green needs to be tweaked to better get all of the green out of the shirt without affecting the green tint in the window over the detective's shoulder. She explains her qualification:

Fig. 6.42 Source image from *Chasing Ghosts*. Image courtesy of Wingman Productions, Inc.

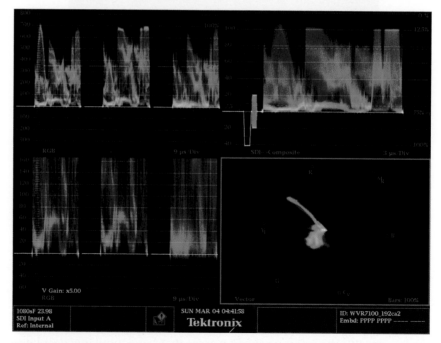

Fig. 6.43 Scopes showing source image from Tektronix WVR 7100. Upper left is RGB Parade. Lower left is RGB Parade expanded to show black level. Upper right is composite waveform. Lower right is a vectorscope at standard zoom.

"I like green. A lot of people don't like green. Normally, what I would do is qualify it based on that that's a darker color or a more colorful color. That's why I was trying to pull up the bottom end of the luminance to eliminate the darker green in the door from the qualification in the shirt. What I would normally try to do is get the greener parts of the shirt. Let the tie stay beige. But there's green in here," she says as she points to the shadowed folds of shirt (Figures 6.46 and 6.47). "If I make a qualification that's stronger on the green parts and maybe a little bit grayer, like not so much of a qualification on the white parts, so that when I make the color correction, it affects more of the greens, the stronger greens. And it might affect the lighter parts too, but not as much. I personally don't want to affect [the green in the window of the door] unless the client or somebody told me, get rid of the green in the window."

When I ask why she doesn't simply use a vignette to save the green light in the window of the door she responds, "Usually it's easier if you can do something without windows, because you never know where you're going to end up later. Maybe we'll come back to this shot later

Fig. 6.44 Falcon's primary correction.

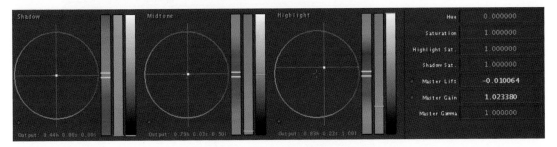

Fig. 6.45 Data from the primary correction in FinalTouch UI.

and he'll be up and standing in front of that or moving around, walking. So to the extent that you can do it with a color vector qualification, you never have to follow it with a window and track it. So I always try to do everything first without a window and then if you have to put in a window, then put in a window. And depending on what this is for, I might put a vignette on him to focus attention on him." Falcon sets up a new secondary with a circle, softens it, and corrects outside of the circle (Figure 6.48).

Fig. 6.46 This correction pulls some of the green out of the more midtone areas of the shirt.

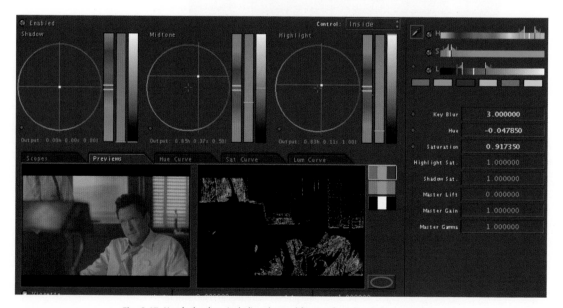

Fig. 6.47 Here's the data, including the qualification for Falcon's first secondary.

The amount of color correction; the shape of the window; the softness of the window. All those things play together.
– Janet Falcon, Shooters Post

Fig. 6.48 **The effect of the correction to the** *outside* **of the second vignette.**

I point out the different "camps" of colorists who prefer adding softness to the vignette early or later. Falcon walks the fence on this decision, though she seems to land in the "soften early" camp. "I like to get the window positioned the way I think I'm going to want it and then I go back and forth. For me they all go together. The amount of color correction; the shape of the window; the softness of the window. All those things play together. I know a lot of other people do it the other way. They'll put the color correction in first and then do the luminance key. I know Kevin Shaw does that." Kevin Shaw is a prominent color correction trainer and consultant. "If he wants a luminance key of the sky, he'll make a color correction in a circle, then create a luminance key and bring that correction into the luminance key. I create the key as close as I think I can get it and then I color correct it. Then I go back and touch up the softness and the positioning. I do a lot of back and forth. I know I work differently than other people. I've seen people do it the other way and I can't understand how they can do it that way."

Falcon tweaks the aspect and rotation of the circle to include his face and some look room and darkens outside of it. Then she pulls a secondary HSL key on the highest chroma part of the banker light. "I think it helps to knock that light down a little bit." I can tell she's not quite happy with her correction because she's unfamiliar with using FinalTouch/Color.

"I like to be very, very, very specific about what I affect and what I don't affect. Some people aren't that specific. I'm kind of neurotic about it. Like, his face looks like he's sick. It's kind of pink here and green here, and that's because I didn't get a perfect isolation on the pinker parts of the face. I got some of the pink out, but it also got it out of some of the places that I didn't want to affect, Falcon mentions as she points to the detective's forehead. "And in here, not enough, she continues, pointing at the darkened side of the face (Figures 6.49 and 6.50). "So he ends up looking kind of blotchy, but in the end it's better."

Fig. 6.49 Completed correction, including a third secondary to reduce the intensity of the glow in the banker's light.

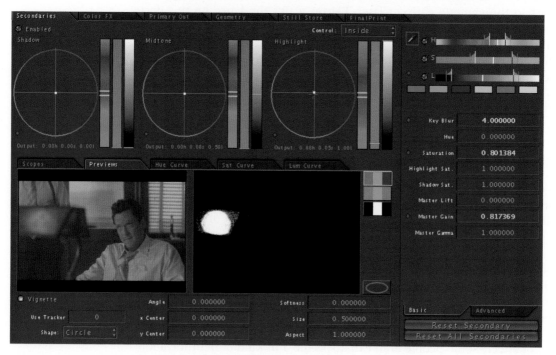

Fig. 6.50 The data from the third secondary, showing the qualified area.

Janet Falcon

Janet Falcon graduated from Tulane University in 1987. She has worked at Teleproductions, Inc. in New Orleans. In 1988 she went to work as Senior Colorist at Limelite/Edefx in Miami and then moved to Miami Transfer before landing at Shooters Post in Philadelphia in 2002, where she is now senior colorist.

Her commercial reel includes work for clients like Volkswagen, Chevy, Miller, Reebok, Time/Warner, and Campbell's Soup. She has also graded music videos for the Baha Men and Wyclef Jean, among others, and has been the colorist on full-length feature DIs such as "Shadowboxer" with Cuba Gooding, Jr., "Teeth," "Perfect Weekend," and "Best and the Brightest." She has also graded episodes of the TV series *Dinner: Impossible*.

Definition

DI: DI stands for Digital Intermediate. It used to indicate that a film had been shot on film, would end up being projected in a theater on film, and in between was a digital intermediate step where the film was digitized (usually by a film scanner) and color corrected, then laid back to film using a film recorder. Now it is a more generic term for digital processing and color correction of an image that could begin digitally and end up being shown digitally.

Secondary Corrections Can Focus Attention

Larry Field of Level 3 Post in Los Angeles used a vector qualification to place the attention where it was needed in the scene I call "Music Video Overhead" which was shot by Charles Vanderpool (Figure 6.51).

Charles Vanderpool

Charles Vanderpool began his career as a theater lighting and set designer off-Broadway in the late 1960s and early 1970s before lighting for still photographers and then TV commercial directors.

For the past 20 years, he has been producing and directing films in addition to his role as cinematographer. He produced films for Kodak that helped launch many of the new motion picture film stocks they've released in the last 15 years.

His production company, Vanderpool Films, boasts an impressive client list, including the American Red Cross, Bank of America, the Discovery Channel, Kodak, HBO, IBM, NASA, PBS, Orion Films, Sony Music, Toyota, and the United Way.

Before he begins, Field jokes about the general look of music videos, saying, "So no one's afraid of contrast in a music video. What I would do if [the strong color of the floor] was a concern would be to grab a color isolation on just that color and desaturate it after everything else was balanced and that would send your eye to her better. But first I want to start at a position where everything is where we want to be instead of starting with just that color and everything else is out of balance. I start basically with primary color correction.

Do the contrast and the basic feel first. It doesn't matter who you're with or where you're at; people are going to enjoy the image a lot better once the primaries are balanced, and you're in the ballpark where you need to be. Then you can start playing in the secondaries,

Fig. 6.51 Source image courtesy of Vanderpool Films and Charles Vanderpool.

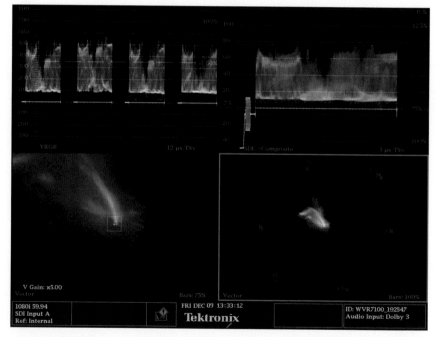

Fig. 6.52 Scopes showing source image from Tektronix WVR 7100. Upper left is YRGB Parade. Lower left is vectorscope zoomed in 5x. Upper right is composite waveform. Lower right is a vectorscope at standard zoom.

effects, windows, keys, masks. That stuff is always secondary to me. It's always after I have it balanced and I have an idea of where I'm going and what we're doing.

Fig. 6.53 Scene after secondary correction, reconstructed from watching a videotape of the session.

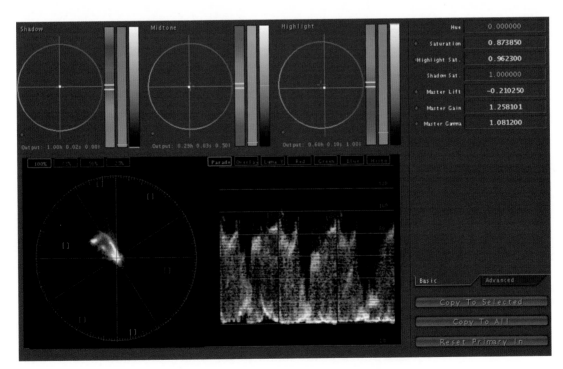

Fig. 6.54 The data from the reconstructed primary correction.

Fig. 6.55 Field just talked through this secondary correction during the session. I reconstructed it later using his instructions.

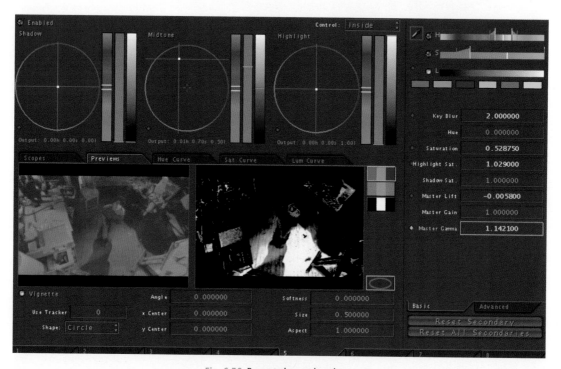

Fig. 6.56 Recreated secondary data.

"Then use a secondary to pick the narrowest range of the floor, so it isn't affecting anything else and desaturate it and maybe swing towards red a little bit to blend in with the shadows more. With the secondary, look at the matte to see what part of the picture you're affecting."

Larry Field

Larry Field works out of Level 3 Post in Los Angeles, where he was the senior colorist on *24*. His credits also include an impressive array of prime time shows including *The Simpsons*, *Scrubs*, *Star Trek: Deep Space Nine* and *Star Trek: The Next Generation*, *Third Rock from the Sun*, and *Murder, She Wrote*. Also, *Terra Nova*, *Bones*, *The River*, *Perception*, *Shameless*, *Melissa & Joey*, and *Wedding Band*.

His current color grading kits of choice are Lustre and DaVinci.

In addition to prime time episodes, Field did live color correction for N'Sync's performance at the 43rd Grammy Awards and hundreds of grades on TV spots and network promos.

Previously, Larry worked at Editel/LA and Unitel. He graduated from Northern Arizona University.

Using Secondaries to Match

We have an entire chapter devoted to matching shots (Chapter 9), but here we'll point out several ways that secondaries can help resolve tricky matching problems. Robert Lovejoy from Shooters Post in Philadelphia used just about every type of secondary qualification as he tried to match the "Art Institute Lions—Cool" scene (Figure 6.59) with the "Art Institute Lions—Base" scene (Figure 6.57).

Like most colorists, he started with the basics before moving to secondaries. Lovejoy explained his opening steps: "I'm balancing blacks, balancing whites, and spreading my tonal range. I'm looking at the steps and the building façade." He sets up a split screen between the correctly shot image and the cool image and then positions the split down the middle of the lion. He starts by trying to match the base that the lion is standing on, adding some red to the midtones (Figures 6.61 and 6.62).

His primary correction to the cool image turns the sky a freakish color (Figure 6.61). This is where secondaries come in handy to fix problems created in the primary correction. Lovejoy qualifies the sky in the upper right corner with a luminance only matte, then desaturates the highlights within the qualification, taking the sky back to pure white (Figures 6.63 and 6.64).

Instead of simply trying to match the base scene with the cool scene, Lovejoy also improves the base scene, then grabs a still of the improved base scene and wipes between it and the cool version he's trying to match (Figures 6.65 and 6.66). Instead of relying on scopes, he's using just his eyes, the video monitor, and years of experience. "It's very close. There are subtle differences in the lion. Secondary could be my friend on that."

Fig. 6.57 Source image of "base" Art Institute scene.

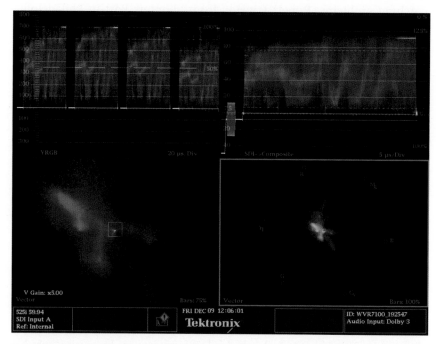

Fig. 6.58 Scopes showing source image from Tektronix WVR 7100. Upper left is YRGB Parade. Lower left is vectorscope zoomed in 5x. Upper right is composite waveform. Lower right is a vectorscope at standard zoom.

Fig. 6.59 Source image of "cool" Art Institute scene.

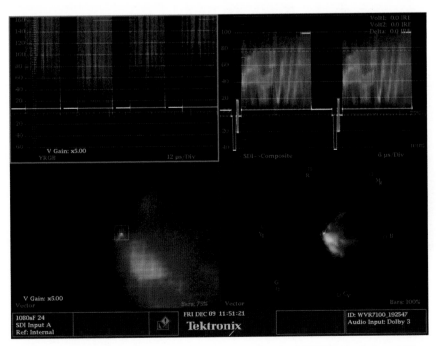

Fig. 6.60 Scopes showing source image from Tektronix WVR 7100. Upper left is YRGB Parade. Lower left is vectorscope zoomed in 5x. Upper right is composite waveform. Lower right is a vectorscope at standard zoom.

Fig. 6.61 The cool lion corrected with a primary correction.

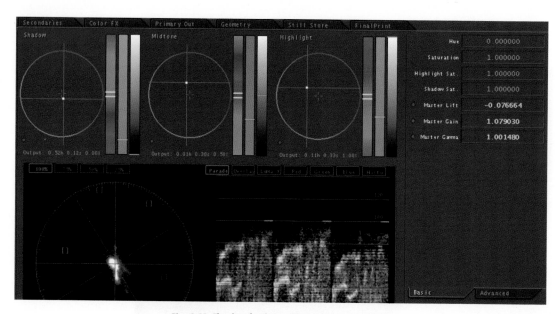

Fig. 6.62 The data for the cool lion primary correction.

Fig. 6.63 This secondary pulls the sky back to white.

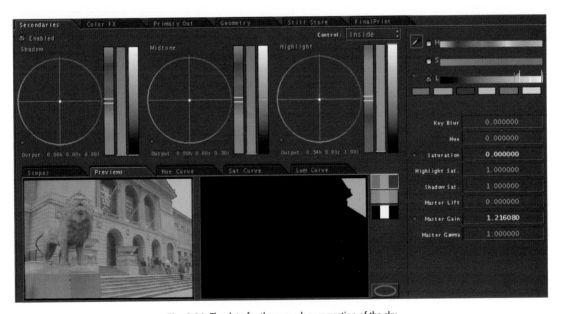

Fig. 6.64 The data for the secondary correction of the sky.

Fig. 6.65 This is the base, semicorrect image with a primary.

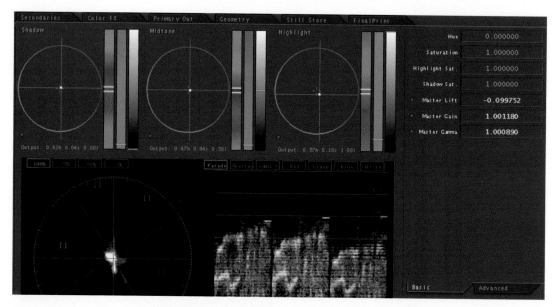

Fig. 6.66 This is the data for the primary correction on the base image.

To create his secondary correction on the lion, Lovejoy combines two qualifications. First he qualifies the lion using an HSL key. His HSL qualification goes a little "broad," selecting some portions of the image beyond the lion, so he adds a circle vignette around the lion as a "garbage matte." With the lion qualified, he lowers the saturation of the lion. "It's hard to get a perfect match out of two widely divergent sources. You can see here that the base (that the lion stands on) is cooler." Using the Tangent Devices CP-200-BK panel, he warms up the midtones and highlights within the secondary qualification, ending up with a very close match. (Figure 6.67)

Fig. 6.67 Second secondary correction, desaturating the lion to make the match.

Fig. 6.68 The data from the second secondary correction.

Secondaries Use Is Changing

When I first started learning about color correction, the prevailing wisdom was that you "saved" your secondaries. In other words, you wanted to just use a secondary color correction for something that really needed it. However, that was the wisdom when additional secondaries were either nonexistent or came as options at a *very* high premium. Bob Sliga and I discussed how this wisdom is changing with products like Apple's Color, which allows what would have been considered as 16 or more secondaries in a color corrector from the 1990s. According to Sliga, "The secondary in Color is not the same as traditional secondary in film to tape transfer. You can go back to the days when we didn't really have secondary color correction, when we could only grab the six vectors and change saturation and hue and maybe luminance a little bit. That was the typical secondary color correction where you could isolate a color until DaVinci changed the game in secondary color correction by isolating a color by using a luminance key or an HSL key or by putting a window around something—which wasn't traditionally called a secondary, but they called that Power Tiers.

"In Color, the secondary room is not just picking colors. We can use it as eight separate levels of full color correction. We're creating a color as opposed to just enhancing it, and that is how the game has changed. Having eight secondaries—I think I've filled them up *once*, where I've run out of room. If you're that far down, either (a) the shot was totally mis-shot, or (b) the effect you're trying to create was 'you better be paying big money per hour,' because if you're using all eight windows and secondaries per scene on a feature or on a commercial, that's a long time for color correction. Does every job need all the complexity? No. But it's good to have the headroom if you need to be able to take something or push something a different way or a different color. I think the colorist that learns these tools and is more flexible and thinks outside the box' will be effective longer."

So, in addition to using the Secondary room as a true secondary, it's also possible to use the secondaries as "layers" of primary correction, where you don't even bother making a qualification before doing adjustments. This allows you to easily enable or disable the various "layers" as you perfect your grade.

Using a Luma Key to Build Contrast

Bob Sliga shows how to use secondaries to create a unique high-contrast look using the "football center" scene (Figure 6.69) from Artbeats' Sports Collection.

In addition to the traditional method of stretching out the tonal range in primary color correction, it's possible to create even greater contrast by grading inside and outside of a luminance key.

First Sliga takes us through the traditional method, starting with some primary-type corrections that Sliga decides to do in a secondary. Sliga exams the source footage and begins, "If you go to our original picture, it's balanced out pretty decent. So the primary room would be the basic,

Fig. 6.69 Source footage courtesy Artbeats.

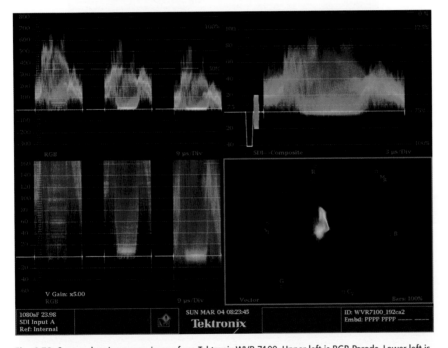

Fig. 6.70 Scopes showing source image from Tektronix WVR 7100. Upper left is RGB Parade. Lower left is RGB Parade expanded to show black level. Upper right is composite waveform. Lower right is a vector-scope at standard zoom.

just starting it out, getting it in the ballpark. I'm just looking for a clean black and I've got one. Now this is a little warm, so we could bring the red gamma down, but the truth of the matter is that if we graded film to look like what it should be, people would not like their film. I mean, everyone loves things warm." Sliga makes a primary correction, but it is so slight that it is hard to perceive, especially on the printed page.

The truth of the matter is that if we graded film to look like what it should be, people would not like their film.

– Bob Sliga, Apple Color

Because the original image is balanced and in a good place, Sliga moves to secondaries to modify the original, using secondaries like layers of primaries without any qualification. (See the "Secondaries Use Is Changing" sidebar.) "Now I'm just going to pull the gammas down like this. Really compress the blacks. I'm gonna crank up some more contrast by raising the highlights. I don't care about these highlights," Sliga explains, pointing to the white tape on the center's fingers (Figures 6.71 and 6.72).

Fig. 6.71 The secondary correction with no qualification at all.

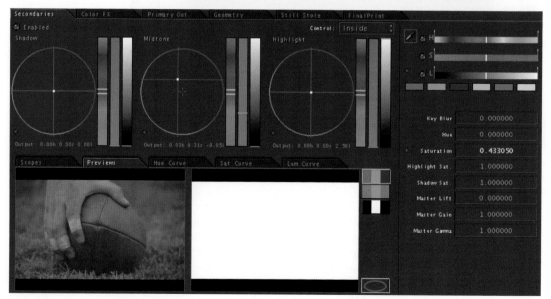

Fig. 6.72 Note the numbers under the color wheels.

"I'm creating an effect. I'm blowing them out. I can pull the blacks down even further if you want. But you can see as we pull the blacks down that it's going to kind of naturally funnel in. That's why sometimes I really won't do that. That's why I do a lot more with the gamma. Pull that saturation back down. Maybe warm the gammas back up a little bit."

Switching gears from the more traditional method of building contrast, Sliga attacks the image by using the secondaries as they're designed to be used: *with* a qualification. "Now let's use it as more of a secondary tool. We're going to create a luminance key." Sliga sets the luminance

Fig. 6.73 Secondary correction on both sides of the luminance qualification.

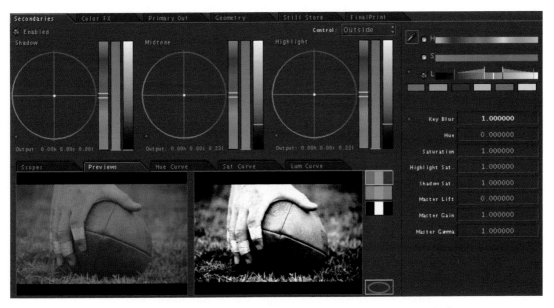

Fig. 6.74 Data for the outside of the secondary. Note the numbers under the color wheels.

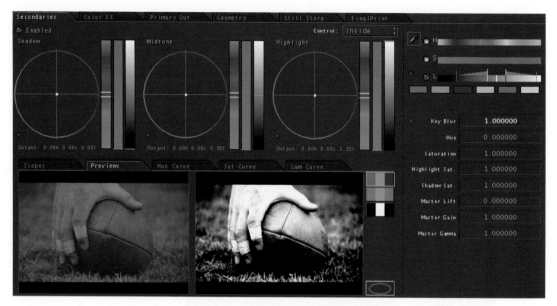

Fig. 6.75 Data for the inside of the secondary. Note the numbers under the color wheels.

key so that basically half of the image is black and half is white. Then he selects to work on the outside of the selection, which is the black part of the qualification. He brings both gain and gamma down. "By creating a luminance key, I've kind of created some contrast naturally without even raising the whites. I didn't make the blacks black. I just darkened the gammas down and pulled the luminance value of that down. So now I can actually go back and choose inside and kick him back up [bringing gain up]" (Figures 6.73–6.75).

Use a Secondary to Soften Skin Tones

One of the important skills for a colorist is to be able to soften skin tones and beautify the people in a shot. This task goes beyond color correction because it also involves creating a blurred, softened skin tone that is then keyed through using either a simple qualification of skin tones or a skin tone qualification combined with a garbage matte to protect other similar colors or flesh tones in the same shot.

Bob Festa walked me through one of these corrections using the footage of the "sleeping_woman." Other colorists explored this same image, showing various techniques from day-for-night to "relighting." It creates some unique challenges for colorists, so it's a great tutorial shot. My good friend, veteran Denver-based director of photography Rich Lerner, shot this image. We've pulled the shot out of context and are trying to prepare it for uses that it was originally *not* shot for, but that is a fairly common occurrence in spots, TV episodic work, and features. What was originally written as a daydream or afternoon nap can be recast by the editors and producers after the fact as a nighttime scene or something else.

Running through the tutorial materials, this shot (Figure 6.76) caught Festa's eye as a good candidate for some secondary correction.

He starts out with a base grade, looking at what he calls his "signposts" for the elements that give him a clear direction for where to place blacks and whites. With that done, he hones in on the skin. The first thing Festa does is zoom in on the woman's face to get a better look at what he's going to try to do, which is to soften the texture in her face and really create a glow to enhance the beauty of her face and skin. Festa walks us through his next step, "I'm going to open up another channel, soften the shot to where I think her skin looks good."

This "channel" he's referring to is something that would need to be done in Apple Color using the ColorFX Room, creating a node that completely blurs the entire shot. In Resolve, this would be another node in the node graph. He blurs the image, keeping an eye on finding a pleasant skin texture. With that done, he puts a garbage matte around her face (Figure 6.77). This matte will keep any other elements of the picture outside of the matte from being affected by the qualification he's about to make. To me it's interesting that he decided to add the garbage matte before the qualification because—at least for me—it's hard to tell what else will be selected by the qualification, and sometimes the garbage matte won't be necessary. Obviously, Festa has a lot more "seat time" than I do and knows exactly what will happen when he does the next step in the correction.

With the garbage matte created and softened, Festa uses one of his favorite tools, the 3D Keyer, to color pick (eyedropper) on her face

Fig. 6.76 Footage courtesy D.P., Rich Lerner.

Fig. 6.77 Garbage mask to protect everything but the face from the correction.

Fig. 6.78 UI showing 3D Keyer.

(Figure 6.78). The 3D Keyer provides Festa with a great way of visualizing the qualification he's made (Figure 6.79). The qualification defines a shapes approximating the shape of the woman's face. He then softens the key (Figure 6.80).

This key serves to selectively blend the original footage to the blurred channel, allowing the blurred image to be blended only through the key created with the 3D Keyer skin tone selection protected with the garbage matte. The effect is a beautiful softening of the woman's face (Figure 6.81). This is a great use of secondaries.

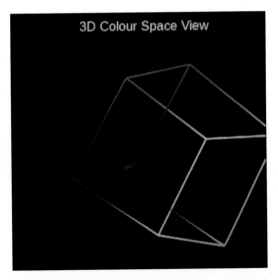

Fig. 6.79 Close up of 3D Keyer showing the skin tones selected.

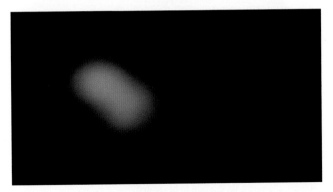

Fig. 6.80 Softened key of the skin tone selection.

Fig. 6.81 Final softened skin tone.

Multiple Windows and Masks

Festa continues grading the Artbeats shot of the Marines. He grades some of the warmth out of the original, bringing the shot to a more neutral or base look. Festa says that even if he brings some of the warmth back into parts of the image, he wants to start from a more neutral place.

After the initial primary grade, the first thing that he attacks is the sky, which is bright and relatively featureless in the original. He creates a garbage mask first to protect the highlights that are lower in the frame (Figure 6.82).

With the garbage matte in place, Festa qualifies the sky with a luminance key and blurs the resulting selection (Figure 6.83). He darkens and saturates the blown-out sky inside the qualification. The softness of the garbage mask at the horizon creates a gentle gradient from dark at the top to brighter at the horizon (Figures 6.84–6.87).

Fig. 6.82 With a curve, the bottom portion of the image is protected from the correction. The softness trails off to the horizon, allowing a sky gradient to be created.

Fig. 6.83 A luma qualification of the brightest portion of the sky, blurred.

Fig. 6.84 Sky with window and luma qualification is graded to darken and saturate the sky.

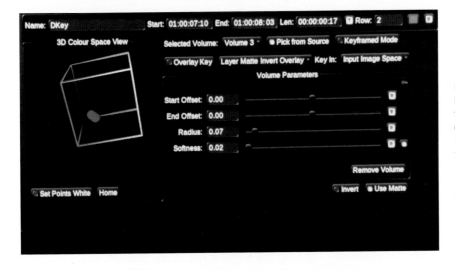

Fig. 6.85 From there, Festa wants the soldier front and center to stand out more as the "hero." He qualifies the soldier's face with a round window (Figure 6.86) and a 3D key (vector qualification) of the skin tones (Figure 6.85) and the rest of the image is darkened slightly outside the window, drawing the eye to the center soldier.

Fig. 6.86 Initial qualification of the hero Marine with a round window. (The strange color artifacts are due to capturing this image with an SLR shooting the video monitor, not the grade itself.)

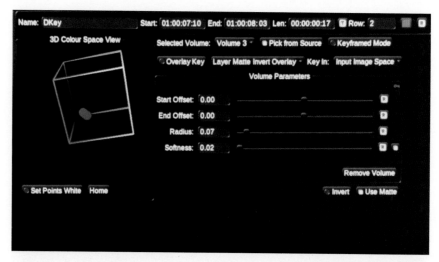

Fig. 6.87 The 3D Keyer shows the qualification of the warm, saturated skin tones that were selected.

Creating Depth and Texture

For Encore's Pankaj Bajpai, it's a cardinal sin for an image to leave his suite "flat." Bajpai explains as he examines the "sleeping woman" shot, "So, the first thing you want to get away from is the image looking flat. To me, flat images are just flat images, and part of it comes from having been so closely involved in photography and photographers. Aesthetically the first goal for me—which I think is the goal for most colorists—is to get away from being a flat image. This is a generic image, it doesn't feel like life, so the first thing would be to just build that image from being not as contrasty.

"We have to make us feel present in this world, so right off the bat, I lower the contrast—I got myself some meat in the picture. I also lowered the gamma. A lot of the magic lies in the midtones. That's where a lot of your play happens. So right off the bat, we do that. At this point I'm going to go in and organically cut it up" (Figures 6.88 and 6.89).

Bajpai softens his hand-drawn shape and corrects outside of the mask, darkening the image and giving a sense of lighting (Figure 6.88). He explains, "We have gone and created a sense of depth, and I've done that in this organic way. I could take the saturation and actually go a touch warmer. So now with that little desaturation happening, you are starting to feel more in that world. I also use a lot of keys. I do a lot of masks. At this point, I will see if I could get to the really light where she is sleeping, so now you see how her skin has suddenly become radiant. That feeling of three-dimensionality: it feels human.

"I could just break up the face just a little bit and then soften it, so now you can see that even on that face, I have broken it in highlight and the

Fig. 6.88 With a pen, Bajpai draws an organic shape.

Fig. 6.89 Levels outside the organic shape were lowered.

shadow and you can see what I was talking about in that you can take an image and completely make it feel like you're there. The whole scene could play in this atmosphere and when I'm doing things, I know that it's not just this one shot, there's a whole scene, so its okay for her to look like this, but if you can't pull that off for the other 50 shots coming after this, you're in trouble."

Bajpai is aware that in this instance, he's kind of relit the scene, and like most colorists, is concerned with what the DP may think. He asserts, "In many ways, when you're on set and you're a DP working with a director, the director isn't always telling you everything in the minutest detail. They want you to be able to convey the feeling that they are going after."

I understand his concern that he's walking a very fine line between (1) the kind of completely relit the image which may piss off the DP and (2) the DP had no time because they were running behind schedule and all they had time to do was to throw up a quick light and get the thing captured on film, so he didn't really mean to light it like this, so he looks for the colorist to help him make it look better.

Bajpai relates his experience with many DPs: "That's where it becomes a matter of trust and faith in that I am not intending to relight a DPs work. That is not the idea. The idea is to enhance it and in that enhancement, if you look at this image versus where it started, the light's already in there—the lamp is already lit that way—so when you're looking at that and you're looking at this, it is more like what that lighting needs to be in the context of that scene or the emotional feel that happens to be in that scene."

The DP isn't the only concern for the colorist. For example, with actors and actresses, he needs to be concerned with maintaining continuity in the look from week to week. If this image were of a star actress, the color of her hair would be critical.

Bajpai agrees, "Absolutely. No question about that. It's very important. I did *Sex and the City* for a couple of years, and it was just as important, I mean the producers were more concerned and if the shade of dye on the set were different from one day to the next, I would get phone calls. It's very critical, especially with blonde hair. We can finesse the hair based on the tool set. I can tweak the shape of the mask (Figures 6.90 and 6.91) and take out the red so I won't affect the redness of the face. And then at the point, the yellow-green part can be separated and I can go in and take out the green" (Figure 6.90).

Despite the windows and qualifications of various vectors (greens in hair and reds in the skin), Bajpai considers this primary color correction. I ask him for clarification. His answer: "I don't necessarily like to call these secondaries. These are like layers so in any layer, what you're doing is shifting that pixel value. I go along with people when they call

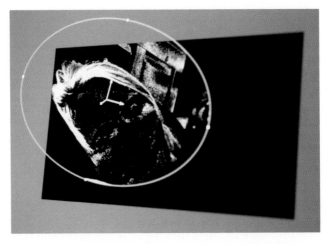

Fig. 6.90 The initial qualification of the hair, in order to remove some of the green cast.

Fig. 6.91 The keyer selects the yellowish/green shade of the hair, allowing it to be corrected.

it 'secondary.' I use a lot of masks. I create masks on layers. That is the true nature of what I do and then I apply 3D keying into that. My work is making it real, getting it three-dimensional, and then taking the cues from the lighting that was done on set and then enhancing that with masks and layers. That's my approach to doing what I do."

Seeing how these talented colorists harness the power of their systems to grade with great specificity to achieve the results they desire is a testament to the importance of color correcting tools that provide you with the most control possible.

Though each colorist attacked the problems encountered in the image in a different way, clear methods and a strategic approach made each step a logical progression towards the goal.

CHAPTER 7

Correcting Shots

Many colorists disapprove of the term "color correction" because so much of their talent extends well beyond simply "correcting" bad color. But the truth of the matter is that when working on an image, the first order of business usually *is* "correcting" the scene.

Also, an even larger part of the job of an *aspiring* colorist will be trying to correct bad video images. So this chapter will be devoted to making bad images look okay, making decent images look good, and taking good images "over the top."

Four More Grades of the "Banker's Light" Scene

Pete Jannotta, one of Chicago's veteran and most respected names in postproduction, is a colorist at Filmworker's Club. Pete chose to work on the same scene from *Chasing Ghosts* that Janet Falcon tackled in the last chapter. (Figure 7.1). He provides a detailed explanation of how he approaches this image mostly in primary, with forays into secondaries that are a nice transition from the previous chapter.

Jannotta evaluates the image, explaining, "My feeling would be that I'd want to make more out of this banker's light being warm and then leave some green on the outside. I also feel like this is plain too much green, even if it is fluorescent-lit and we want to have that office feeling. So I know that's in the mids—most of it." Jannotta starts to push warmth into the banker's light using the midtone trackball, also pushing towards magenta and away from green, explaining, "If anything interacts, like the black gets pulled up a little out of whack, then adjust it. I did not do what I said to do first, which is to get the brightness and contrast kind of set where I want it." Jannotta completes the basic primary correction and continues. "This is starting to feel a little better already."

But when he cuts back and forth between his current correction and the source, he sees something that he didn't see before. "I went too magenta with it. I went overboard. I feel like my monitor and my vectorscope

Fig. 7.1 The "Banker's Light" scene from *Chasing Ghosts*. Image courtesy of Wingman Productions, Inc.

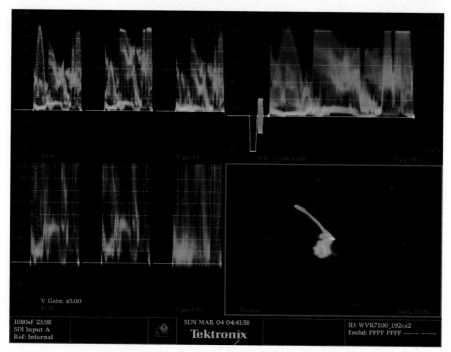

Fig. 7.2 Tektronix WVR7100 screengrab. Upper left corner: RGB Parade. Upper right corner: composite waveform. Lower left corner: RGB Parade, expanded to show black level. Lower right corner: standard vectorscope image.

are telling me two different things." Unlike most of the other colorists, Jannotta did his corrections with my standard 17" Panasonic LCD HD monitor instead of eCinema's grading monitor. In my monitor, Jannotta is seeing magenta, but the vectorscope is not showing magenta. "But assuming that the monitoring is set up properly," he explains, "no matter

what the vectorscope says, this"—here he is pointing to the monitor—
"is the end. But these"—pointing to the RGB parade and vectorscope—
"always help me get there."

The fact that Jannotta's correction was too magenta is common for an
image with a strong green cast, as magenta is the opposite of green. This
effect is a worthwhile thing to note: as you are correcting for a certain
color cast, like green, you must beware of going too far in the exact opposite direction. So in this instance, you must consciously wary to not let
the image become too heavily magenta. The same is true for other colors:
guard against going too yellow for images that start too blue.

*I like less saturation because it would be more realistic, I think, for it
not to be very saturated.*

— Pete Jannotta, Filmworker's Club

Jannotta continues to evaluate the image. "He's got a really interesting
face, and I think there's too much distracting around him to be focusing
on him, so I like less saturation because it would be more realistic, I think,
for it not to be very saturated. It's not a real super colorful situation, but
rather than green . . . it's more like drab office lighting. You can still feel
some green, but I like that better.

"Now what I think I want to do is get him to be more the central focus."
I ask Jannotta if secondaries is the way to accomplish that. "Yeah. And
it looks like my blacks are up too high. It looks milky in here." Jannotta
points to the pants under the banker light and the edges of the banker light.
"When I look at the RGB Parade, it looks like it's kind of high, and blue-
black is kind of low, and that looks better when I fix that. It's always when
you see something there [on the RGB parade] and you balance it, then you
look at the screen and you say 'Yeah. That's it. That did do it.' Sometimes
your eye helps and sometimes the scopes." Jannotta also dials out some saturation and compresses the mids while stretching out the highlights. "Make
more out of it. Make him a little more interesting. I feel like I'm seeing a
little blue in the lowlights, so I'm taking that out" (Figures 7.3 and 7.4).

"Okay. So now I'm going to go and do a secondary," Jannotta explains.
"I'm going to vignette, and I'm going to draw a window." Jannotta indicates the shape he wants with his hands on the monitor before using
custom shapes in Color's vignette tool to create the shape.

*What I like to do is draw the shape and then move it around so I can
see how the light is working.*

— Pete Jannotta, Filmworker's Club

The shape is vaguely triangular, but is similar to a short, wide oval. I ask why an oval wouldn't be acceptable, as it's less effort. Jannotta responds, "I always prefer to draw them; even in DaVinci, I don't use a fixed circle ever anymore. What I like to do is draw the shape and then move it around so I can see how the light is working. I don't care what the shape is, but if it's an oval, then it's fixed and I can't control it. I could do an oval, but what if I want to give his tie a little more light? If I make a user shape, then I can pull that section down, because I'll have it set up."

Fig. 7.3 Jannotta's primary correction.

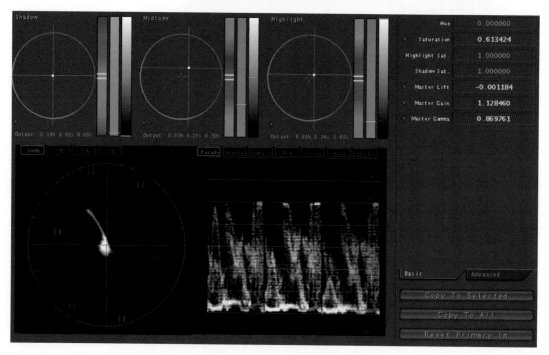

Fig. 7.4 Primary room data for Jannotta's correction.

I'm always wanting to be able to move the shape around as if you were pointing a light."

In the discussion of whether to soften vignettes before or affecting them, Jannotta falls far into the "soften first" camp. He explains, "If you get all done and you have it hard and then you feather it and you don't have what you want then you have to go back and do it anyway. That's why I soften it first, and then I decide if I want to add more softness or take some of the softness away. But I always like to see it start [with softness]" (Figures 7.5–7.7).

Fig. 7.5 Final correction with secondary vignette.

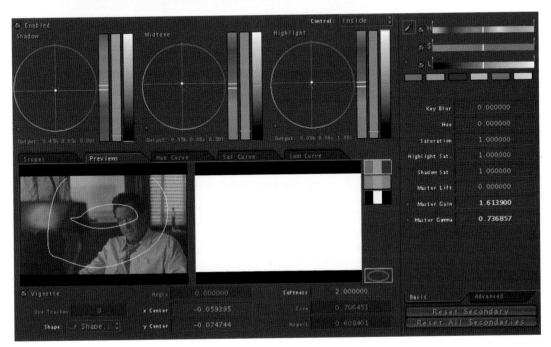

Fig. 7.6 Secondary room data for the *inside* of the vignette.

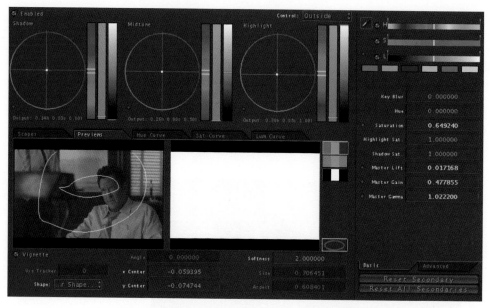

Fig. 7.7 Secondary room data for the *outside* of the vignette.

Chasing Ghosts

The footage of Sony Picture's *Chasing Ghosts* is provided courtesy of Wingman Productions, Inc., and the director of the feature, Kyle Jackson.

The story behind the movie is an interesting one. When Jackson and his producing partner, Alan Pao were looking for a company to do the DI (digital intermediate), they couldn't find anyone who would work within their deadline and budget of $125,000. So they hooked up with the DR Group in Hollywood (who coincidentally helped with equipment for this book) and they learned about a fledgling company that was doing color correction for DI on a Mac G5.

Chasing Ghosts became the first feature film to use FinalTouch2K, and when it was done and word got out about the DI for the movie, many other indie producers wanted them to do the DI for their films as well. That's when the producing/directing team decided to open a post house and start doing DIs based on their workflow for *Chasing Ghosts*. That company is called Tunnel Post, and they've parlayed their knowledge into a steady stream of work that includes features like *Machine Gun Preacher*, *Seven Days in Utopia*, and even work on *X-Men Origins: Wolverine* and *The Day the Earth Stood Still*. They've also branched out into TV work, including *Body of Proof*, *The Big C*, and *CSI: NY*.

According to Jackson, "The workflow hasn't changed a lot. On *Chasing Ghosts*, we scanned in—at an outside facility; though, since then we bought our own scanner—at 2K and then use Final Cut Film List. We wrote a simple Excel macro to translate those film lists into a text file that FinalTouch can read in and then go through the process of grading for 40, 60, 80 hours depending, while we're doing titles and effects stuff at the same time. Then we're rendering to video deliverables, and film out and web previews and trailer all at once instead of having to go through an IP [interpositive] and then video transfer and downconvert. It saves a lot of money in the end."

For more on the film's look, check out the sidebar "The Director Speaks: *Chasing Ghosts*" in Chapter 8.

Neal Kassner of CBS also graded this image. "The first thing I want to do—as my background is in painting cameras—I want to balance the blacks the white and then the mids. So the first thing I want to do is look for something dark in the frame—in this case, it's the pants over there on the left—and I'm going to move the primary color corrector around until I begin to null it out. Somewhere in there," he explains, as he works with the shadow trackball.

"Now his shirt is supposed to be white. If it helps sell the story, I might leave it a bit greenish. In my normal work, we don't want to see that green, because it's news and the object is to enhance visual reality without distorting it. So what I'm going to do in that case is to take the green out of his shirt," Kassner explains as he uses the highlight trackball to balance out the shirt.

> *Normally what I would do is I have my waveform monitor set to magnified, and it's an overlaid display, so I can watch the colors null out.*
> *– Neal Kassner, 48 Hours*

As he does this, I ask what he's watching. Kassner responds, "I'm watching the vectorscope, primarily. Normally what I would do is I have my waveform monitor set to magnified, and it's an overlaid display, so I can watch the colors null out. At this point, what I would want to do is cut between the graded image as it is now and the raw image and see where I am."

Kassner continues, "So now, what I might want to do as well is—since there's a lamp in the foreground, that's going to motivate some light in his face, so I want to brighten things up just a little bit. And this is where Power Windows [a DaVinci trademarked tool] or a mask would come in handy."

Kassner goes into secondaries and adds a small soft circle vignette over the lamp, explaining, "So I'm going to crank down the gain here, to counteract what I did to bring him up. And this obviously is a judgment call as to how much is too much. Then we go back and forth to the 'before and after' just to compare the luminance of the lamp."

After switching back and forth between his current correction and the uncorrected source, Kassner determines that he needs to soften the vignette on the lamp even more. "I don't want to go too far, because I don't want it to affect his face particularly. Now I'm going to cut back and forth between them. It's still there if you know what to look for, but if you're not doing a side-by-side comparison, it looks better. I like that. There's still a little bit of yellow left in his shirt . . . well, a little more green and yellow."

Fig. 7.8 Kassner's primary correction.

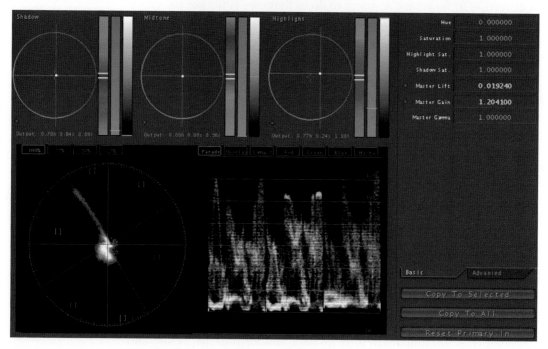

Fig. 7.9 Data from the Primary room.

Kassner chooses to fix the color on the outside of the "lamp vignette" instead of going back to primaries. "Looking mostly at the vectorscope in this case, I'm getting a little more of the green out," he says, using the highlights trackball. "It doesn't have to be pure white. And actually his skin tone is going a little bit reddish, which is not bad, but maybe a little bit too red. So what I want to do now is pick a red secondary" (Figures 7.10 and 7.11).

Fig. 7.10 This secondary brings down the light luminance inside the vignette and slightly pulls highlights away from green outside the vignette.

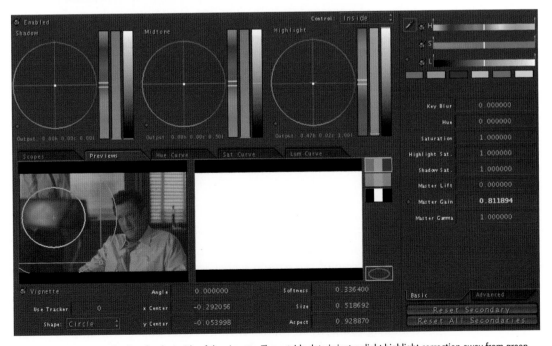

Fig. 7.11 This is just the data for the inside of the vignette. The outside data is just a slight highlight correction away from green.

Neal Kassner

Neal Kassner's first brush with fame was in college when he lit the audition reel for his classmate, Al Roker, while they attended Oswego State University in upstate New York together. After college, he worked on Richard Donner's *Superman* and Milos Forman's *Hair*.

Eventually, he was hired at ABC Television, where he matched multicamera shoots for shows like *World News Tonight* and *Nightline*. He also worked on the soaps *All My Children* and *One Life to Live* in addition to providing fill-in roadwork on *Monday Night Football*.

In 1981, he joined CBS Television and worked for 14 years as a video operator and technical director. That was when he began building towards a career in color correction, starting in 1995 with *Eye to Eye with Connie Chung* and documentaries for CBS Reports. He also graded for *Public Eye with Bryant Gumble* before starting work on *48 Hours*, where he's been ever since.

Kassner has also graded recap shows for *Survivor*, *America's Next Top Model*, and *Jericho*.

Kassner qualifies the face with a red color pick and a vignette before he rolls the midtone trackball away from red. "I just want to make his face look a little tanner" (Figures 7.12 and 7.13).

Kassner continues with a helpful tip: "I do a lot of switching between graded and ungraded. It helps you just see where you're at. Some people like to use a split screen. I find that that is not helpful to me. Because of my training as a video camera tech, you didn't have a split screen capability. You had a switcher that allowed you to cut back and forth between cameras. The quicker you cut, the more you could see a difference between the two and that's the way I grew up learning, so that's what I do here."

> *I do a lot of switching between graded and ungraded. It helps you just see where you're at. Some people like to use a split screen.*
>
> *– Neal Kassner, 48 Hours*

I ask Level 3 colorist Larry Field to take the same image in a different direction: more "straight sitcom." "Well, to do that, I'd defer to the scopes," begins Field. "Make sure the blacks are balanced. One reason I like at least one of my parade scopes expanded out is so I can really see that black balance coupled with the expanded vectorscope. Then the next thing is to neutralize the shirt and white balance and bring his shirt away from green." As he pulls the scene towards a proper balance, he seems to be looking primarily at the zoomed-in vectorscope. "I'm kind of looking at everything simultaneously. One of the bad things that happened to this

Fig. 7.12 The final correction, with the addition of a secondary to pull some redness out of the skin tones.

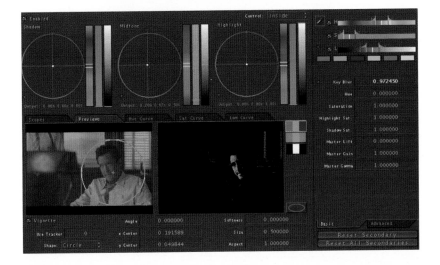

Fig. 7.13 The data for the inside of the qualification, pulling midtones slightly more yellow.

shot as I corrected it was that the background started going magenta, which is natural as I'm trying to bring his shirt from green. If we need to neutralize the shot, I can then affect that area separately if I need to. And everything's interactive somewhat, so I'm looking at all my scopes at one time."

I ask him about his use of the RGB Parade scopes in trying to achieve color balance. "I'm looking at RGB. I'm also looking at black in the middle of the vectorscope—as well as white—and also separation on the chroma side of the split waveform but again: all at one time" (Figures 7.14 and 7.15).

> *One reason I like at least one of my Parade scopes expanded out is so I can really see that black balance coupled with the expanded vectorscope.*
>
> *– Larry Field, Level 3 Post*

Fig. 7.14 This image was recreated by watching the videotaped session with Field and re-executing the grade. This is the primary correction.

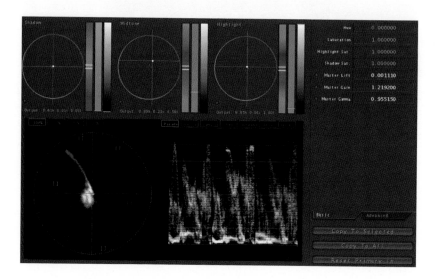

Fig. 7.15 Rcreated data from the Primary room.

Field is not happy with his correction yet, as it's veering toward magenta. Instead of continuing with the correction, I ask him to simply explain what he would do next. "I think it's that window up there where you can see things are going magenta," Field mentions as he points to the vectorscope. "That looks pretty hot up there, so I'd put a key on that," he explains, pointing at the window over the talent's left shoulder. "Then I'd bring it to neutral. Or I can use the Power Window with a soft edge. Or I could put a Power Window over his shirt and white balance the window out. A few different techniques, all of which would work" (Figures 7.16–7.19).

Encore's Pankaj Bajpai demonstrates another approach. "With this image, I would probably use a preset curve that desaturates and gives me higher contrast very quickly. I do use a lot of presets. This is a cocktail of elements I created" (Figures 7.20 and 7.21).

Fig. 7.16 This is my grade following Field's suggestion to pull a key on the window (and shirt), eliminating even more of the green, then adding a garbage matte to the HSL qualification to bring the windows down in master gain.

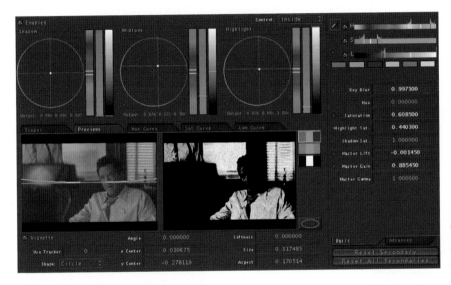

Fig. 7.17 Here's the Secondary room data on the inside of the HSL qualification, plus a garbage matte on the windows.

I point out that Festa is also unapologetic about his use of presets. "Exactly, I designed them. There's no sense doing that work over and over—and I wouldn't be able to get through the volume of work I have without using them," Bajpai continues, though he is quick to point out that he is working without the context of the story.

Bajpai narrates, "I can see that there is this nice mica feel to the picture and again I'm thinking of the light source now. And I'm looking at the window. With light coming in through the window, I'm going to enhance what they have already shot, I'm going to go in and use a mask [Figure 7.21], and it also allows me to go outside of that and create that three-dimensional depth. I don't like losing texture." He also adds a mask around the banker's light to bring that element down (Figures 7.22–7.24).

Fig. 7.18 A secondary with a vignette to pop his face out of the background.

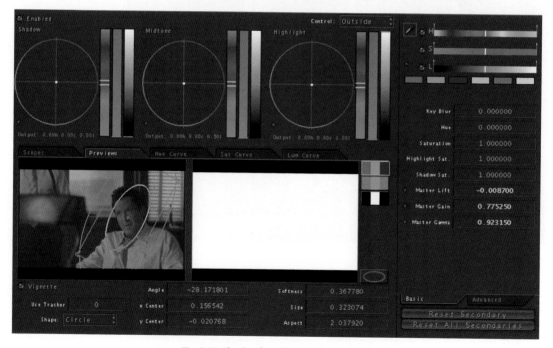

Fig. 7.19 The data from the second secondary.

Saving a Shot with Bad Color Cast

Neal Kassner, colorist for CBS's *48 Hours* was drawn to the challenge of the "flowerbench" scene (Figure 7.25).

"Obviously, it's very washed out and it's very green. There's some whites there. There's actually some blacks as well. So I'm going to crank down the black level and then bring the gammas down a little bit as well.

Fig. 7.20 A preset curve adds contrast and lowers saturation.

Fig. 7.21 Organic-shaped mask shapes the light coming in from window.

There's a lot of green in the blacks there, so I'm using the primary color corrector and watching the vectorscope to a certain extent, I'm just going to walk this in."

By using the phrase "walk this in," I assumed he was using the vectorscope to get the blacks into the middle. Kassner responds, "Well, kind of. That's what I started to do, but the foliage in the shadow areas is not really, truly black. There's still supposed to be a green cast to it, so now I'm going to go by eye until it looks a little bit better. Then maybe bring down the master blacks again. Now I can attack the whites. There's a nice, big, fat, white post there that I can use to get a white balance on, essentially." Kassner looks at the standard composite waveform monitor and watches as the trace that represents that white area "compresses," indicating that it is getting more neutral. Check out the "Kassner's Balancing Tricks" sidebar for more on this technique.

*It's all interactive;, whatever you do in one area may affect the others,
so I'm going to go back and tighten up the whites.*

– Neal Kassner, 48 Hours

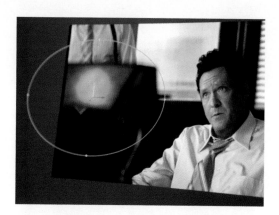

Fig. 7.22 Mask on
banker's light.

Fig. 7.23 Starting point.
(taken from Bajpai's com-
puter monitor with a DSLR).

Fig. 7.24 Finished grade.
(taken from Bajpai's com-
puter monitor with a DSLR).

Mike Most

Mike Most started as a tape op in Los Angeles in 1978 and graduated to working tele-cine and post at Lorimar Television, working on shows such as *Dallas*. He moved on to Encore Video as colorist for shows like *L.A. Law* and *NYPD Blue*. He left color correction for a while to supervise visual effects (VFX) on such TV shows as *Ally McBeal* and *Without a Trace*. Now he works at Next Element by Deluxe, grading shows such as *Covert Affairs* and *The Gates*.

Fig. 7.25

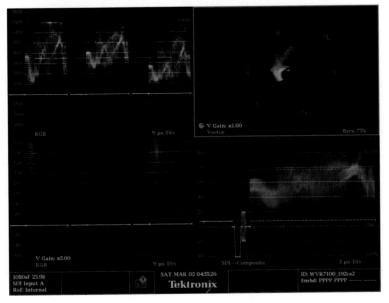

Fig. 7.26 Tektronix WVR7100 screengrab. Upper left: RGB Parade. Upper right: vectorscope. Lower left: RGB Parade expanded to show black level. Lower right: composite waveform.

Fig. 7.27 Kassner's final correction.

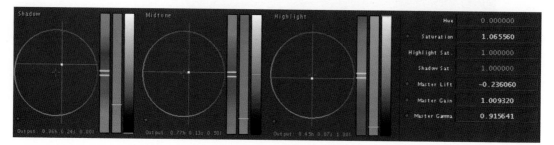

Fig. 7.28 Data from the Primary room.

Kassner's Balancing Tricks

One of Neal Kassner's favorite tricks for balancing whites and blacks was developed long before he became a colorist. His previous career involved "shading" cameras for multicamera shoots. That practice is similar to color correction but takes place with multiple live cameras *before* the shoot—and continues to some extent *during* the shoot.

Kassner blows up the composite waveform *horizontally* to five times normal zoom. Then he positions the waveform so that he can see an area of the screen that he believes has white or black in it. A composite waveform in flat pass mode—or YC waveform—not only purely displays luminance values but reflects chroma as well, which is represented by the excursion of the trace. What does that mean? Well, if the line that represents black or white is thick, then there's chroma or color in it. If the line is as narrow as you can get it, then the color has been eliminated.

Kassner expounds on this idea with another one of his tricks for balancing shots. "Now here's a cheat that I use and I don't think anyone else uses it. In the DaVinci, I use a Power Window to isolate the black or white areas of the picture. So if I make a Power Window and center it over a black area of the picture, I get a truly black area in the shadows. Then, by repositioning the window to a white area, I can do the same kind of thing. So now I've got a rough white and black balance. From there, I can trim as necessary. Isolating that helps, because sometimes in the waveform display, the area that you're trying to sample just gets lost in everything else that's in there. It's hard to separate out a white shirt against a blown-out sky."

This trick is possible in Color by going into the Geometry room and zooming into an area you believe represents white or black. With the overlay waveform monitor active—or, better yet, an external composite waveform in flat pass mode—adjust the highlights or shadows to flatten the trace as much as possible. This can be done with the hue offset wheels or with the red, green, and blue channel controls in the Advanced tab.

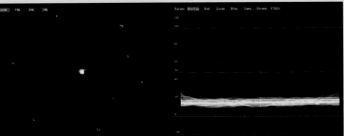

Fig. 7.29

"Now I'm going to bring up the gain in there because that's the hottest thing in the picture. This has also altered the color cast of everything else. It's actually made things a little more yellow. So, I'm going to back that off in the blacks. I'm going to do this by eye instead of by the scope, because this is one of those places where you could do it via the scope, but you're going to end up with an uninteresting looking picture. So I'm just going to play around with it until I see something that looks good. Now I'm playing with the gammas just to kind of even out the midtones a little bit because they were still a little bit yellow-looking. Now I want to increase the overall saturation. The magenta really pops. And maybe just bring down the overall gamma a little bit to make it pop a little bit more. Now, of course, it's all interactive; whatever you do in one area may affect the others, so I'm going to go back and tighten up the whites. So this is where a magnified H display would really help me dial that in nice and tight. But that's close enough for here" (Figures 7.27 and 7.28).

Four Trips Down the "Alley"

I call this scene the "Chasing Ghosts alleyway" shot (Figure 7.30). What follows on the next few pages are four different colorists' takes on this same shot. Actually, almost all of the colorists who took part in the book

Fig. 7.30

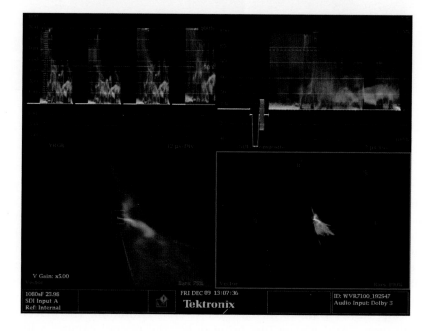

Fig. 7.31 Tektronix
WVR7100 screengrab.
Upper left: YRGB Parade.
Upper right: composite
waveform. Lower left:
vectorscope expanded 5x.
Lower right: standard zoom
on vectorscope.

took a shot at this image, but the four who were the most descriptive about what they were doing as they corrected it were Chris Pepperman, Neal Kassner, Greg Creaser, and Mike Most.

We'll start out with Kassner's grade. As usual, the colorists want some kind of storyline or reference about how they should be grading. But I asked them to grade it the way they saw fit. "The hair in the lower left edge of the frame is blue, so I'm going to eliminate some of that blue. This is by looking at the vectorscope and the picture monitor. If I go too far, it starts to turn a little bit reddish, and if I start to go too far the other way, it starts going magenta. What I would do here, then, even though he's in shade, I'd bring him up a little bit, just so he reads a little better on the screen. And then with the gammas—gammas are your friend, I have found—you can do a lot of things in gammas where you might contaminate the picture too much using highlights and lowlights. Gammas are good for skin tones, I find. I'm trying to get it natural here. I'm not going for a 'look.' So, maybe I went too far there, because now it doesn't look so shady, so I'm going to back off the red in the gamma. Cool it off just a little bit. Somewhere between where it was originally and where I went. Some place, kind of a compromise, because he is in shade."

Gammas are your friend, I have found.

– Neal Kassner, CBS

As you can see, the idea that you need to take a correction *past* where it should go to see where it really wants to end up is a common thread among all of the colorists (Figures 7.32 and 7.33).

Fig. 7.32 **Kassner's primary correction**

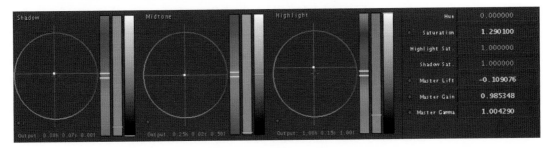

Fig. 7.33 **Data from Primary room**

Kassner reinforces my common analogy of focusing a camera to making grading adjustments. You would never look in a manual-focus camera viewfinder and just leave the focus where it was, even if it looked in focus. You would move the focus ring a bit in each direction in order to find the sweet spot for the focus. This is exactly the approach to take when grading: go too far in each direction to help establish where the correction really wants to "sit." As I sat in with Bob Festa at New Hat, he put his own unique spin on this concept, providing the adage: "You don't know if you don't go." I loved the simplicity and memorable rhyme of this. Put another way: you can't tell if you've gone far enough until you've gone too far.

> *You don't know if you don't go.*
>
> *– Bob Festa, New Hat*

NFL Films' Chris "Pep" Pepperman takes the next shot at the scene. "When I look at something like this, what comes to my mind is that it's definitely a flat light. There's some clipped areas in the building that regardless of what we do we're not going to bring back, simply because that's the way it is on tape. I'll explain that to the client. But I won't necessarily say that right away because I don't want to start right off the bat by saying, 'Well, I can't do this.' Mostly I try to say 'I can, I can, I can.' And if I can't do it, I'll say 'I can' . . . slowly," Pep jokes.

> *If I can't do it, I'll say "I can" . . . slowly.*
>
> *– Chris Pepperman, NASCAR*

"Right now, I'm bringing the blacks down to 0 and I want to bring the video level completely out of clip." Pepperman uses the term "video" or "video level" throughout his session, referring to gain or highlights. He points at the RGB waveform monitor as he lowers the gain. Then he continues, "I'm assuming I'm out of the clip now. What I'm saying is that I'm not electronically clipping it. And once I establish that I'm not, I'm going to come back up a little bit. Now, I'm a little flatter than what I want to be. But I don't want to clip anything now because I want to be sure my reds, greens, and blues are balanced. Now—just by looking at the picture—take the overall video and peds and start to swing that on the warmer side. And as I do that, I'm liking what I see."

As Pepperman sets the levels, he's careful to keep the video levels just under 100IRE. "We clip at 100 percent here," he explains. "At Manhattan Transfer, we used to clip at 103 or 104 percent. Some colorists like to see all of the detail that's in the film element. I like to see what's important, what's relative in the film. Meaning, if something looks good to me and the background's clipped out, then I don't care about the background clipping out. I care about somebody saying, 'That's visually pleasing to me.' And that's what film is about. As far as I'm concerned, that's the beauty of film, being able to do those things. And that's where the art of color correction is different. I always try to look at the picture, interpret what's the most important part of the picture in that image—especially when it's commercial work and I want your eye to go there.

"For me, what is this picture all about? It's all about him talking. So visually, as you're watching this, you're not going to be watching the background. You're not going to be looking at the building. You're going to be looking at him. So let's make him the subject. Let's make him the priority. Let's make him look good. Whatever happens in the background happens. Now with the tools we have, I balance him, make him look good, *then* I work on the things that surround him. So I start with the primary subject and then I work my way around the picture and decide what else is important to me. So right now, all I'm concerned about is him. Right now, I want to make him look good. So now I'm going to start to brighten him up again and I'm going to start adding some warmth, because I still feel that it's cooler."

> *So I start with the primary subject and then I work my way around the picture and decide what else is important to me.*
> *– Chris Pepperman, NASCAR*

"Now I feel like the warmth in the midrange would help. As I'm looking at this, I'm starting to see red in the blacks, so I don't want to bleed too much, but I like the skin tone in him." At this point, Pepperman cuts back and forth between the current correction and the original source footage.

Pleased with his progress, he continues, "Now, I'm taking into consideration the fact that he's in a shadowed area. So you're not going to want it to be real bright. I typically don't use high and low sat. Only when I'm dealing with very rough film. What I mean is very underexposed or overexposed, cause sometimes I feel like I have to add warmth overall to the picture, but sometimes it affects the peds. So then I have to clean the peds up, so that's when I use that tool. But primarily, I wouldn't use that (Figures 7.34 and 7.35).

"So, here's where it becomes subjective. If a DP wants it on the cooler side, I'd add more coolness. If he wanted it warmer, I'd add some warmth. But I would like this a little bit on the warm/neutral side (Figure 7.34). The

Definition

sat: A common abbreviation for saturation, especially when describing the application's controls for saturation. "I lowered the high sat so the clouds would go white."

peds: A common abbreviation for pedestal or blacks.

Fig. 7.34 Pepperman's primary correction.

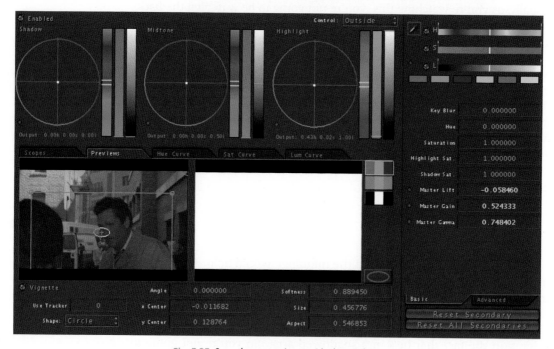

Fig. 7.35 Secondary correction outside the window.

second thing that I would do is isolate about three-quarters of the picture. I would build a window around him and her and knock the background down. Because what I want to do is bring that clip down and I also want to add some depth, some midrange to the building in the back, and try to give it a little more guts. The background I would consider as thin and I want to try to help that out. The way I would do that . . . well, there are a couple of ways, but the easiest way for me quickly is just to build a window around

Fig. 7.36 Secondary to lower highlights on bricks in upper left of picture.

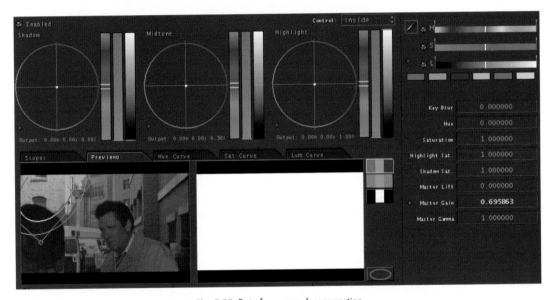

Fig. 7.37 Data from secondary correction.

him, grab the outside of that window, and start coming down see what would happen. So I'm going to position the circle around him and her and soften it. Now I want to affect the outside of the window" (Figure 7.35).

In the continuing saga of correcting with sharp or softened edges on vignettes, Pepperman lands in the "keep it sharp so I can see it" camp. "All I'm doing right now is going down as far as I can to see what the background looks like (Figures 7.36 and 7.37). I'm liking what I see, because it's bringing those subtle details. I like the coolness temperature on the building. I like the fact that the midrange is really helping it out. I like the fact that I'm seeing the areas of the picture that were clipped before.

I would typically build a circle just about where it is right now. I tend to go a little deeper with my shapes as far as overall correction, and as I soften it, I'll make the decision of whether I need to add something or take something out. So what I'm going to do now is I'm going to go back inside the circle. I just want to clean up the black areas a little bit."

Pepperman lowers the low saturation setting inside the window as he explains his change from his earlier stance, "I typically wouldn't use low sat or high sat here, because you can build yourself into a corner. Because what happens with a DaVinci is that the color correction that you apply to the scene will go to the next scene. I just don't like painting myself in a corner that way."

> *I want to go to the point where I don't see emulsion anymore, what we consider emulsion in the blacks, but I still see detail.*
> *– Chris Pepperman, NFL Films*

Finally, he softens the edge of the vignette and moves it up a bit from where it had been. "Now I want to go inside the circle and increase the video (highlights) a little bit. And I want to come up on the peds (blacks) a tad. I want to go to the point where I don't see emulsion anymore, what we consider emulsion in the blacks, but I still see detail."

Next, industry veteran Mike Most of Miami's Cineworks Digital Studios, takes on the "alley" scene: "The whole thing is timed a little cool for my tastes, so once again I'll go through my usual. And I'll look and see if there's anything that warrants being white, and in this case it probably does. In this case, I wouldn't be afraid to let some of the white areas clip. Normally, you try to hold those in check if you can. But in point of fact, the grayscale of this—if I start pulling it up, the picture just looks flat, so I probably want it down where it was and yet I want his face to look right. So I can do that either with a window, or more likely, I'll do it by just clipping the white areas and then fixing the flesh tone a little bit. The reason I prefer to do it that way is simply because it gives me a little more kick. I mean, he's clearly in a shadow anyway, so you don't want him too bright. But there's nothing up there that you need to see, so I would just kind of let it go," Most states as he points to the sky in the top left of the picture.

Mike Most

Mike Most has an extensive background in both color correction and visual effects. His color correction credits include *L.A. Law*, *Murder One*, and *NYPD Blue*. He has also served as visual effects supervisor for shows like *Ally McBeal* and *Charmed*.

Currently, he supervises visual effects at Miami's Cineworks Digital Studios.

Now Most leaves the Primary room to hone in on the flesh tones.

Joining me at the session with Most was Roland Wood, founder of FinalTouch, which later became Apple's Color. *Chasing Ghosts* was the first feature graded on FinalTouch, and Wood used the footage to do demos and training with hundreds of colorists around the world. He was impressed by Most's correction (Figure 7.38), saying, "That's the best correction I've ever seen on that shot. And I've seen this shot done a lot."

Most takes the compliment with typical modesty, "Well, you notice that I haven't used any windows. I tend to use windows for two reasons: I have a real problem. I have a blown-out sky or a blown-out window. Something very specific. Or creatively, like I did in the other shot, where it was clear that to emphasize where the key was hitting and to emphasize the shadows would improve the shot. But on something like this, I know guys who would try to do a window around the hot area."

Greg Creaser, an LA freelance colorist who specializes in grading DIs, shows his take on the "alley" scene as well.

Fig. 7.38 Most's final correction.

Fig. 7.39 Source scene from *Chasing Ghosts* courtesy Wingman Productions, Inc.

I'm attacking the midtones again right away because it's an opened-up image.

– Greg Creaser, freelance colorist

"I'm attacking the midtones again right away because it's an opened-up image. I mean there's a lot of range in there. Midtones are going to be fine for the brunt of it. He's looking a little cool to me. Let's give him a little more flesh tone back somewhere in there. The highlights may be a little bit hot. There's a couple ways to attack that. We could pull them down here," he says, referring to the highlights in primaries. "Then pull the mids back up. Not much we can do with that hotspot. That would be another key situation. Or you maybe wanna throw a shape in there to knock it down if your eye is getting drawn to it. If we wanna little more bite in there, we can dip the blacks a little bit more. I think this image can handle it. Bring the mids back up just a little bit.

"Now let's check out before and after. It's just kind of normalized. I'd like to see a little more bite to the image, but I'd be a little afraid of the hair going away. Sometimes, if I'm grading a film [for DI], I'd use a pixel picker to see where we were in our 10-bit data. Since we're working in HD, I would leave it where it is or we'll get ghosting in the blacks, which is what would happen if you force it too far. I like it."

Creaser cuts back and forth between the source and his correction. "We lessened the contrast just a little bit and gave it a normal look. They're in the shadow, so they wouldn't have a lot of contrast here" (Figures 7.40 and 7.41).

When you're working on film, you can be a little more bold on things. But if you're working in 8-bit video, you have to watch it.

– Greg Creaser, freelance colorist

I ask Creaser what clues or hints that he's seeing in the picture to decide what an image should look like. He responds. "He's in the shadow, even though he's lit, of course. It'd be flat light because he's not getting any kick from highlight of the sun. So the first place to attack this would be lessening the contrast, because I felt it to be a little bit too much in the original. It doesn't look correct that way. I mean, if you were standing there looking at this guy, would it be that contrasty? I don't think so. So you back it out just a little bit and it looks a little more natural. And we didn't kill it and we took the blue out. When you're working on film, you can be a little more bold on things. But if you're working in 8-bit video, you have to watch it."

Fig. 7.40 Creaser's final correction.

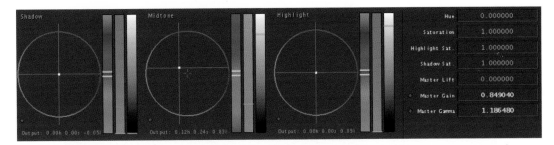

Fig. 7.41 FinalTouch UI data for correction.

Three Passes Over the Barn

Three colorists approach Randy Riesen's documentary scene of an ultra-light flying over a barn (Figure 7.42).

First up on this video-originated scene is Mike Matusek of Nolo Digital Film. "I guess there's two approaches to this shot. What I would do

Fig. 7.42 Image courtesy Randy Riesen.

Randy Riesen

It's a brave thing for any good cameraman to offer their stuff up to be color corrected in front of the world. Luckily, Riesen is confident enough of his considerable skills with a camera to allow me to go through hours and hours of his personal footage looking for a few seconds of less-than-perfect footage.

Randy Riesen has shot in Chicago for more than two decades now. In addition to shooting numerous music videos for bands like the Smashing Pumpkins and the John Mathie Band, and serving as DP for countless documentary projects, he has also racked up an impressive number of credits shooting for more than 25 of the country's top national shows, including *Investigative Reports with Bill Kurtis*, *Entertainment Tonight*, *America's Most Wanted*, *The Daily Show with Jon*, and *The Jane Pauley Show*. He has also shot spots for Leo Burnett and Twitch Films.

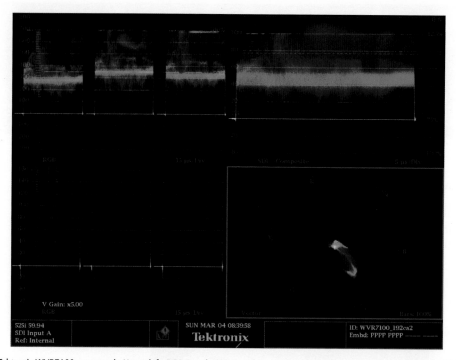

Fig. 7.43 Tektronix WVR7100 screengrab. Upper left: RGB Parade. Upper right: composite waveform. Lower left: expanded RGB Parade to see black balance. Lower right: standard vectorscope.

here, because I like the highlights on the barn, is to warm it up and give it a golden hour kind of look (Figures 7.44 and 7.45). Again, since golden hour is more about the highlights being golden, I'm going to go to the gain controls because right now they're kind of bluish-white. At golden hour, there's much more contrast between the shadows and the

Fig. 7.44 Primary color correction, imparting a "golden hour" look.

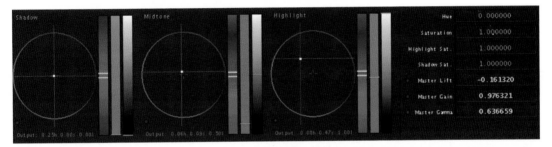

Fig. 7.45 Primary room data.

highlights, so I might crush the blacks a little bit. When you crush the blacks, you're saturating the blacks. When you increase the gain, you're saturating the highlights, which is good for this image because it's washed out." However, with most images, this increased saturation is something that you would need to counteract, especially when dealing with footage that requires extreme changes of blacks or gain.

At golden hour there's much more contrast between the shadows and the highlights.

– Mike Matusek, Nolo Digital Film

"So now what I would try to do is grab these highlights individually, because I'm trying to push more warmth into the highlights, and what I'm doing is whacking out the midtones a little bit, and they're getting a little too yellow and ugly, so I'd probably grab those [the whites of the buildings], blur them, and get that magenta out of there" (Figures 7.46 and 7.47).

Fig. 7.46 Secondary correction to move highlights away from pink.

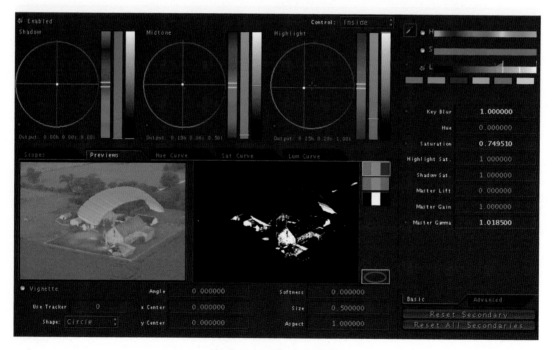

Fig. 7.47 Secondary room data.

At this point, Matusek enables a secondary and pulls an HSL key on the building façades. "So instead of pushing artificial warmth into it, I'll desaturate it a little bit and warm it up like that. So it goes from that pink to a little more white, but there's still some warmth in the highlights. It looks a lot more lush than it was," he concludes.

Mike Most takes the next shot at the "barn" scene. He explains his approach: "Usually when I'm tackling a shot that I know to have all kinds of problems, I try to give myself something to latch on to. I mean, I'm seeing dark shadows in the trees that I can probably boost the contrast of a little bit. I'm seeing white on a barn that I can try and grab, and it's also on the parachute a little bit. So I'm going to try to use that for a rough white balance. I'm seeing green on the bottom that I probably can't get through primaries alone, so I'll try to get that through secondaries. And once again, boosting contrast will help me separation-wise. You don't want to go too far on your whites, because you're just throwing away detail and ultimately you're going to need some of that detail. Crushing the gammas a little bit would not be a bad thing. There's going to be a little bit of green in the blacks. If you look at the Parade display, that's exactly what I have."

I notice that although he'd pulled the blacks down quite a bit to increase contrast, he brought them back up a bit after looking at the RGB parade. Most explains his change of heart, "Yeah. You play. You don't always know exactly where you're going to go. Sometimes you do, but sometimes you don't. You see what you've got and then you figure out what you want to do. So in terms of my starting point, I'm pretty much there" (Figures 7.48 and 7.49).

With his primary correction complete, he moves to secondaries, explaining, "I'll try to pull something that's green here. What you see as green isn't always green. I mean, it's more yellow than green, but what I'm going to try to do is find the center of most of the grass and trees." Most qualifies a green area that mostly selects the trees behind the barn,

Fig. 7.48 Most's primary correction.

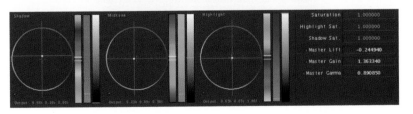

Fig. 7.49 Data from primary room. Original FinalTouch grades brought in to Color for screengrabs.

then adds a little key blur before starting his adjustment of the qualified area. "I'll try boosting the saturation to the keyed area then I'll try swinging the hue around. See what it gets me, if anything. Swinging it away from yellow. At that point, you can go back to the primaries because you've got the secondary on. If you increase that towards yellow, you're going to get more green because you've got a secondary working on top of it. Like I say, it's all about separation and contrast, so now I've got something that may not be the kickiest-looking picture in the world, but it's a lot better than what I started with" (Figures 7.50 and 7.51).

> *It's all about separation and contrast.*
>
> — *Mike Most, Cineworks Miami*

Most talks through his other options. "The other thing I might do is go into another secondary—I hate using multiple secondaries. I honestly do, because I think it's a crutch. I think you've got to get things separated by balance before you start going into secondaries, but when you've got

Fig. 7.50 Secondary correction of the foliage.

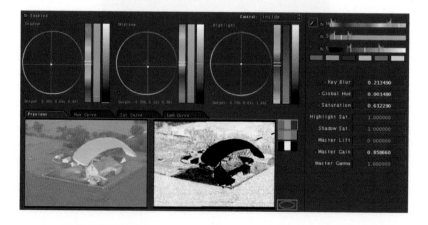

Fig. 7.51 Data from the Secondary room.

something like this that had so little contrast on the original and so many colors as a result that are overlapping each other, that's about the only excuse I can think of for using multiple secondaries. And so what I would probably do here is try to go in and grab another secondary and maybe start with a cyan grab on the parachute and see what happens. Try and separate out the parachute completely, so that I'm only working on the parachute." Most qualifies a beautiful secondary, isolating the parachute. "Right in there seems to get it. Blur the key a little bit. Then what I can do is try and swing that away from the greenish/cyan back towards a blue. It just makes it stand out more. Not sure I can do much with the saturation, but I probably can in the primaries, now that I have it separated. Once again swinging it more towards a pure blue than the cyanish-blue that we were getting before. That creates separation" (Figure 7.52).

Fig. 7.52 Secondary correction of the parachute.

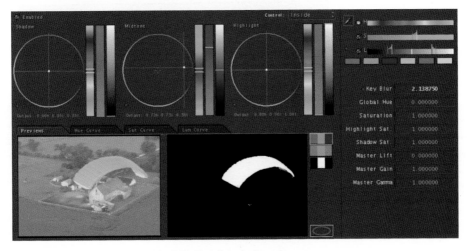

Fig. 7.53 Data from the Secondary room.

Bob Sliga also takes a pass at this image. Before Sliga starts to balance out the image, I ask if he likes to use the expanded, or zoomed, RGB Parade waveform display that so many of the other colorists liked to use when balancing blacks. "No. I use the vectorscope for that. I mean, you can. Every person does it a little differently. But it gives me the ability to see what I need to see here," he explains, pointing at the center of the vectorscope, which has been zoomed in four times. "I'm looking for a nice tight ball there. That gets me where black is black, but we're still so far blue balanced," he says, looking at the shadows of trees above the farm.

"Now I'm going to richen this up something like that," he says as he lowers the gamma and then warms it up. Then he pulls blue out of highlights and touches on the shadows briefly. "I time more on the richer side—little heftier blacks, heavier gammas, just to give you more pop through it. Letting the highlights blow out. It's just the theory that if you don't like that, it's very easy to time back" (Figures 7.54 and 7.55).

At this point, Sliga goes to Sat Curve in Color's Secondary room and cranks up the green point. "You'll see that the green and yellow secondary color correction will blend together."

Fig. 7.54 Primary correction only.

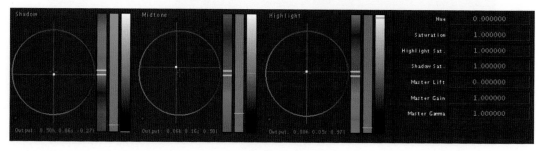

Fig. 7.55 Data from Primary room.

Because not everyone has access to Color's Sat Curve tool, I ask Sliga to walk me through doing the correction with it. In response to the challenge, Sliga creates a qualification based on green that picks the grass and trees. "Once we have that qualification, we aren't limited to anything. We can change the gain, the gamma. Very powerful." Sliga makes the grass a nice green color before adding, "And now let's go outside and if we want to make it more contrasty." Sliga brings the gain up outside of his green qualification before showing us the difference his secondary correction makes (Figures 7.56 and 7.57).

Fig. 7.56 Secondary correction on foliage.

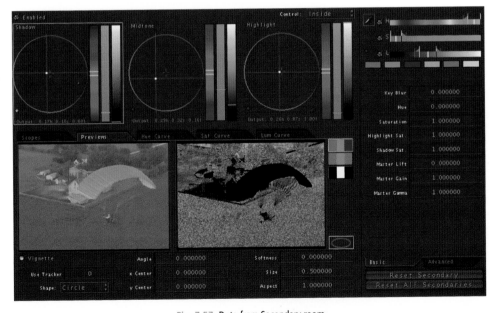

Fig. 7.57 Data from Secondary room.

Sliga's original Sat Curve alteration essentially selected a green color along a color bar with the entire range of hues, then allowed him to raise or lower the saturation of just that "vector" or hue. The other curves in Color's Secondary room work similarly, but instead of raising or lowering saturation, the Hue curve allows a specific hue to be "swung" to a different hue, and the Luma curve allows you to raise or lower the luminance of a specific hue.

Sliga also pulls a qualification on the parachute wing for a final tweak (Figures 7.58 and 7.59).

Fig. 7.58 Secondary correction on parachute.

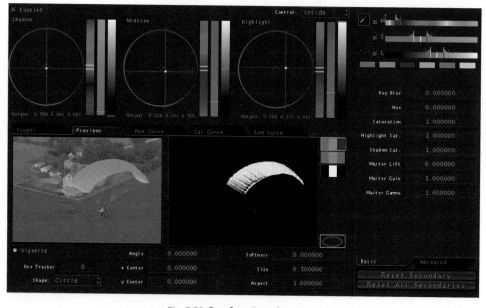

Fig. 7.59 Data from Secondary room.

Building Up a Weak Piece of Video

Figure 7.60 is an image that I should be embarrassed to have shot. It was done as a "one-man-band" interview for a documentary I produced about my family's 1977 bicycle trip across the United States. The subject is my brother Brian. It was shot around 1995 on BetaSP.

We will be returning to this shot in Chapter 9, because this interview started in bright daylight and went into twilight. So in that chapter, we'll

Fig. 7.60 Original image from naturally lit BetaSP footage.

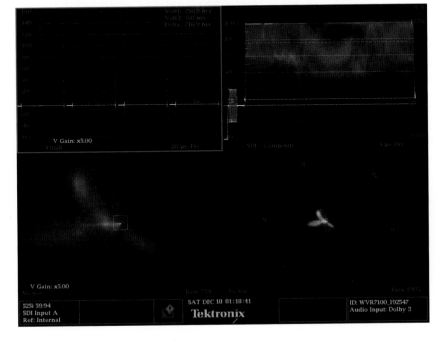

Fig. 7.61 Tektronix WVR7100. Upper left: RGB Parade zoomed 5x to show blacks. Upper right: composite waveform. Lower left: vectorscope zoomed 5x. Lower left: vectorscope.

discuss how to match the interview footage from earlier in the day to the footage shot near dusk.

For this chapter, though, Chris Pepperman tries to turn the washed out footage into something broadcastable. "The first thing I'm going to do is take the blacks and the mids and start crushing at the same time. So the midrange is going to give you all the facial tones."

I tried to gauge how low Pep would take the blacks and mids, asking him, "So you're taking it down until you see some noise that you don't like, then you stop?"

"Exactly," he confirmed. "When it gets too crushed. Right there, it's too crushed. So now I'm going to bring the midrange up a little bit to where I like it. Right there. And I'm going to bring the black levels back up to where I like it . . . right there."

As Pep takes the blacks and mids from one extreme past the proper point and back into a comfortable range, he follows the same "focusing" analogy that I've espoused in previous chapters. "Now I've got to balance. I'm going to overall balance the image. And what I'm doing is looking at the vector and the waveform and I'm touching the peds, the gammas, and the video and I'm just balancing everything." As he gets closer to what he wants, his eyes move from the scopes back to the picture monitor as he tries to find a pleasing skin tone. "I'm seeing that it's still a little blocked up now, so I'm going to come up on the peds." He confirms that by "blocked up," he mean that the blacks are too dark. "So now I'm coming up so I can see all of his hair." Pep's visual clue that the blacks were blocking up came when the hair above Brian's forehead started to lose detail. "I'm looking at the front lock of hair. I'm not looking at his eyes, because his eyes are going to be darker. He's not getting fill light into his eyes, so if I were to bring up his eyes, everything else is going to go. Like his eyes are good there, but it's too flat. So I'm looking at his hair, his eyebrows, and that tree in the back. So I'm kind of liking where that is right now. I'm also liking overall balance. I might warm it up a tad in the skin tone." He cuts back and forth between the original and his current correction. "So we're seeing a significant difference (Figure 7.62). Now let's get into the nitty gritty."

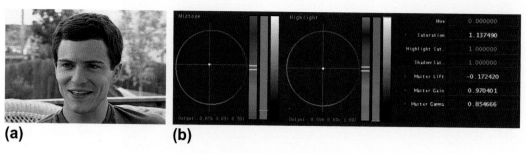

(a)   **(b)**

Fig. 7.62 a) Pepperman's Primary correction.
b) Data from Primary room.

Leaving the Primary room, Pep creates a secondary and enables a vignette, creating a tall oval shape around the subject's face. "Now I'm going to go outside and I want to crush just the midrange and the blacks, leaving the highlights alone right now. And now bringing the highlights down a little bit to where I can see detail in everything. Now I'm going to bring the midrange down, down, down. Now I'm going to bring the black levels up. I'm just seeing . . . it's a feel, you know?"

Always going past the sweet point and then coming back. It's like rack focusing. You have to go past, so you know to come back.
– Chris Pepperman, NASCAR

As I watch Pep dial in his correction, I assume that one of the signposts he's using is the amount of "grit" and noise that begins to appear in the trees. "That's exactly what I'm trying to do. I don't want to see any noise yet, but I want to see detail. And I want your eye to go toward him, obviously. I'm just playing around with the background right now so I don't get any noise. And now I'm just cranking down the video levels, and I'm cranking down the blacks too. I really like that. So what I want to do is now is just open my window [vignette] a tad, move it down, and soften it." His vignette almost perfectly describes the subject's face, hair, and neck. "Now I love it (Figure 7.63). The only thing that's bothering me is the sky. The sky looks like it was clipped and brought down. It doesn't look natural to me. So all I'm going to do is stay on the outside and brighten up the gain a little bit until it starts to look natural. Just about there, so it looks like a bright day and it doesn't look like it's clipped and brought down. It's bright back there, so it's going to clip. *Let it clip!* Take it up to 100. Maybe even a tad bit more. Now the last thing I'm going to do is go back inside and just bring up the blacks, because I want to see where I have them. Then I want to bring them back down to right about here."

Pep and I discuss the boundaries he was reaching as he tried to determine the black level. On the low side, the blacks were creating "grittiness" and noise, but when he brought them up, the blacks became muddy. "That's when I brought it back down," he explains. "Always going past the sweet point and then coming back. It's like rack focusing. You have to go past, so you know to come back. Same thing here applies. Once again, if I was to do anything else here, I might go back to primary and try overall saturation and add just a tiny bit."

Fig. 7.63 Pepperman's Secondary correction, bringing out the face.

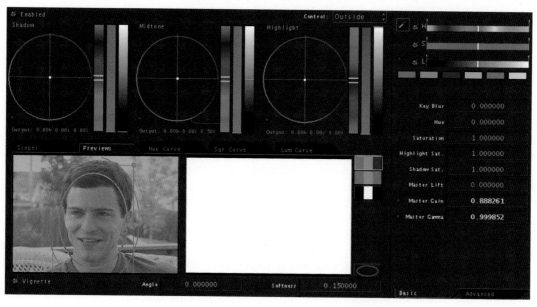

Fig. 7.64 Data from the outside of the Secondary vignette.

Using Many Tools to Fix a Shot

Using another of Randy Riesen's ultralight documentary images
(Figure 7.65), Bob Sliga uses just about every tool in the shed to tweak a
shot that isn't bad to begin with. Before taking too many clues from this
experienced Color operator and veteran colorist, you may want to take

Fig. 7.65 Source image
courtesy Randy Riesen.

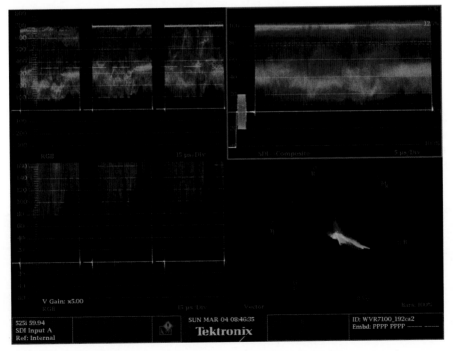

Fig. 7.66 Tecktronix WVR7100 screengrab. Upper left: RGB Parade. Upper right: composite waveform. Lower right: vectorscope. Lower left:
RGB Parade expanded to see black balance.

another look at the sidebar "Thinking about the Budget" from the end of Chapter 2.

To begin his correction, Sliga checks the highlights to see if there's anything that he can "unclip." He decides that there's not much that can be done to rescue detail in the highlights, so he starts balancing the blacks in the image using the shadow trackball on the Tangent Devices control panel. After balancing them, he takes the blacks down to around 0IRE before he warms up the gammas using the red channel gamma level adjustment in the Primary Room Advanced tab. Then he brings the reds in the blacks down again using the red channel lift slider to compensate for the interaction with the gamma adjustment (Figure 7.67).

With the image in the ballpark, Sliga moves to secondary corrections. But for Sliga, his use of secondaries at this point is more closely akin to another layer of primary correction, because he doesn't qualify anything before he starts tweaking. "This jacket has a nice little highlight of blue on it, so I want to keep that. We're going to use that to our advantage a little later."

Fig. 7.67 Sliga's primary correction is minimal due to his workflow of using secondaries as additional layers of primaries.

Fig. 7.68 Data from Primary room. Note the information under the wheels and that he did some corrections in the Advanced tab with individual color channels.

"We're gonna richen this up," Sliga states as he pulls down the gammas, "and warm this up a little" (Figures 7.69 and 7.70).

Sliga attempts to "green" the grass a little bit using the Hue curve, but undoes the correction. Then he pulls a luminance matte on the sky and pushes the highlight wheel towards blue. "Then let's go outside of it and warm it up a touch." Sliga selects outside of the qualification and pulls the gamma wheel to red (Figures 7.71–7.73).

The grass is quite reddish/yellow/green at this point. "So we've gone from there to there," he says, checking the original shot against his correction. "Feels like it's nice and warm and the sun is low."

Fig. 7.69 Secondary correction.

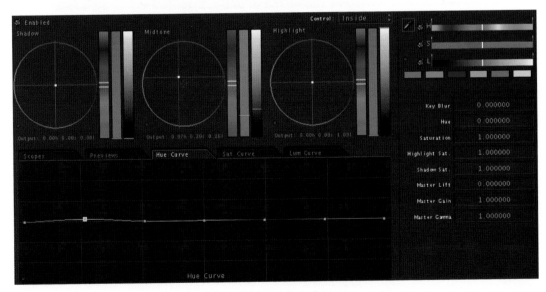

Fig. 7.70 Data from Secondary room.

Fig. 7.71 Second Secondary correction, cooling the sky and warming everything else.

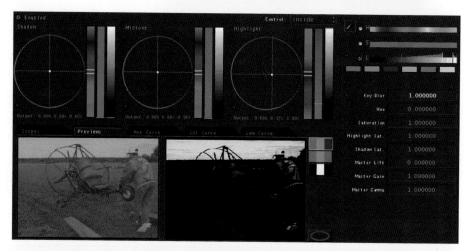

Fig. 7.72 Data on the correction from *inside* of the sky qualification, cooling the highlights.

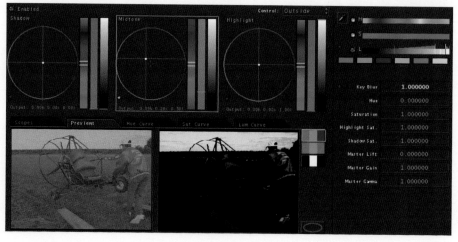

Fig. 7.73 Data on the correction from the *outside* of the sky qualification, warming the rest of the image in the midtones.

At this point, Sliga leaves Color's Secondary room for a foray into the Color FX room. "Let's do a highlight blur. So we're going to need an alpha blend, we're going to need a blur, and we'll need a key. So I generally drag black and white into scale and just adjust the scale creating a highlight key." Sliga drags a Blur to the output of the scale node and blurs it, adjusts the blur, then connects that to the key channel of the alpha blend node.

"Now we have another blur here, and we'll take this blur up big time. If I drag the blurry image into the *light* section of the alpha blend, which is source 2, then press alpha blend, it's going to blur the *highlights*. But if we drag it to the *other* input of the alpha blend node, it'll blur the *shadows*" (Figure 7.74).

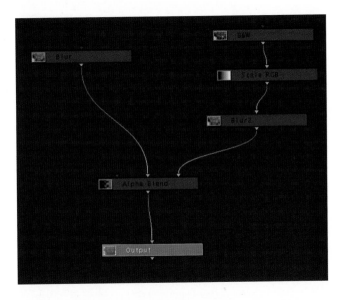

Fig. 7.74 Apple Color's ColorFX Room node tree.

Grading with Curves in Primary

As I mentioned earlier in the book, Terry Curren was one of the few proponents of using curves, which are now available in Color's Primary In room. But when I was interviewing colorists for the book, I was using Color's predecessor, FinalTouch, which did not have Primary curves.

For this correction, Curren worked out of his suite at Burbank-based Alpha Dogs on an Avid Symphony Nitris, but you can follow along with his work method in any application that has curves.

Curren begins by explaining his working setup. "I generally work with two scopes up. I use a vectorscope laid over a luminance waveform and then I also have the RGB parade waveform. I go for the black and white

Fig. 7.75 Boat on the Chicago River in Chicago.

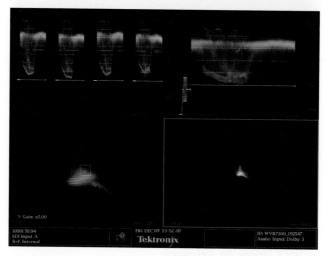

Fig. 7.76 Tektronix WVR7100 screengrab. Upper left: YRGB Parade. Upper right: composite waveform. Lower right: vectorscope. Lower left: vectorscope expanded 5x.

level first out of the two. And since I don't have four scopes to look at, I tend to watch the RGB Parade to see if my blacks are in balance instead of the center dot on the vector."

I tend to watch the RGB parade to see if my blacks are in balance instead of the center dot on the vector.

– Terry Curren, Alpha Dogs

"My first step would be to get down to black with at least one of the colors, whichever is the lowest," Curren explains as he uses the Master Curve to drop blacks down overall. "Then bring the others down. In this case, the blacks are a little green. I can instantly look and see the bulk of the image is here," he says, as he points to the bottom of the RGB Parade. "I can see that in the picture too," he says, pointing on the monitor to the dark water.

"The gamma needs to be bumped, so I can grab that and I'm bringing up the gamma and not the blacks or the top (highlights) any. I can see that the overall picture has a blue tint to it. For most scenes, in the gamma on the RGB parade it goes like that," he says placing a pen across the RGB Parade shapes in the gammas, showing a slight downward angle from the red to the blue side of about 10 to 15 degrees. "In other words, it's not equal red, green, and blue in the middle. But the RGB here is straight across the gammas. So I can see that the blue gamma is high and reds are a little low. That warms the image up a bit. If I wanted to, I could go into the secondaries and pull out some of the green in the water or make it *really* green" (Figures 7.77 and 7.78).

Fig. 7.77 Curren's screenshot of his curves correction shows his primary correction in the center and the source image on either side. The master saturation has been increased, but all other color correction was done with the four curves. This correction took less than 30 seconds.

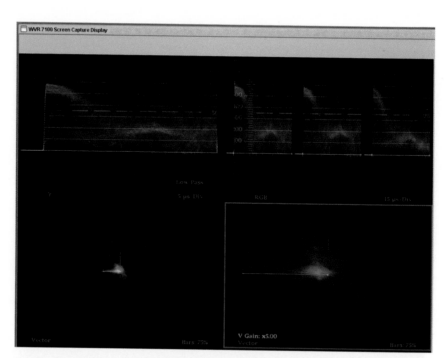

Fig. 7.78 The scopes for the corrected footage. Composite low pass waveform in the upper left, RGB Parade at the upper right, 5x zoomed vectorscope in the lower right and a standard vectorscope in the lower left.

Terry Curren

Terry Curren is a principal and editor at Alpha Dogs in Burbank, California. He hosts a popular series of gatherings in Los Angeles known as the Editor's Lounge.

He began his career in the early 1980s by directing, editing, and producing music videos as well as a successful direct-to-video feature film, *Interview with Terror*.

In 1986, he began work at Matchframe Video, a Burbank-based postproduction studio, where he spearheaded the creation of the studio's edit bays while perfecting his editing and color correction skillset under the tutelage of top-tier DaVinci colorists.

With the introduction of Avid's Symphony online nonlinear edit system and the introduction of its powerful color corrector, Terry saw a golden opportunity. He proceeded to hone his color correction and effects skills with this new toolset until he became a respected colorist in his own right.

Seeing the future, Terry started Alpha Dogs, Inc., in 2002. They currently provide audio and video finishing and graphic design on a wide variety of formats from feature films to television, documentaries, and commercials.

Curren continues exploring the scene called "Blue Sky Tree" (Figures 7.79 and 7.80) using the curves in his Symphony Nitris.

Fig. 7.79

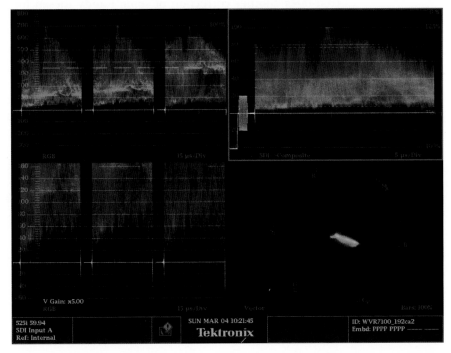

Fig. 7.80 Tektronix WVR7100 screengrab. Upper left: RGB Parade. Upper right: composite waveform. Lower right: vectorscope. Lower left: RGB Parade expanded to show black balance.

"So this is why I'm in curves so much. For me, I want to bring out the gamma in this to get more life in the picture—make it pop more. Now, there is a lot of blue in this. Of course, it's a blue sky, but there's also a lot of blue in the blacks, too," he demonstrates, pointing to the bottom of the RGB parade. "The red black is down there, the green is a little higher, and the blue is up here. Generally, I see the gammas weighted the opposite way," he says, demonstrating the angle again. "But right now it's weighted *this* way," he comments, showing that the angle is the opposite of the way he wants it.

"You can tell by looking at it that it's a very blue picture. So basically, what I've done is this: I've brought up the gamma, I pulled some blue out, and I've added a little red," moving the high/mid blues down on the curve and the high/mid reds up barely. "Then, if this was a commercial, they'd probably want the sky to pop more, so this is where the secondaries would come in for me, in the skies, to bring them out more. Just drive the sky more blue while holding blue out of the clouds. That's where I really find myself using the secondaries the most—on skies. Sky looks great like this as a dark blue, but usually it's much brighter. So if you can grab it and bring the luminance down on it without affecting the rest of the picture, that's really nice" (Figures 7.81 and 7.82).

Curren does another correction of some Randy Riesen footage with curves in Symphony (Figures 7.83 and 7.84).

"Again, I'm going in to pull up gamma," he says as he uses the master curve about one-third up from the bottom. "I'm going to bring the highs down lower because they're clipped anyway. I find when they're already clipped, I like to get them down below 100IRE. It seems to not be as offensive. Obviously, the picture is blue, but I can see, looking at the bottom of the RGB Parade, that both the green and blue are much higher. So in the reds I can bring up the gamma and I can bring both the blue and the green down in the blacks. Basically, I've pulled all the blue cast out of it. But you might not want that, because this is a downtown city, which is always kind of blue in the middle of the day, because you never see the sun until it's directly overhead. Again, this all depends on what was wrapped around it. Left to my own devices, this is where I would go, because it's the closest to normal," Curren concludes (Figures 7.85 and 7.86).

Fig. 7.81 Symphony color correction UI. Center image is the final.

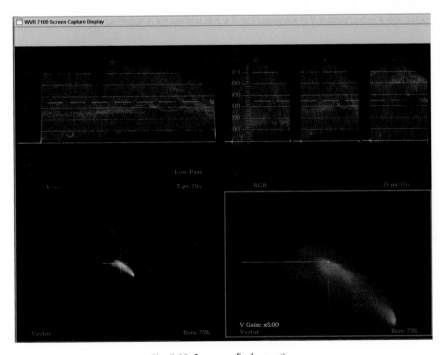

Fig. 7.82 Scopes on final correction.

Fig. 7.83

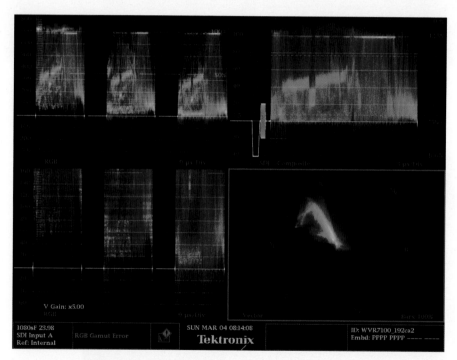

Fig. 7.84 Tecktronix WVR7100 screengrab,. Upper left: RGB Parade. Upper right: composite waveform. Lower right: vectorscope. Lower left: RGB Parade expanded to see black balance.

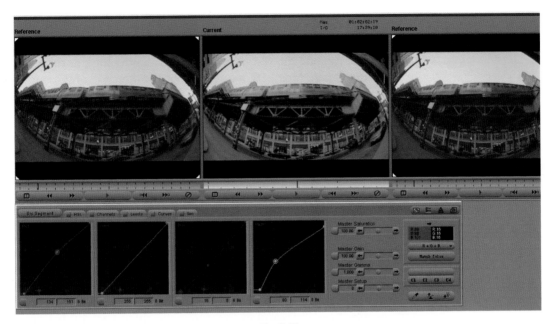

Fig. 7.85

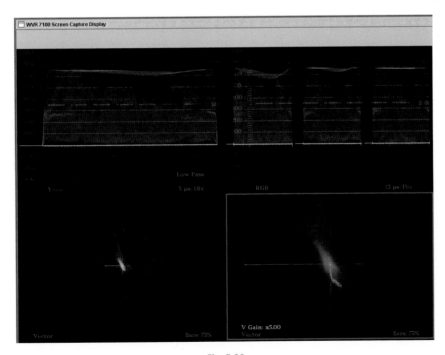

Fig. 7.86

Broadening the Color Palette

Mike Most uses the "Chasing Ghosts—Diner" scene (Figure 7.87) to explain how a colorist can add interest to a shot by broadening the color palette of the shot. Once again, Most is working without the direction of the cameraman, so he must guess about the intent of the shot (Figure 7.88).

> *You need to widen the color palette to get rid of the monochromatic thing.*
>
> *– Mike Most, Next Element by Deluxe*

"On shots like this, I find that most cameramen are going for mixed light. And if you find the mixed light, you bring a lot of life to it, and here it seems a little more of a blue cast. But if I start throwing a little more warmth in the mid range and the highs and keep the coolness in the blacks, it takes on a little more life. If I looked at where it started, it looked a little bit monochromatic, but in most situations like this, the key on the people is usually warm to counteract the bluer daylight that's coming through the windows. Once you throw in a little bit of warmth, and I probably went a little too far here, it tends to separate things better. And it's not a matter of bright and dark; it's a matter of color, because you need to widen the color palette to get rid of the monochromatic thing. Now, it happens that he may have been going for an intentional monochromatic look for mood, but this makes it more visually interesting, at least to me. By adding a little bit of warmth, I separate the curtains by the window. I separate the foreground biscuit tray or croissants or whatever they are and I make the faces come out a little bit more. I also put a little bit of color into the back window and wall, which may or may not be appropriate. In this case, it's more a sense of set lighting and aesthetics that's guiding me, because I have no idea what's going on in the story. The reason they put that foreground in there is to make a more interesting frame. It has no other reason to be there. In this case, there's some color to it, so filling out the color is a good thing" (Figures 7.89 and 7.90).

Fig. 7.87 Source image from *Chasing Ghosts*, image courtesy Wingman Productions, Inc.

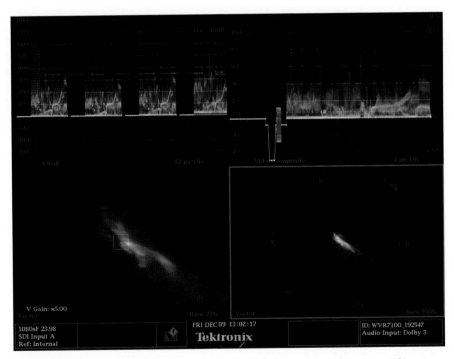

Fig. 7.88 Tektronix WVR7100 screengrab. Upper left: YRGB Parade. Upper right: composite waveform. Lower right: vectorscope. Lower left: vectorscope expanded 5x.

Fig. 7.89 Most's primary correction. The subtlety of this correction may be difficult to discern in print.

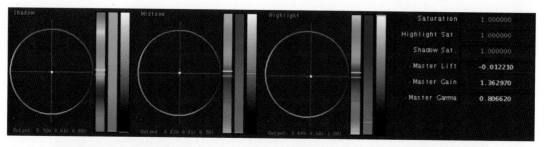

Fig. 7.90 Data from the Primary room of Color. The original correction was done in FinalTouch2K on the actual film scan and was later saved and copied to the HD image in Color.

Mike Most on Scopes versus Eyeballs

Mike Most, senior colorist at Next Element by Deluxe in Burbank, California, explains that getting a good black balance is usually about using the scopes. "The reason for using scopes is that—although I can do it largely by eye—depending on what time of day it is, where I've been in the last 20 minutes, what I've just seen and my mood, I'm not going to be as exact as the scope is. Scopes don't lie. So for times that you're absolutely looking for pure balance, a scope is your best friend. I know a lot of people who tend to stay away from the scopes, and personally I think it's kind of a mistake. I think you get a certain sloppiness that you don't need to have by doing that. I don't think you need to be a slave to scopes, because a lot of it is just feel. But there are a lot of absolutes, and black balance is an absolute. Either the blacks are balanced or they're not—and scopes don't lie. So that's the one thing that I really do.

"You'll see me glance over to the scope on my first correction almost all the time. I trust the parade display. The vectorscope is a good rough guide, and when I first started learning how to do this stuff was back in 1979; we did it with joystick panels on the fly on Ranks. The beauty of the vectorscope is that you could walk yourself into something with a quick, sideways glance while you're still looking at the picture. So you were able to keep yourself relatively balanced with a relatively quick glance to something, and over the years I tend to regard it kind of the same way. It kind of tells me an overall. If I'm trying to push a little greenish-yellow toward a little reddish-yellow, it's actually kind of a nice guide. Out of all the scopes, it's the best guide. But for black balance, the Parade display has to be the bible."

CHAPTER 8

Telling the Story

Most of this book has been a fairly one-sided discussion from the perspective of the colorist. As I've pointed out before, though, color correction is a very collaborative art form or craft and one of the main collaborators—and the originator of the image itself—is the director of photography.

In addition to my conversations with colorists, I also spoke to several DPs, including David Mullen, ASC.

In this chapter, we're going to discuss how the colorist helps to tell the story, which is arguably one of the most important points of color correction. How does the colorist get the viewer into the story using color and keep the viewer's attention and focus in the story? What can the colorist add to the visual process that was started by the director and DP?

"The majority of movies today are shot in a style that could be called romantic realism," begins Mullen. "Sort of naturalistic lighting and photography, but naturalism pushed to kind of its most dramatic or interesting. So we try to make things look realistic, but manipulated for the mood of the story. Sometimes when I'm breaking down a script, I'll list the obvious visual devices that the script seems to call for, then I ask myself if those are clichés and whether the *opposite* is really what the film needs. It's like the Hitchcock thing where he liked to set a murder scene in a sunny field with flowers, just those kind of opposite choices. But this is all stuff you have to talk about with the director. Sort of bounce these ideas off of them. Sometimes they want kind of off-the-wall suggestions that kind of spark new ideas, but generally there are certain cultural associations like warmth for passion or coldness for badness or isolation or something like that. It's not always true.

I'll list the obvious visual devices that the script seems to call for, then I ask myself if those are clichés.

– David Mullen, ASC.

"I've read interviews with directors from northern Europe who feel that cold colors are pleasant and relaxing and warm colors are aggressive and disturbing. You can pick a symbolic style for the film in terms of color and contrast and as long as you clue the audience as to what your symbolism means . . . I mean it's sort of like a code, when someone comes up with a code in the spy business, they also have to come up with a key to break that code so the person at the other end can decipher that code. So you can decide that red symbolizes something or blue symbolizes something and as long as the audience is told in the beginning what that structure is, they sort of accept it for the rest of the film. When you look at *Little Buddha*, Storraro has all of the scenes in Seattle in very cold, blue/gray colors, and wherever possible he tries to have the scenes set at twilight with deep blue light out the windows. So there's always a blue accent in the frame somewhere. And all of the scenes in Tibet are very golden. And sometimes you can flip those two ideas."

Mullen continues, "I remember in the film *Dolores Claiborne* where they shot the modern scenes on Kodak film with a blue, uncorrected tungsten look and the flashbacks all on Fuji film with a warm, saturated color scheme. Now, one could say that you could shoot the flashbacks on Kodak and shoot that saturated and the present on Fuji and make that desaturated and cold. Maybe the present should be saturated because that's the colors of real life and the past is manipulated and desaturated to suggest a distant memory where the colors are missing. But as long as the filmmaker has a kind of structure, it doesn't mean that everyone has to use the same palettes for everything. So that's how I break down a script. I think of it as a sort of series of color and contrast arcs that match the plotline of the story. Some stories are structured in what I'd call an 'AB' comparison and other stories are structured in an 'A to B' arc. Some visual designs of a film is a character starts at one point and ends at a different point, so you try to create a gradual change throughout the film. And other films more intercut the lines of two characters, or one world versus another world, so your visual structure is more of a back-and-forth thing. And there are some films that have no visual arc in terms of color and contrast.

> *But as long as the film maker has a kind of structure, it doesn't mean that everyone has to use the same palettes for everything.*
> *– David Mullen, ASC.*

"You just try to create a single, solid world that has a consistent structure and look to it: a cold, desaturated look, let's say. A film like *Letters from Iwo Jima*, let's say, which has a consistently almost black and whitish look to it. A relentless kind of look. They don't lighten it or darken it that much from scene to scene to scene, so it's kind of meant to be oppressive. 'Cause the world there was oppressive and it never really changes. So, there isn't like one way to approach a film but mental games that you can use to spark ideas, basically. Sometimes I play a game of opposites, you know. I think of all the opposite ideas for a scene: wide angle or telephoto, blue versus red, fast movement versus slow movement, static shots versus moving shots, lots of cuts versus very few cuts. And I break down a scene and try to think which one of those ideas is most appropriate," Mullen concludes.

David Mullen

David Mullen has worked as a cinematographer on numerous feature films and television episodes, beginning in the early 1990s. His feature work includes *Twin Falls Idaho*, *The Hypnotist*, *Northfork*, *D.E.B.S.*, *Shadowboxer*, *Akeelah and the Bee*, *The Astronaut Farmer*, and *Solstice*.

He was nominated for the Independent Spirit Award for Best Cinematography twice for *Twin Falls Idaho* (2000) and *Northfork* (2004). He was also nominated for a Chlotrudis Award Best Cinematography for *Northfork*.

He became a member of the American Society of Cinematographers in 2004. In 2007, he was invited to join AMPAS.

I asked Bob Festa if he felt that there are visual clues to story that the audience expects. "I think so. I think generally if you look at American cinema, Americans are trained on some really stupid levels. They see a dark blue picture and they know that's evening even though it's day-for-night. I think those types of associations are pretty popular. But I work in a primarily commercial and music video environment, so I'm pretty much product driven. So if you look at the types of things I do that tell the story, they are generally based around selling the product. The things that I might do and I might be influenced by are things that heighten or bring to the surface the product focus. I might use traditional dodging and burning techniques to bring the product up and not really be so concerned about the general tone because I'm here to sell things."

I argue that commercials need their stories told even faster than films and that if the story of the commercial is "Your life sucks until you use our product," should one start the spot cool and desaturated until the product arrives, then have the images go warmer and more pleasing once the product "saves the day"? "I think in my world where I've got 30 seconds to tell a story, that's a little too vague," states Festa. "I think I practice it on a small scale, but 9 times out of 10 I'm going to blow the product up and stick it in front of your nose and hit them over the head."

> *With 24, if one of the main characters is doing something bad, we'll make it a very gritty and aggressive look to go with the action.*
> *– Larry Field, Level 3*

Level 3 colorist Larry Field explains one of the ways he works with color to promote the story in his work. "With *24*, if one of the main characters is doing something bad, we'll make it a very gritty and aggressive look to go with the action."

So the question is: what should the shot look like to tell the story? Mullen responds, "Everyone wants context. Without context, you can make a billion different choices, but as soon as you know the context of the shot, it narrows the choices. To me to know whether that scene is late in the day, or whether a character turned off half the lights in the office, so this office is not as bright as it normally is. So if they haven't seen the shot where the character turns off the lights, they might try to match the look of the office from the last time they saw the office in the movie, so you need the kind of story context in order to make the final decisions on stuff. Especially since some cinematographers shoot a kind of flat image and then create the look later, the DP definitely needs to be there to give an idea of what the intent of the scene was."

> *Without context, you can make a billion different choices, but as soon as you know the context of the shot, it narrows the choices.*
> *– David Mullen, A.S.C.*

CBS's Neal Kassner agrees, "You've got to know the story, because color is part of the storytelling tools." Kassner related several stories about how he had corrections go off track because he sometimes started grading before he understood the story.

I continued this train of thought with Encore's Pankaj Bajpal. I asked, "When you try to tell a story through color correction, do you feel like there are specific visual clues that the audience will always understand or do you feel like you can give any clue, and as long as you stick with that clue, then the audience is clued in? For example, take the Artbeat's shot of the boxer. What if we said he was sad because his mother died? Do you color correct it differently than if he's getting ready for the big fight? What are some of your storytelling thoughts?"

Bajpal responds: "Rather than going into the specifics of that, I'll tell you aesthetically what I need to get to and it could be any situation. For me, there is a point where realism meets that something else and it is very critical for me. When you're looking at [an] image, do you feel like in that circumstance, in the moment in the story, are you physically there? Does the image feel three-dimensional enough? If somebody is a good storyteller, you forget that you're sitting in the chair and you're transported into that world, so for me the rule of thumb, the guiding principle in any and every circumstance of storytelling is to be able to break that barrier down.

"You can do it in a very stylized way: for instance, if you're working in science fiction, you could have very high contrast, all these punchy blues and cyans and greens and all of that, but you're transporting that person into that science fiction place, so you're transporting them into that environment and it has to feel real because just by crushing that contrast and painting everything in cyan, it may not have any soul. How you do it, I couldn't tell you, often I don't look at the buttons, I don't look at the dials, it just happens naturally, but the mindset 'Are you able to transport that person?' and it doesn't have to be realistic; in fact, more often than not it isn't."

Company 3's Stefan Sonnenfeld agrees that there is no specific color that tells a story: "First of all, there is no strategic kind of sit-down where we say okay, what are the complimentary colors and this is what we are going to do. This is why you have to try things. There are accidents that happen and I have learned through accidental process. That is in my information bag and I can go back to that and that is where some people without that process fall short. I can say I did this once and it worked great, (so) I can try this. Sometimes guys like Tony Scott will just let me do my thing and he will look at it and he will say, 'I never would have done that for this scene, but it works really well, so let's keep that.' Whoever gets anything right on the first go? That is another thing to remember. There is always trial and error. You have to try things."

Color Changes the Story

When Shooters' colorist Janet Falcon looks at the Artbeats image of the Marines in the desert (Figure 8.1), she believes that the image could tell two different stories, depending on the color scheme.

"I look at this and I think, 'It's the desert and it's hot,' and it came up really warm, so without any direction my feeling is that it should be brownish, goldish, not so blue-sky."

That's why clients are important. Because you need somebody telling you . . . where something's supposed to go.

– Janet Falcon, Shooters Post

Fig. 8.1

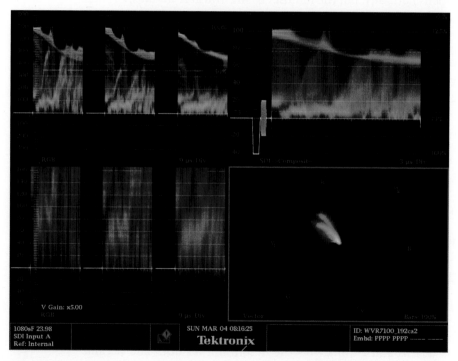

Fig. 8.2 Tektronix WVR7100. Upper left: RGB Parade. Upper right: composite waveform. Lower right: vectorscope. Lower left: RGB Parade expanded to see blacks.

Again, for Falcon, it's all about context. "That's just a judgment call; if I had to start somewhere," she explains as she desaturates the image. "That's what I'm trying to go for: this tobacco look. I could be wrong. That's why clients are important. Because you need somebody telling you—like that story you told me about where something's supposed to go," says Falcon, referring to a story I told in my other color correction book about how Bob Sliga was working on an image before the client arrived. It was a beautiful image of a woman in a flowing dress carrying milk jugs under a green tree toward a big red barn. With no input from the client, he began by turning into a pretty Kodak moment. But when the client arrived, he told Sliga that the woman had cancer, so Sliga switched gears and took the saturation out and changed the warm look to something more cool and depressed.

Returning to the image of the Marines, Falcon continues her assessment, "I mean, it doesn't look like a happy moment. It looks like a more serious moment." With the context of "a serious moment," I ask Falcon what she would do. Her assessment: "You think less saturation. More contrast probably. Serious moments don't have to be low color, but I think it definitely helps to convey a message" (Figures 8.3 and 8.4).

Fig. 8.3 The primary correction reduces saturation and lift while cranking up gain to create contrast.

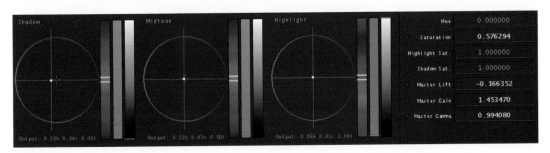

Fig. 8.4 Data for Primary room.

Serious moments don't have to be low color, but I think it definitely helps to convey a message.

– Janet Falcon, Shooters Post

She adds a vignette and darkens the edges (Figures 8.5 and 8.6). The darkened vignette serves several purposes for the image: It focuses the attention on the Marines. It gives some depth and texture to an otherwise flat, burned-out sky. And it also creates a degree of tension by claustrophobically "surrounding" the soldiers.

Fig. 8.5 First secondary gives texture to the sky and focuses attention.

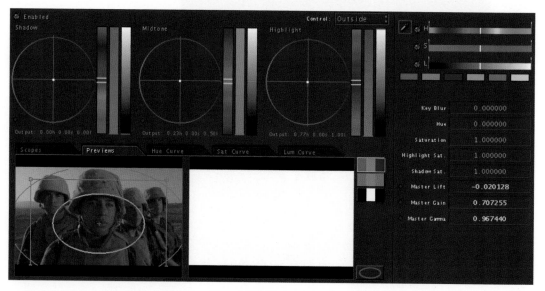

Fig. 8.6 Data for outside of first secondary correction. Lift, gamma, and gain on the edges of the image have all been lowered.

With the vignette done, she qualifies an HSL key on the bright skin tones, blurs the key, and pulls the saturation out (Figure 8.8).

Fig. 8.7 Second secondary qualifies and brightens skin-tone highlights.

Fig. 8.8 Data from inside of second secondary.

"Let's see if we can do a luminance key to the sky." She pulls a key and blurs it. "I'm trying to make it look like a nuclear holocaust. Now if I lift up the blacks, it gives it a ProMist-type look. And I was trying to get some yellow in there, but I think it's just clipped out. Okay, there's my nuclear holocaust" (Figures 8.9 and 8.10).

Fig. 8.9 Falcon's third secondary qualifies the sky and blows it out.

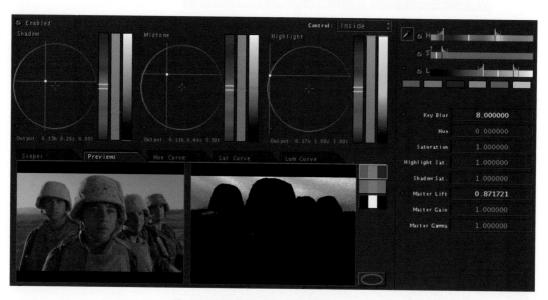

Fig. 8.10 Data from inside of the third secondary.

Here's another look at the same image from Falcon's colleague at Shooters Post, Bob Lovejoy. Lovejoy worked quickly and barely spoke as he went through this correction, saying only, "This one speaks to me. Often in the absence of direction, I just let the picture just take me. It's a subconscious process" (Figure 8.11).

In addition to the primary correction, I believe this image also shows the effect of a Color Effect that was placed on the image to give it the blown-out look. Due to a bug, I couldn't get the Primary correction to show without the Color Effect (Figures 8.12–8.17).

Fig. 8.11

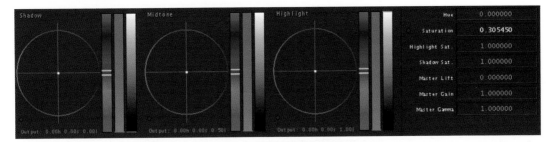

Fig. 8.12 Primary data.

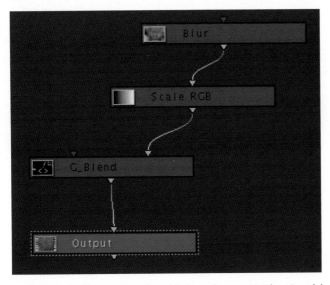

Fig. 8.13 Color effect tree. The blur was set to about 1.5, the scale was set to about 2, and the Nattress plug-in "G_Blend" was set to blend as a "screen."

Fig. 8.14 The first secondary was an HSL key with a garbage matte to qualify the sky and bring the gain down.

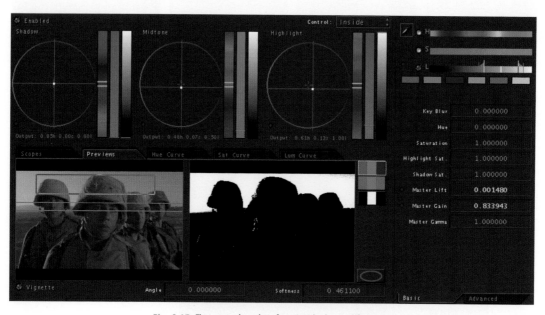

Fig. 8.15 First secondary data from inside the qualification.

Fig. 8.16 The second secondary was a vignette to focus attention and give texture and depth to the sky.

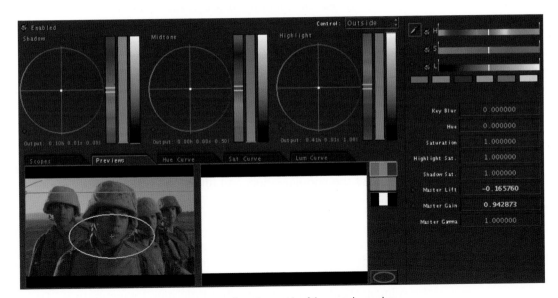

Fig. 8.17 Data from the outside of the second secondary.

Talk Like a DP

One thing to note as Falcon was describing the image was that she often used terms that a director of photography could relate to. The creative arts are filled with jargon and specialized language and colorists, and DPs are no exception. The trick in becoming an effective communicator and collaborator is to learn the language of your collaborator, who in this case is the cinematographer.

> *The trick in becoming an effective communicator and collaborator is to learn the language of your collaborator, who in this case is the cinematographer.*

Specifically, Falcon mentioned the words "tobacco" and "ProMist." Both of these are filters that a DP could relate to. Cinematographers like photographic terms, so learning these terms is a valuable thing. Instead of referring to a general sense of how bright something should be, cinematographers will often describe is specifically in terms of f-stops, saying, "That needs to be a stop brighter." Or sometimes they'll discuss an image in terms of the film negative, as in, "That image seems a little thin." A thin negative is the result of underexposure or under development. The resulting print will be muddy and low contrast.

Understanding color in terms of some of the filters that a DP uses is a valuable skill. Although some filters vary in color, you should be familiar with some of the popular colors and filters and what affect they have on an image.

David Mullen, ASC, explains that the relationship can go both ways: "I find that the more I sit in on color correction sessions, the more I can talk to a colorist on their level. I don't tell them how to turn the trackballs on a DaVinci or any of that stuff, but generally when you're looking at a scene, you're either adding or subtracting primary or secondary colors, so I tell the colorist, 'That warm light needs a little more magenta in it.' Or 'It's warm, but warm with a yellow bias.' Or 'It looks like the shadows have a little cyan in them.' If you talk in terms of red, green, or blue—a little more or a little less, it sort of gives them a good idea of what you want. If you start talking to them in terms of colors that don't have any photochemical or electronic sense, if you say, 'I want that light more turquoise with some chartreuse color cast or burgundy' then everyone's going to start to wonder, because we *sort* of know what those colors are, but we don't sort of all *agree* on what those colors are. And there's another tendency for cameramen to use photographic terms, like filters, like 'That's a coral filter.' Well, a colorist may not have any photography background, and they might not have ever seen a coral filter, and even coral filters don't match each other from manufacturer to manufacturer, so it can be a meaningless term when you get into the color correction space. I've seen cinematographers say to colorists, 'I shot this with an antique white filter and you got rid of all of it.' And I'm like, 'What's an antique white filter to a colorist?' You have to talk to them in terms of colors that *they* understand, which is red, green, blue, cyan, magenta, and yellow. When you start getting things like brown, let's say, that's a very tricky color to create in post and my theory is that brown is really warm minus saturation."

Another popular reference for cinematographers is the way film is processed—for example, bleach bypass or cross-processed, or which film stock they want it to look like. We'll discuss those in more depth in Chapter 10. Cross-processed looks come from having one type of film stock developed in a chemical bath or process that is meant for a different film stock, such as processing "slide" or "positive" film stocks in baths of chemicals meant for a negative film. As a reference, check out Tony Scott's 2005 film *Domino*.

The Story Is the Script

LA freelance digital intermediate colorist Greg Creaser takes on the same scene from "Kiss Me In the Dark" that Mike Matusek covered in Chapter 6. Creaser believes the story to be so important that he likes to read the script before he works on a film.

The Director Speaks: "Kiss Me In the Dark"

In this sidebar, "Kiss Me In the Dark" director Barry Gilbert describes trying to color correct this image himself. (Also see the sidebar on "Kiss" in Chapter 6.)

"With the husband kissing her, we've established that she is lonely to the point of perhaps being obsessive in her attempts to recapture her memories with her husband. And we've made it clear to the audience that this person is dead and that she is a grieving widow. We see her fall onto her side in bed and cover her face in her hands, then we cut outside and see the lightbulb on the porch. Then we see her house through the surveillance monitors and the light goes out. Her eyes flutter open and he appears in the frame and they kiss. I really wanted to crush the blacks and get him to emanate out of the shadows. I spent more time coloring that shot than any shot in the movie. If there was any shot that I wish that I'd had the power of full-scale correction [he originally graded it in Final Cut Pro], it was that one. Because I found it very challenging to crush the blacks without having the color range., because I was working in DV. To have a nice skin tone and crush the shadows without it looking ghastly, I just couldn't do it. I wanted to have that shot be as shadow-filled as possible, and that was difficult. This is the first project that I'd shot that was all about shadow. The projects I'd shot before were all comedies and very poppy and that was quite easy to color because the neg was good so it was really just a matter of taking what you had and plussing it."

"I think story is really important. I know any time I'm going to grade a film—if I'm doing a DI—I'd either like to read a script or at least see a cut of the movie before I do it to know what's involved or to know what the genre is, because I think that has a lot of say on the color as well. I think that's really a key. I think that's extremely important to do that," states Creaser.

> *I think story is really important. I know any time I'm going to grade a film—if I'm doing a DI—I'd like to read a script.*
> — *Greg Creaser, freelance colorist*

He doesn't have that option as he starts grading the bedroom scene from "Kiss," though, so he has to make up the story as he goes. "If I were the DP on this, I'd want more of a mood, so it'd be definitely warmer. And I would probably dip right into the shadows with this and probably the midtones: probably want to drop it down a little bit density-wise." (Note that Creaser uses the photographic/cinematographic term "density" to describe the brightness of the image. "Density" is also the term used by the original "colorists"—negative timers.)

"I'm just going to look at the highlight color and see if pushing it to the warm side makes it nicer. I think that makes more sense," he says as he checks back from his grade to the original image (Figure 8.18). "That's a little cyan for me," he comments, then switches back to his grade (Figure 8.20). "That's a little more in the mood. I'd leave it there to start with for the client" (Figure 8.21).

I point out that pretty much all of the colorists who worked on this image warmed the shot up and darkened it. Creaser adds, "That's the whole point of this. Somebody—the DP or director or producer—is making these choices. Somebody's got to say, 'My taste is to have this shot darker or warmer.' And you know what? I think that's what makes a good colorist. I think being able to have that interaction, being able to help the client make creative decisions—a lot of time they maybe don't. I've heard from clients about being in a room where they didn't get what they wanted and they kind of didn't even know what to do with a shot themselves—so it's kind of helpful if you help them with that a little bit."

Fig. 8.18 Source image courtesy Seduced and Exploited Entertainment.

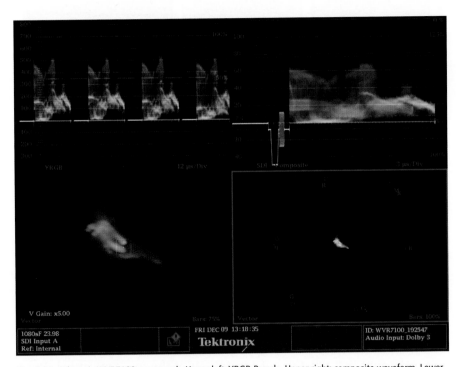

Fig. 8.19 Tektronix WVR7100 screengrab. Upper left: YRGB Parade. Upper right: composite waveform. Lower right: vectorscope. Lower left: vectorscope blown up 5x.

Fig. 8.20 Creaser's final correction.

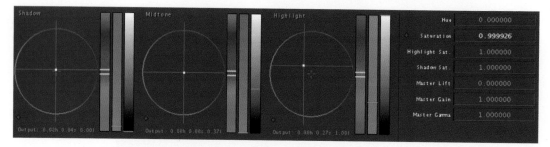

Fig. 8.21 FinalTouch UI of data for correction.

Emphasize Elements to Further the Story

Filmworker's Club colorist Pete Jannotta sees an interesting storytelling challenge in the shot from *Chasing Ghosts* in a basement corridor of a museum (Figures 8.22 and 8.23). Due to the very dark nature of the correction, it is difficult to reproduce the effect of the video monitor image on the printed page. I have enhanced the print images to closer match the video image. My apologies to Pete for having a very nice grade compromised by CMYK color on paper.

"The first thing I would do is make sure I'm getting as much out of the bottom as I can," Jannotta begins, digging into the blacks with the master setup control. "Stretch a little gamma out of there, pull the whites down to make sure that what ever I can get out of the top, I'm getting. But I know if nothing comes down where it's clipped, it's clipped . . . clipped on the source material." Jannotta points out that the fluorescent tubes in the image are clipped. "But for shadow detail, depending on how much noise it generates, I would always try to pull up whatever is hidden towards the bottom, just so I know what's in there. Except, for this shot, stretching it isn't going to do me any favors. Just set black on the baseline and

Fig. 8.22 Basement scene from *Chasing Ghosts*. Image courtesy Wingman Productions, Inc.

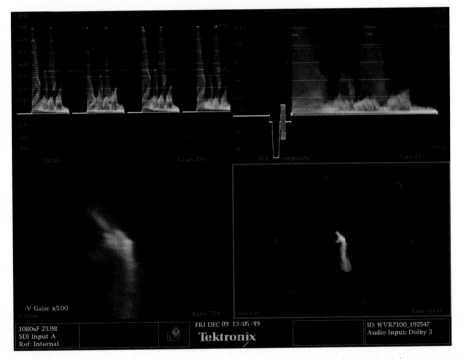

Fig. 8.23 Tektronix WVR7100 screengrab. Upper left: YRGB Parade. Upper right: composite waveform. Lower right: vectorscope. Lower left: vectorscope expanded 5x.

compress the gamma. Push all the stuff from middle black down, toward black, because when I'm looking at this shot, it's asking for much more mystery than the way it comes up, to me. And I don't particularly care for it green. I see it more cold to neutral, and I see him more lit up. Make more out the flashlight stuff and less out of the side walls. And less out of this up here for sure," he says, pointing to the ceiling detail (Figure 8.24).

When I'm looking at this shot, it's asking for much more mystery than the way it comes up, to me.

– Pete Jannotta, Filmworkers Club

"I'm just looking at the vectorscope now and pulling the vectorscope away from yellow, without making it overly blue, which it looks like it's getting. I constantly go between looking at the image and looking at the vectorscope . . . and the waveform."

Definition

ENR: a film process originally developed by Technicolor for cinematographer Vittorio Storaro for the film "Reds."

The Director Speaks: *Chasing Ghosts*

Kyle Jackson, the director of *Chasing Ghosts*, gives some backstory and look direction. "We wanted to create a kind of a noir look, letting it fall off, letting it be kind of a ENR skip bleach kind of look. It's supposed to look like New York, but we shot in Los Angeles.

"The basement scene was supposed to be an old museum that had long since been shut down. High contrast. We wanted to show that the place was long-abandoned.

"Throughout the film, there are basically four looks. There's the police station look that should apply to that 'banker's light' shot. It's a look that we went for any time Michael Madsen's character was alone at his house or in the police station. It should be kind of a smoked tobacco look. Like a refined cigar. Then the exteriors kind of did their own thing because they were less controlled because of the budget. So that was just trying to give it a grit. Then there are a bunch of flashbacks that are super contrasty and grainy, with Gary Busey and Michael Madsen," Jackson explained.

"The SWAT scene was just a basic exterior. But it should look like New York.

"The green cast to the film was the result of a bad film scan. That bad scan is one of the reasons that Tunnel Post bought their own film scanner."

Jannotta is getting comfortable with where he's taking the image, except for the wall in the foreground. But he decides to attack that in secondaries instead. "Maybe push a little blue in the grays, this way. Because that's mostly the middle of the grayscale," he says, pointing to the shadowed foreground wall on the right side close to the camera. "Also I see that this blue waveform"—indicating the RGB Parade scope—"is, or was, a little more compressed than the other two channels in that area," he adds, indicating the shadows. 'So that's a pretty good spot for just a general balance, I think. Let's see if I can put a little more blue into it, 'cause I don't mind if he's a little cold.

"Then maybe compress the grays a little bit," Jannotta continues, moving the gamma lower. "I want to make it look a little more mysterious."

Fig. 8.24 Jannotta's primary correction.

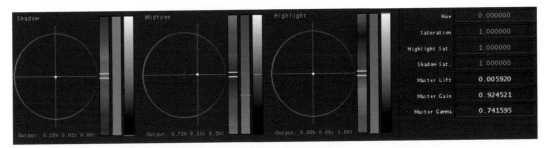

Fig. 8.25 Data from Primary room.

"What I'm thinking I would do in secondary is take that green . . . isolate that greeny/yellow stuff and take it down," he says as he goes into secondary and selects the bright highlight on the right foreground wall with the eyedropper and then customizes his selection (Figure 8.27). "Now I want to bring the saturation down in that area. I didn't like the green stuff. I want to take that matte and make the gain come down. That's what I want. So I'm just seeing what I can do with contrast in that matte. I'm just seeing what I can do that looks natural" (Figure 8.26).

I notice that as he's trying to dial in his correction, he's constrained in where he can take it by some funkiness that's happening in the highlight on the wall under the fluorescents. "Yeah. I'm seeing edges that I don't like, but I'd like to bring it down. I want to snap him out and make more of this light made by his flashlight spilling on his clothes and that light," he says, pointing to the pool of the flashlight on the floor (Figures 8.28–8.30).

Jannotta also wants to diminish the detail in the image above the actor's head. He decides to do this with a window, or vignette. Jannotta draws a custom vignette shape and softens it (Figures 8.31 and 8.32). "I would make him a little warmer. But first I want to change the shape so that it

Fig. 8.26 First secondary correction lowers the glare on the wall and hides detail in the shadows.

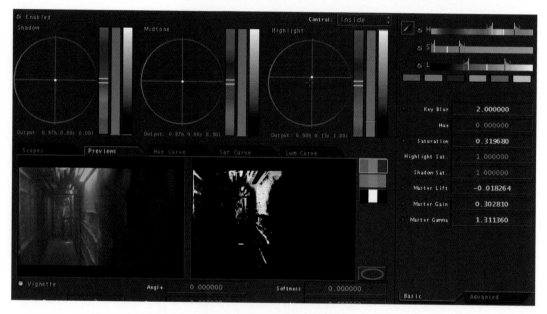

Fig. 8.27 Data from first secondary.

covers less of the top of him and is bigger at the bottom where the flash-light pool is. So my thought is to keep his head cooler, and it will be more interesting if more of the warmth comes from the bottom," he explains.

"I'd like to keep his head cool, and it's too dark up there," Jannotta continues as he plays with the original shape to better define the beam and pool of the flashlight. "So I'm just trying to now to see if I can—even though it's not like a flashlight beam—try and have it feel more like a source light. I'm pulling out the softness on the bottom, 'cause I really want to feather that bottom."

Fig. 8.28 Second secondary focuses on the flashlight.

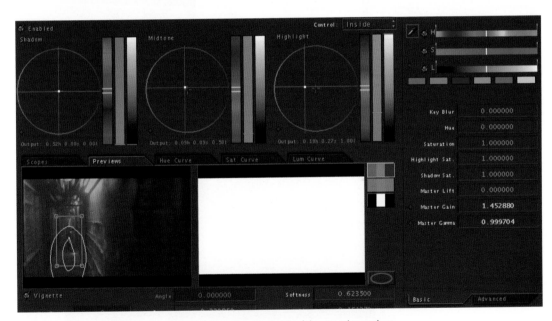

Fig. 8.29 Data from the inside of the second secondary.

Jannotta creates another secondary vignette. "What I think I'm going to do now is get his head with a triangle kind of thing. So they'll be overlapping, but this one on top is going to be so I can light up his head a little bit, but keep it cool. I like the way that shot feels now."

Continuing with his definition of the image using secondaries, Jannotta draws an upside-down dome along the top middle of the picture, selecting the bright practical lights near the top of the frame then pulls the highlights down (Figures 8.33 and 8.34), explaining that he didn't like emphasis on the bright lights over the actor's head. "That looks more

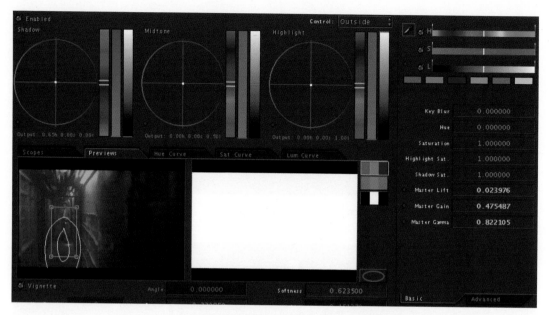

Fig. 8.30 Data from the outside of the second secondary.

Fig. 8.31 Third secondary focuses some attention on the face.

interesting to me. To me this tells the story better. This guy's looking for something . . . he's looking for trouble. It's all about being in a dark scary place with a flashlight. So I brought all of the shadow detail down and it becomes more about him and his flashlight."

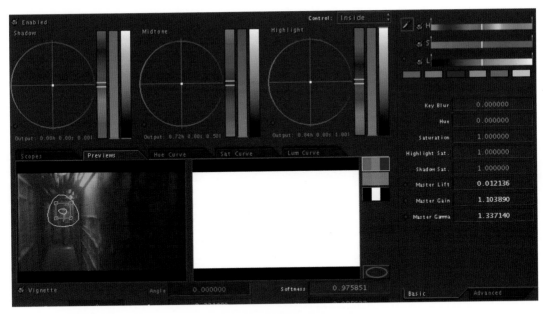

Fig. 8.32 Data from the third secondary.

Fig. 8.33 Fourth secondary lowers gain on lights, helping focus attention on the subject.

I stepped in briefly to save Jannotta's grade for him, but before I did, I moved the timeline to a more representative frame of the grade. "So you grabbed a thumbnail at a better place? I do that all the time," Jannotta says approvingly.

So you grabbed a thumbnail at a better place? I do that all the time.
– Pete Jannotta, Filmworkers Club

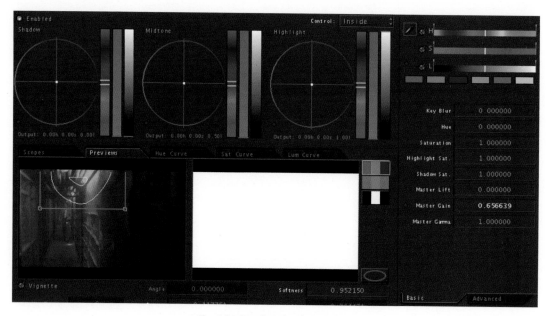

Fig. 8.34 Data from fourth secondary.

Imposing Story on the Boxer

Nolo's Mike Matusek and NFL Films' Chris Pepperman both decided to create their own story around the Artbeats image of the boxer (Figure 8.35).

Matusek begins, "So you wanted me to pick something and make up a story. I just saw *Rocky*, so I'm going to say that this guy is training for the big fight. He looks like a mean guy, so I don't know if he's the villain or if he's the hero, but I'll say he's the bad guy. So I would want to give it a kind of unsettling look, so first I started off by crushing the blacks, basically giving it more contrast. I went a little green with it. Desaturated. Trying to give it a more menacing. Obviously it was lit to be contrasty, because of the difference between dark and light, so I'm just playing on that contrast and seeing how far I can push it. If I crush the blacks too much, I'll lose too much detail."

Matusek looks at the original image. "So that's where it was. Looking a little muddy. I think I crushed it down too much. I think this is a better place for it, but maybe go back to the greens and see what that looks like. Again, this guy's the villain, so give him a more menacing look. Try going a little more warm with it in the highlights. Give it a different look. Basically I started off going kind of going kind of dark with it" (Figures 8.37 and 8.38).

Fig. 8.35 Image courtesy Artbeats.

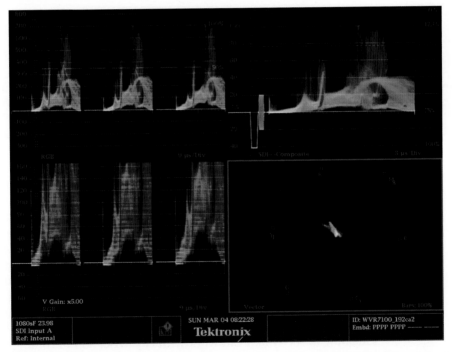

Fig. 8.36 Tektronix WVR7100 screengrab. Upper left: RGB Parade. Upper right: composite waveform. Lower right: vectorscope. Lower left: RGB Parade expanded to see black balance.

"Then I decided I liked it brighter. So the highlights are somewhat clean. I guess they're a little green," Matusek continues (Figures 8.39 and 8.40).

Fig. 8.37 **This was done with just a primary grade.**

Fig. 8.38 **Data from Primary room.**

"Then I decided to go warm with it. I think that's a better fit. It has more contrast anyway. And this one (bright and warm) has the most grittiness to it I think" (Figure 8.45).

Chris Pepperman also worked on this image and had this take on it: "The first thing I think about is what this picture can look like. And I see this guy in an element that is real gritty. I see that it's a monochromatic, almost black and white, with a little bit of color and a very hard shaft of light coming through and he's training very hard. He's getting ready for a fight and he's really intense about it. How can we tell a story with color? I'm going to start by doing what I typically do, and that is adding contrast. I'm going to see what I can work with clip-wise. So I'm coming down on highlights and I'm coming up on setup to see where my detail is," Pepperman explains as he adjusts both tonal ranges simultaneously with the dials around the trackballs that control master gain and master setup.

He's getting ready for a fight and he's really intense about it. So how can we tell a story with color? I'm going to start by . . . adding contrast.
— Chris Pepperman, NASCAR

Fig. 8.39 This was done with just a primary grade.

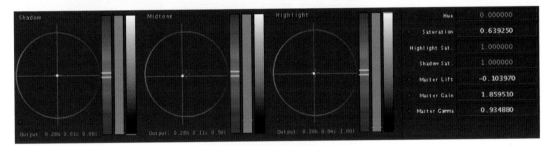

Fig. 8.40 Data from Primary room.

"All I'm doing is seeing what my parameters are. I know what it's going to look like clipped. I'm really seeing what I have in the image. So now what I'm going to do is just add a little bit of contrast to it and start letting the light fall off where it wants to be."

I explain to Pepperman that the image has already been touched by a colorist. "I was just going to say, balance-wise, it's almost there. There's not much to balance."

But I prod him to take the image further by pointing out that we're telling a story, so the balance isn't necessarily important. "Right," he agrees. "And that's just what I was doing. I'm fine-tuning the balance where I am comfortable. So I really want to see that smoke. I really want to see that highlight. So I'm going to start kicking the highlights. I don't care if his back blows out. As a matter of fact, I *want* his back to blow out. I want you to see this really hard, edgy light screaming and kind of cutting him out of the background. And I just want to bury the blacks to where it's not going to hide anything but it's where it wants to be, which I'm going to say is right about there," Pepperman states as he looks into the shadow areas to see if he's losing any important details. "There's nothing back there, so I'm going to get rid of it completely. So I'm going to take the black levels all the way down to about here."

Fig. 8.41 The image with just the primary grade.

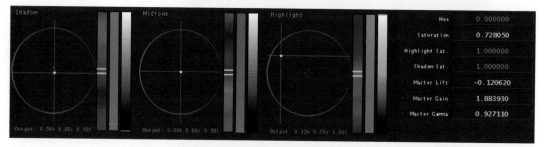

Fig. 8.42 Data from the Primary room.

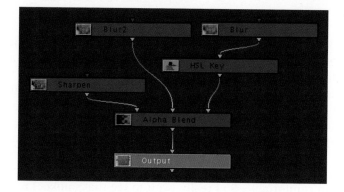

Fig. 8.43 Color Effect tree for highlight glow. Both blurs are set to 5. Sharpen is set to 2.

"That's where I'm going to start (Figure 8.46). The next thing I'm going to do is take the color almost all the way out, then I'm going to come back in a little bit. So I'm liking where I'm going, but I'm still not happy with the contrast."

Anytime you build heavy contrast, you're going to have to come back on the saturation if you want to stay consistent.

– Chris Pepperman, NASCAR

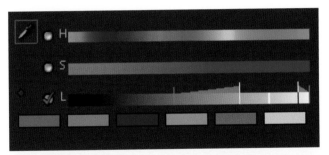

Fig. 8.44 The data for the HSL key in the Color Effects tree.

Fig. 8.45 Final image with primary correction and Color Effect.

Pepperman explains an important point: "When you add contrast, it also affects the saturation, no matter how separated it is. Anytime you build heavy contrast, you're going to have to come back on the saturation if you want to stay consistent. Meaning if you create something that is this green and you like that color, but then you stretch that signal and make it more contrasty, inherently that green is going to get more saturated, so you have to pay attention to that. So I'm going to add more contrast and I'm going to come down on the midrange a little bit. So I like that. Now what I want to do is accentuate that shaft. I want it to be really warm light. I want it to look like it's late August. Like it's this hard, hot, humid day. This is how I envision it."

Pepperman enables a secondary and a vignette and creates a shape diagonally across the screen in line with the shaft of light. "Now I'll go inside and kick it up a notch." The highlight on the fighter's neck really starts to look good. "Keep coming, keep coming. I want to see how far we can go with this. That's what it's about. Now I want to warm it up," he says as he pushes warmth into just the highlights and midtones (Figures 8.48–8.50).

"So that gave me what I wanted," he concludes. "That was pretty easy, actually. Let's talk about what I did. First I checked to see where my range

Fig. 8.46 Pepperman's primary correction is largely a drop in saturation as the image was already nicely color corrected by Artbeats.

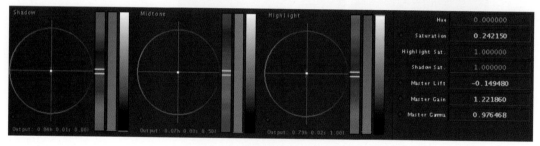

Fig. 8.47 Data from Primary room.

Fig. 8.48 This secondary is the one that really imparted the look.

was. Then I added contrast. Then I desaturated it. Then I created the window. I brightened the inside. I went back and darkened the outside. I kept going back and forth until I go the ratio that I wanted between outside and inside the vignette. Then I applied overall primary warmth to it."

As he explains his finished process, Pepperman decides to add a few more touches. "Now let's just say I like the warmth in the highlights, but

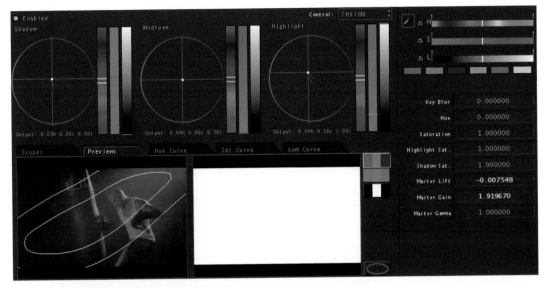

Fig. 8.49 Data from inside of the vignette.

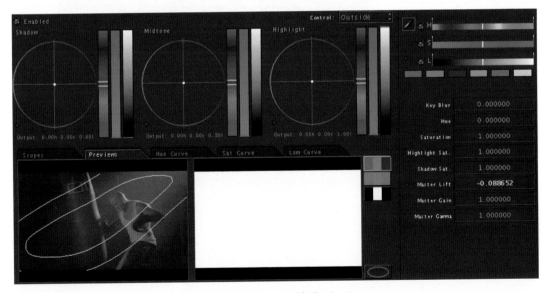

Fig. 8.50 Data from outside the vignette.

I want to grab his skin tone and mess around with his skin tone. So now I'm going to go to another secondary."

Pepperman grabs an HSL key based on the fighter's skin tone and plays with it. "Finding that key is all trial and error. That's really what that is," he states as he adds a vignette to the same secondary, creating an oval to garbage matte the skin tone and eliminate the punching bag, which is also a skin-tone color.

With the skin tone qualified, Pepperman starts to tweak. "I'm actually trying to eliminate the red in his skin tones without affecting the highlighted areas of the smoke. As opposed to doing an overall correction, I'm trying to see if I can grab that skin tone without affecting anything else and just desaturate it. I liked where I was overall, I just wanted to desaturate his skin tone a tiny bit. So I really like what I've done here (Figure 8.51). I like this feeling of 'It's hot. It's warm. He's sweating.' And that's where I really wanted to be."

Fig. 8.51 This secondary is a slight desaturation of the skin tones.

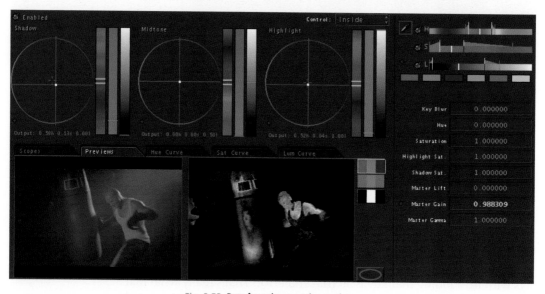

Fig. 8.52 Data from the second secondary.

Well, not quite. Still seeing yet another tweak, Pepperman continues his correction with and additional secondary. "Okay, I want to try one more thing. I like this a lot but I just want to see the blue in his pants a little bit more. So why don't we do this. Let's go into yet another secondary." Pepperman draws a square, resizes and rotates it, and positions it over the fighter's shorts. "So right now I'm opening it up to see how much I have and I want to add a little artificial blue," he says as he pushes blue into the shadows of the square vignette, then softens the shape. "That's much better" (Figure 8.53).

Fig. 8.53 A minor tweak to the color of the boxer's shorts.

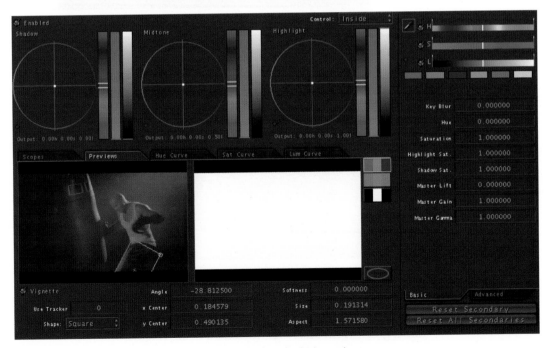

Fig. 8.54 Data from the third secondary.

In an effort to save time with the colorists and have them touch as many images of interest as possible, we didn't follow all of these corrections through the entire process that would be needed to truly finish them. In this case, each of these windows would need to be tracked to the motion of the shot.

New Hat's Bob Festa also delivered three different story lines on the boxer shot. He describes his three looks: "The first one is *Raging Bull*. High contrast, black and white, noisy, grainy, ratty" (Figure 8.55).

"Then it's *Rocky*—1970s, well-balanced, strong" (Figure 8.56).

Fig. 8.55

Fig. 8.56

"And in this third image: Clint Eastwood. *Million Dollar Baby*. Desaturated, green wash #2, 1998 written all over" (Figure 8.57).

Fig. 8.57

Story Epilogue

For me, the thing that stands out in this discussion of color correcting to help promote story is that the colorist really needs a strong sense of the story to focus the direction of the corrections. Without context, as David Mullen mentioned, the creative choices are unlimited. Context helps to focus those creative decisions.

There are several books that attempt to define the emotional clues that color delivers. Patti Bellantoni's *If It's Purple, Someone's Gonna Die* (Focal Press, 2005) is a prime example of this school of thought. Another excellent example is Bruce Block's *The Visual Story* (Focal Press, 2001).

I don't believe that defining hard-and-fast rules about what specific colors *always* say is valid, due to cultural differences and trends and fashion, but the colorist definitely has a strong storytelling capability through the use of color and contrast in the collaboration with the other storytelling artists on a film as they attempt to influence and engage the audience.

As an exercise, watch a few films and try to determine whether there is a story-based reason why the director, DP, art director, and colorist are using certain colors and how they are using contrast and tonality to help tell the story.

CHAPTER 9

Matching Shots

This chapter is devoted to one of the basic colorist tasks: matching shots. This skill is critical because it is the colorist's job to ensure that in any scene, all of the shots look like they happened in the same place and time, even though they may have been shot over the course of several hours, days, or even locations. It's critical, especially in a dramatic piece, that the audience doesn't get pulled out of the story because the color or contrast or luminance levels shift from shot to shot inside of what is supposed to be a single contiguous scene.

This area is one of the *least* subjective skills in which a colorist must be proficient. Either the shots match or they don't. You'll see that there are numerous strategies and tips to make these matches easier, but that the more experienced you become, the more you simply rely on your eyes. Until then, learning to match shots is a valuable skill and training method in learning to force a very specific look on a shot with a clearly definable and quantifiable result.

Many times, the need to match cameras is due to some technical mistake during production, but matching shots still needs to occur with even the most skilled director of photography and most diligent crew. The reasons for these matches often have to do with the quality or color temperature of natural light changing over time. But it can also happen on a shooting stage with completely controlled lighting. Sometimes it can happen between lens changes—for example, with a wide shot, on which the actual exposure of a face matches the close-up, but because of the perception of the light levels, the wide shot may need to be adjusted to match the perceived level. Stephen Nakamura said just such a case happened when he did the grading on David Fincher's *Panic Room*. In one scene, the perception of the light level of the wide shot was affected by the light bouncing off of a large wall. But in the close-up, even though the exposure values of the skin on the face were identical, the skin tones seemed brighter, because the eye wasn't taking in as much of the wall.

I presented the colorists with four matching scenes, (which are also available on the DVD). The first pair includes a shot of the lions in front of the Art Institute of Chicago. One was shot with proper white balance (though fairly warm) and one was shot balanced blue. The second pair includes an interview clip and a B-roll shot that need to cut back to back. The third pair includes two clips from the same interview that was shot outdoors as lighting conditions changed. And the final one is a seemingly impossible match of two horribly overexposed and poorly white balanced images of the Chicago Water Tower.

Matching the Lions of the Art Institute

Craig Leffel, of Chicago post house Optimus, starts us out with his take on the match of the Art Institute lions (Figures 9.1–9.4).

Leffel begins by analyzing the images and correcting the "base" image. "I'm looking at these shadows," he explains as he points to the black areas above the three colored banners, "since they're the darkest shadows that I can see the fastest. This," he says, pointing to the shadowed archways above the doors, "is also a good place to see texture; to see if I'm cranking the blacks too hard or too harshly, this stuff will look pretty awful pretty fast. I'm trying to get the blacks not to look milky and trying to get some richness, but richness with separation. Just adding contrast to an image and just crushing the blacks is not the same as trying to get tonal separation and get richness. Especially when I'm working off something that I know is a piece of tape, I try to separate out as much dynamic range as I can. The way I discern that is by the black to midtone relationship and then the midtone to highlight relationship. And to me, when

Fig. 9.1 The "base" shot, though it's a little warm.

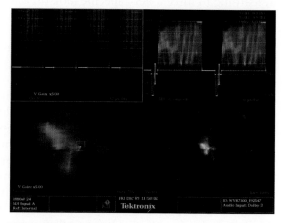

Fig. 9.2 Tektronix WVR7100 screengrab. Upper left: YRGB Parade. Upper right: composite waveform. Lower right: vectorscope. Lower left: vectorscope zoomed 5x.

Fig. 9.3 The "cool" shot.

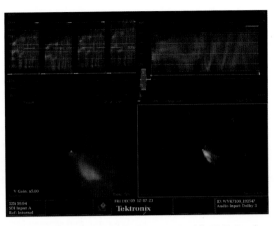

Fig. 9.4 Tektronix WVR7100 screengrab. Upper left: YRGB Parade. Upper right: composite waveform. Lower right: vectorscope. Lower left: vectorscope zoomed 5x.

you start out—it's one thing where you finish—but where you start, it's nice to have as much range between each stage of black, gamma, and white as you can without any clipping, crushing . . . just get as full a tonal range as you can. Imagining it's a photograph and trying to see every bit of the tone from 16 steps of gray that you can or more. Kind of a Zone System kind of a thing. Whenever I'm doing an image I'm always thinking about—not literally the Zone System—but that's pretty much how I judge an image."

> *Just adding contrast to an image and just crushing the blacks is not the same as trying to get tonal separation and get richness.*
> — *Craig Leffel, Optimus*

With the base image looking the way he wants (Figures 9.5 and 9.6), he grabs a still to begin working on the match. Very quickly, without referring to the scopes, Leffel has a pretty close match.

Leffel ignores the fact that the sky in the "cool" image is radically off, knowing that he'll deal with that later. He switches from the split to cutting back and forth between the still store and the correction. "I have a blue shift in my shadows if you look at the bottom of that lion. The color of the building is right, except the contrast is wrong. You can also see the blue in the shadows in the doorways and in the guy's jacket on the stairs. However in a case like this of a mis-balanced camera, there's going to be a trade-off of what compromises you're willing to make in order to make *most* of the image feel good."

Still Store

Any good color correction application or system should have some method of storing and recalling visuals to which you can refer. There are a number of important ways to use a still store. Several colorists grabbed stills throughout their corrections so that they could judge whether the direction they were heading was improving the image. Others grabbed stills of shots they were trying to match exactly or of scenes in which they were trying to maintain continuity. Also, the still store can be used to maintain consistency over long-form programs.

Learn to use the still store in your application using the keyboard shortcuts. Experiment with ways to use your still store or reference images to improve your corrections. It may seem like pulling these stills and referring to them will slow you down, but they can keep you from straying too far down an unproductive path.

Also, as you see by the example of the colorists throughout the book, you need to decide in which cases you want to cut back and forth between the still store and the live image, or whether you want to wipe between it and your working image. Some prefer one method and some prefer the other, but most of them use both methods at one time or another.

DaVinci Resolve's Color screen, where most of the correction is done has a dedicated area devoted to pulling stills and using them. Apple Color has an entire "room" devoted to stills.

"So," I ask Leffel, "Making a perfect match won't be possible in this case because one or more of the color channels has either become clipped or compressed in one area and not another?"

"Yes," he responds. "So you have to say, 'I want to get as much as I can get right.' Like this is already better, just to take that blue out of the black."

> *There's going to be a trade-off of what compromises you're willing to make in order to make most of the image feel good.*
> *– Craig Leffel, Optimus*

I ask him what he sees as the difference in the images. "It's mostly red gamma. But if you start worrying about that particular detail, you're going to lose the rest of it. It's more an overall perception thing. If you just try and watch the whole image, not trying to see too many details, what your eyeball is going to catch is the overall hue shift. Your eyeball is not going to catch, necessarily, that change in the doorway."

I ask Leffel to describe what he did as he cuts back and forth between the corrected and uncorrected cool image. "I looked at that blue and said, 'Most of that is happening in the brightest parts of the picture or gain' and I immediately tried to take out that blue tone and lean more towards the

Fig. 9.5 First Leffel got the "base" image to a place where he was comfortable with it.

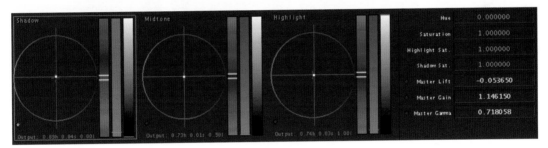

Fig. 9.6 Data from the Primary room.

target image overall—throwing warmth in. Once I had that even remotely close, I started dialing contrast in. So then it was time to hit blacks and gamma and dial in some contrast. Then working black and gamma against each other to try to get full tonal separation again in the shadows and the midtones so that I wasn't crushing or hitting anything too hard."

I press him further, asking, "By saying 'full tonal separation and working blacks against mids,' you mean how far you pull down the blacks and how high you pull up the mids or how high you bring up the blacks and how low you pull down the mids? And you're doing that with both hands. Then you do that on the other side with the highlights?"

"Exactly," he responds. "You open the midtones and darken the whites. It's a lot easier to match an image if you have some full tones to work with so I added black. I added gamma. I added color saturation. I mostly manipulated midtones. I brought the black down, but I also brought the whole midtone down. You can see that the white values don't change a whole lot, but the midtones and the blacks do."

Fig. 9.7 **Primary correction for cool image.**

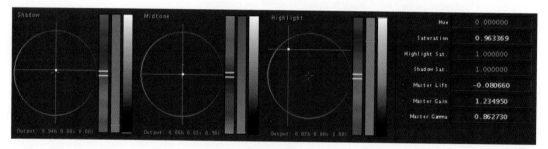

Fig. 9.8 **Data from Primary room.**

The tonal separation really makes the detail pop. "It looks like you can see individual bricks in the façade," I comment.

I still use the Zone System every day.

– Craig Leffel, Optimus

"Absolutely, and that midtone kind of really stretches out. One of the things I tell colorists is that you have to discern rather quickly: where's the white? What's a white point? If you think of the whitest points and the darkest points, and then everything else is kind of midtone. Then if you manipulate that midtone and think of midtone as a curve that you're kind of sliding down, you can sort of round this image out to have some richness. So you've added a bunch of black and stretched out the image, not to the point where it's harsh or that you're clipping anything unnecessarily—in an image like this you kind of have to clip, but— you've stretched it out to have dynamic range: a black, a little-bit-higher

Fig. 9.9 Secondary correction, pulling added warmth out of the sky.

Fig. 9.10 Data from Secondary room.

than black, a middle gray, a slightly-higher than middle gray, something approaching white and then white. If you can get 16 steps of gray into an image, you're doing a great job . . . or at least my buddy Ansel Adams said so," Leffel jokes. "I still use the Zone System every day. I'm really surprised that I do, but I come from printing photographs and the mark of a good printer of photographs is tonal separation. If the creative direction is to eliminate it, then of course that's what you do, but as a base way to color correct or as a base way to approach an image, I always approach it as a full tone image," Leffel concludes.

Bob Sliga also took on the challenge of the Art Institute lions. His approach was that—even though the "base" image wasn't ideal—he would treat that as the "hero" grade and would match directly to the uncorrected, slightly warm shot. This is almost the reverse of Kassner's approach later in the chapter.

> *I like to look at the vectorscope blown up . . . as far as I can go because it helps me find a neutral black and a neutral white.*
>
> *– Bob Sliga*

"I look at the waveform monitor, vectorscope [Figures 9.2 and 9.4]. I like to look at the vectorscope blown up a lot. I blow it up as far as I can go because it helps me find a neutral black and a neutral white. I also look at the RGB Parade display, then I look at the picture. What I have up right now is in the still store; I've saved a picture that I want to match to. The white balance is extremely different. The exposure level is different on the scope. I can see where I have to put the signals in order to help match the image. I'll utilize the wipe to the reference image, then I'll rotate the split so I have a little bit more of the picture," he says as he rotates the wipe so that it goes from the lower left corner to the upper right corner.

"So, I go to primary in and I'm just going to brighten this up really high. So one of the things I'm looking for is a match in the waveform. Then it'll be by eye after that. So you kind of get it in the ballpark of the overall video level. I'm also looking at the black level; how we're higher over here, so it's not balanced out. So as I come back over here to my parade display what I'm trying to do is balance these off as close as possible. To do this, I'm going to start by making my blacks black."

Sliga uses the shadow trackball to balance blacks. "You can see as I move around what happens on the vectorscope. You want to have things coming out of the center. We still have a big-time white balance difference and I'm not even looking at the monitor. I can do this in the joyball area and move all three tonal ranges or I can come over here to the advanced side (the Advanced tab in the Primary room) and grab the channels one at a time. I'm going to bring my red lift down just a little bit more in the blacks. Now that we're in the Advanced tab, it's easier than moving three joyballs at once. This is just another way of doing this."

Sliga switches from adjusting the red, green, and blue shadow levels to working on highlights. "We're just going to try to get the highlights in the ballpark," Sliga states as he checks the waveform monitor. "We need to take some of the blueness out of this, which I can look to do in one of a couple ways. First, I'm going to start with the blue gamma and bring it down into this area here. Then I'm going to bring the red gamma up a tad and then go back and forth."

Sliga changes gears again and jumps from the Advanced tab corrections back to the trackball for midtones. "This is one of those places where it's easier to do with the trackballs, so I'm going to do the rest of the correction over here. We're getting warmer overall. We're probably not going to match it totally 100 percent exactly, but the idea is to get it pretty darn close and we should be able to. If we had to use windows and that, we could. Remember I'm just in the primary in room for this right now. So I'm just going to add a bit of color to it. Looks like we have a little bit of a green balance," he says as he adjusts the highlight trackball. "I'm doing this by eye at this point. Then I'll come back to the gamma with a little bit more green. Now I'm using shadow sat [saturation] and pulling down some of the saturation that was building up in the shadows."

With most of the work done in the Primary room (Figures 9.11–9.14), Sliga moves to secondaries, explaining, "I'm going to use the Saturation

Fig. 9.11 The shot Sliga used for his match.

Fig. 9.12 The primary correction.

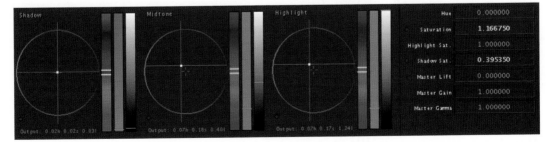

Fig. 9.13 The main primary data.

Fig. 9.14 The data from the Advanced tab of the Primary room.

curve. What I really want to do is deal with that yellow that's coming in to the warmth of the bricks." He pulls the saturation down on the yellow vector of the cure (Figure 9.15).

"When you're actually doing matching like this, you end up trying a lot of things to make it happen because you're forcing one into the other. And so this one here, by pulling the yellow out, it got our stone [the foundation of the lion] a lot closer, except we've got a little bit of color up in there that's different," he explains, pointing to the building façade between lion and first doorway. "So I came back up here figuring I could get away with a gain change, that gets it in the ballpark. And if we wipe between the two just to see where we're at—the building itself is pretty darn close."

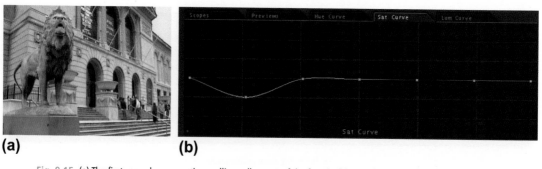

(a)   **(b)**

Fig. 9.15 (a) The first secondary correction, pulling yellow out of the façade. (b) Data for the first secondary correction.

Using another secondary, Sliga tries to bring the color of the lions closer. He positions the split screen diagonally across the lion, then goes to the Saturation curve and moves the cyan point, moving it up and down radically. "That's the wrong point. That ain't gonna work, so I'll try the green point." Sliga lifts and lowers green saturation point radically, seeing that it is affecting the right portion of the image. He settles into a lowered saturation on green. "Maybe somewhere in that area," he determines. "And if we go to the still store and wipe across . . . I pulled too much out, but we can go back to that and raise it a little." A few minor tweaks to the Saturation curve later and his match of the lion is complete (Figure 9.16).

Sliga then added another correction to match the sky, pulling a Luminance HSL qualification and a circular garbage matte (Figure 9.17b).

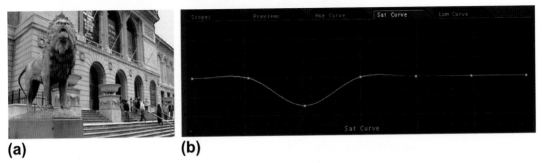

(a)   **(b)**

Fig. 9.16 (a) The second secondary. pulling saturation out of the cool image. (b) The data for the second secondary.

(a)   **(b)**

Fig. 9.17 (a) The third secondary, pulling warmth out of the sky. (b) The matte and vignette for the third secondary.

Neal Kassner takes the next crack at matching the lions. His initial corrections are to the cool lions. "All right, the first thing I'm going to do is try to balance the blacks a little bit. And I'm looking at a combination of the waveform and the vectorscope. I'm going to warm up the gammas a little. Now, I don't know what kind of stone that is [referring to the façade of the building], but I know it's not as yellow as one or as blue as the other, so I'm just going to try to make it neutral. I'm also going to wind down the overall gain and see what that does to the sky."

Fig. 9.18 The diagonal split between the "base" shot and the corrected "cool" shot. The wipe goes just under the red Ansel Adams banner and above the leftmost arched doorway. Notice the "cut" high on the lion's legs.

Then he switches over to the warmer lion shot. "So now what I have to do is go the other way with it. And I'm going to take some of the warmth out of the low lights and also out of the midrange. Okay, so this is where it's getting there, but it's not close, so I'll cut back and forth between this and the still. What I'm going to do is match the luminance using the waveform."

In order to get the contrast ratios right between the two images, Kassner plays the gamma and highlights off each other, bringing gamma down and highlights up, then bringing shadows up then playing shadows up and highlights down at the same time before his correction is in a comfortable range for him. "Okay, the luminance is closer than it was. Now I'm going to concentrate on color.

"Now I'm running into a situation where I like *this* better than *that*," he says, preferring his semiadjusted shot 2 over his completed correction on shot 1.

Kassner starts his grade over using grade 3 in the timeline. I ask him if he's trying to get the shapes in the waveform to line up. "Exactly. So now there's a color cast . . . a little cyan. It appears to be mostly in the gammas. Now I'm looking at the vectorscope, just trying to match the shapes a little better. It almost looks like there's a black stretch going on in this grade. This," he says, pointing at the shadow area on waveform monitor, "up to here is a fairly close match, color aside, just luminance. But then, this," he points at the high midtones, "is getting stretched out more. If I just go and bring up the highlights, it's also dragging up the lowlights with it. So if I work the two against each other . . . now we're getting someplace. That's actually a little bit closer." Kassner has been moving the gammas down

Fig. 9.19 Kassner chose to balance to the cooler Art Institute shot entirely in primary. This is the primary grade for the warm or "base" shot.

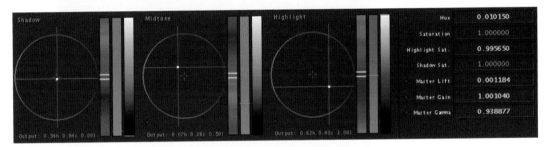

Fig. 9.20 Data from the "base" image in the Primary room.

Fig. 9.21 "Cool" image graded slightly in primary.

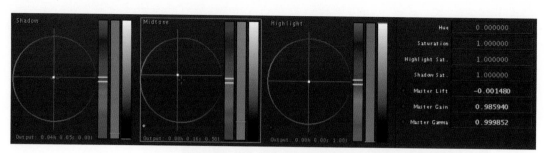

Fig. 9.22 Data for the "cool" image in Primary room.

Fig. 9.23 Split between shots, "base" image is on the bottom.

and the highlight up at the same time. "Then there's just a question of trimming the colors. A little overall hue correction would be a good cheat."

Janet Falcon of Shooters Post is next up. She starts in on the correction with her eyes almost completely on the video monitor.

A lot of color correction is about defining edges and contrast and being able to see what you want to see.

– Janet Falcon, Shooters Post

"I'm just trying to get it somewhere close to a starting point before I bother going back and forth." Falcon wipes between the "correct" and cool lion, deciding, "There's way too much red in the blacks. I need to brighten this up. This one (in the façade) still looks blue. There're actually variations of color (across the front of the building), cooler to warmer shades. And this one looks like it's painted all one color . . . flat. So this one doesn't look as good to me. This one looks more realistic because there are different shades. There are lighter areas and darker areas. This one looks flat, so I'm trying to make this one look like that. So basically I need more yellow in the highlights because there's too much blue in the highlights. Then put a little blue back in the lowlights." Falcon points at the middle of the doorway arch closest to the lion, commenting, "I'm going back and forth between looking here for blacks, here for gammas," as she points to the top edge of same archway. "And up here for whites," she says, pointing to the far right square of building façade above far right archway. "It's a little pinker."

Falcon points out that as you get closer to getting a match, it's easy to forget which side of the correction you're adjusting. She explains that on a DaVinci, when you're wiped over a still, you see a green bar so you know you're on the reference frame. See Figures 9.24–9.27.

Fig. 9.24 Primary correction on the warm, "base" image.

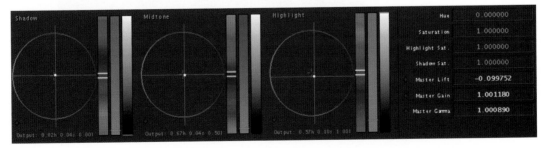

Fig. 9.25 Data from the primary correction to the "base" image.

Fig. 9.26 Primary correction on the "cool" image of the Art Institute.

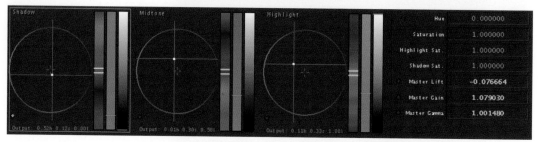

Fig. 9.27 Data from the primary correction to the "cool" image.

Fig. 9.28 Secondary correction to the hue and saturation of the lion.

With the buildings matching fairly close, Falcon pulls a secondary HSL key for the lion and matches it as well (Figures 9.28–9.30). She also adds a simple HSL qualification to both the images to correct for the clipped sky. Those corrections are nearly identical to those done by the previous colorists in this chapter.

Falcon offers a final tip at the end of her matching session: "A lot of color correction is about defining edges and contrast and being able to see what you want to see."

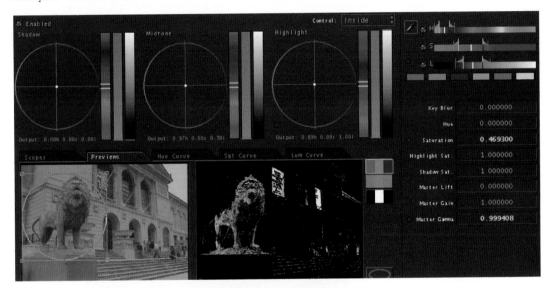

Fig. 9.29 Data for the secondary correction.

Fig. 9.30 Split screen with "cool" Art Institute image on top.

Matching Scene to Scene

This footage is from a project I edited. In that project these two shots—the interview scene of the woman (Figure 9.33) and the B-roll shot of her with her son (Figure 9.31)—were not cutting together well. I tried trimming the shots one way and then the other with no success. Finally, I decided to color correct the shots so that they'd match better. That was the solution. Figuring that our panel of experts could match them better than I could, I included the scenes in the sessions for the book.

Bob Sliga takes the first crack at matching the scenes. He starts by correcting the interview scene first. "I'm bringing the whites down out of clip. Then I balanced my blacks and brought them down a bit, which got me to here (Figure 9.35). I forgot I even did it. Sometimes it seems like my hands think for me."

Fig. 9.31 Source footage of B-roll shot. Image courtesy Exclaim Entertainment.

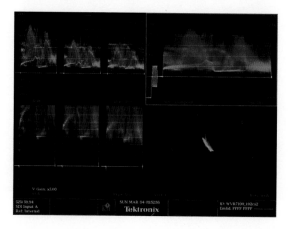

Fig. 9.32 Tektronix WVR7100 screengrab. Upper left: RGB Parade. Upper right: composite waveform. Lower right: vectorscope. Lower left: RGB Parade zoomed in the show black balance.

Fig. 9.33 Source footage of interview shot. Image courtesy Exclaim Entertainment.

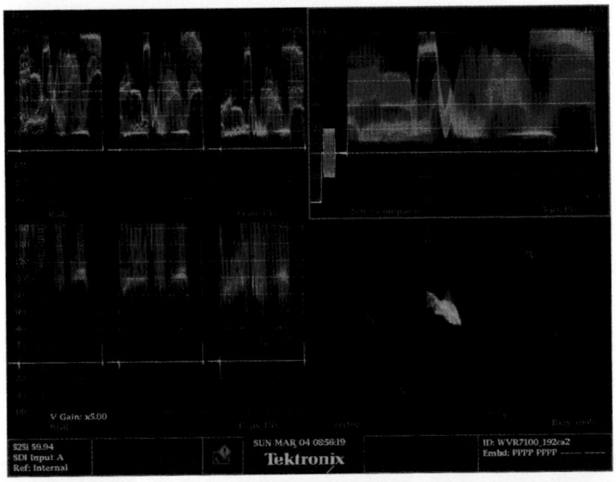

Fig. 9.34 Tektronix WVR7100 screengrab. Upper left: RGB Parade. Upper right: composite waveform. Lower right: vectorscope. Lower left: RGB Parade zoomed in the show black balance.

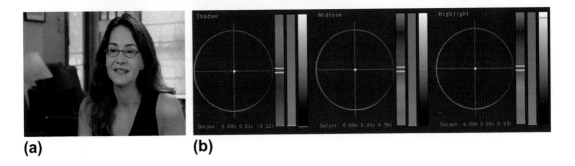

(a)   **(b)**

Fig. 9.35 (a) Primary correction to interview scene. (b) Data for Primary room.

With a basic correction to the interview scene (Figure 9.35), Sliga turns his attention to the shot of the mother and son. "Okay, so now we come over here. I'm going to balance him out too. I'm just going to pull the blacks down to zero. I'm going to bring the overall warmth of this down a little bit in the gain because we see how high that is," Sliga remarks, referring to the red channel in the RGB Parade scope being much brighter than blue or green (Figure 9.32).

A lot of times I'll advance the clip to the next scene and then back it up one frame to see how the shot ends.

– Bob Sliga

"I'm going to choose to do it this time on the individual channel. It's a little easier. Sliga brings the gain of the red channel down, but not so much that it is perfectly even with blue and green. "It is still slightly higher, which it should be because the image is mostly skin tone," he explains. Then he plays the shot through (Figure 9.36). "A lot of times I'll advance the clip to the next scene and then back it up one frame to see how the shot ends."

Sliga returns to the interview shot. "This shot is a lot warmer than the other shot. I could pull the warmth out. People generally look better warmer, so I try to use the warmth to its advantage. I'm going to try to richen her up first, then I'll match the other to this.

"I'm going to keep what I've got here and go to the secondary room. The reason is that if I like where I'm at in primaries, but I want to do some more, then I don't have to sacrifice what I've already done. There's more than one way to color correct with this software and it all depends on the type of job and the type of work that you're doing. I'm going to richen her up a bit by

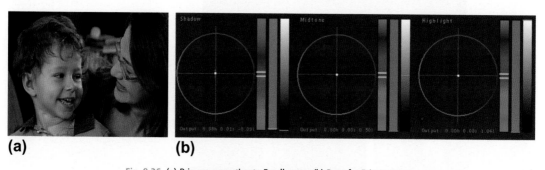

(a)   **(b)**

Fig. 9.36 (a) Primary correction to B-roll scene. (b) Data for Primary room.

Fig. 9.37 Data for Advanced tab of Primary room.

Red Gain	0.857900
Green Gain	1.000000
Blue Gain	1.020300

pulling the gammas down a bit. I'm going to warm it up a tad. The black is looking nice and black and we've got a nice clean white back here. I just richened it up a bit, okay? And by doing that, the saturation kind of came into play on its own . . . I added more saturation by just darkening it down. So I'm going to keep this and hit Control-I, which will make a still of this."

Sliga continues with his explanation of his workflow. "Then I'm going to call up the other scene and cut back and forth to the still. I'm more of a cut person instead of using a wipe. First thing I'm going to do is richen this up, warm it up a little here. I'm going to leave primaries where they're at and I'm going to come into secondaries."

Sliga enables secondary, but doesn't qualify anything at all, using it as another layer of primary. "I'll richen it up a bit," he continues, pulling down gamma. Then he warms the image by dragging the midtone wheel toward red/yellow. "Now I'll kick up the whites a bit, bring my blacks back down. That's going to be a little too warm, I have a feeling," he speculates as he brings red back down in the mids. "Let's just see where this is at," he says as he hits Control-U, checking his match. So I've made this a little bit too warm in comparison," he says, altering the shot slightly (Figure 9.39).

TIP

Sliga explains his workflow for setting his "hero grade": "I copy it to grade number one. There's a reason why I use grade one. It's a quick check. Because we have four grades available, what I'll do is I'll always drag the real grade that I want into grade one. And if I go to the Final Print room and choose add all, I can see instantly that I didn't load the correct grade in because there's a column in Final Print that shows which grade has been selected."

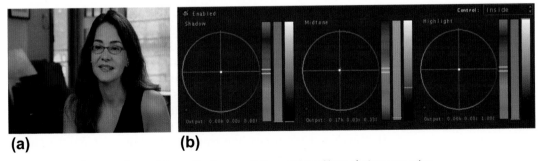

(a)   **(b)**

Fig. 9.38 (a) Secondary correction used "unqualified" as essentially an additional layer of primary correction. (b) Data from Secondary room.

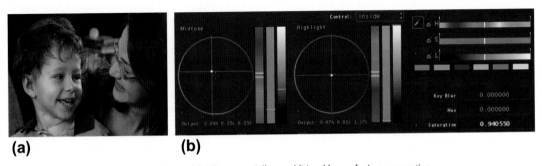

(a)   **(b)**

Fig. 9.39 (a) Secondary correction used "unqualified" as essentially an additional layer of primary correction. (b) Data from Secondary room.

CBS's Neal Kassner is next up with this match. Kassner starts out by still storing the shot of mother and son, then begins correcting the interview shot. Unfortunately, the grades for this match were not saved, so I don't have imagery to accompany the narrative, but I felt there was some good information in having him talk through the match.

"First thing I'm going to do is bring the blacks down a little bit and the gammas down a *lot*. Bring up the saturation. Move the gamma toward red. Just to kind of get it roughed in. Maybe bring the highlights down just a little bit to protect the window. She needs a little more red in the highlights, I think. Maybe drop the master gamma a little bit to give it a little more contrast. Skin tone is a little bit different on the vectorscope. Now I've got it closer on the vectorscope, but it looks wrong. So I'm not going to go with that. The real warm tone in the background elements are a little misleading," Kassner explains.

I point out that there are a lot of colors in the shot that are similar to flesh tones. "Yeah," he agrees, "it's pretty monochromatic. What I'm going to do now is something I should have done in the first place, and that is balance the blacks a little better, 'cause I'm assuming she's wearing a black dress.

"I'm going to use the shot of her and the little boy as what I'm matching to. I'm just going to keep clicking back and forth between that shot and the one I'm working on. I'm using just the primary controls on this. And at this point mostly the gamma. And every once in a while, I'll glance over at the vectorscope more than the waveform monitor. So I'm playing with the gain and the gamma just to get the skin tones to look fairly close. There's different lighting so the contrast is going to be a little different. That's a closer match than it was. We still have a lot of yellow stuff in there. The door and the lampshade are probably where that's coming from."

I ask Kassner if it's times like this that he has to depend more on his eye than the scopes. "Exactly," he confirms. "At this point, I'm just relying mainly on the picture monitor to get her face looking close in the two-shot. And once again it's the gammas and the gains where I'm doing most of my work here. But what I'm a little bit concerned with is that in the interview shot her cheeks are starting to blow out. So I'll back off on that, but then the overall luminance of her face is a little darker. So it's really just a question of walking back and forth until you get it to look right."

Matching When Lighting Changes in a Scene

These shots (Figures 9.40 and 9.42) are from a documentary I produced about my family's bicycle trip across the United States. During the interview, which I shot on BetaSP without lights, the sun started to go down, so the beginning and end of the interview look somewhat different. The

Fig. 9.40 Source footage of interview from early in the day.

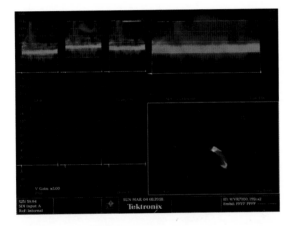

Fig. 9.41 Tektronix WVR7100 screengrab. Upper left: RGB Parade. Upper right: composite waveform, Lower right: vectorscope. Lower left: RGB Parade waveform zoomed in to show black balance.

Fig. 9.42 Source footage of interview from later in the day.

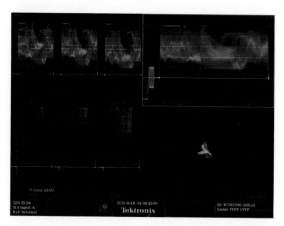

Fig. 9.43 Tektronix WVR7100 screengrab. Upper left: RGB Parade. Upper right: composite waveform, Lower right: vectorscope. Lower left: RGB Parade waveform zoomed in to show black balance.

Fig. 9.44 Early interview footage with primary correction.

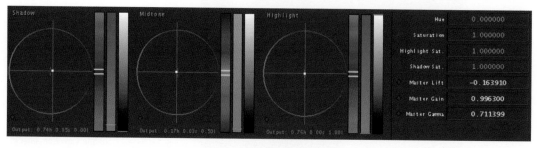

Fig. 9.45 Data from Primary room.

Fig. 9.46 Later interview footage with primary correction.

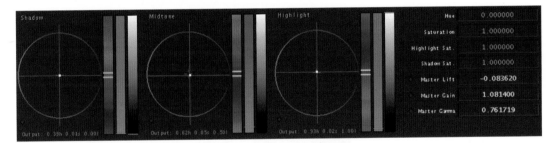

Fig. 9.47 Data from Primary room.

color temperature didn't actually change much, but the contrast as it got closer to dusk definitely changed.

Nolo Digital's Mike Matusek starts by correcting the first shot from the interview, and then he corrects the second shot to match the first. "This would be a combination of midtones and blacks that I'd bring down. Midtone may not have enough range," he says as eyes go back and forth between scopes and monitor as he adjusts.

I ask him what the challenge is in getting these shots to match. "I think you said that the sun was out in this first image and then it started to go down in this second image," he replies. The first shot has more contrast and the highlight of his right side is up, so I'll probably put a window on the left side. Probably increase the contrast on [the second shot] to try to get them closer, then just match the flesh tone" (Figures 9.44–9.47).

Matusek puts a window on the left side and lowers the brightness of the background and the face highlight. "See? That's all it really needed" (Figures 9.48 and 9.49).

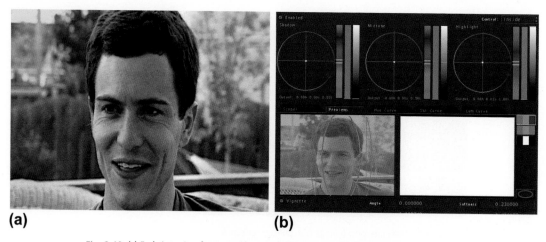

(a) **(b)**

Fig. 9.48 (a) Early interview footage with secondary correction. (b) Data from Secondary room.

Fig. 9.49 The split shows how close skin tones and background tonality match (and this Picasso-like image is sure to make my brother laugh).

Matching AND Saving!

Here's a pretty impressive "save" of a horribly overexposed and poorly white balanced shot. Alpha Dog's Terry Curren made great use of Avid Symphony's Channel Blending capabilities. I'd warned Curren that I had a tricky shot for him, and he knew it as soon as he saw it. "This is the bad guy!" Curren laughs, "This is the one we were waiting for (Figure 9.52). Well, the first thing is, it's clipped. It's obviously clipped up there, so that's a drag."

"Obviously, one of the advantages we have is that you can go in to the channels and look at individual channels and see . . . now the blue's (Figure 9.56) actually got a nice image compared to the green and the red (Figures 9.54 and 9.55), which are really messed up. The red is actually

Fig. 9.50 Source footage of Chicago Water Tower "base" image.

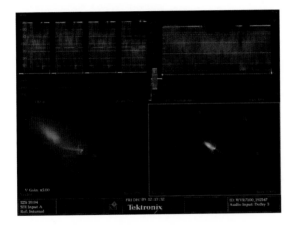

Fig. 9.51 Tektronix WVR 7100 screengrab. Upper left: YRGB Parade. Upper right: composite waveform. Lower right: vectorscope. Lower left: vectorscope zoomed 5x.

Fig. 9.52 Source footage of Chicago Water Tower poorly white balanced and overexposed.

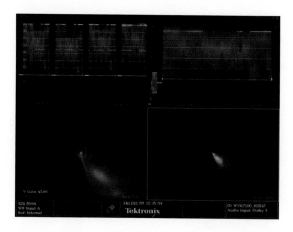

Fig. 9.53 Tektronix WVR
7100 screengrab. Upper left:
YRGB Parade. Upper right:
composite waveform. Lower
right: vectorscope. Lower
left: vectorscope zoomed 5x.

Fig. 9.54 The red channel
of the "base" water tower
image.

Fig. 9.55 The green chan-
nel of the "base" water
tower image.

Fig. 9.56 The blue channel of the "base" water tower image.

way blown out, so I will knock the red down and build some of that chan-nel back with the blue. And the same thing with the green channel. Then I'll add a little bit more blue back in the mids. Even though the whites and the blacks end up even, the mids have this little angle to them (slightly higher reds, mid greens, lower blues). I don't know why, but it just works out that way."

Curren switches to the blown-out, poorly white balanced version of the shot. "Now comes the fun. Once again, I'm just going to get down out of the high areas first," Curren explains, pulling the whites down on the master curve. Now, you can check the channels and it's exactly inverted from the other one. The green channel is the hot one (Figure 9.58) and the blue channel (Figure 9.59).

"I'm going to do the same thing I did on the other one in channels, only in the opposite direction. Now we know the red channel is the good one" (Figure 9.57), he explains as he blends red with the blue and green channels.

"Still got too much blue," he states as he goes to the red curve and pulls the high/mid reds up a bit. "This is one of those cases where you have to start messing up the other one to get them to match." He adds a chroma blur from GenArts' Sapphire plug-ins to better match the differ-ence in contrast between the two shots.

I ask what the point of the blur was in matching the shots. Curren explains, "Basically, I used a chroma blur and I went in and blurred ver-tically because I was seeing all the sharp edges. If we go in and look at the channels individually, you can see these hard edges in here. But the blue is not. The blue is a little softer. So I did a vertical blur on the two channels that were nasty, because the hard edges aren't going that way [horizontally]."

Fig. 9.57 The red channel of the poorly white balanced, overexposed water tower image.

Fig. 9.58 The green channel of the poorly white balanced, overexposed water tower image.

Fig. 9.59 The blue channel of the poorly white balanced, overexposed water tower image.

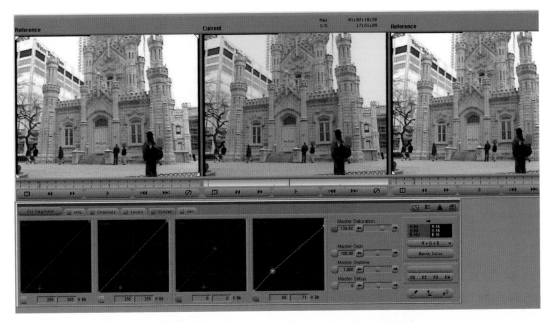

Fig. 9.60 Water tower "base" shot corrected in Avid Symphony Nitris Primary.

Fig. 9.61 Water tower "base" shot in Channel Blending tab of Symphony Nitris.

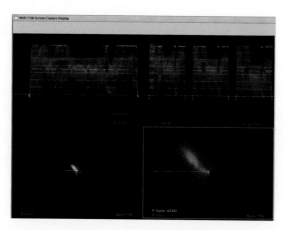

Fig. 9.62 Scopes of the correction.

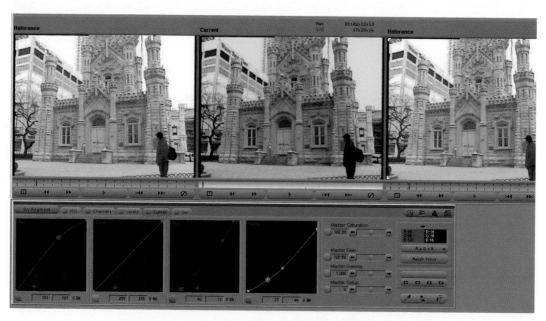

Fig. 9.63 Blue balanced water tower shot corrected in Avid Symphony Primary.

Fig. 9.64 Blue-balanced Water Tower shot in Channel Blending tab of Symphony Nitris (image does not include GenArts' Sapphire blur).

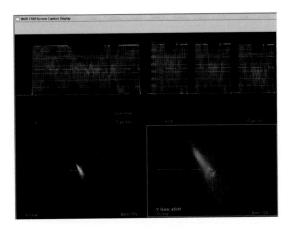

Fig. 9.65 Scopes of correction.

DaVinci Resolve has a tool similar to Avid Symphony's Channel Blending tab. On Resolve, the RGB Mixer tab (Figure 9.66) is on the Color Screen in the Primary section. If you are interested in attempting to match Terry's Symphony correction, you can accomplish it in the Lite version of Resolve.

Fig. 9.66 DaVinci Resolve's RGB Mixer tab works similarly to Avid Symphony's Channel Blending tab.

Matching Conclusion

So many of the guys—and Janet—have such a depth of experience that most of them did these matches very much by eye. Less experienced colorists will find that one of the greatest ways to match shots is by using the split screens and the RGB Parade waveform monitors, matching the various "shapes" in the trace between each color channel or cell.

Another good way to assist your eye in matching is rapidly cutting back and forth. At first, you can look at the overall image and try to ascertain the differences, but as you get closer, your eye will have to isolate various tonal ranges as the shots cut back and forth so that you can determine if the thing making one shot look redder—for example—than the other shot is red coming from the shadows, midtones, or highlights.

And for a completely different viewpoint, Company 3's Stefan Sonnenfeld questions the need to match at all, saying, "I have people who will not let me use stills to match. I rarely use film stills. There are a lot of people who will put up a still, take the still reference and just meticulously match all throughout. I do not even use stills. Now and then I do because people insist on it, but most of the time I do my thing and then watch it and watch it in context. That is what it is all about. It is not just technical perfection. This is where a lot of people fall short or flat. There is a lot more to it. There are guys like Michael Bay who will literally get mad at me if I start to try and match up things. It is not realistic. When you are in an action scene and there is smoke and fire and car crashes and guns and this and that it is haphazard. It is craziness. Why would every little piece of image have to look the same? It is boring when it is one canvas. It is one-dimensional, not three-dimensional. But once in a while, it is appropriate."

CHAPTER 10

Creating Looks

The creation of "looks" is probably why some colorists make as much as CEOs of Fortune 500 companies and drive around in Lamborghinis. This is the sexy stuff. It's also the stuff that is virtually unquantifiable. It's part of what takes color correction from craft to art.

And after a recent trip to New Hat in Los Angeles to visit Bob Festa, I got a glimpse of how it can even be like menu writing at a good gourmet restaurant. As I sat with Festa, he showed me a wide range of looks that he'd created and stored. Like a guitarist with names for each of his treasured axes, Festa did not simply call his looks by some technically accurate name, but with creative descriptive flair that did as much to sell the effect to the client as it did to actually describe it. I saw Brazilian Silver, Cold Steel, Study in Neutrality, and Pearlized Whites. Like a good description of an entrée at a restaurant, they describe the item in a way that makes it desirable.

Pearlized Whites was little more than a simple soft, highlight glow (Figure 10.2). *Any* colorist can give you a highlight glow . . . but *Festa* gives you Pearlized Whites. I think this is more than a mere gimmick. It brands the entire experience and provides a handle for clients that generates creative buy-in to the looks. I doubt that Fuzzy Highlights or Blurry Brights were contenders when he was naming this look.

Festa explains how he created the Pearlized Whites look. He adds a little more contrast to the base shot (Figure 10.1), driving the highlights up. He explains, "Make sure the whites are nice and strong. I'm comfortable with the shape of the shot, the colorimetry. I'm going to add another layer and soften the whole shot. I'm going to isolate just the highlights on her dress, with a nice softness. Now I'm using the 3D keyer and put a garbage matte and a luminance isolation to get rid of the highlights in the curtain." With the softened shot being keyed through the highlights, the whites of the nightgown take on a beautiful, ethereal patina: Pearlized Whites (Figure 10.2).

Festa describes his Brazilian Silver look: "a very desaturated, silvery look that softens the midtones a bit, low saturation. An aggressive,

Fig. 10.1 Base look.

Fig. 10.2 Festa's Pearlized Whites.

contemporary, cross between a bleach bypass and a hi-con black and white look" (Figures 10.3 and 10.4).

Why "Brazilian?" Why not? It's a branding statement that does little to describe an actual color or look, but definitely provides a hook to draw in the imagination—and continued patronage—of a client. Can you imagine this client going to another colorist and requesting Brazilian Silver?

It's similar to the Bozell ad copywriter who coined "fine Corinthian leather" to describe the interior of the Chrysler Imperial and Cordoba back in 1974 when Ricardo Montalban was the spokesman. The leather did not come from Corinth, but New Jersey. But who wants an upscale car upholstered with fine New Jersey leather?

But pitching the look could be argued to be not quite as important as creating it, so we turn to Chicago colorist Craig Leffel of Optimus to

Fig. 10.3 Base look.

Fig. 10.4 Festa's Brazilian Silver.

explain some of his process for coming up with looks. "Well, I think it's always a process of working wider and then narrowing."

I ask if some of the time when he's spinning the trackballs, he's not really color correcting as much as getting a sense of where the image can go. "Yeah. Sometimes when you make an extreme change you see that you've either grabbed the wrong thing or you've grabbed too much. It's certainly the subtle stuff that begins to appear to you when you've made a huge change. Then you can narrow down and narrow down and narrow down from there. Also, sometimes when you're starting to play with a new image, you work in extremes unless you're being told a very specific thing. But if it's up to you to kind of come up with a look, then making extreme, radical changes is sometimes helpful. It may not be helpful to the people sitting behind you, but it helps you kind of see where an image can go. How much it can handle. If you really do make those extreme changes up front, I quite often see things that I didn't think of. Like maybe this image looks really good pink and I never considered that. Or maybe hi-con (high contrast) or way more crushed than you would have ever thought would look good.

Well, I think it's always a process of working wider and then narrowing.

– Craig Leffel, Optimus

"You say, 'Holy moley, that looks great. I didn't really mean to do that. I was just kind of rolling through my ranges but that looks really good. I think I'll work towards that.' Because quite often that first impression of an image, no matter who you are, no matter how experienced you are, no matter how much background you have, the first time somebody says, 'Do something really cool with that.' That first impression that you have may not be the one you really want to go with. And you kind of have to be willing to let yourself find where you might want to go. And obviously it's a collaborative effort with the people behind you, but quite often, if I'm by myself, I don't like to trust my first instinct. I like to kind of challenge myself and see if there's something I didn't think of. I call it 'going through my ranges.' You know, really pushing it around: light and dark, pushing it all the way around the vectorscope.

"If I have a huge time crunch, I don't do it and if I've got someone behind me saying something very specific, I won't typically do it, but I will push for a little bit of time with the film by myself where I do run through those ranges. Especially if it's kind of open-ended, like 'Do something cool with this.'

"So that's my trick," concludes Leffel. "Push it around hard at the very beginning and then narrow down and narrow down and narrow down."

Enough Is Enough

They say that great art is all about knowing when to stop, so I ask Leffel when he knows to stop. "Certainly in my line of work, knowing when to stop . . . there's a point of diminishing returns. I think I'm usually done when I don't see anything objectionable in the picture any more. If everything has lived up to what I was trying to do and I don't see any objections, then I'm usually feeling pretty good about being done. The truth is, you could keep working forever and you'd never be done. You'd just keep going and going and going."

I ask him to be specific about how he knows where his boundaries are. "Those are the hard things to even verbalize. I think if the lighting I've set feels like it's actually motivated by something outside and I feel like that's not going to be able to go anywhere past that. If I like their flesh tones; if I like the details in the image. I'm always scanning the image all over the place to see if something is standing out to me or bothering me or drawing my attention and I'm usually trying to consider all things at once, so in a shot, if I'm really trying to be critical, I'm saying to myself 'Is anything distracting me? Is anything bothering me? Is anything pulling my eye away from what I should be looking at?' When I can answer all of those questions and say, 'I'm not being distracted. I feel I'm looking at what I'm supposed to be looking at. I've achieved the goal that I've set out to do.' If I can answer all those questions, then I'm usually feeling like I'm pretty done."

Preset Looks

Bob Festa was one of the few people that I spoke to who described some of the looks that he starts to show clients. Festa is clearly talented enough to develop these looks from scratch on every shot, but he's also a big proponent of reusing selected elements of these looks as easy-to-apply presets.

> *I'd rather show them 25 things that I can do with a single keystroke than 4 things that I've had to build from scratch.*
>
> *– Bob Festa, New Hat*

"I've been doing this for a long time and I've been the architect of a couple of features in the DaVinci, and one of those is something called PowerGrade. PowerGrade is a browser that lets me keep 20–25 of my top techniques in there, and once I get an image balanced and into a place that I like, then I can ripple those PowerGrade effects back on top of it. Those might be everything from a four-corner pin to a bleach bypass to a cross-process look. These are things that might take five or ten minutes to build up from scratch; I can quickly double-click it and dial it in on top of my base, well-balanced image."

Festa continues, "That PowerGrade library is very influential. And I had a lot of arguments about that with people about 'Should we be able to dial things on top—with just a single keystroke—of images, or should they be rebuilt from scratch?' My feeling is, if you want to give your clients a choice, I'd rather show them 25 things that I can do with a single keystroke than 4 things that I've had to build from scratch."

Definition

cross-process look: The look of film when it is processed chemically in a "bath" or "soup" that is supposed to be used to process a different kind of film—for example, using a C41 development bath on a piece of film that should be developed in an E6 bath, or vice versa. This cross-processing alters the characteristics of the film.

Festa's PowerGrade Library Revealed

Festa generously shared a glimpse at some of his trade secrets. "Some of the things that are in there are prebuilt PowerTiers. Basically, I always start with a nice balanced image. Then I've got a bunch of PowerTiers that I can ripple on top of that. They'd be one or two channels of window or a channel of defocus combined with a key."

Festa is sitting at his DaVinci, walking through the presets with me. "Just to give you an idea off the top of my head what I have in there: in the top row, I have a complete line of bleach bypass, ranging from 20 percent to 70 percent in 10 percent increments. In a single keystroke, I can ripple that on top without having to go through a whole building process. So I can show somebody 20 percent, 30 percent, 40 percent, boom, boom, boom, just like that."

Festa Switches Gears

I've interviewed Bob Festa on three separate occasions for this book. Originally, he worked on a DaVinci 2K +. Since then, Bob has moved from R!OT in Santa Monica to his own shop called New Hat. The move also came with a change in "kit" from DaVinci to Baselight.

Everybody's got a deadline, so why spend it recreating something you know you've done over and over again?

"The DaVinci is really clumsy when it comes to setting up soft effects like ProMists, defocus, pearlized whites," Festa opines. "So I have all of those set up on single keystrokes. Of course, what that does is build a defocus channel and a key channel and a channel of Power Window, just to support it all."

Continuing through the presets, Festa explains, "I have the Pearlizer, which is just soft whites. I have the swing and tilt, which is just the corner's softened. I have the ProMist, and the ProMist is divided up into ProMist 1 through 6. And I also have a Mist with what I call 'demin' added to it, which is like a richer ProMist also. The ProMist settings don't have much correlation to the on-camera ProMist filters.

"Textures, which are really hard to create, like bleach bypass and soft effects—I have all those on single keystroke things," Festa explains. "In addition to those, I have the usual kinds of stuff like Blue Wash #2, duo-tones, day for night 1 and 2, film noir black and white. Then I have my cross-process looks."

Festa describes what his cross-processed looks actually do. "So I have those two things built as layers also and those use multiple layers, because a C41 to E6 look really gives a super golden white with a lot of blue/cyan in the blacks. So I use a separate channel for each one of those effects. One channel to warm up the whites give it a golden, dirty look. And also a channel to get that 'cyan-ey' blue crap in the blacks."

Festa summarizes, "To build any of these effects from the ground up is really a five-minute job. So I found, if I had all of this stuff at the top, I could open up this PowerGrade and just quickly show somebody not only my warm, cool, and balanced looks, but here's some really wacky stuff if you want to stretch out."

I respond, "Everybody's got a deadline, so why spend it recreating something you know you've done over and over again?"

"Exactly," Festa agrees, "That was my thought."

With Festa's switch to Baselight, he's also added a new twist to the speed of his look application. With Baselight, Festa is able to do something similar to the look generation in some of Apple's consumer products, in which you see the source image in the middle with eight choices arrayed around the center. Selecting any of those variations delivers another set of similar choices around the first choice, which now sits in the middle. Using this method, Apple users can dial in a look by simply choosing variations on a theme. Festa does something similar (Figure 10.5).

Fig. 10.5 Nine-way split in Baselight offering up variations on a central look (image courtesy of *Chasing Ghosts*, screen capture courtesy New Hat/Bob Festa).

Preset Looks in Apple's Color

Apple's Color—and many other applications—have this same ability to create preset looks and apply them at the touch of a button. Most of the preset looks that were delivered with the initial release of Color were created by Bob Sliga, who is featured in this book. Bob and I also cohosted DVD training series together for both Apple Color and DaVinci Resolve for Class on Demand. There are also fantastic preset looks available from third-party vendors such as Graeme Nattress, who sells a collection of effects nodes that works in Color. Many of the colorists who are experienced Color/FinalTouch users highly recommend the Nattress plug-ins, which come not only with the effects nodes themselves, but also with entire prebuilt process trees. Sliga also sells a collection of looks for Color called "Scone Looks," including primaries, secondaries, and ColorFX for Apple Color, plus a new series of Powergrades for DaVinci Resolve.

Film Processing Looks

Many of the highly desired looks that colorists are asked to do actually mimic chemical film processes. We briefly touched on cross-processing, and we'll take a deeper look into the electronic "reproduction" of the skip bleach and bleach bypass looks later in the chapter, but the following looks give you a quick overview of some of the ways that various film processes can affect the look of an image. The following images are not color corrections, but motion picture film processed chemically in various ways. Understanding how these processes affect the look of the image will help you build your "visual vocabulary." Because directors of photography are frequent collaborators with colorists, understanding what these processes do to the image will help you communicate better with them.

Often times, DPs will choose to attempt to reproduce these looks electronically in color correction sessions instead of applying them chemically, because these chemical processes are somewhat risky to apply as they can't be "undone," and although Kodak educates film makers in how to execute and utilize these processes, it does not recommend them due to the inherent dangers of developing film in ways that were not intended.

Cross-processing creates higher contrast and saturation and distorts colors in sometimes unexpected ways (Figure 10.7).

"Pushing" film—which overdevelops the negative—is used in combination with underexposing the negative to increase contrast and add grain (Figures 10.11 and 10.12). In color films, it also creates lifted, blue shadows and a color imbalance. It is also possible to "pull" process film, which is essentially the exact opposite of push processing.

Cross-Processing Visualizing Tutorial

The cross-processed images provide an excellent resource for an important tutorial exercise. Look closely at the base images and the cross-processed looks and try to describe the differences in the images. Be specific about how different things are affected by the process. How is contrast affected? What about highlights? Do the blacks or highlights become cooler or warmer? Do the highlights or blacks clip or lift? What color shifts happen in the warmer colors? What color shifts happen in the cooler colors? What color shifts happen in the midtones? What would you name this look if you didn't know if had a name already?

All of these exercises in describing the image help you become better at communicating looks with DPs and directors. It also helps develop your eye for observing the changes in images. A lot of being able to recreate a specific look that you see in a magazine, TV ad, or movie is dependent on your ability to simply describe the image and how it's different from "reality." If you can't describe it, it will be very hard to recreate.

Another exercise comes from Festa's description of his Brazilian Silver look at the beginning of the chapter. New looks can be created by combining looks. His Brazilian Silver was the combination of a hi-con black and white with a bleach bypass. Why not combine a saturated hi-con look with glowed blacks? Mix and match and see what works. And if a look doesn't work, try it on an image with a radically different "base" colorimetry. Sometimes an interesting look works only on images with—for example—small areas of deep blacks, but if the image has a lot of deep blacks, then the look fails. So before you give up on a preset look that you're trying to create, test it on several shots that are radically different—cool, warm, contrasty, flat, dark, light, saturated, desat . . . you may find the perfect combination. See Figures 10.6–10.10.

Skip bleach and bleach bypass are processes in which the film is either not bleached at all to remove silver or is partially bleached, leaving various amounts of silver. The remaining silver increases the contrast of the film. Wherever there is more developed dye, there is more silver, so you get higher-contrast, blacker blacks and less saturation (Figures 10.13–10.15).

Fig. 10.6 A print from Kodak 5245 negative film processed normally with the ECN-2 process.

Fig. 10.7 A print from one of Kodak's reversal films, Ektachrome 5285, which has been processed using ECN-2.

Fig. 10.8 A print from Kodak reversal film Ektachrome 100D processed normally.

Fig. 10.9 A print from Kodak negative film 5279 processed normally.

Fig. 10.10 A print from Kodak Ektachrome 100D cross-processed.

Fig. 10.11 This image is printed from a black and white negative with normal processing.

Fig. 10.12 This image is printed from a black and white negative pushed two stops.

Fig. 10.13 A print from normally developed Kodak 5274 film.

Fig. 10.14 5274 with a bleach bypass processing of the camera negative.

Fig. 10.15 5274 with skip bleach processing of the print.

Now that you've seen how these looks are created photochemically, the following section will describe how to electronically attain one of the most common of these looks: skip bleach or bleach bypass.

Skip Bleach or Bleach Bypass

Bob Sliga did his first pass at this image by simply dropping Graeme Nattress's bleach bypass Color Effects node on it (Figures 10.18 and 10.19).

I ask Sliga if he could reproduce the look just using the primary and secondary rooms. "This shot is pretty nicely balanced, and the blacks all

Fig. 10.16 Original source footage courtesy of Artbeats.

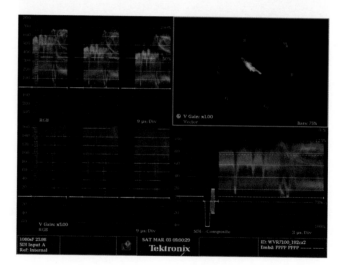

Fig. 10.17 Tektronix WVR7100 screengrab. Upper left: RGB Parade. Upper right: vectorscope. Lower right: composite waveform. Lower left: RGB Parade zoomed in 5x to blacks.

Fig. 10.18 With the Nattress Bleach bypass effect dropped on in Color Effects.

Bleach Effect Amount	0.425800
Over Exposure	0.072000
Desaturation	0.500000

Fig. 10.19 Data from Nattress "G_Bleach_Bypass" node in Color Effects.

match but in the gammas, there's a bit of an angle' with red higher than green higher than blue," Sliga explains. "That's because this shot is balanced a little warm. And there are purists who might say that this shot needs to be balanced perfectly and that those levels should match."

I explain to Sliga that I've been looking at this shot with the basic grade of the original Artbeats' image, so I'm used to seeing it a little warm. Sliga agree, "It should be warm. This shot wants to be warm. When I think of balance, I think of making the blacks black" (Figures 10.20 and 10.21).

Fig. 10.20 Primary correction.

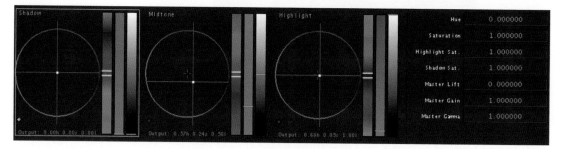

Fig. 10.21 Data from Primary room.

With the shot in a good starting position, Sliga turns his attention to giving it a classic bleach bypass look. "We'll favor the bleach bypass on the cool side," he says as he takes the gamma and highlights toward blue a little with the hue offset wheels. "Then we'll go to secondaries." In a secondary, Sliga doesn't bother qualifying anything before he pulls the blacks down in the entire image—using the secondary like a second level of primary correction (Figures 10.22 and 10.23).

"I'm going to be clipping that blacks and blowing the whites out," he explains as he stretches the gamma back up a bit to compensate for his big black drop. Then he drops saturation in each of the tonal ranges.

Fig. 10.22 **First secondary correction.**

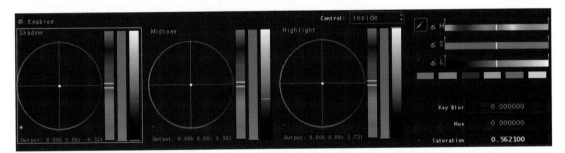

Fig. 10.23 **Data from Secondary room.**

Then adds another secondary and qualifies the brightest portions of the sky and building adding even more contrast, correcting the outside of the secondary—which are the shadows, in this case—making them darker (Figures 10.24 and 10.25).

"It hurts the eyes after a while when you look back and you see how far it went," Sliga comments. "That's one way we could go." Bleach bypass is a matter of crushing gammas, crushing blacks, blowing out whites. How far that you want the blacks to be is really the key. You have to have a broadcast safe filter on it, because you're blowing it all out. If you don't have a broadcast safe filter on it, you're going to get hosed."

Fig. 10.24 Second secondary correction.

Fig. 10.25 Data from second secondary.

With skip bleach, you end up with a saturated/grainy/gritty image. It changes the contrast of the film.

– Greg Creaser, freelance colorist

Greg Creaser expounds on the look of bleach bypass as he drops a bleach bypass effect on the Artbeats Marines scene (Figures 10.26–10.28). "Typically, bleach bypass has more saturation than that, depending on how it was done or how long it was let out of the bleach." To correct it to a more classic bleach bypass look, he goes back to primary, adds saturation, pulls blacks down and pumps up highlights. "It would be a little edgier, like that," he says.

Greg Creaser

Greg Creaser is a freelance DI colorist in Los Angeles with an impressive list of more than 60 feature films to his credit as either digital color timing supervisor or digital intermediate colorist: *The Ring Two, Seabiscuit, Terminator 3, Pirates of the Caribbean: The Curse of the Black Pearl, xXx, Spider-Man, The Fast and the Furious, The Mummy Returns, Hannibal, Mission Impossible II,* and *Gladiator.*

Greg has been working in the industry since 1977, starting in the laboratory as a technician/color timer and moving into upper management by 1985. Greg also studied photography at Art Center in Pasadena, and his father was a cinematographer.

I ask Creaser to define the look of bleach bypass. "That's an interesting question," he says. "There's multiple ways to do skip bleach. You can skip the whole bleach or half of the bleach. What usually happens with skip bleach is that you end up with a saturated/grainy/gritty image. It changes the contrast of the film. It really depends on what kind of film stock it is and how it was bypassed and whether it was overdeveloped or underdeveloped on top of that."

Fig. 10.26 Source image courtesy Artbeats.

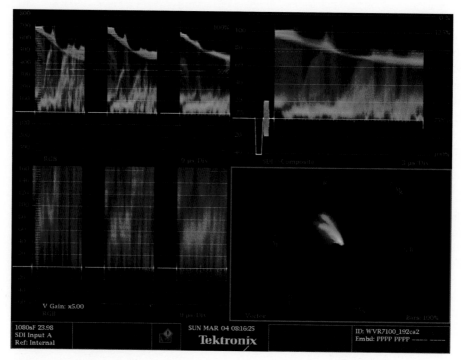

Fig. 10.27 Tektronix WVR7100. Upper left: RGB Parade. Upper right: composite waveform. Lower right: vectorscope. Lower left: RGB Parade expanded to see blacks.

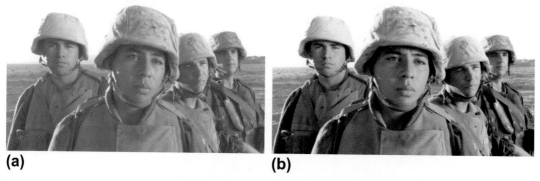

(a)   **(b)**

Fig. 10.28 a) Image with no correction except bleach bypass node in Color Effects Room. b) "Edgier" version after Creaser adds saturation, lowers blacks, and raises highlights.

Match the Look

One of the common requests to colorists is to give an image a look from a popular movie, TV show, or music video. Obviously, for the colorist, this requires a fairly decent command of popular culture and a decent color memory.

I ask Matusek if it's a big help when someone provides visual references to other media. "Do you feel like you have to be up on the latest movies or watch a lot of media or TV so that if somebody says, 'Hey I want it to look like *Crash*,' you can say 'I know what that means'?" Matusek responds, "Totally. I get Netflix. Newer films are a good place to look for looks. With older films, it was color timing and they were not as extreme. Commercials are great resources to look for really pushed looks. I did the GoDaddy spots the last few years and the look we were going for in those spots was *CSI: Miami*. Hypersaturated . . . well, not hypersaturated, but make the sky yellow and the water cyan and push the contrast. Generalizing, that campaign had that look. Or the 'Diamonds Are Forever' spots were kind of contrasty and cyan, duotone with a flesh tone that's desaturated. It's tough to have seen the same movie as your client, or see the same spots as your client. It's mostly about saying, 'Is this what you mean?' and doing a look and then trying something else. Usually you can find something you've both seen."

As for looks from movies that are often requested or copied, Stefan Sonnenfeld has developed some of them that have been copied so much that he almost feels as if the look is being parodied, "There are a lot of looks that I have been teased for. I think I was one of the first or if not the first to do those kind of greenish and orangey skin tones. (Think *Transformers*, though the look goes back at least a decade before that.) Then I did a film like *Man on Fire* and I guess there are three other movies that are literally copies of that."

Matusek picks out the Marines shot from Artbeats (Figure 10.29) and decides to give it a look of another popular movie. "For this image, I'm just trying to give it a more high-contrast, maybe go for a skip bleach kind of a look. Kind of a *Blackhawk Down*—I hate to be cliché, but it is kind of a cool look."

Matusek begins his grade. "So in this shot, I'm just playing on the contrasty image, because there's already nice highlights here. I'm just kind of pushing that. Letting the sky blow. There's some nice blue there. Sometimes a client will have you spend 20 minutes on making the sky blue—the subject is the soldiers" (Figure 10.31).

Matusek points to the highlights on the bright sides of the helmets and continues with a great tip: "I'd probably grab a highlight and defocus some of that stuff, because if you defocus the highlights, you can push the contrast even more. When you do too much, some of these pushed highlights start to look a little clipped, which doesn't look that good. So if you throw a nice, soft defocused highlight, that kind of smoothes out that transition and allows you to go a little more heavy-handed with the contrast."

If you defocus the highlights, you can push the contrast even more.
– Mike Matusek, Nolo Digital Film

Fig. 10.29 Source image courtesy, Artbeats.

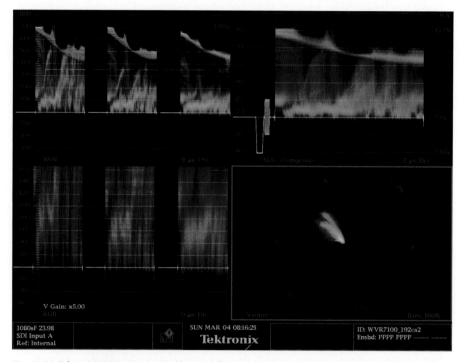

Fig. 10.30 Tektronix WVR7100 screengrab. Upper left, YRGB Parade. Upper right, composite waveform. Lower right, vectorscope. Lower left, vectorscope zoomed in 5x.

Fig. 10.31 Matusek's primary correction.

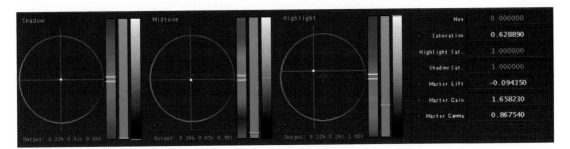

Fig. 10.32 Data from Primary room.

Matusek takes some time working on getting a saturated sky before explaining, "I'm doing what I said I disliked when the clients asked for it, but I'm putting a little blue in the sky. Usually it works out to look pretty good." He creates a big oval window along the top. "I would prefer it without the blue sky, but a lot of clients would prefer that," he says, showing off his newly tweaked sky (Figures 10.33 and 10.34).

Continuing with the soldier/look theme, Matusek comments on a recent project of his. "I worked on a documentary called *War Tapes*. They gave a bunch of cameras to soldiers and they documented their year's stay in Iraq. So what we did was, all the footage in Iraq, we gave it a higher contrast, warmer look. We gave it a little grittier look. And then they would cut from the soldiers to their families. On the home front, it was a little softer, it was more saturated and had truer colors. Just trying to create a separation. And it's all subtle. It was a documentary, so the Iraq footage wasn't like *Blackhawk Down*.

Fig. 10.33 Secondary correction to tweak sky.

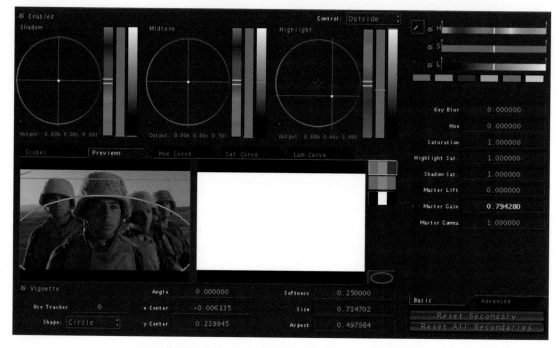

Fig. 10.34 Data from *outside* of the qualification in the Secondary room.

Looks for Promos and Opens

One of the popular images that the colorists in this book chose to give a look to was Artbeats' image of a football being readied by the center (Figures 10.35 and 10.36).

To give some context, I ask Shooters Post colorist Janet Falcon to grade the image as if it will be used in an open for the Super Bowl.

Fig. 10.35 Original source footage, image courtesy of Artbeats.

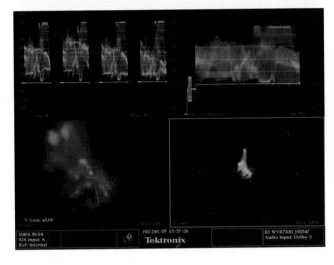

Fig. 10.36 Tektronix WVR7100 screengrab. Upper left: RGB Parade. Upper right: vectorscope. Lower right: composite waveform. Lower left: RGB Parade zoomed in 5x to blacks.

Opens are usually high color. Like if you've seen the open for Survivor. Really bold, wild colors.

— *Janet Falcon, Shooters Post*

She considers the request, then dives in to the grade. "Then you'd go for something a lot more contrasty and a lot more pushed and forced. Depending on what other things are in there, you may stick with normal color. I just want to save it along the way so I can play with a few different things. Every time I get something, I save it. I use my DaVinci notepads a lot. Maybe go with a blue-black if you want not 'off' colors, but not normal colors."

She continues, "Opens are usually high color. Like if you've seen the open for *Survivor*. Really bold, wild colors. You could go something more like that" (Figures 10.37–10.40).

Fig. 10.37 Falcon's
primary correction.

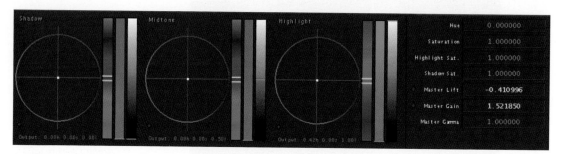

Fig. 10.38 Data from the Primary room.

I ask for a different look because the Chicago Bears were in the Super-Bowl the year we did this: cold and tough. (GO BEARS!) "We could go for cooler. You can shift colors when you're doing master gain and master lift. As you track up and down, you shift color. I usually like to do luminance only in my vignettes and then go in separately and adjust more

Fig. 10.39 Secondary correction.

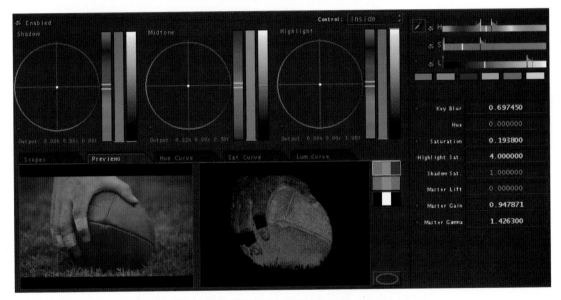

Fig. 10.40 Data from inside the qualification in the Secondary room.

or less saturation." Falcon's last sentence describes a fairly unique ability of DaVinci to affect luminance without affecting RGB. Many other color correctors, including Apple's Color, don't have this capability, so the workaround is to go back and change saturation after gain and setup adjustments that raise or lower saturation.

Fig. 10.41 Falcon's new "Chicago cool" primary correction.

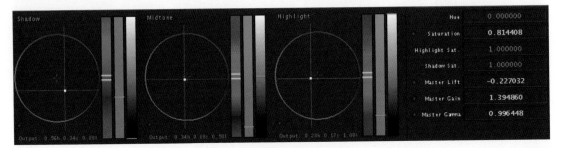

Fig. 10.42 Data from Primary room.

Pete Jannotta also gives the football image a look of his own. He works for a while before I prompt him to tell me what he's doing. "I desaturated it," he explains. "I'm just experimenting. I want this one to feel strong. Not too clean. Feel gutsier, because of his tape, the dirty tape, and go with that suggestion of it being tough." It's a telling point that he derives the direction of his correction from an element of the picture, like the tape on the player's fingers.

White's go up, blacks go down, gamma goes down. It always makes it more theatrical . . . printlike.

– Pete Jannotta, The Filmworkers Club

"Then the other thing I was thinking of with this picture is softening the outside. But then I looked at it, and it's kind of already done. It does

Fig. 10.43 Vignette correction in first secondary.

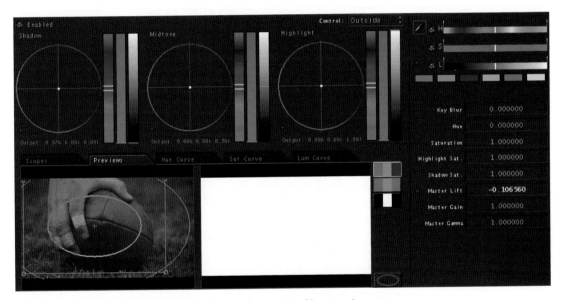

Fig. 10.44 Data from outside of first secondary room.

it naturally. I don't know if I really need to get on top of that and mess it up. But I do think I can do more with the fingers."

Jannotta cranks up the highlights and pulls down the setup. "Maybe just make it burn a little. White's go up, blacks go down, gamma goes down. It always makes it more theatrical . . . printlike. It looks more like it's on a movie screen this way" (Figures 10.47 and 10.48).

Jannotta continues, "I don't like that his hand is so flat. The ball looks good, the grass looks pretty good. His hand's kind of not happening.

Fig. 10.45 HSL qualifica-
tion for second secondary
correction.

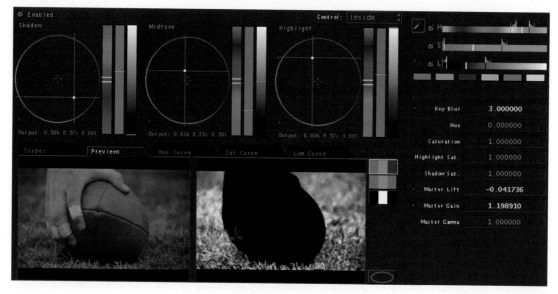

Fig. 10.46 Data from second secondary.

Boring. So I'm going to go into secondaries and put a vignette on, and enable this and enable the vignette and draw something. I'm going to make a sloppy shape around here like this," he says, drawing a mitten shape around the hand. "I'm not sure how it's going to work when he moves, but I'll figure that out later."

He saves his shape and goes back to secondaries to adjust inside the mitten shape. Jannotta spins the mids down a lot and the blacks down some, exclaiming, "Now I've got dirt! Make that dirt pop." He cranks up the highlights. "On the outside of the hand vignette, I might

Fig. 10.47 Jannotta's primary correction.

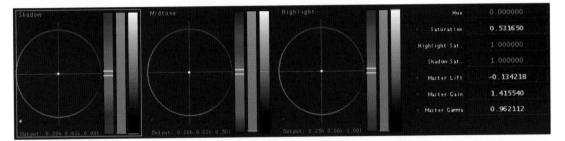

Fig. 10.48 Data from the Primary room.

desaturate that a bit. I like what's happening there. Maybe not the *areas* it's happening in, but I like that blend of the warm with the more neutral. Let's watch it as it moves. Yeah, not too bad," he says approvingly before he pulls down the mitten shape to include more of the football (Figure 10.49).

Pete Jannotta

Pete Jannotta has worked in the television industry since 1975 and has been a colorist for almost 30 years. Jannotta has worked with a myriad of color correction systems, including every permutation of DaVinci since its inception.

Jannotta was a colorist at Editel Chicago for 13 years, working on national and international advertising accounts, until becoming a partner at Skyview Film and Video, where he continued to hone his craft for ten years, working with A-list clients from Chicago as well as all over the Midwest and the world.

Currently, Jannotta is a senior colorist at the Filmworkers Club in Chicago, where he continues to work on advertising accounts as well as feature films, documentaries, and music videos.

Fig. 10.49 The final look in secondaries, though the correction to the outside of the vignette is made later.

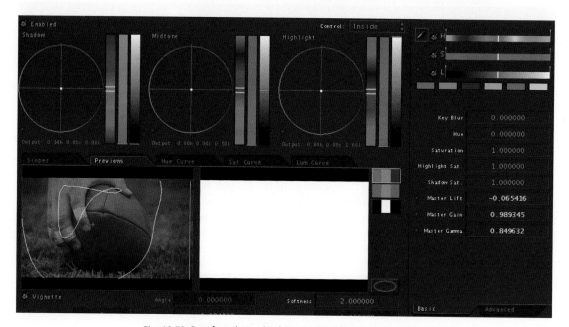

Fig. 10.50 Data from the inside of the vignette in the Secondary room.

"I'm thinking the blacks are too compressed on the inside, but boy, I like the hand that way. Jannotta goes to the color effect room and adds sharpness, bringing it down a little from the default sharpness setting (Figure 10.51).

As a final touch, Jannotta proposes one last change: "I feel like adding blue to the outside. It's going to pop the ball more and his hand. It doesn't necessarily make sense that it's that desaturated on the right side but it's interesting" (Figure 10.52).

Fig. 10.51 Jannotta's color effect is just a Sharpen set to .621550.

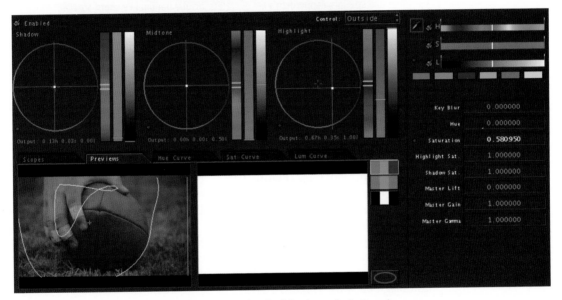

Fig. 10.52 Data from the outside of the vignette in the Secondary room.

Of course, the natural colorist to take on this image is Chris Pepperman, who was a colorist at NFL Films when I sat down with him to grade this shot. Pepperman starts with primaries. "I want to make everything black and white." (The primary correction is simply pulling all of the saturation out.) He pulls an HSL key in secondaries, qualifying warm tones. Then he cranks the contrast, crushing the blacks.

I always want to push the limit and then come back, because I want to know what my range is.

– Chris Pepperman, NASCAR

When Pep realizes that some posterizing was starting to happen in his correction, he stops to refine the qualification of the HSL key, saying, "I always want to push the limit and then come back, because I want to know what my range is. I reference it to a golf club. You swing a nine iron. You swing it as hard as you can. You know how far you're going to hit it. And then, when the target is closer, you soften it up a bit. You don't swing as hard until you get the right distance."

Chris Pepperman

Chris Pepperman joined NFL Films in 1993. In addition to working on NFL Films television series and specials, Pepperman's list of credits include national TV spots, *Survivor: Africa* for CBS, and numerous other documentary and film projects.

Pepperman's partial client list includes: NASCAR, HBO, Harley Davidson, Sprint, Walmart, Comcast, Pepsi, and the US Army.

Before joining NFL Films, Pepperman worked as a colorist for Manhattan Transfer in New York. He has since joined NASCAR as senior colorist.

"What I've done here is just create a contrasty image, and I just desaturated the red a little bit, and I'm really pushing the blacks and I'm giving it a very contrasty look (Figure 10.53) 'cause this is for an open and they tend to be glossy. I might add some blur to it. I might add some grain. I might add sharpness to it. Make it sizzle a little bit. So it gives it a very gritty 8-mm-type look. I see grain structure. I see maybe film scratches. I also like to do desaturated looks where you desaturate everything and then just feather back in a little bit of color. That might work very well here too. Keep everything black and white, then just add a little of the red and black back in" (Figure 10.55).

Fig. 10.53 First secondary correction to the warmer tones.

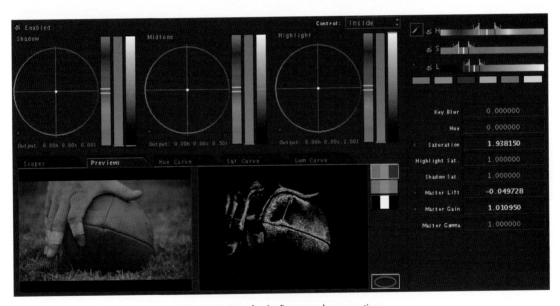

Fig. 10.54 Data for the first secondary corrections.

Fig. 10.55 Second secondary corrections to green tones.

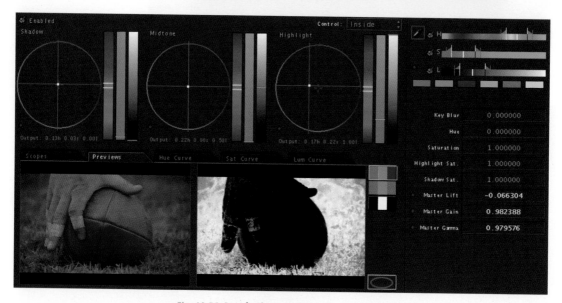

Fig. 10.56 Data for the second secondary corrections.

True Grit

One of the images that definitely called out for a tough, gritty look was the SWAT team storming out of the truck from *Chasing Ghosts*. Several colorists were inspired to give that scene a shot.

Pete Jannotta starts off. "Well, what's coming to mind for me on this one is gritty, desaturated, crispy, which I don't know how to make it on this machine." I ask Jannotta to define "crispy" for me, as it's a term that I've heard lots of colorists use. "'Crispy' is sharpening and highlight accentuation, which I would do with a curve in DaVinci. Really peak the top end only. Stretch it. That makes all the highlights pop up. And sharpening makes the grain pop; it makes all the edges pop. I'm looking at this

Fig. 10.57 Source image from *Chasing Ghosts*, courtesy Wingman Productions, Inc. (The green tint came from a bad film scan.)

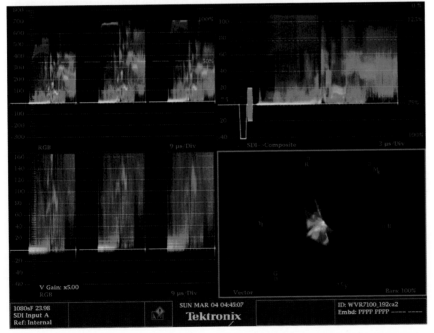

Fig. 10.58 Tektronix WVR7100 screengrab. Upper left: RGB Parade. Upper right: composite waveform. Lower right: vectorscope. Lower left: RGB Parade zoomed in 5x to blacks.

thinking it needs to be meaner. It has to have a mean feel. It's too sweet. So again, we'll look at our contrast on this stuff over here and balance," Jannotta says, checking out his RGB scopes.

Then he points to his vectorscope, explaining, "I see a lot of green down here and I see a lot of green up here." He points to the monitor. I point out that the green is not only coming from the grass behind the truck. Jannotta agrees, "No. It's not just the grass. He looks over at his RGB parade. "Whoa. That's not good. Blue is way out of line in the blacks," he says, before he balances it out with the shadow trackball.

"Now I'm looking at that gray courthouse wall and trying to get a better balance overall than what we had before." He cuts back and forth between source and correction. "Well, that's what I wanted it to do. I just wanted to get it more balanced to begin with, then I can start doing the weird stuff. As long as I know what kind of picture I really have here."

Burn it and compress the bottom end. There's more tension that way, I think.

– Pete Jannotta, Filmworkers Club

Jannotta's ready to move on, saying, "Now I want to desaturate it. Then really stretch the heck out of the top." He rolls the highlights *way* up as he says, "Burn it and compress the bottom end of the grayscale so that everything gets pulled out." Jannotta makes a hand gesture like he's pulling taffy. "There's more tension that way, I think" (Figures 10.59 and 10.60).

With the primary color correction out of the way, Jannotta wants to sharpen the image, so we go to FinalTouch/Color's Effect room and add Sharpening. The process tree was simply a Sharpen node set to 0.671350—a fairly similar setting to the sharpening he did in the last correction. "There you go. Now it's a SWAT team. That sharpening effect is pretty cool. It makes it really dangerous-looking."

Jannotta is pleased with his correction and decides to take it one step further. "I'm going to try, just for fun, a more simple vignette on this one." I notice that his "simple" vignette is—as usual for him—a hand-drawn shape instead of a simple geometric shape. I tease, "And once again, you refuse to use a square or a circle." He responds, "Yeah, I do. I don't like 'em, because I want to have the handle . . . the control and the ability to move."

He finishes drawing a big D shape and darkens the edges (Figure 10.62), then starts adjusting the shape with the correction in place. "I had the shape too tight. But you don't know until you do it. That's why I like these custom shapes and adding the softness up front to the shape."

Jannotta starts pulling out even more saturation. I ask him what the saturation move is accomplishing. He replies, "I want it to feel colder and more scary. More tension. So pulling the color out and adding a little blue to it, making it real crispy like that. Closing it in," he says, pointing to his vignette with darkened edges (Figure 10.61). I note that he's got deep shadows and punched highlights. "Yeah," he says, "I think of pulling the picture like this." He makes motion like pulling a scroll open from top to bottom.

Fig. 10.59 Jannotta's primary correction.

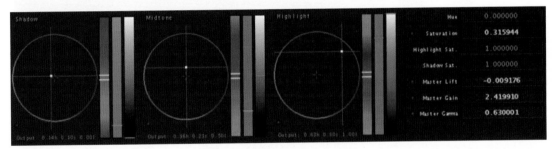

Fig. 10.60 Data from Primary room.

Feeling in his element with the action of the scene, the colorist for *24*, Larry Field, also gives the image a shot.

> *If this were 24, we'd have this nice and warm, desaturated, and as grainy as we could get it.*
>
> *– Larry Field, Level 3*

Field explains his approach, "It's yellow/green. It could be changed to a few different things. I'll just quickly balance it. We can neutralize it somewhere in there. Those white balanced gammas weren't too bad. You may want contrast in a shot like this because crazy things are happening. It would add to the excitement—the intensity of the shot. If this were *24*, we'd have this nice and warm, desaturated, and as grainy as we could get it. Then do a lift of luma-only, which grits it out and gives it a bleachy feel. Then, because it's film, we can really push the grain; desaturate it.

Fig. 10.61 Jannotta's image after the secondary was added.

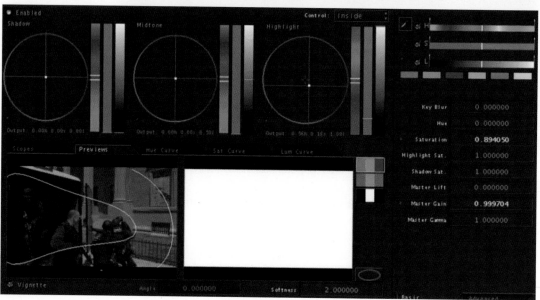

Fig. 10.62 Data from the inside of the qualification.

Very high-con, low-saturation to bring up a grit of it and the intensity." (Unfortunately, the settings for Field's corrections are unavailable, so I can't show the final or the settings he used to get there. From memory, it was similar to Jannotta's correction.)

This shot also appeals to Chris Pepperman, who works on a look for it. Pep starts, "Okay, this is a good shot. I want to make sure I'm out of the clip." He pulls the gain down a bit before continuing, "And I want to balance everything. I know it has a green texture to it. I see that. But what

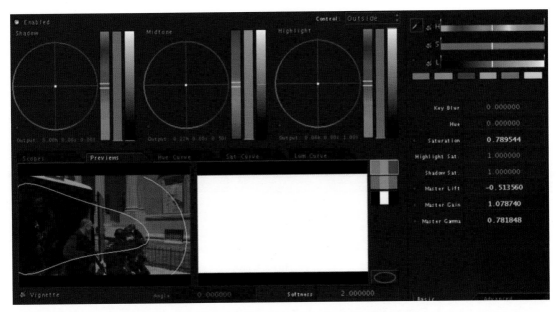

Fig. 10.63 Data from the outside of the qualification.

I'm trying to do is eliminate that and balance it to what it would look normally by eye."

"You're assuming that the green is not something the DP wants," I interject. "That's right. Assuming that that's not what he wants. Now I'm going to take this image and do it like we're doing a very high-contrast almost reenactment kind of scene, and what I would do is, in this particular case, I'm going to take the primaries and I'm really going to go to town and crank the video levels up and bring the black levels down and create this very, very high-contrasty look. As I'm doing that, it's affecting the greens in the highs and the midrange, so I'm going to clean that up a little bit as we go along. I can see it in the wall. The background is almost blue and the pillars themselves almost have a green texture to them, which doesn't bother me. I like it. Everybody tries to stay away from that green green green. I kind of like it where you can really stylize. Everybody always used to stay away from that yellowish-green because it always looked like it was bad video. Looks come and go. Everybody does windows. Everybody does the cross-processed look. It's the guys who innovate and try to melt those looks together and come up with different images.

"Right now I'm adding just a little warmth into it," he explains. "There's still a little contamination in the blacks, so I'm really trying to clean that up a little bit. I'm seeing a little bit of purplish in the blue. I just want to add some cyan. I'm liking what I see, though it's cyanish here," he says, pointing to the shadows in the truck (Figure 10.64). "Now once I got that look, I would isolate the reds and bring the reds down a little bit."

Fig. 10.64 Pepperman's primary correction.

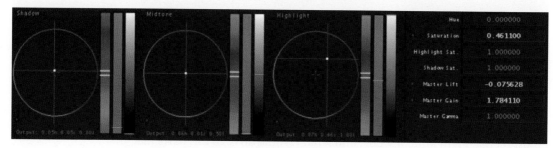

Fig. 10.65 Data from the Primary room.

Pepperman qualifies the skin tones with an HSL key and starts to add a vignette to garbage mask them, when I warn him that the shot is a Steadicam shot that follows the team. Pep continues, "I use vignettes all the time on motion, and I just track it and keep it very soft" (Figures 10.66 and 10.67).

Pep adds another secondary, creating an oval, then rotates it and changes its position and aspect. I notice that Pepperman falls into the "grade-with-vignettes-sharp" camp. He agrees, "Right, because I want to see the difference between the two. I always do softness last. I want to see the difference." He cranks down the gain outside and cranks up the gain inside before softening the oval. "See now I went too far, so I'm just backing off the vignette a little bit. See how I like to go deep, and now I've come off of it a bit. So now you can't see the vignette. It's transparent" (Figure 10.68).

Fig. 10.66 Image after the first secondary was applied.

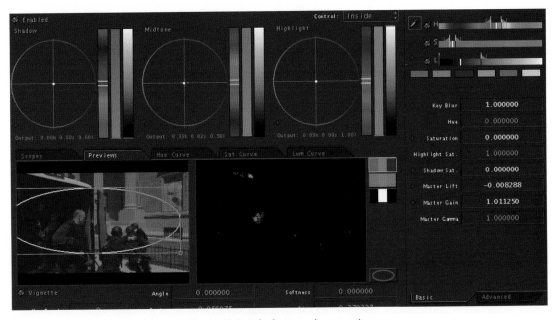

Fig. 10.67 Data for first secondary correction.

In an interesting side note, Pep's vignette was "transparent" on the eCinema display, but on the Dell computer monitors attached to the Mac, it was still pretty obvious. This is one place where the gamma display differences between the computer monitors and the real grading monitor were obvious.

Fig. 10.68 Image after second secondary correction was added.

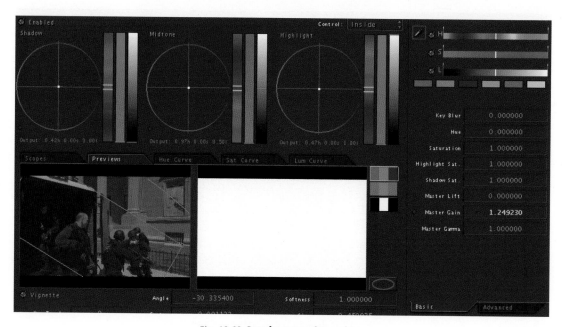

Fig. 10.69 Data from second secondary.

Pep continues tweaking the look of the shot by adding another secondary and qualifies the green grass using an HSL key and a vignette (Figures 10.71 and 10.72), being careful to select the grass but not the green of the pillars.

Fig. 10.70 Image after the final secondary correction was added.

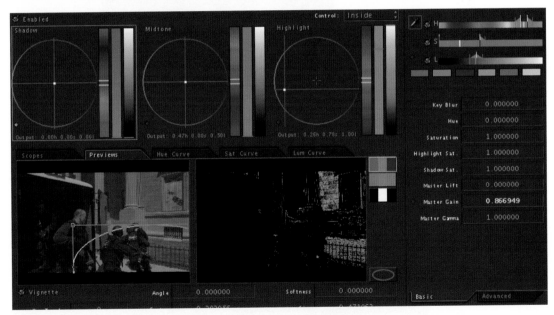

Fig. 10.71 Data from final secondary correction.

"Once again, I'm trying to give it this chromatic look. A high-intensity Ektachrome look. So what I'm doing is I'm almost wanting that green of the grass to glow and look ultra green."

Obviously feeling liberated by the ability to add up to eight secondaries in Color, Pepperman adds yet another secondary, qualifying and tweaking the blue of the SWAT team uniforms.

Graphic Looks

From the frantic energy and grittiness of the SWAT scene, we'll transition to the Zen-like simplicity of Artbeats' image of a man sitting at the end of a pier. It was an image that spoke to Mike Matusek.

"I look at this one and I think of it as more of a graphic image," Matusek explains, "So I'll try doing a few looks. First a silhouette, maybe crush it a little bit and see where that goes. Maybe that'll be too muddy. Then sometimes what I do is bring the blacks to zero and don't crush, but

Fig. 10.72 Source image courtesy of Artbeats.

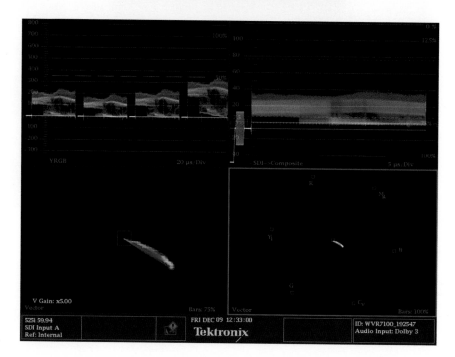

Fig. 10.73 Tektronix WVR7100 screengrab. Upper left: YRGB Parade. Upper right: composite waveform. Lower right: vectorscope. Lower left: vectorscope zoomed in 5x.

I want to get it darker that that, so then I'll go to the midtones and bring the midtones down, so I'm not necessarily crushing the blacks" (Figures 10.74 and 10.75).

> *There's a lens flare there, so that clues me in that the sun is maybe still a little bit out. Maybe get more contrast.*
> — Mike Matusek, Nolo Digital Film

"Sometimes when you go blue, you get kind of hypersensitive to the hue and you see a little pink in there. You almost see a little bit of magenta in the water. So, do you want to go more cyan blue? Do you want to go a little more true blue? If you go to more true blue on the scope, it looks more magenta all the time, at least to me, so I tend to go a little bit more towards cyan. There's a lens flare there, so that clues me in that the sun is maybe still a little bit out. Maybe get more contrast. Throw a vignette on there real quick to see what that does to the mood of it."

Matusek adds an oval vignette with softness and rotates it, then darkens the upper left corner (Figure 10.78). I comment that as I watch a lot of people use vignettes, it is a way to focus attention, but it also seems

Fig. 10.74 Matusek's primary correction.

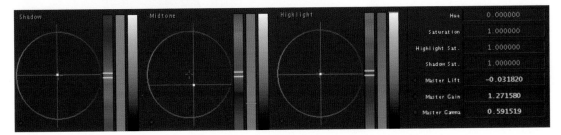

Fig. 10.75 Data from the Primary room.

to be a way to take a flat expanse of color and give it some depth or texture. "Exactly. Once you get a vignette on there, it's a little more shaped. Because it seems just flat and uninteresting, so if you add a vignette to it there's much more depth to it. So now there's more depth *and* it brings your focus to him."

If you add a vignette to it, there's much more depth to it. So now there's more depth and it brings your focus to him.

– Mike Matusek, Nolo Digital Film

Fig. 10.76 Secondary correction was applied to the inside and outside of the vignette.

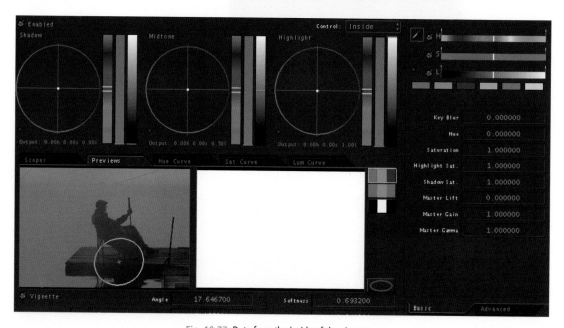

Fig. 10.77 Data from the inside of the vignette.

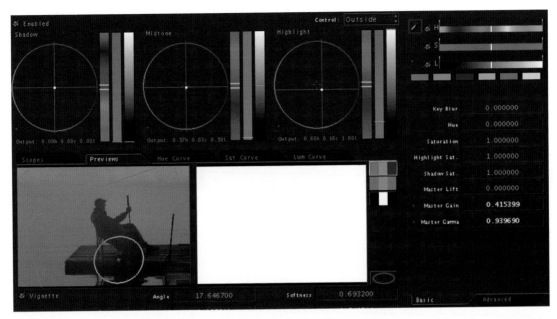

Fig. 10.78 Data from the outside of the vignette.

"He looks like an old guy reminiscing. That's why I went cooler with it. I think if I'd gone golden, that evokes a different emotion." I ask if it wouldn't be hard to get this image to be golden and Matusek seems ready for the challenge.

Matusek starts off by mentioning that his blacks are close to being clipped, and I ask how he knows how to stretch a specific tonal range. "If I wanted to get detail out of the blanket over his legs, bringing the black up would just make it milky, so riding the lift down and the gamma up until I'd stretched that little area and get more detail out of it. If this was shot on video, it'd just be noise."

Matusek continues, "If I'm going to go golden, I'd probably go a little more contrasty with it. This is more of a graphic image, so you don't have to be realistic. You can definitely have some more fun with it. It's really the color of the water and then the guy and the pier is pretty much grayscale. There's not much color information. So you can really be more graphic with it" (Figures 10.79 and 10.80).

Fig. 10.79 Matusek's primary correction for the "gold" look.

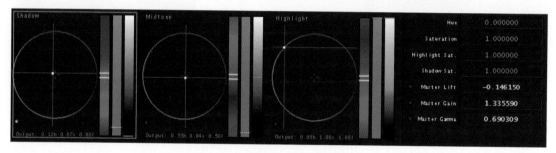

Fig. 10.80 Data for the Primary room.

N o t e

Please check out the Gradient_Look video tutorial on the DVD for another way to create a cool look with this image.

Matusek goes to the secondaries and adds a soft oval in the Upper left corner. "You can do a few things here. Maybe add some more color in there. You can even do this, which is interesting sometimes," he says as he makes the vignetted area cyan (Figures 10.81–10.83).

"So you're playing one color off another?" I ask. "Right," he responds. "That's not creating contrast with luminance, that's doing it with color."

Matusek continues with his experimentation. "I can do one more thing with this, because, as you said, the planks are kind of cool on the pier," he says, increasing the contrast in the planks of the pier, creating a nice texture to the shot (Figures 10.84 and 10.85).

Fig. 10.81 Secondary correction done both inside and outside of the vignette.

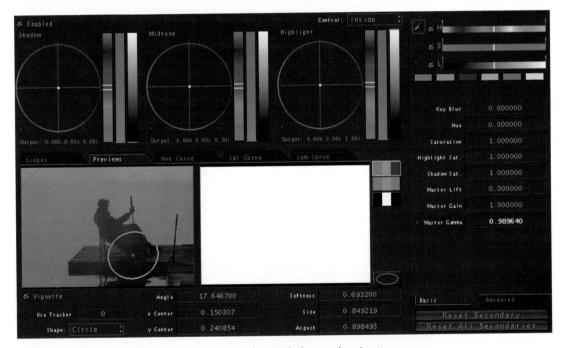

Fig. 10.82 Data from inside the secondary vignette.

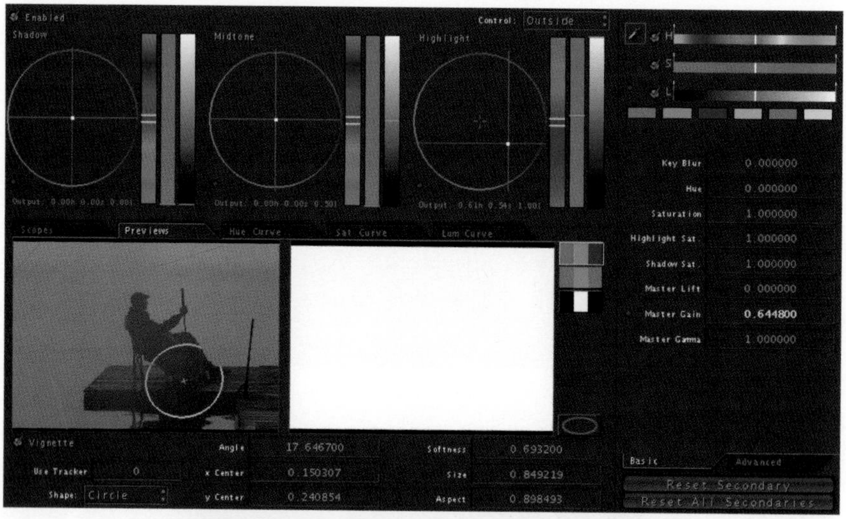

Fig. 10.83 Data from outside the secondary vignette.

Fig. 10.84 Second secondary correction to increase contrast in the planks.

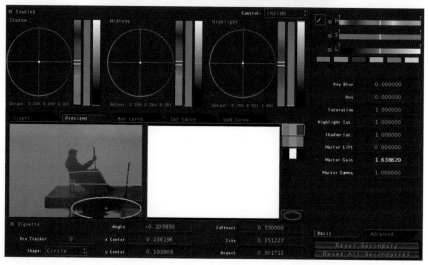

Fig. 10.85 Data from second secondary correction.

Day-for-Night

Day-for-night shots are one of the requests that colorists have to pull off on occasion. We tasked several colorists to walk us through day-for-night shots on several scenes.

Bob Sliga starts on an indoor scene that was shot as camera test footage by my good friend and respected documentary and feature cinematographer, Rich Lerner (from the tutorial footage: "sleeping_woman," Figure 10.86).

Fig. 10.86 Original source footage courtesy of Rich Lerner.

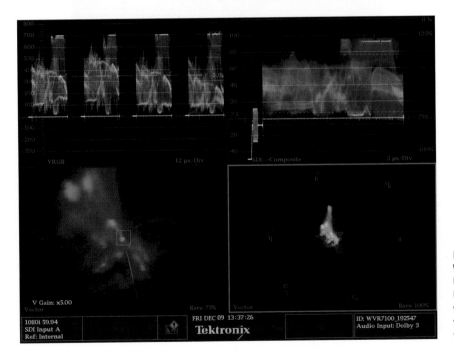

Fig. 10.87 Tektronix WVR7100 screengrab. Upper left: YRGB Parade. Upper right: composite waveform. Lower right: vectorscope. Lower left: vectorscope zoomed in 5x.

"One of the things to remember in day-for-night is that saturation isn't plentiful. A lot of people really overdo blue," states Sliga. "You should feel it, but you shouldn't be hit in the face with blue."

That's how I come across a lot of my looks. I'll walk around and look at things and almost reference them like I have a video scope.

– Bob Sliga

I ask, "So you use the science of how the eye sees at night time?" "Exactly. And that's how I come across a lot of my looks. I'll walk around and look at things and almost reference them like I have a video scope. I mean, I've done it for so long. I'll look into shadows. I'll look into other areas. Overall color textures. Highlights off of building reflections downtown. Then thinking, 'How would I emulate that in here?' Then at night, you go outside; after a while, obviously your eyes will adjust, and you can see more and more into the night, but you never see more and more color. It's not there."

"I remember reading that your eye has a harder time seeing red saturation in low light," I say.

Fig. 10.88 **Primary correction.**

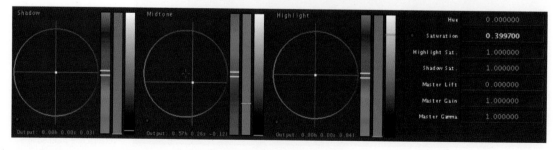

Fig. 10.89 **Data from Primary room.**

"Exactly," Sliga agrees. "So you feel the cooler tones. I'm doing this all in my primary in room, and what I'm doing is throwing away the detail that I don't want to keep. But I'm not clamping it off. I'm not plugging it in the basement," he says as he points to the fact that the blacks aren't incredibly crushed. Then, as Sliga lowers gammas and shadows, the saturation increases, and he compensates by lowering saturation in those areas as well as using the wheels to push a little bit of coolness into all of the tonal ranges.

"Let's go into a secondary room now," Sliga continues. "The first thing I'd like to use on this is a luminance key." He qualifies mostly the lamp and spill on the wall with a little of the highlight on her forehead and arm (Figure 10.91). "Now I'm going to go outside the qualification and throw more stuff away. Now I'm sliding some of that blueness in. Not a lot, just a little bit."

Fig. 10.90 First secondary correction.

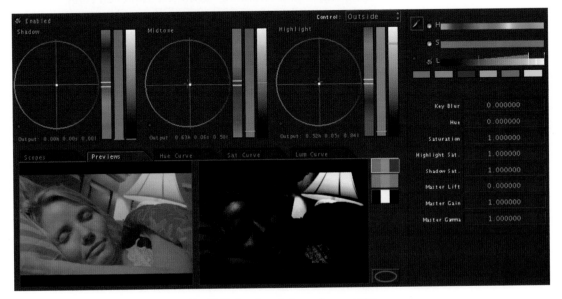

Fig. 10.91 Data from first secondary correction.

Sliga notices the strong red tones of the blanket. "This is still coming through pretty strong," he complains as he goes to the saturation curve in secondaries. "So I'm just going to go in and try to grab reds in the saturation curve and pull them down. Attempting to fix the redness of the blankets with the saturation curve does not create the look he is after, so he resets the curve and tries another tack.

Rich Lerner

Rich Lerner was the director of photography for the Academy Award–winning short documentary "A Story of Healing." He also developed and coproduced "Instinct" with Anthony Hopkins and Cuba Gooding, Jr. He worked on the National Emmy–winning episode of *Nature* titled "Urban Elephant" and has shot more than 1,000 fashion retail spots. He has also worked extensively as a cinematographer for *National Geographic*. He has shot several feature films and feature documentaries. His background was primarily in shooting 35 mm and Super 16 mm film, but he currently does a lot of his work in HD and digital cinema. He's also shot several independent feature films, including *The Torturer* and *Natasha Kizmet: The Movie*.

"I'm going to go into another secondary and pick that red. That's a very strong selection, because it's looking back at the *original* color of the source. I'm going to use the color picker to isolate that down just a little bit more. Then I'll throw a little blur on it. On the inside of that qualification, I'm just going to pull saturation down. We can even come down on the outside of the qualification and bring the red gain down as well," Sliga adds as he goes into the Advanced tab to affect the red gain (Figure 10.92).

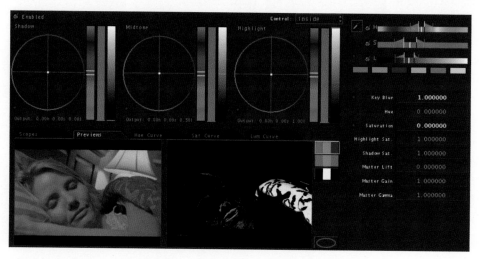

Fig. 10.92 Second secondary correction bringing down the red saturation in the blanket, mainly.

Sliga adds a third secondary to qualify the lamp and the spill on the wall using luminance. Then he softens the qualification, picking up some of the highlights on the woman's skin. With that done, he pushes a good deal of warmth into the highlights, making her face quite warm.

I ask about the change to the woman's face. "You're not worrying about what happens to her face, just the lamp, right?" "Right," he says, explaining, "I'm trying to find something symbolizing a little bit of warmth coming out of that lamp." To fix the face, he creates a soft vignette and positions it over the lamp, eliminating the corrections on the woman's skin (Figure 10.94). "So we came from here to there," he concludes as he checks back and forth between the starting source image and where he ended up (Figure 10.93).

Fig. 10.93 Third secondary correction, bringing warmth to the lamp.

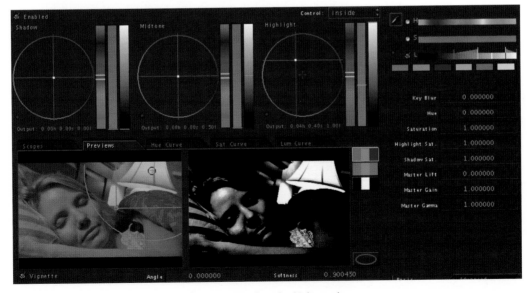

Fig. 10.94 Data from the third secondary.

Mike Most also works this image into a day-for-night.

"What I would do is bring this way down," Most begins by pulling down midtones and shadows. And I've also got to bring down saturation first, because one of the things about night is that saturation is much lower and, point of fact, red saturation is much, *much* lower. It's not so much that things go blue. They don't really, but what they do go is minus red because the red disappears. You don't want it to greenish but cyanish is probably okay. What I'd probably try to do is put a little bit of a window around her. It doesn't make physical sense, but I'm going to play this as if there's another key down here. It doesn't make sense, but sometimes it just works" (Figures 10.96 and 10.97).

> *One of the things about night is that . . . it's not so much that things go blue . . . they go minus red.*
>
> – Mike Most, Cineworks Digital Miami

Most draws an oval around her face, raises the gain inside the vignette, and then softens the edge. "I'd have to do something very different with the outside area," he comments. "What I'd actually like to do with the outside area is make it a little warmer. That whole green thing is driving me nuts. Once again, take some of the saturation out. I'm desaturating the outside" (Figure 10.100).

Most cuts back and forth between the original image and his correction. "Considering that you started from that . . . it's not great, but it's not horrible."

"Looks like night to me," I say.

Fig. 10.95 Source shot—"sleeping_woman" from tutorial footage.

Fig. 10.96 Most's primary correction. (This data was created in FinalTouch2K and reimported into a Color Project. I feel like the correction is not quite the same as the way Mike was seeing it.)

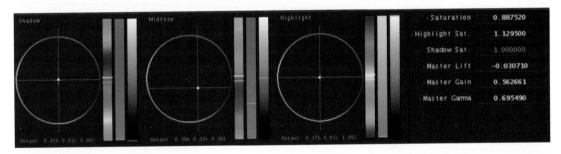

Fig. 10.97 Data from Primary room.

Fig. 10.98 Secondary cor-
rection inside and outside
of vignette.

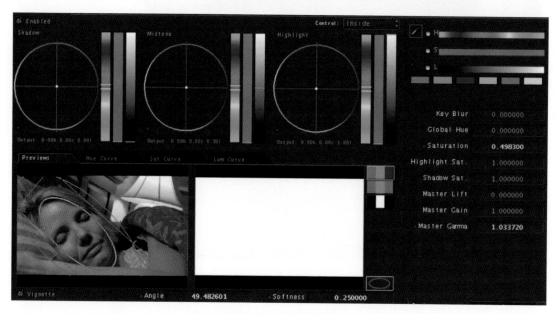

Fig. 10.99 Data from inside of the vignette.

Fig. 10.100 Data from outside of the vignette.

Pete Jannotta takes on the Artbeats scene of the Marines (Figures 10.101 and 10.102) to attempt another day-for-night shot.

Jannotta goes straight to secondaries to try to select the sky. He picks a spot that selects the left side of the sky, then widens the qualification with the HSL selection sliders, grabbing almost the entire sky. Switching the HSL selection so that it used *only* luminance improved the qualification.

Jannotta thinks this selection will be good enough, but it isn't, because as he brings down the luminance in the qualification, it brings down the right side of the sky before it brings down the left side.

Fig. 10.101 Source image courtesy of Artbeats.

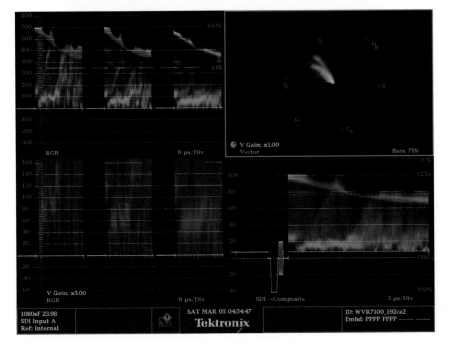

Fig. 10.102 Tektronix WVR7100 screengrab. Upper left: RGB Parade. Upper right: vectorscope. Lower right: composite waveform. Lower left: RGB Parade zoomed in 5x to the blacks.

"A little blue always helps for the suggestion of night. But this," he says as he points to the sky and the way the matte transitions to the helmets, "is not good."

This is a real shot that someone would come in and say, 'I want this to be nighttime.' And whether or not it's easy doesn't matter.
— Pete Jannotta, Filmworkers Club

Instead of being impatient with the mistake, the challenge of the shot energizes Jannotta. "This is fun. This is a real shot that someone would come in and say, 'I want this to be nighttime.' And whether or not it's easy doesn't matter. So it's actually a good exercise."

I ask Jannotta what things he has to do to create the day-for-night effect. "Desaturation, all the levels come down, a little blue added. Pretty much that's it," Jannotta responds. He starts with desaturation. "I'm just compressing the bottom and bringing the highlights up a bit. We could cool those off a bit too. I'm pushing it into the flesh tones. It can get pretty trite to get really blue, because it just looks hokey. But most everyone sees blue and dark and they think 'night.' If you go overboard, then it's sad and sick looking. It could almost be okay to do a little bit of cyan. A little bit of green/blue is okay, too" (Figures 10.103 and 10.104).

Fig. 10.103 Jannotta's primary correction—day-for-night.

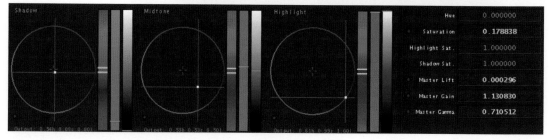

Fig. 10.104 Data for Primary room.

Greg Creaser completes our final day-for-night scene. Actually, it's more of a night-for-night scene as he works on the "nightgown" scene from "Kiss Me In the Dark" (Figure 10.105).

"If this was typical moonlight, it's not going to be warm. We started out a little warm and a little bright, so around in there . . . would be a good starting point. I think this would be a creative decision on the part of the client. I'd stick it there and say, 'Where do you want to go with it?' It'd be maybe more to the cyan side or the bluer side. My own opinion on night stuff is that I don't like to see it always blue. I like to see it clean. Maybe cool yet not blue blue. A lot of time you see night shots and they're just extremely blue. I kind of try to stay away from that, but that's my personal choice, and that's not what a client may want so, maybe I'd put it here and they'd say, 'We want it cooler' or this or that" (Figures 10.105–10.108).

Fig. 10.105 Source image from "Kiss Me In the Dark," courtesy Seduced and Exploited Entertainment.

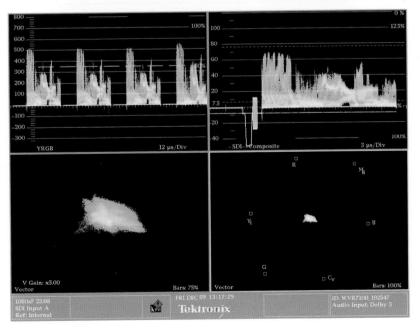

Fig. 10.106 Tektronix WVR7100 screengrab. Upper left: YRGB Parade. Upper right: composite waveform. Lower right: vectorscope. Lower left: vectorscope zoomed in 5x.

Fig. 10.107 Creaser's final day-for-night correction.

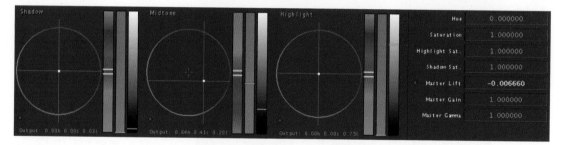

Fig. 10.108 Data for correction in FinalTouch UI.

The Look of the Feature Film

David Mullen, ASC, describes the modern look of feature films. "Most movies nowadays are on the contrasty side, compared to movies in the past. They tend to be a single-source look with a lot of fall-off into the shadows, which is nice because it gives the film a certain three-dimensional quality to it. There's always a technical reason for wanting more contrast, and that is that it makes things look sharper and more three-dimensional. But it's mainly a mood issue. It's like asking a cook, 'How much salt should I put in it?' One of the questions I always get from film students is, 'I'm working with a director and we're trying to make these scenes look dark and we're not agreeing on what that means.' And that's partly because it's completely a taste issue. I mean, one thing I tell people is that you have to define what 'dark' means. Does it mean 'dim,' which can be low contrast and nothing is at key exposure and everything is fairly murky and low key and soft? Or it can mean that there's a lot of contrast, where there are small areas of the screen within the frame at full exposure but there's lots of big areas of the exposure that are black or near black. A lot of them don't realize that the terms are all vague. I remember once telling a director that we should shoot the scene in silhouette and he said, 'Oh, that's great.' So I lit the scene in silhouette, and he goes, 'I can't see the actor's face.' I go, 'That's because he's in silhouette.' And he said, 'Well, can't we have some fill light on him?' 'Well, then it wouldn't be a silhouette!' A silhouette means a dark shape against a bright background. But some people think a silhouette means a backlit person with very dim lighting on them. So that's 'silhouettey' but it's not in silhouette."

NOT Doing a Look

Veteran colorist Mike Most explains that not every colorist "does looks." Colorists often have niches. Most explains, "Look creation is not really my big forte. Everybody's got their forte. My forte is fixing problems and I'm really good at continuity. Making sure that scenes play consistently. The whole look creation thing: that's the Bob Festas of the world, the Jais Theirrys of the world, the Beau Leons of the world, the Stefans of the world. They're really heavily into taking something and making it into something that it wasn't. I've never been that guy. For me, what always came naturally was just bringing out the beauty of something that's already been shot and try to make it more than what it was but not something that it wasn't."

Plug-In Looks

With editors being pushed into service as "colorists" more and more without any formal training, many vendors have seen a market for prebuilt looks and a kind of automated look generation based on plug-ins for common editing software. One of the most common of these is MagicBullet Looks 2, which is available for Adobe After Effects and Premiere Pro, Final Cut Pro, Motion, and Sony Vegas. There were also prebuilt looks from Graeme Nattress and Bob Sliga for Apple Color.

CHAPTER 11

Miscellaneous Wisdom

Consider this chapter to be like the bonus track on a CD from your favorite band. It wasn't in the plans for the original book, but I had many great little nuggets of information left over that didn't otherwise fit into the book but that I really wanted to share.

There's not a great way to tie them all together, so I'll just share them in a stream-of-consciousness sort of way. I hope you find them influencing your corrections in important ways.

Starting Off

Bob Festa describes how he approaches a shot: "When I throw up a shot, the first thing I do, before I talk to anybody, is kind of peer into the corners of the negative and look for my visual signposts; my references in the shot that I look for. I'm actually looking for handles in the film like, 'What would I bring forward? What would I drop back? Is there a white light reference in the shot? Would I sniff around and try to find that and try to find a reference to create a quick dynamic image that we can start to talk with? Basically, I look for signposts that point to balance and white, then I also look for traditional photographic techniques—stuff I can either bring up or bring back. Getting the blacks to a malleable area and getting the whites to a malleable area. When I first put up a shot and get it balanced, I use the blacks and whites almost like a throttle on a motorcycle. Kind of revving the engine to see what you've got. I use the master gains and master blacks to get a feel for how it behaves."

> *You really have to push it around to somewhere you don't want to go to find out where you do want to go.*
>
> *– Bob Festa, New Hat*

I give Festa my camera focusing analogy. "I think that's true," he agrees. "You're looking for the sweet spot. And the only way to find that is to go too far. That's probably true for color correction in general. You really have to push it around to somewhere you *don't* want to go to find out where you *do* want to go. I think that's a good statement.

"Then I can look into the neg and look for things that I can bring to life. So I look at the ratio of foreground and background. But in addition to balancing, I'm also looking at adding value.

"I like to show my commercial clients a whole range of opportunities based on that. The most classic thing I like to do is show three or four different opportunities based on either warmer, cooler exposures, more or less dynamic range, more or less contrast. And then we start getting very, very specific using the classic photographic techniques of the day—dodging and burning—and actually creating the look that's based on that."

Festa continues, "What I like to do is show people some choices. If you give them one, two, or three different choices, they can actually point their finger up at the screen and say, 'I like A, B, or C,' instead of being very general about 'Where do you think you guys want to go from here?' I also like to look at the work picture, just to see what these people are used to looking at. Whether it's right or wrong in *my* mind, they may have fallen in love with it and not even know it to some extent. So I'll give them an option that might have some relationship to the work picture. That makes the dialog a little easier, I think. I think initially I tell them that this is going to be very general, for starters. And it's very broad-stroke based. And once you get dialed in through a series of 1, 2, 3. After a while you get into a very close place. Then the brushstrokes become much more fine and more dynamic, I think."

Communicating with Clients

Festa continues with a discussion on communicating with clients: "It wasn't so much techniques or tools that helped me communicate more with my clients, but I actually started listening. I would actually not say a damn word, but I would tell people, 'Before we get started, tell me in 20 words or less what today's theme is going to be.' I'd rather let them spill their guts for 20 words or 20 minutes and then turn around and deliver the goods, because then I have a good idea about what their perception is and what their ambitions are for the session. So if anything, I've become a good listener in my old age. Also, you give them a choice. Work like an eye doctor. Show them A, B, or C and before you know it, you've worked your way into something that's really in focus. And not only have you listened to them, but you've shown them and they've made the decisions as you've worked your way down into it. So how can they not be happy?"

Chris Pepperman extends this conversation: "Typically, the way I work when I color correct is, I'm one of those guys who verbally expresses or talks out loud what I'm doing. A lot of my clients actually like that because as I'm doing it, I'm talking my way through it and explaining to them what I'm doing. That's a habit that I picked up very early in the business when I was working with guys like Nick Dantone and Howie Birch, who were the principal owners of Manhattan Transfer, and I spent years assisting those guys. I always found it to be a very good tool. I consider myself not to be a technical colorist. There are guys out there who are really technically inclined. Chris Ryan is one of them. He knows these systems inside and out."

Pep continues, "There are two aspects to color correction. One is being able to emulate the aesthetic look or direction that the DP or director is expressing to you and that's essentially your primary objective, right? That's what you want to do. Somebody comes in and they have a visual idea of what they want and you try to give them that. The other one is being able to have the 'room savvy,' and what I mean by that is being able to communicate effectively with the client. It's a personality thing. I try to be personable."

> *You have to have the personality to sit in a room with an A-type personality, understand what they want, and give it to them.*
> *– Chris Pepperman, NASCAR*

Having hung out in a session with one of Pep's clients, I agree: "People like to hang with you."

"Exactly. And I feel that's one of my strong points—why people like to come here. You definitely have to have talent, technical-wise, to be able to interpret what they want visually. But you also have to have the personality to sit in a room with an A-type personality or a B-type personality, understand what they want, give it to them, and all along keep them comfortable."

Company 3's Stefan Sonnenfeld agrees that the interpersonal side is critical: "I think this business is trickier than most people think," states Sonnenfeld. "I say half the people who are doing this really struggle to get what they end up with, because it does not come naturally, and there are technicians so to speak who know how to work the knobs but have a very tough time translating either their own thoughts to the screen or somebody else's thoughts to the screen or a mixture of the two, which is why some people just take forever to get something."

I ask Sonnenfeld if being able to communicate in the language or with the terminology of a DP is important. He answers, "I do not need that kind of specificity. Some people do come in and say, 'Tell me what I should say.' It does not matter. There are people that I work with, like Michael Mann, who give me an emotional rundown of a narrative. Then he says, 'Okay, go.' Here is the story I am trying to tell, here is the emotion that is trying to be shown. Johnny is really angry and feeling betrayed in this scene. It is really just a question sometimes about experience and sometimes being more social.

"I just think there are technicians who just are not somebody you would want to spend time with sometimes. If a guy has no sense of style or just looks like the guy out of the *Hangover* movie in terms of how they dress. Do you want that guy? And if you do not gel with that, how are you ever going to work with that person? If you cannot feel comfortable in the room speaking with that person, then how are you going to collaborate together? A lot of it is social and a lot is understanding others. Part of it also is cultural. I grew up in Europe and went to boarding school and I have been all around the world, I used to speak another language, and I am the first American-born in my family, so I also can empathize and kind of relate to the European crowd. They tell me that I am the first person that they have ever met who can understand what they're thinking. I have traveled in Europe and around the world and that is a huge part of learning. The other part is that I have been fortunate to work with a lot of great people, and every time you work with a person who is great, you are always learning. I have just a whole bag of experience behind me that I have learned from others that I have embellished myself."

As an editor and colorist, I have always believed that the best editors and colorists are a balance of the technical, the social, and the creative. I pose this thought to Sonnenfeld. "There are some technically inept colorists that I know who are pretty successful," he asserts, "The dirty secret of our business is that there are a lot of people who do not really know some of the stuff that they should. From that point of view, I think everybody should have a strong (technical) foundation—and I do—because I worked my way up. I think experience is a huge part of it. The creative collaborative is the majority of it. So, for me, it is really coming to an understanding of what people want. I would say that is the most important thing. Part of it is also trying something and pushing yourself more than you would think. What happens is this inspires you to do different things."

I point out my sidebar from Chapter 1 on the similarities in terms between colorists and musicians and ask for his feedback. "People realize how much [color] impacts the movie, and it is the same way with music. It brings out these emotions in people much more so than color. It is a visceral emotional appeal. It is much more obvious with music. You put on a song and you start to experience all these different feelings, whereas color is a little bit more hidden, but at the same time it does the same stuff. You almost notice it more when it is wrong or not working then when it is actually right and fantastic. Being able to evoke emotion and feeling from people is what it is all about."

Encore's Pankaj Bajpai thinks that the most important communication tool he has is visual. Bajpai elaborates, "For me, it's not so much 'talk' as to be able to show options. The toolsets that I have been drawn to are the ones that typically allow you to *show*, because a picture is worth a thousand words. So instead of saying, 'Hey, this will look really contrasting. This will look great. I will crush the blacks or goose it up.' There are all these terminologies that I'm sure you have heard, but there is really no substitute for showing it. It's like you see that in the context of the images that you're working with, so for me to be able to very quickly display what it is, even if it's not completely finessed, to get the sense or an idea, and that's how I come to a common understanding of what we're doing.

> *The truth of it is that the skill of coloring is about 50 percent of what you do . . . a very huge chunk of it is people management.*
> *– Pankaj Bajpai, Encore*

"The truth of it is that the skill of coloring is about 50 percent of what you do. Navigating when people are not around and keeping people's creative visions and eventually making it all homogenous and whole so that everybody says, 'Yeah,' and they're getting what they want, is the trick in the episodic world. I think a very huge chunk of it is people management. Being able to take ideas, sometimes on the same page or sometimes a very contrary idea and then somehow coming up with a solution that works and being able to cut through the esoteric-ness of it all and then coming up with a solution that is artistic, that you know you can maintain, specifically in episodic."

The Future of Color Correction

I ask Festa about the trend away from telecine color correction—in which the image that is being manipulated is coming directly from the film—toward corrections done from flat data transfers on central servers or from flat transfers to D5 or some other tape. The episodic world of color correction has already turned towards this workflow, as have many digital intermediate workflows. The TV spot world seems to be the sole holdout, and I wonder if spots will join the rest of industry in this regard. (This question was asked back in 2005. Since then spot work has indeed gone file-based.) As Festa is definitely a veteran of the industry, I expect some resistance from him on this point, but he surprises me.

"God, I sure hope so," Festa exclaims. "I really don't know what it's going to take. I really think it's going to be an application like the Color app, where people are exposed to it on a fundamental, early level. The youngsters who are familiar with Final Cut . . . today's runners or assistant editors, they're all familiar with Final Cut—maybe it'll seed the industry at an early age and these people will all be influenced early on that there's no reason to pay big money and spend an inordinate amount of time slinging film. I think it's like anything else, if you look at everything from the Beta to VHS revolution to compressed delivery systems like DirecTV, we're always selling out in little steps, and quite frankly, I'd rather have the flexibility and the speed to make contributions that are possibly not quite the same quality but are equally satisfying on a more artistic level."

Trying to understand his point, I ask, "Because you'd do more color correcting than waiting for the film to get set up on the telecine?"

I've only got so much patience left and I'd rather spend it color correcting something in context than threading film up.
– Bob Festa, New Hat

"Yes. The way I see it, I've only got so much patience left and I'd rather spend it color correcting something in context than threading film up. I think we're really witnessing the Avid-ization of telecine, where hopefully color decisions and color correction as we know it can be a lot more interactive and face to face and project-based as opposed to service bureau–based. Quite frankly, I'd be much happier if I was working on a per-project basis, face to face, much more interlocked with my client as opposed to just acting as a service bureau. I'm excited about the future, because I think that's what it's going to be," concludes Festa.

Festa also discusses the changes in acquisition formats in recent years, "What's become more and more important in digital acquisition is texture: 80 percent of my work is Alexa, 10 percent is RED, and 10 percent is film. Digital acquisition is clean; there's no traditional film grain. I have a library of grain, roll out, flash frames or I could have picked a stock, high speed or low speed or 16mm or Super 8mm. Eight out of the ten jobs I do with Alexa; I spill in a little bit of grain and it creates a less antiseptic look, sometimes putting it in the highlights or the blacks, depending on whether it's underexposed or overexposed."

This change in acquisition formats and in the traditional color correction tools for colorists is illustrated in an informal poll taken by Warren Eagles, an Australian colorist and founder of the International Colorists Academy, which does color correction training. Warren and I do a video tutorial on the DVD for the book. Warren walks through some of the powerful ways to exploit the node graph in Resolve. Warren's poll was done before Adobe acquired and integrated Speedgrade into Production

Premium. Total percentage is over 100% because some colorists use multiple systems. His results are as follows:

Of the 80 respondents worldwide on the day of the poll in late 2011:

- 40 percent were grading on Resolve
- 17 percent were grading on Film Master
- 13 percent were grading on Baselight
- 7 percent were grading on Color
- 7 percent were grading on Lustre
- 5 percent were grading on Scratch
- 3 percent were grading on DaVinci 2K
- 3 percent were grading on Pablo
- 3 percent were grading on Avid DS
- 3 percent were grading on Pandora
- 3 percent were grading on Pogle
- Resolve, Lustre, and Film Master were the primary US systems.
- Nearly all of the Baselight users were in Europe and Britain.
- Most of the Color users were in South America.

The footage being graded came from RED/EPIC (~20%), Alexa (~18%), followed closely by Canon DSLR footage, XDCAM, and film (~15% each). The rest included various flavors of SD and compressed HD video.

Taking It to Extremes

When I see them trying to get a certain color, I say, "Just go overboard." Show me beyond what we're talking about.

– David Mullen, ASC.

David Mullen, ASC, explains how he likes to communicate with colorists. "When I see them trying to get a certain color, I say, 'Just go overboard.' Show me *beyond* what we're talking about, because when you're fiddling with something subtle, it's sometimes a problem that you're not quite seeing the effect you want. It's better if you just overcrank it for a moment and then pull it back down."

This is similar advice to Festa's adage: "You don't know if you don't go."

Festa extends the analogy, "I use it like a motorcycle, I mean I want to rev this up a little bit and see where the blacks are going to take me or rev the whites up and see where they go. Just constantly pushing things and sniffing around. I probe for the extremes, always seeing where the image is going to either: (a) fall apart or (b) come to life.

Then always going back and looking at the original to see what the original intent was."

The Importance of Color Contrast

Pete Jannotta explains that the *traditional* way to think of contrast is certainly not the *only* way. "Luminance contrast is important, but *color* contrast is just as important."

Jannotta is examining a shot that he's trying to tweak. "Before, when I was looking at it, I wasn't feeling the color contrast was right. It was too much in one part of the palette. It looked kind of brown, so it needs a little blue and green back into it. I've taken too much green out of it."

> *Luminance contrast is important, but color contrast is just as important.*
>
> *– Pete Jannotta, Filmworkers Club*

"This is a real common thing that I do all the time," explains Jannotta. "What did I have to start with? So: 'Am I ruining anything?' 'Am I taking away something that I want to retain?' I'm always looking for that."

Maintaining a Look

Neal Kassner talks about one of his biggest challenges. "My show—*48 Hours*—has to match itself from one segment to the next and the characters reappear all the way through, even though the same source reels are used by as many as six different editors working on different Avids. The first time I correct a character, I grab a reference of it, and each time that character appears, even in the same segment, I'll reference back. Because I've found that when they're shooting, it's not unusual for the camera guy to adjust the iris. So the same character, even in the same setting may be a little darker or a little brighter than the first time I saw him. So I want to keep it consistent all the way through."

Encore's Bajpai agrees: "It's no good to take one frame and make it look super good and go wow and then do that over 5 years on 65 episodes so you can come up with something that's super good but then has to fit into your ability to repeat it again and again, indoors, outdoors, day, night, multiple storylines. That's always challenging with a new show is where you set that."

The other challenge, according to Bajpai, is access to decision makers and a revolving door of characters involved with any given episodic series. "DP's can't be here (in the color suite)," states Bajpai. "It could be the executive producers that take over. Then how do you balance all of that with a director who is there for only a single episode and then there's another director. There is a lot of variation in the input, but then at the end of the day, the show can't be one thing one week and the next thing another week and the next thing another week. It has to be consistent. Plus, with TV episodics, you have ten pages [to shoot in a day] and whether it goes bad, you're going to shoot those ten pages any which way you can because you're on these tight deadlines, tight budgets, and tight schedules. On a feature, nine times out of ten, you would to be able to go back and do a reshoot. But with episodic, it's 'move on, move on, move on,' so in that sense, a lot of the things we end up doing in here are basically fixing production issues. Scripts change in the middle of editing and a scene goes away and suddenly a scene that was shot in the day now has to play as night. On a feature, you would probably go back and reshoot it. On a commercial, you're shooting on a two day thing and you're done, you're moving on to a whole new thing, so what color for episodic is, is a whole other animal, and the duties and responsibilities of being a colorist on an episodic show is being able to navigate that."

Looking at Real Life for Inspiration

Neal Kassner tries to look at real life for inspiration in the color suite: "One of the things I find helpful to do is look at life as objectively as you can, he says. You need to look around. You have a white barn in the middle of a field. At noon it's going to be white. Late afternoon, it's still going to be a white barn, but it's not going to look white to your eye. Your brain is going to filter what your eye sees. In news, that's a kind of fine line that I walk. Do I make it a white barn in the afternoon and destroy the overall look and feel? Or do I maintain that? And what I often end up doing is sort of splitting the difference. There's a way in the DaVinci to put in two color corrections and mix between them."

> *One of the things I find helpful to do is look at life as objectively as you can.*
>
> *— Neal Kassner, 48 Hours*

Smoke

As Leffel prepares to work on the Artbeats image of the boxer, he discusses what he considers to be the bane of the colorist. "This shot's got all the bad things colorists hate, like smoke. God knows I hate smoke.

Photographers love it, but I hate it. Light doesn't travel predictably through it. So when you filter a light source—especially if you mix incandescent or mix practicals in a lighting scenario, like right here— you've got this green light coming from maybe a practical, maybe a lighting source and you've got this cleaner source over here and if you were to walk through there his skin and his face and his body would change color because smoke dissipates the light quite a bit, so it quite often corrupts whatever it is that you're trying to do. And most of these color correctors are set up with hue, saturation, and luminance, and the smoke affects HSL in a way that's really unpredictable, and color correctors have a really hard time with it—which makes *you* have a really hard time with it," Leffel concludes.

Keeping Butts in the Seats

In the end, the colorists that make the most money are the ones that keep the butts in the seats. In other words: new clients coming in the door and old clients coming back.

Chris Pepperman describes what he thinks delivers that desired result. "Clients respond to colorists who work quickly. Colorists who get them what they want and stay within their budget and deadline. I assess what I have: I look at the rough cut. I look at the film. I look how it's shot and I say, 'This isn't going to take as long,' or 'This might take more time.' But I typically always run quicker than slower. Because I'm the kind of guy who, once I get an image the way I like it, I'm gone. I'm not dicking with it. If you like it and you're happy with it, I'm moving on. I'm not going to teeter around with it any more. I go to the next scene. And then, depending on the kind of client you are and what you like, because all my clients are different, I tend to move quickly, and therefore, instead of doing the job in eight hours, I've done it in five and they're still getting what they want. I want to get it done, because if something goes wrong, now we're ten hours into a project. My eyes are tired. I'm compromising the look of my project the longer I'm in the room, the more frustrating it becomes for the client. For me, once I like the image and they like the image, we're moving! If that takes five minutes, then it takes five minutes. I'd rather always have the extra time in the back end of the session to say, you know what, I wasn't happy with this shot, let's go back and tweak it, rather than get to the clock and have five shots still to go and then you've got to rush through them. And that's something I learned in New York, working under the gun with agencies just kind of lined up at your door, waiting to come in, four or five a day, because you can really get yourself in a tizzy if you're slowing down and it's five o'clock and there are still clients out there waiting."

I color and image enhance and color correct for maximum reemployment.

— Bob Festa, New Hat

And for Festa, keeping butts in the seats is what it's all about, business-wise. "Here's the deal," Festa begins, "I've learned a long time ago that I color and image enhance and color correct for maximum reemployment. We have an expression: 'time for the mortgage payment.' So it doesn't matter what I think, so much as what the client thinks. So I'm all ears in the session, especially early in the session—I listen to everybody in the room, but just between you and I and the book, I probably weight my hearing more towards my repeat client, the people I'm going to work with, the people I know are coming back. And I listen to the client and as much as I'd like to turn this into the green cyan kind of thing, I really like to listen to the client a lot. If they think it needs to be a study in neutral or cold steel or something, goddamn it, that's the direction it's going to go whether it's going to work or not because we're timing for maximum reemployment.

"We don't work in a vacuum; there's always somebody here with an opinion or who was there on location who certainly has an opinion, and I think the film should do the same thing. It shouldn't just be a witness; I think every shot should have an informed opinion, a direction, something it's trying to say. With a documentary, you might want to step aside and not leave a mark on the film, but hopefully you can be an objective colorist and make an informed approach without leaving footprints; you never want to leave your signature."

Books of Note

Here's a short list of books about color and color correction in my library.

Of course, my previous book with Jaime Fowler, *Color Correction for Digital Video* would be at the top of the list! This book is now in its second edition and the title has changed to:

- *Color Correction for Video* by Stephen Hullfish and Jaime Fowler, Focal Press, 2008, ISBN-10: 0240810783, ISBN-13: 978-0240810782.

Also:

- *Apple Pro Training Series: Encyclopedia of Color Correction—Field Techniques Using Final Cut Pro* by Alexis Van Hurkman, 2006, ISBN-10: 0321432312, ISBN-13: 978-0321432315.

- *The Art of Color—The Subjective Experience and Objective Rationale of Color* by Johannes Itten, John Wiley and Sons, 1961, ISBN 0-471-28928-0.
- *Color Correction Handbook: Professional Techniques for Video and Cinema* by Alexis Van Hurkman, 2010, ISBN-10: 0321713117, ISBN-13: 978-0321713117.
- *Color, Light, Sight Sense: An Elementary Theory of Color in Pictures* by Moritz Zwimpfer, Schiffer Publishing, 1985, ISBN 0-88740-139-2.
- *Designer's Color Manual: The Complete Guide to Color Theory and Application* by Tom Fraser and Adam Banks, Chronicle Books, 2004, ISBN-10: 0-8118-4210-X.
- *Digital Color Management* by Edward J. Giorgianni and Thomas E. Madden (color scientists at Kodak), Addison Wesley, 1998, ISBN-10: 0-201-63426-0.
- *If It's Purple, Someone's Gonna Die: The Power of Color in Visual Storytelling* by Patti Bellantoni, Focal Press, 2005, ISBN-10: 0-240-80688-3.
- *Pantone Guide to Communicating with Color* by Leatrice Eiseman, Grafix Press, 2000, ISBN-10: 0-9666383-2-8.
- *Photoshop Color Correction: The Essential Guide to Color Quality for Digital Images* by Michael Kieran, Peachpit Press, 2003, ISBN-10: 0-321-12401-4.
- *The Visual Story: Seeing the Structure of Film, TV, and New Media* by Bruce Block, Focal Press, 2001, ISBN-13: 978-0-240-80467-5.

Color Correction Training on DVD

- *Class on Demand, Basic and Advanced Training for Apple Color.* Hosted by Steve Hullfish and Bob Sliga.
- *Class on Demand Total Training for DaVinci Resolve.* Hosted by Steve Hullfish and Bob Sliga.
- *Fxphd's Resolve Fundamentals* with Warren Eagles (http://www.fxphd.com).

Conclusion

I hope this glimpse into the worlds of some of these great colorists inspires you to dig deeper and delve into the world of color correction with renewed confidence.

Getting to meet and watch these talented men and women was really a treat, and I've been excited throughout the nearly decade-long journey of writing and researching this book to bring their experience and wisdom to you through this book.

Happy coloring!

CHAPTER 12

Tutorials

With Adobe SpeedGrade still in the wings (as of the writing of this book) and Apple Color's discontinuation, the most universally available color correction application is probably DaVinci Resolve. In order to get through the most material, I'll be doing all of the tutorials in this chapter using DaVinci Resolve 8.1. But regardless of whatever color correction system you have access to, or prefer to use most frequently, you should be able to follow along and translate the methods from this chapter to your own favorite system.

As I was writing this, Adobe did start to show off the capabilities of their version of SpeedGrade. It seems like it will be a standalone product for the time being instead of being integrated into Premiere. There are numerous analogous tools between Resolve and SpeedGrade. And for those still using Apple Color, the tools will also be very similar.

The goal with these tutorials is to walk you through several corrections from start to finish so that you start to develop a comfort level with the tools and techniques. These tutorials will build on each other.

Start out by loading all of the footage. On page xvii is a thorough explanation of how to load the tutorial material from the DVD onto your system and prepare it for grading in DaVinci Resolve. If you haven't already, follow those instructions before continuing.

Primary Color Correction

1. With the DVD footage loaded into Resolve, click on the Color button at the very bottom of the screen (Figure 12.1). This gets you to the Color Screen.
2. Scroll through the timeline, in the center of the screen, and find the "Ghost_SWAT" shot (Figure 12.2).

Fig. 12.1

Fig. 12.2

3. With the "Ghost_SWAT" shot in the viewer window, right-click on the viewer and select Waveform options, putting checkmarks in the waveform options you want to see (Figure 12.3). I've chosen RGB Parade and Vectorscope. You can choose as many as you like, but choose at least those two.

4. Notice in the RGB Parade that the strongest channel is the green channel (Figure 12.4 and 12.5). This should confirm what your eyes are telling you: that there's a distinct green cast to the image. This cast could come from the small patch of green grass to the right side of the picture, but the grass is only on the right side, and the strength of the green channel in the RGB Parade goes all the way across the image. We can also see by looking at the very bottom of the RGB Parade that the blacks are probably pretty well balanced because none of the channels is higher than another. This could be because they're all crushed, so the best practice is to use the shadow controls—like the thumbwheel under the Shadow color wheel in the 3-Way Color tab—to lift the blacks to see if they all stay the same relative to each other as they are lifted. They do, so that tells us that our blacks are balanced. Return the blacks to 0 or press Command-Z to reset. Or, from the Session pulldown menu, choose any of the Base Memory options to get back to your starting point.

There are three base memory keyboard shortcuts: Shift-Home is the standard Base Memory (clears the grade from the selected node); Option-Home is for Base Memory All (clears the grade from all nodes, but leaves the nodes); and Command-Home is for Base Memory Reset (total reset, deleting all nodes and grades).

Fig. 12.3

As I have professed several times throughout the book, external scopes are critical to good color correction work, especially for colorists without a *lot* of experience under their belts. Make a note of the detail difference between the Tektronix scopes (Figure 12.4) and the Resolve internal scopes (Figures 12.5 and 12.6).

The Tektronix scope is showing four different views. The top left is a straight RGB Parade waveform. Directly underneath that is another RGB Parade waveform image zoomed in and repositioned to show great detail in the shadows. The top right shows a composite waveform, for basic levels, and the bottom right is a standard vectorscope. Note the difference in the quality of information between the Tektronix scope and the internal scopes.

As you can see from the shadows at 0 and highlights at 100 percent—or 1023 on the DaVinci RGB Parade—there is a good spread between highlights and shadows, but we should play with the gammas/midtones to determine the feel of the shot and how much detail we're able to see in the shadows. Use the center thumbwheel in the 3-Way Color tab (Figure 12.7). Taking the gammas below 0 (look at the numbers between the colored rings

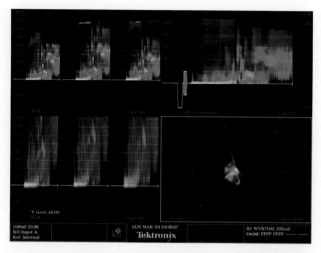

Fig. 12.4 Tektronix waveform monitor of "Ghost_SWAT" image.

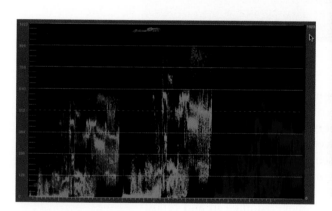

Fig. 12.5 DaVinci Resolve internal RGB Parade waveform monitor.

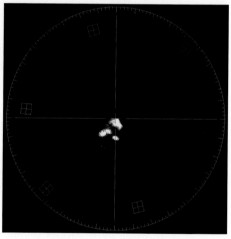

Fig. 12.6 DaVinci Resolve internal vectorscope image.

and the thumbwheels) starts to give a very dark feel, and the detail in the shadows becomes completely lost. Bringing it up to the 0.15 range makes the action seem like part of a sitcom. It's much easier to see good detail in the shadows though. And if you take the gamma level *way* up to the 0.40 or 0.50 range, you can see in the RGB Parade that there is actually quite a bit of cyan in the shadows. You'll see that the weakest (closest to 0) channel is the red channel and that the green and blue channels are higher. Green plus blue is cyan and the opposite of red

Fig. 12.7

is cyan. Let's leave the midtones at 0.06. This leaves some meat to the image, but allows us to see some of the weaponry in the shadow details.

5. The blacks of the uniforms seems pretty well balanced, and we can't be sure of a true white. The top of the truck might be white, but it could be painted some slightly different color or could be reflecting the sky. So to try to balance out the green/cyan, we need a neutral color. The best choice could be the door to the SWAT vehicle. To confirm exactly where that is in the waveform image, let's zoom into it. At the bottom of the Resolve screen, click on Format (Figure 12.8).

Fig. 12.8

6. Move the Zoom slider to 4.0 (4x) and use the Pan slider (Figure 12.9) to move the image in the right viewing window (the output) so that the door is on the right edge of the screen (Figure 12.10). I did this in the Input tab. But if you use both the Input and the Output tabs, you can zoom in even further so that the door completely fills the frame.

7. In the RGB Parade Waveform, it's easy to "see" the door as the thinnish line on the right side of each color channel just under the dotted line in the middle of the waveform monitor. And it's evident that the strongest channel is green, followed by blue, with the weakest channel being red (Figure 12.11). Switch back

Fig. 12.9

Fig. 12.10

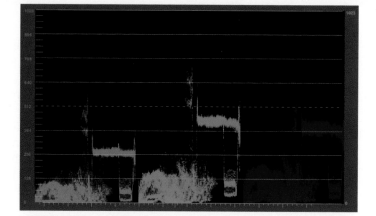

Fig. 12.11 Internal RGB Parade shows that the red channel is weak and the blue and green channels are stronger, indicating a cyan cast in the midtones.

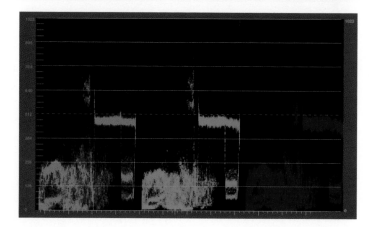

Fig. 12.12 The internal RGB Parade after the Custom Curve correction.

to the Color screen. Try balancing this in a number of ways. You could use a point in the middle of the green and blue Custom Curves. You could use the midtone sliders in the Primary tab, or you could use the wheels in the 3-Way Color tab. To do the midtone correction in Custom Curves, first right-click under the curves and uncheck the Gang Custom Curves checkbox in the contextual menu. The goal is obviously to get the part of the RGB waveform that represents the door to be even across all three channels (Figure 12.12). Remember that by raising the red and blue channels to match the green channel, you are also raising the overall gamma. I took green down a bit and red and blue up a bit to make my match (Figure 12.13). Experienced colorists will be able to do this match by eye, but we need to use the basic tools to get start to create a solid level of experience and a confidence in our eyes.

With a still loaded, you can toggle the wipe to your live source off and on using the keyboard Command-W.

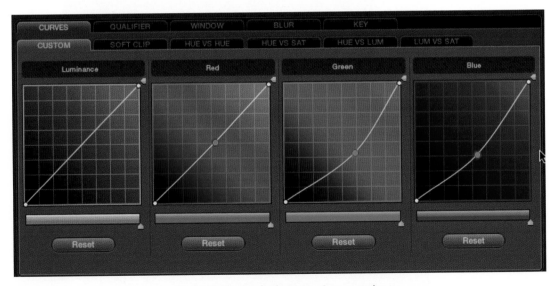

Fig. 12.13 The data for the Custom Curve correction.

To do this same correction in the Primary tab, first reset your grade (Session > Base Mem), then adjust the red green and blue gamma sliders (Figure 12.14).

To do this in the 3-Way Color tab, reset to Base Mem and use your mouse to move the center Gamma-Midtones wheel. Pushing it up toward red (11 o'clock) will add red and slightly drop the green, but do little to balance the blues. To get the blue channel to balance, slide the mouse straight to the right. The other two channels should not move and the blue channel should rise (Figure 12.15).

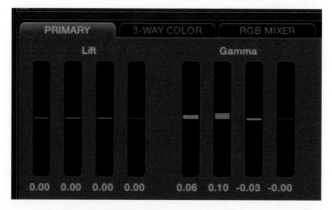

Fig. 12.14 Note the numbers under the red, green, and blue gamma sliders.

Fig. 12.15

Fig. 12.16 The split is at the middle of the door. The green cast to the right is the "before." The warmer tones to the left is the "after."

The image may seem a little warm. You can dial back some of the warmth with the entire image visible. On the gamma color wheel, just pull straight down toward the center position until you feel balanced (Figure 12.16).

Secondary Correction

Let's add three secondaries or nodes to this image. The first one will be a vignette to just darken and blur the edges. The second will be a window that will help highlight the one SWAT face that we can see. We'll pretend he's the hero of this shot, so we'll help call a little more attention to his face. The final one will be an HSL qualification to punch up the grass. I don't think this shot really needs that treatment, but we'll do it as an exercise.

First, the vignette:

1. In the Color Screen's Window tab (Figure 12.17), check the "on" button next to the Circular choice (top choice) and click the second box next to it to grade outside the window instead of inside. This selection will put three colored circles in the viewer window. The middle green circle is the center of the softness. The outer yellow circle is the outside softness. The inner yellow circle is the inner softness. You can either use the sliders in the Window tab or click and drag on various handles of the circles to change the size, shape and softness of the circle (Figure 12.18).

Fig. 12.17

Fig. 12.18

2. Use the standard color correction controls to lower the highlights, gammas, and shadows outside of the selected window. You could also lower the saturation or even open the Blur tab and blur the image outside of the window. To see the image without the colored circles, deselect the small box icon button to the left of the eyedropper button under the viewer (Figure 12.19).

Fig. 12.19

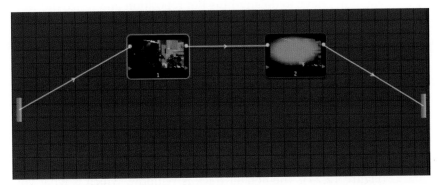

Fig. 12.20 First node selected, ready to add serial node for the tracking window.

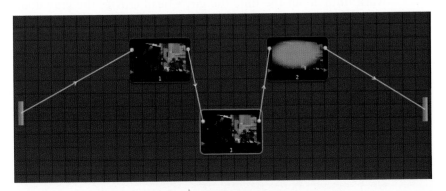

Fig. 12.21 Third node added between first and second nodes.

3. Let's add the window that will highlight our hero. We will track this window because the man moves through the shot. I want to do this secondary before the vignette that we just created is applied, so in the node graph, select the primary node and choose "Add serial" (Shift-S) to add a new node between the primary (first) node and the vignette (second node). Note that the first node is selected by the blue outline (Figure 12.20). After adding the third node the node graph should look like Figure 12.21.

> **TIP**
>
> It's possible in the Node menu to add a node that already has a circular window applied and ready for use press shift-C instead of shift-S.

The keyboard shortcut for adding a serial node is Shift-S.

4. With node 3 highlighted as in Figure 12.21, create another circle window in the Window tab by checking the box to the right of the Circular style. This time, we'll grade the *inside* differently, instead of the outside. Grading the inside of windows is the default, so you don't have to do anything but reposition and resize the window so that it surrounds the hero's head (Figure 12.22).

5. Use the thumbwheels in the 3-Way Color tab to slightly increase the highlights and gammas, maybe increase saturation, and you could even push some warmth into the gammas with the color wheel (slightly pushing the color wheel cursor up toward about 11 o' clock).

6. Switch over to the Viewer Screen with the Viewer button at the bottom of the screen and click on the Show Object Tracking Controls arrow near the bottom right corner of the screen (Figure 12.23).

7. This brings the tracking controls up on the right side of the screen (Figure 12.24). The default track is Window, which is what you want. Click the Fwd button to start the track. The track should work until about the time the guy's head crosses the gray door. Because the shape of his head has changed as he turns the corner, the track gets lost.

Fig. 12.22

Fig. 12.23

Right and left arrows on the keyboard are the shortcuts for Step One Frame Forward and Step One Frame Reverse.

Fig. 12.24

8. Turn on the Show Track checkbox in the tracking controls and step through the track using the single-frame advance button under the viewer, two to the left of the pause button in the middle of the screen. There are a number of ways to fix the track from where it gets lost. Because there are only a few frames left in the track, we'll fix them one keyframe at a time. To do this, under Adjust, the Global choice is the default, but we want the Key Frame option, so select that. Now you can simply step through the shot one frame at a time, manually adjusting the position of the window to keep it centered on our hero.

9. Let's punch up the grass. To do this kind of secondary, the first job is to qualify—or select—the grass. In the node graph, select the first node and press Shift-S to add a serial node that will go before the other two secondary corrections. We don't want either of the other secondaries to affect the grass qualification, so we want it to be first. We could even have it before the primary if we wanted to.

10. With this new node selected (outlined in blue in the node graph), click on the Qualifier tab in the same area of the screen as the Curves, Windows, and Blur. With the "deck controls" under the viewer, shuttle forward to about two-thirds of the way through the show, where you can best see the grassy area. Then use the color picker (eyedropper tool in the Qualifier tab) and drag the

Fig. 12.25

cursor around in the area of the grass to select it. You'll notice in the Qualification tab that the HSL bars show the selected color vector of the grass, defined by white lines in the bars (Figure 12.25). The white lines in the HSL bars show that the qualification is in a tightly defined area of Hue, fairly low saturation (to the left of the Sat bar), and in the midrange of the Luma bar.

11. To see the specific portions of the picture you've selected, check the Highlight checkbox in the Qualifier tab. The default is to show the selected area in the viewer as a color (green for grass) and all nonqualified or nonselected colors are shown as gray. My selection picked up on some of the green cast of the pillars in the building, which I don't want. So use the Low sat and High Luma controls to try to dial in a better selection, or use the "–" button to the right of the eyedropper control and click in the areas you want to subtract from the selection. If you like a nice high-contrast key to see your selection, go to the Config screen in the Settings tab and check the box for "Mattes display high contrast black and white" (Figure 12.26).Without the hi-con matte option, the qualification looks like Figure 12.27 in the viewer. With the hi-con matte option, the qualification looks like Figure 12.28 in the viewer. Use whichever one helps you make the best qualification.

To make the best adjustment of this qualification, turn off the checkbox for Highlight in the Qualifier tab so that you are viewing the image in full color.

12. In the 3-Way Color tab, drag the gamma color wheel down toward green (7 o'clock) and adjust the gamma and highlight

Fig. 12.26

Fig. 12.27 Default view of qualified portions of an image.

Fig. 12.28 Hi-con view of qualified portions of an image.

thumbwheels to richen the colors. Again, for this shot, it's probably not appropriate to pump up the greens, because this is supposed to be a dangerous assault, not a golf documentary, but this is an exercise to show that it can be done and how to do it.

Use the up and down arrow keys to enable or disable all nodes.

To sum up, we balanced the shot in our first node, vignetted the edges in the second node, highlighted and tracked an actor in the third node, and qualified a specific vector (the green of the grass) and punched it up in the fourth node (Figure 12.29). We could have actually created them in the order they ended up: grass, then actor, then vignette, but this order gave you a chance to learn a little about the node graph.

The first node is the primary, the second node (4) is the grass qualification and adjustment, the third node (2) is the vignette, and the fourth node (3) is the tracked "hero" window.

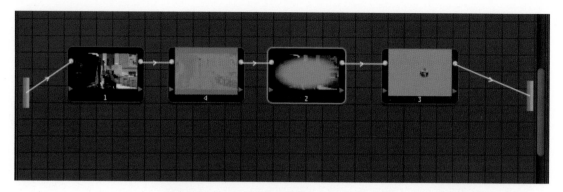

Fig. 12.29

(a)

(b)

Fig. 12.30 (a) Original film scan. (b) Finished look.

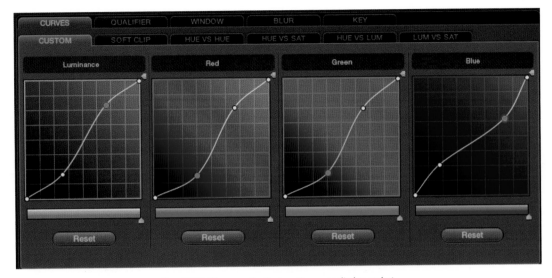

Fig. 12.31 These are the Custom Curves applied to node 1.

Creating Looks

On top of the work we just did, we also want to create some looks. I am fond of the Brazilian Silver look that Bob Festa did in Chapter 11, so we'll try to replicate that. He described it as a bleach bypass mixed with a black and white hi-con look. So let's try to recreate that.

1. Save our secondaries grade before we add any looks on top of them. Right-click on the viewer and, from the contextual menu, choose Grab Still. Or memorize the *very* useful Option-Command-G keyboard shortcut to Grab Still. This places it in the Stills tab to the right of the viewer window in the Color Screen.

   In the Color screen, you can switch from the Stills Tab to the PowerGrade tab and save the grade directly to a PowerGrade in a single step with Option-Command-G.

2. Using the buttons at the very bottom of the screen, switch to the Gallery screen. Drag the thumbnail of your saved SWAT still to the Memories tab to the left, dropping it onto the A position. Then click on the PowerGrade tab and drag the thumbnail from the Memories tab to the PowerGrade tab. There is a more direct way of doing this, but I wanted to show you how these various tabs interact and save grades. You want to save grades as PowerGrades so that they can be used in future sessions. Stills are

available only to the current session. You can also save grades to the Memories (the lettered thumbnails) with Option-# (where the # is the number 1–9, for A–I) and recall the Memories with Command-# (where the # is the number 1–9).

In the Gallery Screen, you can save and transfer Stills, Memories, and PowerGrades.

3. With your grade saved as a PowerGrade, go to the Session menu and choose Base Memory Reset. You'll notice in the node graph that your secondary nodes are gone and that your primary node has been reset.

Many colorists grade images while they're still, but grading while looking at a moving image is beneficial. The keyboard shortcut for Play is the period key. The keyboard shortcut for Stop is the spacebar. The keyboard shortcut to toggle looping is Command-L.

4. To create the basic bleach bypass, we'll create two nodes blended together as layers. The first node will have some funky color alteration that cross-processed chemical looks tend to have. I borrowed this color curve look from a tutorial I saw in *Layers Magazine*. Go into the Custom Curves tab and right-click under the Curves (near the reset buttons) to get a contextual menu; uncheck "Gang Custom Curves," which is on by default. Then click and drag on points on the graphs to make them look like Figure 12.31. Note that the luma, red, and green curves all have the bottom point pulled down and the top point pulled up and that the blue graph is the reverse. Also, because this image has so much green in it anyway, I didn't pull up the top green point as much and I pulled the bottom point down more. But that's just for this image with more green to it. If you want, you can really do this part much more subtly than I did it.

5. A real bleach bypass or skip bleach effect is done by processing film and skipping the bleach bath that is typically used in the normal processing of the film. Sometimes, instead of completely skipping it, the film is just left in the bath for less than the recommended time. The lack of bleach means that the silver in the film is retained. The effect of this is basically a contrastier, grainier image, because the layers of colored emulsion also have a layer of silver. To create this effect, we're going to create a contrasty black and white and layer it on our weird color node. Press Shift-P to create a parallel node. The bottom node should already be selected, so just pull saturation all the way down.

Fig. 12.32

6. Click on the Parallel node. Right-click on it and choose "Morph into Layer Mixer Node" in the contextual pulldown menu. (Or you can shift-L to create a Layer Mixer node directly.) In the contextual menu, under Composite Modes. You can choose several options, but I like Add and Screen the best. Screen is a little more subtle. Add gives it some attitude. Remember that if you don't quite like what you're seeing, you can go in to the individual nodes and do some tweaking. For example, the highlights are too blown out for me, so I'll go back into the first node (the Curved one) and lower the highlights.

7. Festa says he takes a bleach bypass look—which is already contrasty and layered with black and white—and combines it with another layer of black and white. We'll add a bit more coolness to the additional layer.

8. Right-click on the "grid space" in the Node Graph (Figure 12.34) and choose Add Node > Corrector from the contextual menu.

9. Right-click on the Layer Mixer Node and choose Add One Input from the contextual menu. You'll notice that there are now three little dots (inputs) on the left side of the Layer Mixer Node.

10. Click on the top left dot on the newly created Corrector node (which looks like a rainbow colored globe) and drag back to the input bar on the far left side of the node graph. Release it when the line turns solid white.

11. Click on the top right dot on the Corrector node and drag it to the newly created input dot on the Layer Mixer node. Your node graph should look like Figure 12.34.

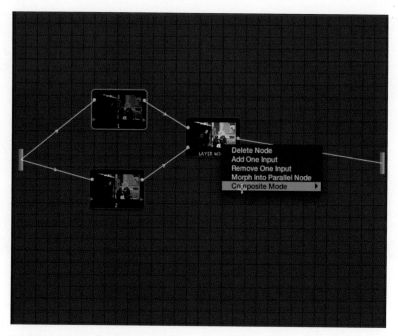

Fig. 12.33 The node graph for the bleach bypass look. The Curves from Figure 12.31 are applied to node 1. Node 2 is black and white. Node 3 has a Composite Mode of Add.

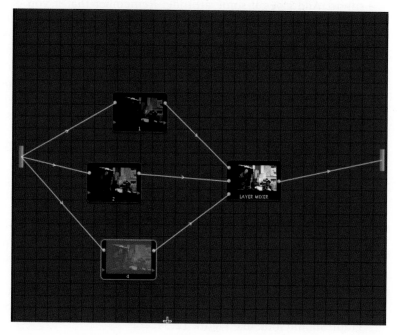

Fig. 12.34

12. This step really amps up the brightness. Click on node 4 (which has changed from a rainbow colored globe to a thumbnail of the SWAT team) and pull saturation down to almost nothing. Don't go all the way, because we want to add just a touch of coolness in the midtones and the highlights using the color wheels. Dial the thumbwheels for midtones and highlights down to a comfortable level. Or you can leave the levels where they are and experiment with the Key tab in the secondaries area, adjusting the Gain and Offset controls to regulate how much of the image is being keyed through in the Layer Mixer.

So that's my version of Brazilian Silver (Figure 12.35). It's possible to do a similar look in fewer steps, but the tutorial shows some good concepts for combining corrections. Definitely experiment with the Modes in the Layer Mixer. Screen and Add work best with this particular correction, but each image and each combination of corrections will be different.

Save this correction to your PowerGrades and use it on other images. Save the still to one of the Memories (Figure 12.36) by pressing Option-3 (for example, to save to Memory C, or Option-4 to save to Memory D).

Then move to another shot in the timeline and press Command-3 to put Memory C onto that shot.

If you want to apply this look to several shots in the sequence, select the shots, right-click, and choose "Add into a new group." A Group Name dialog will pop up. Type a name for the group, such as "Bleached," and click OK. Press Command-3 to assign the Brazilian Silver look to the group.

If you find other shots that you want to be in the group, just right-click them and choose "Add to Current Group."

Fig. 12.35

Fig. 12.36

Compositing Modes for a Better Look

For the final tutorial on looks, I direct you to the DVD. The number of options and possibilities and the need to see things in real time instead of as "snapshots" made writing out this final tutorial almost impossible. Please see the Compositing Mode tutorial for an explanation of how to create some truly amazing looks by the creative combination of nodes, node types, compositing modes, and selective qualifications.

The basis for this tutorial was another Bob Festa look: Pearlized Whites. I don't really do his look justice, but the basic concept is there, and you may be able to perfect the recipe for yourself once you see all of the ingredients laid out.

The basic concept for the look is to use the Artbeats image of the boxer—or the same "Kiss_nightgown" shot that Bob used—to make the highlight areas of the image glow. The quick explanation for this effect is:

1. Select the first node. Press Shift-P to create a parallel node.
2. In node 2 (the one underneath your first node), use the Blur tab to blur it pretty heavily by cranking up the Radius sliders (leave them ganged).
   You can also choose to add some color—blue or yellow—to the highlights using the highlight color wheel in the 3-Way Color tab.
3. Select the Parallel node. Right-click it and choose "Morph into Layer Mixer Node." Or use the shift-L shortcut to launch straight into Layer Mixer node.

4. Right-click on the newly renamed Layer Mixer node and select Composite Mode > Add. Another mode that works for this image is Screen. Experiment and see which you like better. You may also have to come back and try different modes after you've completed the next two steps, as the next two steps will drastically alter the results of these modes.

   Please also experiment with other mode choices. Each one does something different depending on the brightness or color of certain parts of the two nodes feeding into the Layer Mixer.

5. Select the second node (the blurry, bottom node) and experiment with various highlight and midtone levels using the thumbwheels under the color wheels in the 3-Way Color tab.

6. Experiment in the Qualifier tab with various Luma (bottom bar) qualifications, changing the sliders for Low, Low Soft, High, and High Soft. If you don't add some High and Low Softness, this effect will look really ugly. As a starting point, put Low, Low Soft, and High Soft to about 50 and High to about 80 or 90.

Final Thoughts

I hope that this book has inspired you and that you realize that the techniques shown here are simply the starting recipes for you to create your own amazing grades.

I created this book because I felt that there were so many better people to learn color correction from than me—a mere converted editor. I hope that being exposed to the dozen or so top-tier colorists on these pages has shown you that there is no *one* way. There is simply experience and trial and experimentation and the thrill of discovery that can come only from sitting in a dark room and trying things—pushing the limits and remembering my favorite line from this book:

You don't know if you don't go.

Index

Page references followed by 'f' indicate figure, and by 'b' indicate box.